"The most important, best documented, and most convincing indictment of Opus Dei ever written."
—*Misterios de la Historia*

"This sympathetic autobiography is so persuasive, so convincing, because María del Carmen Tapia only reports on what she herself lived through and experienced."
—*La República,* Venezuela

"A dispassionate and accurate description of the inner life of Opus Dei. The author's high position in the hierarchy of Opus Dei and her meticulous concern for detail make this the best book on Opus Dei."
—A. Ugalde, Professor of Sociology,
University of Texas-Austin

"When it came to the cause of beatification of Monsignor Escrivá, Opus Dei...did everything to keep at bay the number of unfavorable witnesses. Special efforts were made to stifle the voice of María del Carmen Tapia."
—*La Reppublica,* Italy

The picture which the author paints of Opus Dei's founder...is far from that of the holy servant of God which his beatification proclaims him to be. She found him egocentric and self-absorbed, in addition to being authoritarian, haughty, and having a violent temper.
—*Frankfurter Allgemeine Zeitung*

If it were not for the great intellectual sincerity that the entire book breathes, much of what we read here could seem exaggerated, as though drawn from experiences endured in the prison of a totalitarian regime. The book is exceptional...written without hatred but with great sensitivity.
—*Historia y Ciencias,* Spain

The insights that this book provides into the secrets of the Roman headquarters of Opus Dei — from its secret-service-like membership list to the specific spirit of the founder of Opus Dei — are unique. Whoever gets to know the founder through María del Carmen Tapia will also better understand Opus Dei: its rigorous asceticism, its shadowy financial practices, its indoctrination of fourteen-year-olds, and its strict segregation of its celibate men and women."
—West German Radio

"[Tapia] portrays the cult which formed around [Escrivá] during his life and shows how, in the so-called Work of God, the Founder is more spoken of than God or Christ. The book is absorbingly written."
—South German Radio

"About Opus Dei everything always seemed bleak. But after reading María del Carmen Tapia's book, the bleakness acquires the face of fanaticism, misogyny, and a total absence of love....The book is a journey to the secret horror of facts that nobody dared to speak about but only the courage and astonishing memory of María del Carmen have been able to bring to light."
—*Presencia Ecumenica*, Venezuela

"The book has provoked and still provokes great uneasiness inside and outside the strong Catholic organization of [Opus Dei]."
—*Il Mattino*, Italy

"Here a highly sensitive woman describes in a highly detailed and unusually elegant manner, without hatred and with the distance of over twenty years, a religious madhouse by the name of Opus Dei, which she came to know intimately like few others."
—*Spiegel Spezial*, Germany

"María del Carmen Tapia offers authentic insight into the personality and work of the founder of Opus Dei. She reveals unsparingly the truth about the churchly 'mafia,' from its questionable methods of recruitment to the psychic terror it practices on its members....A truly shocking document of contemporary church history."
—*Vereinigung für Geschichte im öffentlichen Leben*,

Germany

BEYOND THE THRESHOLD

A Life in Opus Dei

MARÍA DEL CARMEN TAPIA

CONTINUUM · NEW YORK

1999

The Continuum Publishing Company
370 Lexington Avenue / New York, NY 10017

Printed in the United States of America

Library of Congress Cataloging in Publication Data

Tapia, María del Carmen, 1925–
  [Tras el umbral. English]
  Beyond the threshold : a life in Opus Dei / María del Carmen
Tapia.
     p.   cm.
  Includes bibliographical references and index.
  ISBN 0-8264-1096-0 (pbk)
  1. Opus Dei (Society)   2. Escrivá de Balaguer, José María,
1902–1975.   3. Tapia, María del Carmen, 1925–   . I. Title.
BX819.3.068T3613   1997
267'.182'092—dc21   96-51695
                                                      CIP

A Dominique de Ménil,
qui tient si profondément
au coeur les droits humains.
Pour son encouragement,
toute ma gratitude.

M . C . T .

Desde el llano adentro vengo
tramoliando este cantar,
Cantaclaro[1] me han llamado.
¿Quién se atreve a replicar?[2]

Far from the plains I came
tuning this song
Cantaclaro I was called
who would dare to respond?

1. Although literally "Cantaclaro" means *to sing clearly,* to a Venezuelan it means *to tell the truth.* Similarly to the minstrels, Cantaclaro represents the popular singer from *el llano* (the Venezuelan plains) at village celebrations. In his songs he relates stories, events, romantic involvements, and even political gossip of other places in the area. When the feast is over he leaves at the break of the day.

2. Rómulo Gallegos, *Cantaclaro*, Obras Completas, Tomo I (Madrid: Aguilar, 1976), p. 807.

Contents

Acknowledgments

The affectionate support of relatives and friends made this book possible. Each played a special role as the book appeared in different languages.

To Dr. Roberto de Souza, professor of the University of La Plata, and to Dr. Carlos Albarracin-Sarmiento, professor of the University of California, goes my deepest gratitude for their generosity in dedicating their yearly vacations to reading, evaluating, and correcting the Spanish manuscript. Héctor Chimirri, editor of Ediciones B in Spain, with his personal and enthusiastic collaboration made possible the first Spanish edition, which also owes its existence to the intelligent direction and guidance of Blanca-Rosa Roca, director of Ediciones B.

My friend Laura Showalter-Astiz accompanied me in search of many of the documents included in this volume. Matilde de Urtubi corrected and clarified the text with her acute criticism. Despite an ocean between us, my oldest nephew, Javier, supplied constant data from the Spanish media.

The Portuguese edition was born in the marvelous city of Lisbon, thanks to the warm and efficient supervision of Tito Lyon de Castro, my editor at Publicações Europa-America, and to his colleague Ana Sampaio. To both of them my deepest appreciation.

In Germany this book appeared so satisfactorily thanks to Markus Fels, editor at that time of Benziger Verlag. He fully understood the book's message. To him goes my gratitude for his efficient work, his enthusiasm, and his understanding. I am also grateful to Dr. Tulio Aurelio, the current editor at Benziger, for his perseverance in the new German editions as well as to Klaus Eck, of Goldmann Verlag in Munich, who launched the German paperback version.

The understanding and collaboration of very dear friends in Italy, some of them lawyers and scholars from Milan, who knew well the importance of the topic, encouraged and helped me to have the book published in Italy. I keep the warmest memory of my encounter in Milan with Dr. Alessandro Delai, editor of Baldini & Castoldi, who from the very beginning saw the importance of the book for the Italian reader and successfully brought it out just a few months ago. The Italian edition awoke many personal memories and a special thought for the late Professor Enrico Castelli Gattinara, of the Institute of Philosophical Studies of the University of Rome, who told me, many years ago, of his fear that Opus Dei would cause serious problems within the church, giving rise to unnecessary controversies among Catholics. On his advice, I visited Cardinal Gabriel Maria Garrone, prefect of the Sacred Congregation for Christian Education, who told me that he had never received any information about Opus Dei's plan of studies.

At long last the English-language edition! My intention was to publish it many years ago, before the Spanish version, as Christine Hopper Warsow and Professor John Roche, of Oxford University, well know. Both helped me very much at that early stage. Subsequently, without the assistance of several friends from the United States, who prefer not to be mentioned at this time, I could hardly have had access to important sources of information.

I have to thank particularly Rosalie Siegel, my agent, whose advice and encouragement I dearly appreciated. Last by not least, I owe Frank Oveis, my editor at Continuum, profound gratitude for his efforts in undertaking this English edition. He endured with admirable patience and professionalism the shortcomings of an author expressing herself in a language acquired as an adult.

Once more my heartfelt gratitude and affection go to Dominique de Menil to whom I dedicate this book. When I met her many years ago for the first time, she understood my concerns and, because of her deep love for human rights, encouraged my idea of bringing the experiences described in this book to the printed page.

To know how to say thanks properly is an art. But to know how to be thankful in matters of the spirit entails a very special sensitivity. I would dearly wish to master both art and sensitivity and to be able to offer them to all my friends around the world who helped me bring this book into being so long awaited and so much needed.

PREFACE TO
THE ENGLISH EDITION

The present book has its own history. I began writing it in English, although the Spanish, Portuguese, German, and Italian editions appeared before the English version. As the book has appeared in various editions, I have been moved by hundreds of letters, which I keep with deep respect, from persons who spent many years in Opus Dei, others from persons who never joined the institution as well as from parents of students at Opus Dei schools and clubs. They all asked me, with understandable anxiety, how to escape Opus Dei's orbit or how to remove their children from their schools without subsequent reprisals. Many letters were from men (some of them priests), former Opus Dei numeraries or supernumeraries, who, on leaving or being fired by the institution, also became estranged from God and the church, while others went on to a humble priesthood far from former pomp and circumstance. Servants, who with great courage and after many years in Opus Dei, wrote that they left the institution without receiving any kind of financial or social help. However, it has been very rewarding to know that many people have learned through my personal experience that they need not abandon God because of the peculiar doctrine of this institution.

On May 17, 1992, His Holiness John Paul II beatified Opus Dei's Founder, Monsignor José María Escrivá, a step that does not imply a public cult. Several questions linger about the process of beatification itself, about the behavior of its judges, and the long-standing cultic reverence of the Founder by members of the institution. According to Kenneth Woodward, "a Vatican source said, contrary to established procedures, no published writings critical of Escrivá were included in the documents given to the judges of his cause; nor did the congregation investigate Escrivá's celebrated conflicts with the Jesuits, reports of his pro-fascist leanings, and Opus Dei's involvements with the Franco government. Incredibly, 40 percent of the testimony came from just two men: Alvaro del Portillo [who died in March 1994] and his assistant, Father Javier Echevarría [who was actually elected Opus Dei prelate less than a month later]."[1]

The beatification and its procedural irregularities were scandalous.

Some friendly criticisms have convinced me of the need to make a few comments on the nature and genesis of this book. Shortly after my separation from Opus Dei, as a healthy way of putting the pieces of my life together, I began to make notes of some of my experiences in Opus Dei.

Years later, although studies of the institution have appeared, my profound concern about human rights and freedom made me regret the lack of material about women in Opus Dei. As a close witness I had a privileged vantage point and a duty to explain my experience in Opus Dei. Thus, I began to write. The advice and fears of a friend (who figures in the story) kept me from trying to publish and this probably delayed the book by some eight years. Ironically, the Spanish publication date, April 1992, coincided with the controversy about the beatification of Monsignor Escrivá. However, the reason for writing this book transcends the occasion of the beatification.

Although I have used the thread of my life as a young woman who joined the institution, became a fanatic, and was brutally disillusioned, this book is not a biography nor a comprehensive study of Opus Dei or of Monsignor Escrivá, but rather testimony about my years in Opus Dei. Consequently, my life after Opus Dei, except for a small part involving revealing brushes with the prelature, is beyond the scope of my book. A secondary prudential reason for not alluding to that post-Opus Dei life is that Opus Dei consistently makes personal attacks on its critics to distract attention from substantive issues.

Canonists and theologians will perhaps some day be able to write a complete study of Opus Dei and Escrivá. Works prepared by Opus Dei are uncritically apologetic, given that outsiders and members have no normal access to key internal Opus Dei documents.[2] I wish it were possible to give more of a sense of Monsignor Escrivá's occasional charm and magnetism. The adulatory biographies by Opus Dei members do a poor job. Moreover, as early as the 1940s a great deal of

---

1. Kenneth L. Woodward, *Newsweek,* May 18, 1992, p. 47.
2. See, for example, Vittorio Messori, *Opus Dei: Un'indagine* (Milan: Mondadori, 1994), and Pilar Urbano, *El hombre de Villa Tevere* (Barcelona: Plaza y Janes, 1994).

enthusiasm for Monsignor Escrivá was generated among Opus Dei members by an indoctrination imparted under the heading "filiation toward the Father." The image of Monsignor Escrivá propagated within Opus Dei is largely a fabrication, as writers such as Luis Carandell, who is not a member of Opus Dei, have shown.

Some critics complain about the absence of sensational revelations about political, economic, or other scandals. The sociologist Alberto Moncada has gathered and written invaluable testimonies on this score. Two points, however, need to be made: First, information within Opus Dei is restricted and obsessive secrecy or "discretion" is the rule. Most Opus Dei members, particularly the young, have no knowledge of their Founder's bad temper or of Opus Dei's political maneuvering and nepotism in Spain under the Franco era Plan de Desarrollo.[1] The testimony of former members can contribute pieces to this mosaic. Second, the abuses are primarily important in so far as they reveal the lack of freedom and autonomy of Opus Dei members. It is not the case that Opus Dei pretends to be a religious movement but is really financial or political. Nor is the main problem that it occasionally lapses into unethical political or financial activities. I can guarantee the readers who do not themselves belong to a strong religious tradition that there has never been an Opus Dei director who said anything like: "For public consumption we claim to be interested in prayer, but what matters is the stock market, or the next election." The Spanish philosopher Ortega y Gasset distinguishes between the defects of political systems due to abuses and those due to uses as the result of the normal functioning of the system. That distinction may help us understand that the problems of Opus Dei stem from its normal functioning. My testimony attempts to portray part of its normal functioning.

Because I have given a detailed account of the life of women in Opus Dei, the publication of my book disturbed Opus Dei so much that it made several attempts to abort, or at least delay, the first Spanish edition, and to challenge the first Portuguese edition. Needless to say, Opus Dei tried to silence me because I touch on sensitive issues such as the lack of freedom within the institution or the process in which it turns members into fanatics. Through its vicars in the countries where Opus Dei is established, it officially declared that I was lying. It also issued a long statement, signed by the central directress of the Opus Dei Women's Government, to which I have replied point by point in the *Expresso* of Lisbon, September 25, 1993.

---

1. Yvon Le Vaillant, *Sainte Maffia: Le dossier de l'Opus Dei* (Mercure de France, 1971), pp. 213–227.

To refute my book would imply refuting Opus Dei's own documents, some of which are included in the text of this book, others in the Appendix; the originals are mine.

Curiously, two years after the Spanish version of my book appeared, Pope John Paul II published a book responding to a series of questions from an Italian journalist, titled *Crossing the Threshold of Hope,* so reminiscent of my title, yet so different in content.[1] I only know that the figurative threshold into Opus Dei and the literal threshold into the women's central house on Via di Villa Sacchetti were indeed thresholds of hope for me and many others. As it turned out, of misplaced hope and trust.

After so many years of living in the United States, I am troubled by the limited critical information about Opus Dei available. It has become apparent in recent years that there is a general tendency of Opus Dei to cultivate high-ranking members of the hierarchy of the church, looking indeed for their support. Opus Dei publicizes its recognition as a personal prelature and the beatification of its Founder but hides its system of recruiting and the day-to-day life of its members in the shadows. The English-language edition is my personal contribution to shedding light on this hidden and manipulative presence in the country where I live and which I consider mine.

Santa Barbara, February 2, 1997
Feast of the Purification of Our Lady
MCT

---

1. His Holiness Pope John Paul II, *Crossing the Threshold of Hope,* edited by Vittorio Messori (New York: Alfred A. Knopf, 1994).

INTRODUCTION

Few people walking down Via di Villa Sacchetti in Rome's fashionable Parioli district would feel impelled to stop at the sealed door at number 36. The building to which it gives access fits unobtrusively into the restrained classical architecture of the street. But looking up from a little farther down the street, turning back toward Viale Bruno Buozzi, one is struck by the tower "il torreone," rising from the building next to number 36—a modern building whose front, as it turns out, is Viale Bruno Buozzi, 73; it is apparent that both are part of an immense, interconnected structural complex. The passerby might be struck by the odd combination of architectural styles but he or she would never guess that this was the world headquarters of Opus Dei.

The Spanish word *puerta*, from the Latin "porta," is defined by the dictionary as an opening in a wall that lets you go from one side to the other. The door to number 36 Via di Villa Sachetti is tightly sealed.

The purpose for writing this book is to allow you to pass the threshold and into the house of the Women's Branch of Opus Dei, where I lived as a numerary (full member) for almost six years. What you will learn is far more interesting than the way the buildings are interconnected, or the size of the place. José María Escrivá de Balaguer, the Founder of Opus Dei was proud of its approximately twelve dining rooms and fourteen chapels and used to say, jokingly: "It shows that we pray more than we eat." The largest of these chapels can accommodate hundreds of people, men or women who, although separated, live in the complex. Monsignor Escrivá remarked that he could "bring a Cardinal in by the front door in the morning, travel fast through the house, stop thirty minutes for lunch, continue the tour and let him out through the back door at dinner time, without having seen half of the whole compound."

The Founder of Opus Dei, henceforth Monsignor Escrivá, built tombs for a few close associates as well as for himself in one of the underground chapels. I heard Monsignor Escrivá say many times that two tombs will be above his. One was reserved for Alvaro del Portillo, president general of Opus Dei and subsequently "prelate" until his death on March 23, 1994. Monsignor Escrivá used to say, "And Alvaro will be close to me even in death." I also heard Monsignor Escrivá say, "I come from sitting on my tomb and not many people could say that."

The remaining tombs were for Jesús Gazapo, the architect of the Opus Dei headquarters, and for Opus Dei's first two women numeraries. It was always assumed that one of them would be Encarnita Ortega. For many years she was the central directress of the Women's Branch of Opus Dei, but lost favor with Monsignor Escrivá after a scandal involving her brother Gregorio. (Gregorio Ortega, an Opus Dei numerary, was Escrivá's man in Portugal. In October 1965 he escaped to Venezuela with money and jewelry. He stayed in the best hotel in Caracas. Reported by a prostitute, and traced by the police, he was deported. Opus Dei superiors took him to Spain under allegations of insanity.)

Since Monsignor Escrivá's death his tomb has become a place of pilgrimage for members of Opus Dei. Night and day, women and men pray around the tomb. Women usually wear the traditional short Spanish "mantilla," used to cover their heads in church. Opus Dei members will touch the tomb of the Founder, where "El Padre" is etched in bronze. They also pass out a portrait of the Founder with a "particular prayer" for private devotion. On the back of the portrait there is a summary of his life and virtues. Favors granted by Monsignor Escrivá are reported at greater length in a Bulletin published by Opus Dei in several languages as evidence to support his beatification. Fresh flowers, mainly roses, always grace the tomb, regardless of the season. Members of Opus Dei from all over the world come to Rome to visit the grave, especially after his beatification on May 17, 1992. Sometimes the superiors of Opus Dei invite selected outsiders to visit the tomb of Monsignor Escrivá, and pray.

Curiously, he used to tell Opus Dei superiors: "Do not keep me here too long [after my death] since too many people might bother you. Take me to a public church so you can work peacefully here." On May 14, 1992, Monsignor Escrivá's coffin was taken to the Basilica of San Eugenio, where people had free access to enter and pray. The coffin was inside a glass case covered with a red cloth. On May 17, 1992, the glass case was removed and the coffin could be seen. In the afternoon of May 21, 1992, Monsignor Escrivá's coffin was taken in public procession from the Basilica of San Eugenio to the oratory of Our Lady of Peace, now called "Prelatic Church of Our Lady of Peace." Monsignor Escrivá's coffin is now relocated in a glass case under the altar of this oratory,[1] whose entrance is roughly under the door of Viale Bruno Buozzi, 75, in Opus Dei's headquarters.

This book describes my life in Opus Dei from 1948, when I asked to be admitted as a numerary (full member) in Madrid, until 1966, when I was compelled to resign in Rome. My years in Opus Dei and the persecution to which I was subjected for several years after I left reveal the inner nature of this institution.

What is Opus Dei? To say that it is an association of more than 72,375 members from 87 countries, including both priests (approximately 2 percent) and lay people dedicated to a life of Christian action in the world, is both accurate and superficial.

For those who wish to know more, much has already been written, both for and against Opus Dei, some in good faith, some not, some supported by knowledge, some not.[2] Accounts by those who have not belonged to Opus Dei have almost always concentrated on the secrecy of the group, its supposed political orientation, or on a few prominent members. The recent book by Robert Hutchinson offers for the first time detailed information on the political and financial life of Opus Dei.[3] Until now, research into the association's finances (its participation in international banks and other related enterprises, assets and real-estate holdings, and the personal property of members closely linked to the organization) was based on limited hard data including a good deal of inaccurate information. However, books written by those who are or have been members of Opus Dei are either uncritically adulatory or concentrate too narrowly on particular issues and deal mainly with men in Opus Dei.[4]

Hardly anything has been written about women in Opus Dei. When non-Opus Dei authors speak about women, they usually repeat something I have said or written.[5]

1. See *Bulletin on the Life of Msgr. Escrivá: Special Edition* (New York: Office of Vice Postulation of Opus Dei in the United States, 1993), p. 22.

2. See the Bibliography on Opus Dei, p. 360.

3. Robert Hutchinson, *Die Heilige Mafia des Papstes: Der wachsende Einfluss der Opus Dei* (Munich: Droemer Knaur, 1996).

4. See Alberto Moncada, *El Opus Dei: Una interpretación* (Madrid: Indice, 1974). Also by Moncada, *Historia oral del Opus Dei* (Barcelona: Plaza y Janés, 1987), and the novel *Los Hijos del Padre* (Barcelona: Argos Vergara, 1977).

5. See, for instance, Michael Walsh, *The Secret World of Opus Dei* (London: Collins Publishers—Grafton Books, 1989, and San Francisco: Harper Collins, 1992). Walsh quotes, without permission, parts of a conversation I had with him years earlier.

Other than María Angustias Moreno, and then only for Spain,[1] nobody has yet to describe in concrete terms what takes place inside the women's houses of the association, now juridically a personal prelature. I have come to realize that my years in Opus Dei, the range of my responsibilities in the organization, the fact that I lived and worked close to Monsignor Escrivá for several years in Rome where I was one of a few women whom he tried to mold in the spirit of Opus Dei, and my subsequent opportunities within the association in several countries, make me an important witness. I held executive offices in the central government of Opus Dei and also within the Women's Branch in Spain and Italy. For several years I worked in Rome directly with the Founder of Opus Dei. I headed the women's section of Opus Dei in Venezuela for more than ten years. I visited Colombia and Ecuador. I also visited Santo Domingo to explore the possibilities of a new foundation of Opus Dei women in that country. I was in close contact as well with the women of Opus Dei in such countries as Colombia, Peru, Chile, and Argentina.

I have been in a position which allows me to present an overall picture of Opus Dei's Women's Branch, relating my own experiences as one who entered the Opus Dei with enthusiasm and high spiritual ideals and who spent eighteen years within the institution.

As I recount my life in Opus Dei I shall use real names, except in a few cases to protect members still living in Opus Dei houses. In one case only will I refer to a person by her first name alone.

For many years I thought that what happened to me during my years in Opus Dei was important only to me personally. I have now come to realize that my experience has importance for others, especially for women, as well as for anyone with idealism and good faith who might consider entering Opus Dei in any country of the world nowadays. First, my story might help families of Opus Dei members that know little about the characteristics of the group their children have joined. Second, it might be useful to the Roman Catholic Church, which needs to understand Opus Dei *from the inside,* not from visits that have been carefully prepared by Opus Dei superiors, or through information provided by these superiors. Third, it concerns Christians, non-Christians, and nonpracticing Catholics alike, who have connections to Opus Dei and might become Opus Dei "cooperators," giving financial aid to the association. Finally, given the sectarian characteristics of this group, the account may interest society at large.

---

1. María Angustias Moreno, *El Opus Dei: Una interpretacion* (Barcelona: Planeta, 1976). The author was the object of a defamatory campaign by Opus Dei. See also her *La otra cara del*

Opus Dei is in the process of establishing new houses in the United States of America, mainly on the West Coast[1] as well as in Eastern Europe, and the Nordic countries. Fundraising on a large scale is taking place, as Opus Dei profits from the independence from the church in its new status as a "personal prelature."[2]

Nowadays, all the efforts of Opus Dei, from its prelate to the most recent member, concentrate on having its Founder, Monsignor Escrivá, declared a saint. To this end, the members pray earnestly and make use of every tool possible such as hierarchical contacts, Vatican influences, the naive piety of the unwary and, of course, their considerable financial resources. On April 9, 1990, Opus Dei had him declared "Venerable." On May 17, 1992, he was beatified. However, I hope that the material in this book will inform the Holy Father, His Holiness John Paul II, of the misdirected or one-sided information he has no doubt received about Monsignor Escrivá's life, before taking the final step of canonizing Monsignor Escrivá. Such a declaration would cause a painful confusion among millions of Roman Catholics and a sad scandal to Christians of all denominations. The simple truth is that Monsignor Escrivá's life was not an example of holiness, nor was he a model to be imitated by the women and men of our time.

I certainly can testify that in Rome and behind the door of Via di Villa Sacchetti, 36, a giant puppet show is staged: Opus Dei superiors pull the strings to manipulate their members, men and women, all over the world, invoking their legal commitment of obedience or using the strongest order available to Opus Dei superiors: "It is suitable for the benefit of Opus Dei."[3]

Would it not be an act of irresponsibility and a crime of complicity to file my experiences away in my heart and leave them to oblivion?

To be silenced by Opus Dei because of fear of reprisals would be to act against my strong belief in the defense of spiritual freedom and human rights.

Opus Dei (Barcelona: Planeta, 1978). The latter includes my "Open Letter to María Angustias Moreno," pp. 104–111.

1. See *San Francisco Chronicle,* June 1, 1986, p. A-10.

2. See Bustelo, "Interview with Monsignor Javier Echevarría," in *Diario 16,* April 1994.

3. "Conviene para el bien de la Obra." The verb *conviene* (it is suitable) is the strongest order a member can receive in Opus Dei.

1

MY ENCOUNTER
WITH OPUS DEI

Opus Dei is a socio-religious phenomenon bound up with the political situation following the Spanish Civil War (July 1936 to April 1939). By the end of the war, the hopes and dreams of the country's youth had overcome the animosities and hatred of the adults. We were filled with personal, political, and religious aspirations. We had grown up during the Civil War years, remembering years of hunger, bombings, and often the destruction of our own homes. We had suffered the loss of loved ones, not on a "glorious" battlefront that seemed less and less "glorious" as time went on, but by the deadly butchery wrought by fanatics and criminals of the lowest type, whether communists or fascists.

If only the warm waters of the Mediterranean, the cemetery walls, the river banks, the outskirts of many towns, the park trees, the dirt roads could talk! They would tell the story of mass executions, of anonymous corpses whose families even to this day cannot have the consolation of crying at their graves. There were also isolated places whose mute solitude hid those unjust firing squads.

I still remember one morning in December 1936 during the siege of Madrid by Franco's troops. Our house had been destroyed in one of the bombardments; we had lost more than thirty close relatives to the so-called communists. My mother was pregnant and the communists were looking for my father, an engineer for the Spanish railroad. We were staying with friends (Carlos Anné, a colleague of my father's, and his family) in a neutral zone—so-called because of the belief that Franco would not shell it. The zone included Serrano Street, a few adjacent streets, with residential neighborhoods like El Viso, Colonia de la Residencia, and Cruz del Rayo. I left home very early that day to look for some food for my family; since I was only eleven, I was glad to have the company of two older friends, Elvira (Viruchy) Bergamín and Chelo Sánchez-Covisa, who were both fifteen. We took a shortcut through a street that had only been opened a few months before the war started. We walked silently, remembering that people had recently been killed in the area at night. Suddenly someone said, "Watch out!" There was a pool of blood in the middle of the street. I had to look away but I had already seen something I shall never forget: a murder had been committed at dawn by the communists.

We kept going, soon arriving at the place where we were to collect the food. Several times we had to drop to the ground, once because there was a sniper who was prepared to kill anyone in his line of fire, and twice to avoid the artillery shells from Franco's troops besieging the city, which apparently occurred every morning in that area near a garrison.

I cannot catalogue all the sufferings. There was hunger, lack of housing, financial hardships, and when the war was over there were purges, the need for political affidavits, the discovery of betrayal by former friends; for many there was an even greater torture: banishment. Many were expelled from Spain, and others from their own home towns. A human being can put up with incarceration and even face death, but the torture of banishment can break even the strongest.

As children of those years, we had to put away our toys and grow up ahead of o   time. We had learned that a careless word could mean danger or even death to our parents and friends. But we did not become callous and cynical; having learned to overcome our fear we were ready to sacrifice our own lives for a noble ideal. Our personal experience made us want to end violence and betrayal; wealth seemed less important than kindness and loyalty to a noble cause. We were religious. Although we had great ambitions we knew how to be happy with very little; we were poor and deprived due to shortages caused by World War II. Because of Franco's political ideology, Spain was boycotted by all European countries except Portugal.

The disruptions of the Civil War had caused young people to lose years of school; we were now eager to learn and rushed to take advantage of crash courses that were being organized everywhere in the country. We had lost the habit of study, but not the eagerness to learn. We did not have the money to buy new books; we had to sell the book we used in one course in order to buy another for a subsequent course. We would break books into sections so that several of us could copy it by hand (there were no copying machines at that time). Sometimes, we even went to the trouble of copying an entire book for a companion who did not have the time to do it. Many young women made extra sacrifices, surrendering their chance of going to college or university in order for their brothers to continue their studies.

Perhaps some of those reading these lines will find aspects of their own lives reflected in some portion of this odyssey. Those children and adolescents of the Spanish Civil War—youngsters from 1940–1950—initially filled the ranks of Opus Dei.

At that time, Opus Dei was practically unknown. Father Escrivá's recently published *Camino*[1] was a provocative invitation to postwar youth with practically no literature available other than religious books and the required textbooks approved by Franco's censorship. I did not know then that Father Escrivá was the Founder of Opus Dei nor did I then see the internal contradiction in this book where the frequent use of military language was combined with passages from the Gospel.

Father Escrivá offered the great adventure: to give up everything without getting anything in return; to conquer the world for Christ's church; a contemplative life through one's everyday work; to be missionaries, without being called such, but with a mission to accomplish. Students were challenged to excel in their chosen endeavor, turning study time into prayer, with the aim of attaining a high position in the intellectual world, and then offering it to Christ.

It was not a question of becoming nuns or monks, but a real challenge to lay people who had never considered a religious vocation. Our apostolic field was our own environment, among our friends. There were no special headquarters and nothing needed to be said. What counted was example, silence, discretion. Escrivá's book, *The Way*, reflects this approach. All these factors constituted a distinctive style that helped create a genuine ebullience among the young men and women who joined Opus Dei during the decade of the 1940s and who, in Opus Dei jargon, are known as "the first" or "the eldest." Indeed, the phrase is a kind of badge of honor within Opus Dei.

Sometime around 1945, I heard references to Opus Dei for the first time. They were very negative. Several people suggested that it represented a subtle danger to the Roman Catholic Church. More than one acquaintance, playing on the widespread Spanish hostility to Masons as members of a secret society, used the expression "white freemasonry." Some alleged that Opus Dei was envious if not hostile to the two most significant Spanish Catholic lay groups, Catholic Action

---

1. José María Escrivá, *Camino*, first edition (Valencia: Gráficas Turia, 1939). The first edition was published without the normal "nihil obstat" of ecclesiastical censors. It had the "imprimatur" of A. Rodilla, G. Vicar. English edition: *The Way* (New York: Scepter, 1979).

(Acción Católica) and the Spanish National Association of Propagandists (Asociación Española Nacional de Propagandistas). I even heard stories of young men from Opus Dei who courted young women, with no intention of marrying them, merely for the purpose of recruiting new members for the association!

Because of what I had heard and because of my personal concern for the church, I asked about Opus Dei during a conference at St. Augustine, my parish church in Madrid. The pastor, Father Avelino Gómez Ledo, said that he did not know enough to offer an opinion and would rather not discuss it. It was a discreet reply that somehow hinted at an unfavorable judgment on the group.

A few months later, in October 1946, I finally met someone from the mysterious Opus Dei, a priest named Pedro Casciaro, who officiated at the marriage of my first cousin in Albacete. He was a friend of the bridegroom, Javier Sánchez-Carrilero. The priest spoke in such a low voice that only the bride and groom could hear his homily, and he slipped away before the wedding luncheon was over without saying goodbye to anyone except the newlyweds.

I was intrigued about Opus Dei, and discussed it at length with my fiancé. He told me that he had heard the same rumors as I had, but that one of his classmates at his engineering school was a member and seemed perfectly normal, though he did not socialize with women. My fiancé admitted that nobody at the engineering school knew what membership in Opus Dei entailed or what life was like at the group's student residence.

In 1947, a year before our intended marriage, my fiancé, now a forestry engineer, accepted his first job in Morocco. To relieve my boredom during his absence and to pursue my own intellectual interests, I accepted a position at *Arbor*, the general cultural journal of the Council of Scientific Research, CSIC (Consejo Superior de Investigaciones Científicas) in Madrid. I was an assistant to *Arbor*'s associate director, Raimundo Panikkar.

When I was introduced to him, I was quite surprised to find a priest in such a major cultural post. I was even more surprised that he was an Indian with a Catalonian accent. Although only recently ordained and still a young man of twenty-eight, he was highly regarded at the CSIC as one of its founders. Everyone considered him brilliant; he had an astonishing capacity for work. I was told of a number of articles he had written for *Arbor*, in particular an essay on the thought of Max Planck.[1] He was well known for his mastery of languages, modern and

---

1. Raimundo Panikkar, "Max Planck (1858–1947)," *Arbor* (24) 1947:387–406.

classical. As an Indian, he was a British citizen. He wore the usual cassock like any other priest at that time. He was kind, although extremely serious with the staff of *Arbor*, with whom he very seldom used more words than those essential for greetings and work.

I began work at eight o'clock, an hour earlier than the other members of the staff, and I also left an hour earlier. One morning I was called by Dr. Albareda, the general secretary of the CSIC.[1] His own assistants were not due to arrive for at least an hour and he had an important and confidential letter to write immediately. When he started dictation I was very surprised that the letter was addressed to Monsignor José María Escrivá de Balaguer, the author of *The Way*.

Absorbed in my own thoughts I went back to my office. By then, my two co-workers were there, and they started pulling my leg with typical Iberian irony and asked me if I had been promoted.

"Promoted?" I replied. "What I was doing was taking a letter for the author of *The Way*.

"Of course," they said, "as a member of Opus Dei, Albareda has to send a report to its Founder."

"What did you say?" I asked, astonished. "That Escrivá, the author of *The Way*, is the Founder of Opus Dei and Albareda is a member?" Everybody laughed at my ignorance.

"Didn't you know," they went on, "that Florentino Pérez Embid,[2] the secretary to *Arbor*, is a member, too, as well as Rafael Calvo Serer."[3]

"No, I did not know any of this."

"And that Dr. Panikkar is a priest of Opus Dei?"

"Are you sure about Dr. Panikkar?"

"Positive. And so is the director of *Arbor*, Sánchez de Muniáin."

"But Sánchez de Muniáin is married," I protested.

"So what? He is a member too. He belongs to the married ones."

---

1. José María Albareda, one of "the first" in Opus Dei, was a professor of edaphology at the Universidad Central in Madrid (now called Complutense). Because of his professional prestige and age, Monsignor Escrivá suggested Albareda's name to the Spanish Minister of Education, José Ibáñez-Martín, for the position of CSIC general secretary. Albareda was ordained an Opus Dei priest around 1960 with the idea of posting him as rector of the University of Navarra, recently constituted by Pope John XXIII as a university of the church. He died in Madrid in the late 1970s.

2. Florentino Pérez Embid, well-known member of Opus Dei, was a monarchist who played an important role in bringing Prince Juan-Carlos de Borbón to Spain to receive a royal education as future king. Pérez Embid held important positions in the Franco regime, such as General Director of Fine Arts. He was from Seville and died in Madrid in the Opus Dei house of Monte Esquinza in late 1974.

3. Rafael Calvo-Serer was an atypical member of Opus Dei, one of the few members of Opus Dei publicly acknowledged as such. His political views were much discussed. Opus Dei used him as a tool to demonstrate the "political freedom" of Opus Dei to the world at large. He died a few years ago.

"What is going on here?" I asked angrily. "Is everybody here part of that organization? Are you two members too?"

"Certainly not." They laughed. "But almost everybody on the top levels here at the Council is a member."

I was appalled at the news that the author of *The Way,* a book read by many young people at that time, was the Founder of such a dubious group as Opus Dei and that the CSIC, the main Spanish center for research, was a platform utilized by Opus Dei. And since I had such a positive opinion of Dr. Panikkar, I was angry to learn that he was an Opus Dei priest.

The possibility of talking directly with Dr. Panikkar regarding Opus Dei and its control of the CSIC was little less than utopian. I had worked at *Arbor* for five months and the only words I had exchanged with Dr. Panikkar were formal greetings on arrival and departure and bits of information about work. So, a serious conversation on this matter seemed out of the question.

An opportunity presented itself, however, when Dr. Panikkar asked me to work the following Saturday, since he had a backlog of correspondence that had to be answered. After three hours of dealing with his correspondence, Dr. Panikkar suddenly said: "May I ask you why you work here?"

Astonished at the question, I said that I was planning to get married the following year and hoped to make my fiancé's absence more bearable by working at something that interested me.[1]

Dr. Panikkar made no comment, and we resumed our work. When we finished at lunch time, and I was locking the doors, he started another conversation, this time about Barcelona, where he had been recently.

"The weather was beautiful there," he said.

"I know," I replied, "my parents just returned from Barcelona and said the same thing."

"Why didn't you go with them?" he asked.

"For the simple reason that I am working here."

"I would always give you time off to go to Barcelona," he said, half-jokingly.

"I am so busy this year," I answered seriously, "that I do not even have time to make my spiritual retreat."[2]

"I am going to lead two groups next month, so if you would like . . ."

"With you? No thank you."

---

1. Although many today might smile, it was customary at that time that when a young woman was engaged her life was rather secluded.

2. Many Roman Catholic young people in Spain had the habit of making a spiritual retreat, perhaps of five to seven days, usually during Lent.

"I am not asking you to make your retreat under my guidance," Dr. Panikkar continued calmly. "What I meant was that you can have a week off at that time."

There was an embarrassed silence on my part. I did not know whether I should apologize because of my reply or how to pursue the conversation.

Finally Dr. Panikkar broke the silence with the question:

"May I ask why you said 'not with me'?"

"Because you are with Opus Dei," I answered frankly.

"Oh! I see. And what do you have against Opus Dei?"

"Personally nothing, but I think it is against the church."

"All right, all right," Dr. Panikkar said slowly. "Thank you for coming today. I think that we will have to talk about this matter again." And with his usual formal smile, he walked away.

Over the weekend I worried about whether I had been rude. I had been brought up to show reverence for the clergy and had never before challenged a priest so directly. But when I came to work the following Monday, Father Panikkar greeted me affably, saying he was ready to resume our discussion.

"Would you please explain to me your negative attitude to Opus Dei?" he asked gently.

I recounted all the things I had heard about Opus Dei: that it was a "freemasonry" because of its mysterious way of doing things such as not disclosing the identity of its members, where its residences were located, or who in those residences were members and who were not. That Opus Dei plotted to "capture" chairs at the university, hoping to preserve them for members and were ruthless about getting rid of anyone who was in their way. I even mentioned Father Casciaro's strained behavior at my cousin's wedding, and repeated the stories of male members who courted young women simply to recruit them for Opus Dei.

Father Panikkar heard me out without betraying any emotion, but his reply, when it came, was forceful:

"Do you know the meaning of slander?"

"Yes," I answered haltingly.

"Well, everything you have heard, everything you have repeated here, is nothing but slander."

Somehow, the assurance with which Father Panikkar spoke was more convincing to me than the accusations I had just made.

2

VOCATIONAL
CRISIS

What I will narrate in this chapter is not just my individual story, but reflects the way Opus Dei has always operated and how it still provokes a vocational crisis in a young woman. Persons or countries may vary but the strategy has not changed throughout the years. Opus Dei still describes recruitment in terms of "hunting" and "fishing." The same persuasiveness and subtleties are used to corner the prey.

In January 1948, Dr. Panikkar invited me to collaborate with him in preparations for the International Congress of Philosophy, which was to take place in Barcelona in October and of which he was the general secretary. This was a new position at the Luis Vives Institute of Philosophy that involved a two-year commitment and subsequent preparation of the proceedings for publication. Although I would still be working at the CSIC in Madrid, I would leave *Arbor*. I was pleased with the job offer since it was more challenging intellectually and the salary was better. The loss of employment security after two years did not matter, since I expected to be married by then and would no longer be living in Madrid.

I shared Dr. Panikkar's sense that this congress might well be the most significant intellectual gathering in Spain since the Civil War. Professor Juan Zaragüeta was president of the congress. I was administrative assistant in charge of public relations and the editing of three volumes of the Proceedings.[1] Father José Todolí, O.P., was not officially a member of the team organizing the congress, but as secretary to the Luis Vives Institute, was always willing to lend a hand. At about the

1. *Actas del Congreso Internacional de Filosofía* (Barcelona, 4–10 Octubre, 1948): *Con motivo del centenario de los filósofos Francisco Suárez y Jaime Balmes,* 3 vols. (Madrid: Instituto "Luis Vives" de Filosofía, CSIC, Bolaños y Aguilar, 1949).

same time Dr. Panikkar was elected secretary of the newly founded Spanish Society of Philosophy.

Although busy at work, I tried to get ready for married life. Daily attendance at Mass did not seem enough; I felt the need for an intelligent priest with whom I could share my ideas and questions about my forthcoming marriage. A number of my friends had a Jesuit as a spiritual adviser; I had considered seeking advice from Father Panikkar, but after that morning at *Arbor* when I voiced my criticisms of Opus Dei, I had never talked to him on personal matters of any kind.

My high regard for Father Panikkar was largely based on the letters I typed for him to a number of people whose names I never knew since Father Panikkar would write their names and addresses by hand. His letters were powerful testimony to his Christian faith. He was never authoritarian, but had empathy for a person's weakness; his intelligence was lively, open, and discreet.

Almost every day I also typed two to three pages of his personal writings, published much later in 1972 under the title *Cometas* ("Comets") and kindly dedicated to me.[1] These brief reflections touched on events at the university and in the world. I always looked forward to reading them, and still remember the one he wrote after Mahatma Gandhi was assassinated.[2] Another of his manuscripts, *Religion and Religions*, introduced me to the idea of the plurality of religions.[3] When Dr. Panikkar gave me this manuscript to type, I noticed the plural form "religions." Because of my strict Catholic education, I assumed that there was only one true religion and asked him to correct the spelling error.

"Why do you think there is an error there?" he asked, smiling.

"Because you wrote 'religions' in the plural, as if all religions are true."

"How many 'religions' do you think are true?" he asked.

"There are many religions, but only one true religion: Roman Catholicism."

"If there is only 'one true religion,' what would you call the others?"

"Just 'natural religions,'" I replied.

"Oh!" he said with some amusement, "I did not know that you considered Roman Catholicism an 'artificial religion.'"

---

1. See Raimundo Panikkar, *Cometas: Fragmentos de un diario espiritual de la postguerra* (Madrid: Euramérica, 1972).

2. Ibid., pp. 245–46.

3. Raimundo Panikkar, *Religione e Religioni* (Brescia: Morcelliana, 1964), *Religion y Religiones* (Madrid: Gredos, 1965), and *Religionen und die Religion* (Munich: Max Hueber, 1965). Curiously, the original was written in English but has not yet been published.

Work with Dr. Panikkar broadened the horizon of all of us on the team, which included Roberto Saumells and José Gutiérrez-Maesso.

As I mentioned earlier I could not find a spiritual adviser and I knew that once married I would live in Morocco, and I deeply wished to understand the people there. I must make explicit here something that I consider very important: I was profoundly moved by Father Panikkar's spiritual qualities and I was also confident that a priest would not be influenced by institutional ties when giving spiritual guidance.

So one fine day I asked Father Panikkar whether he would be willing to be my spiritual adviser. Father Panikkar was obviously surprised and said:

"Very well, but you should know that I am very strict. I am afraid we will have to talk at the Opus Dei's women's residence."

The following day we had an early morning appointment, and he gave me the address, Zurbarán, 26, and mentioned that the name of the directress was Guadalupe.

Because of all the criticisms I had heard about Opus Dei, I arrived at the students' residence with both suspicion and curiosity. When I rang the bell, I realized that I only knew Opus Dei men and priests, and now I was going to meet Opus Dei women.

I was surprised to see the door opened by a maid in a black uniform with a small satin apron. That kind of "uniform" was appropriate only in the evening. I told her that I had an eight o'clock appointment with Father Panikkar, and I followed her up the white marble steps covered with a red carpet and had to pass her to enter the living room. She asked for my name and motioned for me to sit down and left with the door ajar.

Half an hour's wait gives you time mentally to rearrange a room from your chair! My first impression was that the room was unattractively furnished and did not look at all like the living room of a residence for university women.

The room was not appropriately lit. The couch was pushed against one wall and a piano against another wall, from which direction I could hear the prayers of Mass being said. I noticed a crystal lamp and two Victorian-style arm chairs upholstered in a pale damask tea rose. On the right was a dark folding table standing by what I took to be the wall of the room whose closed door I saw on my left as I followed the maid up the stairs. On that table lay a volume of *Camino*. On another chest there was a picture of a lady whom I assumed was the foundress of the Women's Branch of Opus Dei. I was soon informed that Opus Dei had no foundress and that the woman in the picture was the Founder's mother, whom members called "the grandmother."

There was also an easel with a classic Spanish painting of a Madonna graced with fresh flowers. On the wall was a photograph of Father Escrivá.

At the end of Mass, a tall, smiling young woman joined me. She introduced herself as Guadalupe Ortiz de Landázuri, directress of the residence.[1] With her round face and oblique eyes, she had an Oriental look. She seemed capable, self-contained, and affable, but I was unprepared for her directness and her many questions: Was I a student? Where did I live? Did I work? I gave her only the briefest answers. I also said that I had an appointment with Father Panikkar. She always recalled our first encounter saying, "You were so distant!"

When Father Panikkar arrived, she left. In this first conversation with Father Panikkar as my spiritual adviser, I tried to speak of my goals in life as well as of my concerns. He listened carefully, trying to understand my personal situation.

The first spiritual reading he recommended to me was *The Story of a Soul* by Saint Thérèse of Lisieux. Despite my continuing suspicion of Opus Dei, the session with Father Panikkar reassured me. I told him that I was looking forward to getting married and hoped he would help prepare me for my new responsibilities.

The relationship with Father Panikkar as my spiritual adviser did not affect our daily work. Our work for the International Congress of Philosophy was distinct from his spiritual guidance.

As I continued my visits to Zurbarán to see Father Panikkar, I found the atmosphere at the women's residence both friendly and attractive. I had also met several classmates who also sought spiritual guidance from Father Panikkar.

I was 22 years old at the time and life held every possible promise of happiness. Father Panikkar would say that this happiness was the reflection of a normal, happy childhood. I was optimistic, curious about learning, passionate about reading and interested in art, mainly modern art. I was open to any challenge; I loved and felt loved. I was able to move freely in any circle because of my social upbringing. I had a more cosmopolitan point of view than most young Spanish women: my father had been educated in England and many close relatives had married persons of different nationalities.

In March 1948 I decided to attend a retreat for young women that Father Panikkar was to give at the residence of Zurbarán. My hope

1. Guadalupe Ortiz de Landázuri was finishing her doctoral dissertation in chemistry. Since I liked and trusted her, she had a lot to do with my decision to enter Opus Dei. She was convincing, refined, and persistent. In 1950 she founded the Opus Dei's women's branch in Mexico, returning to Spain in 1964 where she died in Madrid a few years later.

was that it would help my spiritual life before taking on the new responsibility of marriage. My fiancé and I had often discussed our ideal of a Christian marriage, happy and open to other people who might need our help. I had always been very much concerned about social problems; to help others was of primary importance in my life. As a teenager, I thought that this might be a sign of religious vocation, but I soon realized I was not called to be a nun. At this point I was not afraid of making a retreat organized by Opus Dei because I was totally confident in Father Panikkar's spiritual guidance.

My fiancé was in Morocco, and just before the seven-day retreat, several of his colleagues came to my home, imploring me not to attend the retreat. They spoke bluntly of their fear that Opus Dei would try to enroll me in their ranks. Their insistence offended me, since I was convinced I would see through any attempt by Opus Dei to proselytize.

I disregarded the advice of my fiancé's friends and replied that I would never give up my future husband to become a member of Opus Dei.

My parents also had misgivings about the retreat.

Nevertheless, I went to the retreat with confidence, knowing that I would be under the guidance of Father Panikkar.

At the registration desk I met a friend, Carmen Comas-Mata, who seemed surprised and irritated:

"What the hell are you doing here?" she asked.

"Why should I not be here?" I replied. "You are here, too."

"Yes, but 'they' are not trying to sign me up. And I am sure that they will go after you, and make your life complicated."

"Don't be ridiculous! I came for the retreat and that is all."

"Please, don't talk to anybody," she said mildly.

I was getting tired of all this advice. Even though I did not completely trust Opus Dei women, I trusted Father Panikkar; I was sure that Opus Dei priests were concerned only for the souls in their care.

The retreat started normally enough; the atmosphere was very pleasant, the meals carefully prepared, the table served with exquisite taste, and the house immaculate. During the first two days I found the Opus Dei women polite and discreet. Three days later, when Guadalupe asked me if everything was all right and whether I had any questions, I answered:

"I am fine, thanks."

In retreats of this kind, the priest usually gives meditations on death, charity, and religious vocation.

Father Panikkar's meditation on death was superb, with no hint of terror. He even made us laugh when telling us about a priest at his econdary school who always used to talk about death as the last topic of the day before going to bed. I do not remember what he said on charity and there was no meditation whatsoever on religious vocation during the first three days. Then, on the fourth morning, Father Panikkar started the meditation by reciting the lyric of a popular song of that time:

> They say that John Alba's daughter
> Wants to be a nun.
> They say that her fiancé refuses
> But she replies: "No matter!"

The audience's first reaction was laughter. But suddenly the priest repeated the last sentence more forcefully: "But she replies that it does not matter! That it does not matter!" (what her fiancé thinks).

Father Panikkar continued his meditation by drawing on the parable of Lazarus and the rich man (Luke 16: 19–31), the poem by Rabindranath Tagore, *The Chariot of the King:* "What hast thou to give to me?"[1] And he ended it with the marvelous poem by Oscar Wilde: *The Nightingale and the Rose.*[2]

Naturally, the examples, the stories of generosity in the meditation, were taken to heart as a challenge. Did I have anything to do with John Alba's daughter? No! I had no desire to be a nun. But what about the nightingale, the little bird who allowed the rose tree to take its blood to give the student the chance to do what the young woman he loved had asked: find a red rose in the middle of winter? What did Father Panikkar want to convey with these examples?

The issue had been raised. A seed had been planted. That meditation was the most serious event of my entire life and the point of departure for a vocational crisis that totally changed my life.

Lost in my own thought, I suddenly heard Guadalupe ask:

"How would you interpret the meditation in your case?"

"Oh!, it doesn't apply to me, because I don't want to become a nun."

"Haven't you ever considered religious life?" she continued.

"Yes, when I was a kid. But it isn't my vocation to be a nun; I have been clear about that for some time. Besides, I am not John Alba's daughter," I said somewhat sarcastically.

"That is true, you are not," she went on. "But I am not talking about 'religious life' as such. As you noticed, in Father Panikkar's stories, one

---

1. See Rabindranath Tagore, *Gitanjali,* No. L, in *The Collected Poems and Plays of Rabindranath Tagore* (New York: Macmillan & Co., 1967), p. 19.

2. See Oscar Wilde, *The Nightingale and the Rose,* in *Poems, Fiction, Plays, Lectures, Essays and Letters,* ed. H. Montgomery Hyde (New York: Clarendon Press, 1982).

person's gift to God may be his wealth, for somebody else life itself, for another ... a fiancé. ... Have you ever thought about the possibility of dedicating your life to God's service as a lay woman? The Gospel needs to be read in terms of our individual situation; it is always a question of generosity."

I was confused because what was being presented to me was not a religious vocation but an act of personal generosity. Was God speaking to me through Father Panikkar's meditation? Were Guadalupe's words an Opus Dei "trick"? I certainly tried to be a good Catholic, but was quite aware that I was not a saint. Why would God ask something special of me who was preparing to be a good Christian wife?

I decided to speak with Father Panikkar. There was anxiety in my voice but my questions were clear and direct: was his meditation something I should consider for my own life despite my deep love for my fiancé? Why shouldn't I just get married and work to help others? Shouldn't his meditation be totally disregarded in my case?

His answer was unambiguous: I should not disregard the possibility of dedicating my entire life to God's service. On the contrary, I should consider it seriously and act accordingly, "at any cost," he emphasized.

"I will pray very hard for you," he added. "I will ask God, who has given you so many things in life to help you to be generous to him. Tomorrow is the first Friday of the month; tonight," he continued, "I will pray for you especially before the Blessed Sacrament."

The point of being generous with God bothered me tremendously: all the responsibility was on my shoulders, since I was told by Guadalupe that they did not pose that challenge to everybody.

I finished the retreat in a sea of tears and with tremendous anguish. Mine was an impossible dilemma: to give up my forthcoming marriage for God's sake, or go ahead with my marriage knowing that I had refused God's invitation to a life of dedicated service to him in Opus Dei.

A couple of days later Father Panikkar told me that during the retreat several girls had asked him to write a brief note on the back of a religious picture. If I had asked him, he told me, he would have used a couple of lines from Tagore: "If you shed tears when you miss the sun, you also miss the stars."[1]

After the retreat, Guadalupe repeatedly called me at home and at work, asking me to discuss "my problem" with her. She and Father Panikkar suggested that I ask my fiancé for a waiting period, a delay in which to consider this unexpected possibility without outside pressures.

---

1. See Rabindranath Tagore, *Stray Birds,* VI, in *Collected Poems and Plays,* p. 22.

I prefer not to describe in detail the surprise, pain, and disappointment this request caused my fiancé. He was stationed in Tetuan, Morroco, and finishing his compulsory military service there. He was initially unable to obtain leave from the army. However, when he managed to come to Madrid for a couple of days, we spoke, and then he talked with Father Panikkar who stressed that he also had to be generous and accept God's will. As a good Catholic he felt trapped and unable to fight with the people representing God.

I shall always remember his sadness as he told me: "If you were leaving me for another man, I would break his head, but what can I do to a God to whom I kneel every day?"

I loved my fiancé deeply and his unhappiness and anguish made me feel terribly guilty. Meanwhile in Opus Dei Guadalupe and Father Panikkar told me that suffering was required by God as a sign of purification. They stressed over and over that suffering was the cornerstone for anyone entering Opus Dei at the "foundational stage" and insisted that I had to place my whole life in God's hands without asking for anything in return. They spoke of all this quite naturally. Guadalupe would remind me that I should follow her indications as well as those of my spiritual adviser. She told me that the Founder was accustomed to say that "Opus Dei was the manifestation of God's will on earth" and that "Opus Dei was the way of converting the world to God" and that "the day in which we put Christ above all human activities, God will convert the world to him."

Since there were married men in Opus Dei, I asked Guadalupe why I couldn't marry and remain in Opus Dei. "Perhaps there will be married women members someday," she replied, "but who knows when?" She also added "That is not the vocation to which you were called."

I was repeatedly told to be generous to God and committed to Opus Dei. But I felt I needed a clearer picture of my vocation and an understanding of Opus Dei, and asked Guadalupe for a copy of the Constitutions.

"Why do you need it?" she laughed.

She didn't give me a copy; she didn't even tell me that the Constitutions of Opus Dei had yet to be written. However she emphasized that, by virtue of the Vatican's 1947 promulgation of the Constitution *Provida Mater Ecclesiae*,[1] Opus Dei was the "first secular institute of the Roman Catholic Church" and that a few days later it had also received the *Decretum Laudis*.[2] She also remarked that because it was a novelty in the church

---

1. *Constitutio Apostolica Provida Mater Ecclesia*, February 2, 1947, in Dominique Le Tourneau, *Que sais-je? L'Opus Dei* (Paris: Presses Universitaires de France, 1984), p. 59.

2. See *Decretum Laudis*, February 24, 1947; in Giancarlo Rocca, *L'Opus Dei: Appunti e documenti per una storia* (Rome: Edizione Paoline, 1985), pp. 38ff. and original texts, pp. 159–163. Also in A. de Fuenmayor, V. Gómez-Iglesias, and J. L. Illanes, *El itinerario jurídico del Opus*

and few people would be able to understand it, it was necessary to be "extremely discreet"—silent—about Opus Dei.

In the beginning Opus Dei presented itself as the most modern, innovative, and *avant-garde* institution in the church. Its members were laywomen and laymen; they did not wear a religious habit but ordinary clothes. Nor did they change their names, as was required of members of religious orders. Opus Dei houses were not convents; no canonical community life was required. As prospective members we were told to continue our regular work since it would be by means of this work that we would exercise a fruitful apostolate, convert the world, and achieve our personal sanctity.

After months of being told over and over again that "my way was clear and that I had been chosen by God for this new apostolate," I broke up for good with my fiancé and I wrote the required letter to Monsignor Escrivá, the president general of Opus Dei, asking him to be accepted as a numerary (full member) in Opus Dei.

The directress of the Opus Dei women's residence made it quite clear that in accordance with Opus Dei policy, I could not breathe a word about my letter, *which implied a decision for life,* to anybody, especially to my family or to any priest outside Opus Dei.

The struggle over this decision exhausted me, and I was still so confused about God's will for my life that I decided to go abroad to think things over. Guadalupe did not want me to leave, but Father Panikkar supported my decision. So I went to France and Switzerland.

In the summer of 1948 I went to Paris and stayed at the residence of the French Dominicans, whose school I had attended in Spain. I visited Mortefontaine-sur-Oise, the Mother House of the French Dominicans of the Holy Rosary, a lovely old chateau in a very peaceful and beautiful setting in the countryside near Paris. I was happy to have the chance to speak at leisure with the mother general, Mère Cathérine Dominique, a tall, elegant woman from an old Parisian family. She was very intelligent and an excellent listener. She knew me from my school in Spain. At the end of our conversation she strongly recommended that I review my situation with another priest not linked to Opus Dei.

I also spoke with Mère Marie de la Soledad, who had encouraged me to come to France and to Switzerland. She had known me since I was twelve, when I entered the French Dominican School in Valladolid. Young, bright, and understanding, she had a doctorate in mathematics and had long been my teacher and spiritual confidant. Neither she nor Mère Cathérine

---

Dei: Historia y defensa de un carisma (Pamplona: Ediciones de la Universidad de Navarra, 1989), pp. 532–35.

Dominique clearly understood Opus Dei's policy and goals, but were respectful of the institution, since it had been accepted—if not yet finally approved—by the Roman Catholic Church. They were concerned about my future, however, and did not believe life in Opus Dei would be appropriate for me; I should keep praying to God for guidance and review my situation with my parents as well as with another priest who was not a member of Opus Dei.

I went on to Lucerne, Switzerland, where I decided to write my fiancé asking him to come to Madrid on my return so we could talk things over. I never understood how he managed to get permission from the army and the director of his company, where he worked as a forest engineer, for a week's visit to Madrid. We talked at length and were soon reconciled.

I asked Guadalupe Ortiz de Landázuri to disregard the letter I wrote earlier to Opus Dei's Founder and I phoned Father Panikkar to inform him of my decision to continue the relationship with my fiancé. It was September 14, 1948, the Feast of the Exaltation of the Holy Cross, a day of religious celebration in the church and a special feast day in Opus Dei. Father Panikkar reacted with sadness and told me that my decision made the burden of his own cross heavier since he was full of apostolic expectations with regard to my vocation. Years later I realized that this kind of reaction was typical in Opus Dei when new members tried to leave the institution.

I was convinced, however, that from now on everything would be easy, but once again I was wrong: Guadalupe and Father Panikkar kept insisting I had failed to be loyal to Christ's call. When Father Panikkar learned that my fiancé was coming to Madrid for two weeks, he made part of my penance not to use makeup or nail polish during his visit.

All this time I was still working for the International Congress of Philosophy and about to leave for Barcelona for the big event. One day I received a call from José María Hernández-Garnica, the priest in charge of the Women's Branch of Opus Dei, asking me to come to Zurbarán, the women's residence, because he wanted to ask a favor. I went without any idea of what was involved. I knew, however, that he was the priest in charge of all women in Opus Dei (central priest secretary) and one of the first three priests ordained for Opus Dei in 1944. He was known among Opus Dei's men by the nickname "Chiqui." Father Hernández-Garnica was a tall, pale man with black hair and thick glasses. He did not look directly at people. Although he belonged to an old Spanish family, his way of speaking was too colloquial, not at all refined: he used lots of "muletillas" (verbal crutches). Rather rude while speaking to Opus Dei women, he was, however, as I came to realize over the years, honest with us.

After a brief greeting and without preliminaries of any kind, Father Hernández-Garnica asked me not to go to Barcelona in October for the International Congress of Philosophy that I had helped organize.

I was tempted to give a sharp answer but held my tongue before saying that I could not comply with his request because the organization of the congress was my full-time work.

Hernández-Garnica said that he was asking me not to go to Barcelona as a "favor" since I was not an Opus Dei member; to members he would simply issue an order. The reason for his request was the severe criticism of Opus Dei in Barcelona. The fact that Father Panikkar's assistant at the congress was a woman could be an occasion for gossip against Opus Dei.

In my naiveté I could not then understand how important it was for Opus Dei not to have one of their priests next to a young woman. In my years in Opus Dei I learned that in accordance with its Constitutions, the separation between men and women members is total.[1] This separation is particularly stressed between Opus Dei priests and women members; to my understanding, this is a reflection of Monsignor Escrivá's sexual repression.

The request from Father Hernández-Garnica put a damper on my enthusiasm for the congress, to which I had given the best of my abilities and much of my time. The congress committee's decision to allow me to attend the sessions in Barcelona would have given me the opportunity of meeting the world's leaders in philosophy and the humanities.

When Father Hernández-Garnica understood that I was unwilling to yield, he resorted to blackmail: he said that if I insisted on going to Barcelona, Opus Dei superiors would forbid Father Panikkar to attend the congress. I realized that this meant that the congress would be a total failure; Panikkar was not only the general secretary, but able to communicate fluently in all the official languages to be used at the congress.

Realizing that he had left me no choice, Hernández-Garnica added that I should offer a gracious excuse to the president of the congress without revealing the real reason.

The anger with which I related this conversation to Father Panikkar led him to say that, if I wanted to attend the congress, he would be willing to renounce going to Barcelona; but as an Opus Dei priest, he was obliged to obey its orders. It was a sincere offer but I had no choice: whatever my disappointment, I could not do anything that would endanger the success of the congress.

My excuses for not going to Barcelona were kindly and discreetly accepted by the committee in charge of the congress. My absence was

---

1. See Rocca, *L'Opus Dei*, pp. 51, 163–65, where he includes Opus Dei's *Internal Rules for Administrations* in its first version. Around 1954, in Rome, I copied and printed the new version prepared by Monsignor Escrivá. It was longer and more detailed.

sincerely regretted, but Father José Todolí, O.P., who as secretary of the Luis Vives Institute had been deeply involved in all the preparations, was not fooled and remained convinced that my decision was the result of an Opus Dei trick. It goes without saying that, from that day onwards, Father Hernández-Garnica was not exactly my "cup of tea."

In turn, I discovered that the strategy used on me was not an isolated case but the result of an oath that all Opus Dei priests, superiors, and members called *inscribed—inscritos*—(the numeraries who have a position on the Opus Dei governing or indoctrination board) are obliged to take. It is called a "promisory oath." This oath, taken with one hand on the Gospel, entails that any member in such a position must always consult with his or her respective superior on important matters such as whether or not a governmental, professional, or social position should be accepted. Since political activities are often related to social matters, this means that an Opus Dei member cannot accept a government appointment or agree to head a corporation, for example, by himself or herself alone. In virtue of the "promisory oath," the members are first obliged to ask for advice from the assigned Opus Dei major superiors.

Theoretically, Opus Dei members are free to accept or reject advice received from their superiors. But Opus Dei superiors are also empowered to move an Opus Dei member to the other end of the world if they consider that any failure to follow "their advice" might interfere with Opus Dei's interests. All Opus Dei priests have to take this oath, which clearly shows the great farce and the fraud of Opus Dei "freedom."

From October to December 1948, Opus Dei launched an offensive to regain my "lost vocation." Over and over I was told that I was going against God's will and therefore I could never again be happy or be able to make my husband happy. Father Panikkar told me not to invite him to officiate at my marriage ceremony since such an invitation would be tantamount to participating in a crime, and Guadalupe said that my idea of consulting a priest who was not a member of Opus Dei was diabolic. These are practical manifestations of Opus Dei doctrine taught by its Founder.

As "new vocations" in Opus Dei, we were told not to disclose to our own families the commitment we had made to the institution. This often led to serious conflicts and even lies to our parents. Unfortunately, this Opus Dei policy continues in force to this day. As far as families are concerned, the Opus Dei idea of "discretion"—a practice of being secretive—consequently tend to make them suspicious.

Opus Dei had the appeal of not rejecting the secular world but of calling rather for the sanctification of ordinary work, through which you could both serve humanity and achieve your own salvation. To be a missionary without going to a remote land was attractive to me. I was taken with the idea that through ordinary work we could bring peace and salvation into the world.

For us Catholics who went through the turmoil and horrors of the Spanish Civil War, Opus Dei's perspective was not only attractive but able to awaken our inner generosity. I had now been invited to participate in this adventure.

Once again I heard that giving to Opus Dei our life, our youth, our love, sacrificing a possibly brilliant future for the sake of God, was a fair price to pay. In the 1990s Opus Dei repeats the same arguments to potential recruits: generosity to God, yes, but through Opus Dei. I came to realize that Opus Dei does not undertake any apostolate unless it entails proselytism for the institution. By way of example, the visits to the poor which Opus Dei recommends to girls attending its schools are always manipulated by the numeraries directing this apostolate into an occasion to bind those girls closer to Opus Dei centers, rather than exhibiting real interest in the poor and their suffering. A true apostolate, as it is understood in the Roman Catholic Church, purely for God and the church, is not Opus Dei's primary intention. Nowadays, when all humankind trembles at the lack of basic human rights such as freedom, housing, food or basic reading skills, the Opus Dei doctrine continues to reflect an embarrassing lack of Christian concern for the poor and their suffering. No member of Opus Dei, much less an Opus Dei priest, enjoys the freedom to join a group of citizens in a demonstration for justice for a minority group.

But, coming back to the thread of my story, on Christmas Day 1948, the mail brought me a card with a beautiful picture of the Madonna with the printed legend: *Ecce Ancilla, Behold, the handmaid of the Lord.* Below was a handwritten sentence by my spiritual director: *Will you become one?*

It had been a struggle, but Opus Dei had won. On New Year's Eve 1949, I made a clean break with my fiancé, believing that by entering Opus Dei I was doing God's will. Many people rebuked me for my behavior toward my planned marriage. I was told by relatives and friends that I was "a woman without feelings, without heart!" God knows well the painful crisis I went through until I finally surrendered to "God's will," as I understood it.

Without doubt, Opus Dei presented the vocation to me on the basis of my own passionate temperament and the fact that they knew I liked to do things wholeheartedly. They saw my thirst for an apostolate and successfully channeled it toward Opus Dei. They emphasized the dilemma of apostolic limitations that marriage implies. It was also stressed that because of my family and its social connections, I could move in a wide range of social circles in Spain, giving me the opportunity to help young women of similar backgrounds and, eventually, even married women. My capacity for leadership was another gift from God. I was asked whether I wished to keep these gifts to myself or offer them to God. All these ideas were intermingled in my heart and in my mind, and, finally, I decided I must give to God whatever he asked me for, even if it meant giving up my future marriage and inflicting deep hurt on the man I loved.

Many people judged me harshly for my decision. Many friends and even close relatives said I had treated my fiancé frivolously; these were people I was not to see again for almost twenty years, when I had left Opus Dei. Their attitude would probably have been different if I had joined one of the established religious orders; at the time Opus Dei was largely unknown and regarded with considerable suspicion. Despite my mother's negative attitude toward my vocation, a few relatives and friends of mine, as well as my father and my brothers kept in touch, either by sporadic correspondence or by meeting me briefly when I passed through Madrid on a move from one house to another.

I remember how touched I was when my youngest brother, who was twelve, managed to come with our housekeeper to visit me while I was living at Los Rosales, an Opus Dei study center in Villaviciosa de Odón, near Madrid.

During the eighteen years I remained in Opus Dei my parents never came to visit me, nor was I ever allowed to go to my parents' home. Two facts are evident: (1) Opus Dei always kept me away from Madrid, and (2) Opus Dei superiors never had the basic human decency to visit my parents to explain to them what Opus Dei was. The meager explanation I gave to my parents was completely inadequate. At that time Opus Dei's Constitutions as such did not exist; there was no official or written information on the institution, which in fact had not yet received official and final approval by the Holy See. I learned about this years later while in Rome working close to the Founder as an Opus Dei major superior.

The real attitude of the organization was shown by Opus Dei superiors and priests who frequently told us that parents were often a "tool" used by the Devil to destroy or take an incipient vocation away.

New vocations were told to answer the question: "What are Opus Dei people like?" Reply: "As everyone should be."

In the following chapters I shall give details of Opus Dei's structure and procedures that I was unfamiliar with when I joined the institution. A few specifics of which I was unaware on Opus Dei's *modus operandi* are worth mentioning here:

a) I did not appreciate how my family's name and social circumstances made me a good "catch." Opus Dei's interest was recruiting women from the social élites.

b) I did not know that my giving up a forthcoming marriage was going to be used as an example for future potential members to encourage them to do the same.

c) I did not know that the reason Guadalupe Ortiz de Landázuri laughed when I asked to read Opus Dei Constitutions was because the Constitutions were not yet written nor even submitted to the Vatican for approval.

d) I did not know that the secrecy of Opus Dei—called "discretion"—was due to fear because of the weakness of Opus Dei's legal status within the Roman Catholic Church. Escrivá did not want to become involved in disputes within the social circle represented by the new candidates' families. But it is important to explain here that new vocations are still required to keep silent (discreet) about Opus Dei to their families, despite the current approval of Opus Dei as a personal prelature. Opus Dei still considers the candidate's family as the worst enemy of an incipient vocation, especially now that they proselitize teenaged girls.

e) I also did not know why Opus Dei women and priests labeled those of us who went to their residence for Mass, confessions, or study circles as "the St. Raphael girls," their jargon for "possible vocations."

Looking back from a distance, I must say that I consider totally immoral Opus Dei recruitment policies requesting people to assume a lifelong commitment as members of this prelature without first letting them read what in my time were the guidelines of the future Constitutions as a secular institute, a draft document called *Praxis,* whose existence was kept totally secret from us as new vocations, to which only the directress of the house had access. Even now Opus Dei's approved Constitutions as a personal prelature are not made available—indeed have not been translated from Latin. Then, after reading over these documents, candidates should be given time to reflect and consider the responsibility their commitment would entail.

Ironically, whereas in the conservative atmosphere of the 1940s and 1950s Opus Dei presented itself as *avant-garde,* it has since become the most retrograde and sectarian wing of the church. Opus Dei remains the same in its inner structure: its eagerness to be seen as "different"; its effort to convince the Pope and the hierarchy it is a providential institution for our time, while, in fact, Opus Dei exploits the church for its own purposes.

Significantly, when Opus Dei fought the big battle to change its status from secular institute into personal prelature, whose main characteristic is precisely the freedom and independence (Opus Dei calls it "harmony") it enjoys from the hierarchy of the Roman Catholic Church throughout the world, it became an *ecclesiola in Ecclesia,* a sect.[1] Without leaving the

---

1. See chapter 10, especially nos. 11, 12, and 13 of de Fuenmayor et al., *El itinerario jurídico del Opus Dei.*

church but as a church inside the church, Opus Dei has all the characteristics of a sect.[1]

Just as Monsignor Escrivá was virtually worshipped in life as the incarnation of the spirit of Opus Dei, the goal of Opus Dei today is to elevate him to the altar.

---

1. See Bryan R. Wilson, *Patterns of Sectarianism* (London: Heinemann, 1967), pp. 22–45.

3

THE MAKING
OF A FANATIC

During a slow and subtle process of several years Opus Dei superiors mold people's souls. Following a period of formation—I would call it "indoctrination"—people begin to change until they acquire the "good spirit" Opus Dei talks about so much and become mere robots in the hands of the organization. In the following chapters, I will attempt to describe in detail how Opus Dei superiors brought about this change.

What I am about to describe might be familiar to persons who belonged to religious orders before the "aggiornamento" occasioned by Vatican II took place. One cannot compare Opus Dei, however, to the procedures of any religious order, since they are juridically different. Monsignor Escrivá himself was not in total agreement with Vatican II and the notion of a possible "aggiornamento" in Opus Dei is totally foreign to the spirit of the institution. The Constitutions of Opus Dei can never be changed or modified.

After I wrote the letter to Monsignor Escrivá seeking admission, my directress, Guadalupe Ortiz de Landázuri, stressed that I should say nothing to my parents about the letter I wrote or my intended vocation, or my visits to the Opus Dei residence. God's will would be revealed to me by Opus Dei superiors, who knew what would be best for me and knew me better than my parents. So, under the guise of discretion, our vocation in Opus Dei started by lying to our parents.

Many years later, in 1979, when Opus Dei submitted to the Vatican its petition to change from being a secular institute to a personal prelature, it stated: ". . .Opus Dei has a lay body composed of simple faithful or common citizens, united by the same specific vocation *rite probata.*" What is meant by *rite probata* is that the superiors of Opus Dei are the only ones who know the spirit of the institution; they alone can screen the vocation of any possible new candidate.

Guadalupe said that, since I had not yet taken any vows, I could simply tell anybody, if asked, that I was not a member of Opus Dei. To mention our vocation to our parents would have meant breaking one of the strictest rules of Opus Dei: discretion. For this reason I became almost "mysterious" to my family and friends.

My parents noticed that I had changed; I had stopped socializing, not even attending family events like weddings or birthday parties. My parents knew only what I had told them, following Opus Dei guidelines: I had broken off my engagement because I was considering the possibility of joining a religious order and possibly Opus Dei. My mother, who is very astute, became infuriated at my behavior and said that it was a ruse to join Opus Dei, since the change had begun during those "blessed" days of recollection I attended.

When the Saint Raphael's girl gives her life to Opus Dei, she is on probation for the first six months. She now belongs to "Saint Michael's work," and as such she is now a new member of the Opus Dei family that will become more important to her than her blood relatives.

By "Saint Michael's work" is understood all the indoctrination (education, studies, personal work) that an Opus Dei numerary undertakes from the very first day she requests admission to the institution. The numeraries (the élite members of Opus Dei fully dedicated and living permanently in the houses of the institution) are under Saint Michael's protection. The archangel is also patron of the associates (formerly called oblates, members with full dedication to Opus Dei who only rarely live in Opus Dei houses) as are all Opus Dei priests.

The *Instruction of Saint Michael* is an internal document, written by Monsignor Escrivá, and printed at the Opus Dei headquarters in Rome in the 1950s. Although brief, it explains in detail the specific reasons and ways of indoctrination for men and women numeraries and aggregates.

Six months from the day I wrote the letter to Monsignor Escrivá requesting admission and although still living with my parents, I was allowed to go through the first stage into Opus Dei, the "admission." The ceremony took place in the small oratory of Lagasca 124, in Madrid.

An Opus Dei priest, the central directress (Rosario de Orbegozo), and the very first numerary of Opus Dei (Lola Fisac) attended the ceremony. It was a simple ceremony in accordance with the Opus Dei *Ritual.* You kneel in front of a wooden cross, common to all Opus Dei oratories, you respond to the questions read by the priest, set down in the *Ritual.* When the question and answer period is over, you kiss the priest's stole and the wooden cross. Finally, all recite the Opus Dei official prayer, the *Preces,* which all members must recite every day, collectively if possible.

The admission means only that you are now officially "on probation"; it is a moral but not a legal commitment to Opus Dei. During this period, Opus Dei superiors can advise you to leave, and you are also able to leave Opus Dei without breaking any law, although superiors always subject persons who try to leave on their own initiative to a kind of emotional blackmail. For a year from the day of admission, you must adapt to the rules and duties of Opus Dei. That means that if during this year on "probation" you start to change your lifestyle and adopt the "good spirit" of Opus Dei, the numerary may be granted permission to take the first temporary vows or commitments, called the oblation. This is granted by the regional vicar with the deliberative ballot of the regional advisory. These vows or contracts, as they want to call them now, are taken for the period ending on the nearest March 19, the Feast of St. Joseph. From then on the vows are renewed every year on March 19. The oblation consists of two parts. First, it is customary to take the vows during morning Mass. If the oratory is exclusively for numeraries, at the Offertory time, the numerary taking the vows kneels in front of the altar and reads the following: "In the presence of God, Our Lord to whom all Glory is due, with confidence in the intercession of Holy Mary and of our holy Patrons and with my Guardian Angel as witness I, [here the complete name of the person], take the vow of poverty, of chastity, and of obedience until the next feast of St. Joseph in accordance with the spirit of Opus Dei." Second, in the afternoon or evening of that very day, also in the oratory, another portion of the oblation takes place. It is attended by an Opus Dei priest, the directress of the house, and possibly another numerary. You read the brief texts in dialogue with the priest. When the dialogue is over you kiss the priest's stole and also the wooden cross. The ceremony ends with the recitation of the *Preces* by all in attendance. After five consecutive years of renewal, there are the perpetual vows, called fidelity, which require the confirmation of the prelate.

Madrid: Zurbarán

From January 1949 to January 1950 my life as a new Opus Dei numerary focused on my job at the Council of Scientific Research and on my obligation as a new vocation to make a daily visit, or as often as possible, to Zurbarán, the Opus Dei students' residence, to speak with the directress and to help in the house.

I came to enjoy my conversations with Guadalupe Ortiz de Landázuri more and more. She encouraged me to speak openly and understood me very well. I admired her intelligence and kindness; she was also socially gifted and very persuasive. I trusted her and considered her a real friend. Years later, when I was no longer a member of Opus Dei, I met her in Madrid at the Church of El Espíritu Santo; she had then returned recently from Mexico. Despite the change of circumstances, I valued her friendship and I was deeply saddened when, subsequently, I learned that she had passed away. I believe that she and Father Panikkar were the two most important people behind my decision to join Opus Dei.

"Helping in the house" meant doing menial work to aid the numeraries in charge of the administration of the residence.

After my work day, I would head to Zurbarán. On arriving at the house I saw almost nobody, since at that hour the residents would be in the study room. The maid would tell Guadalupe that I had arrived and I would be instructed either to go to the living room to speak with her or to the administration to help the numeraries there.

In the administration I was asked either to set the dinner tables for the residents, or to help the numerary in charge of the laundry with ironing or prepare the oratory for Mass the following day.

María Jesús Hereza, the second numerary of Opus Dei, and a delightful person, also lived at Zurbarán while completing her doctoral dissertation in medicine. She introduced herself to me as a student in awe of my uncle, Dr. Antonio García-Tapia. My uncle mentioned to me that he respected her very much both as student and young professional. During my years in Opus Dei I was often in touch with her and always found her honest and sincere. She left Opus Dei several years before I did and we have always maintained a close friendship.

Father Panikkar had a day assigned for confessions and chats at Zurbarán. At that time it was still possible for women to speak with an Opus Dei priest, or spiritual adviser, outside the confessional. Other young women whom I knew from outside the residence were present that day and the atmosphere of the house was joyful and pleasant. During the rest of the week the house seemed serious, and I did not see anybody.

The conversations with Guadalupe took place either before or after helping in the house, either in the living room or in her office and dealt mainly with my spiritual life. She always challenged me to consider who among my female friends and relatives might be possible members of Opus Dei. We also discussed my spirit of sacrifice, of mortification, and the practice of flagellation. Guadalupe gave me my first cilice, rather, she sold it to me, since the "non-giving apostolate" is customary in Opus Dei.

The cilice is a belt worn around the thigh. The "generosity" of this mortification depends on how much one tightens the cilice. If firmly tightened, the cilice is quite painful and produces small wounds that necessitate alternating the thighs to prevent the possibility of infection.

The "discipline" is an autoflagellation tool. It is a kind of whip intended for use on the bare buttocks, never on the back to avoid damage to lungs and ribs. To use it you must kneel, aiming it over your shoulders so that the lash strikes your buttocks. The degree of self-punishment relies on the strength you use to deliver the blows. I kept both the cilice and the discipline in my office at the CSIC. I did not dare to keep these instruments at home since my parents would have been outraged to discover them in my room. Opus Dei superiors advise new vocations to perform flagellation only on visits to Opus Dei houses.

In addition to those informal conversations with the directress, there were also required weekly meetings with her then called "confidence" and nowadays "fraternal chat." This weekly "fraternal chat" is obligatory for all Opus Dei members, priests included. Monsignor Escrivá used to say that for him "the confidence was more important than the confession and that the only difference he made between the two was that the confidence was not a sacrament."

During the "confidence" or "fraternal chat," all members of Opus Dei are obliged to address three main topics: faith, purity, and vocation. It is also recommended that you discuss Opus Dei devotional life, recruitment to Opus Dei, and your work, be it professional, housekeeping, or internal (work done by Opus Dei superiors as such), or anything that might have bothered us during the week.

It is totally forbidden in Opus Dei to have any confidential exchanges with anyone outside Opus Dei or even with a member who is not the appointed directress. Such a confidant Monsignor Escrivá described as a "sewer," not the correct channel where we could place our spiritual concerns. The reason why confidential conversations among numeraries are forbidden is to avoid the possibility of "special friendships," which could be construed as lesbian. This means that genuine friendships do not exist in Opus Dei. If a numerary dared to speak with another on a personal matter, both would be obliged to report it to the directress and repeat the conversation to her in detail. In Opus Dei it is also deemed wrong to speak to your family about intimate or personal matters.

I recall raising many questions with Guadalupe regarding secularity and freedom in Opus Dei: I could not understand why it was that once we were numeraries, our vocation remaining fully secular, we had to check everything with the directress, even on such matters as whether or not to attend a lecture or concert. Friends and relatives could not understand why we would respond to an invitation by saying that we needed a day or two to think about it (to check with the directress, in fact). While working at CSIC I observed many differences between Opus Dei men and women. It was obvious that Opus Dei men enjoyed more freedom than women in regard to attending cultural events or going out to meals. When women received invitations or wanted to attend any given event, we were often discouraged and told it would be a waste of time.

At that time female numeraries had no freedom whatsoever: you had to consult, check, and have authorization to do anything at all. This has changed and Opus Dei women today apparently have more freedom to participate in conferences or social events related to their work.

Before proceeding further I want to clarify the meaning of freedom in Opus Dei in the light of my own experience and that of many other former members. In Opus Dei there is a theoretical freedom, similar to that described by Solzhenitsyn in *The First Circle*.[1] Members of Opus Dei do not enjoy freedom because they are not free at all. To put it differently, they have the same capacity to choose as the militants of any radical organization; in other words, their possibility of choosing is limited to the options offered by Opus Dei itself. In practice, the freedom of Opus Dei members is always controlled and subordinated to indoctrination of a "formative" kind. Here follows one example: confession.

Theoretically, a member of Opus Dei may confess to whom they please, in accordance with the stipulations of Canon Law[2] and even with what is said in the Opus Dei Constitutions itself.[3] In practice they cannot! Opus Dei members must confess to the priests assigned as ordinary or extraordinary confessors to the house where they live or the center where they belong. This practice is recommended for religious women by the Roman Catholic Church but it is *never* compulsory.[4] In Opus Dei, however, if a member should make confession to a priest unaffiliated with Opus Dei, even with ministerial licences from his bishop, it would be considered a serious offense against "good spirit." It would equally be considered inappropriate for an Opus Dei member to make confession to an Opus

---

1. Aleksandr I. Solzhenitsyn, *The First Circle* (New York: Harper & Row, 1969).
2. "Cuius christifideli integrum est confessario legitime approbato etiam alius ritus, cui maluerit, peccata confiteri." *Code of Canon Law* (Washington, D.C.: Canon Law Society of America, 1983), p. 362, no. 991.
3. *Constitutiones Societatis Sacerdotalis Sanctae Crucis et Operis Dei*, approved June 16, 1950, hereafter *Constitutions*, 1950. Reference here to no. 263, chapter V, n. 83. The *Constitutions* have been published in a bilingual Latin/Spanish edition, translated by Maltilde Rovira Soler: *Constituciones del Opus Dei*, vol. 1, 1950, and vol. 2, 1982 (Madrid: Tiempo, 1986).
4. *Code of Canon Law*, p. 236, no. 630, 3.

Dei priest not assigned to that member. In this case the director or directress must report the fact to the immediate Opus Dei superior or even to headquarters in Rome. Very recently, Opus Dei women have been allowed in particular cases to go to confession to an Opus Dei priest assigned to a public church.

For the sake of the secrecy and seal of the sacrament of penance, Roman Canon Law forbids the confessor to betray the penitent by word or in any other way.[1] However, during all my years in Opus Dei it was common practice to provide the assigned confessor with a list of names of the women numeraries, agreggates, supernumeraries, or outsiders, who in the order stated in that list would make their confessions that day.

Are Opus Dei priests limited in hearing confessions? Yes! Opus Dei priests are ordained primarily to hear confessions of Opus Dei members in the houses they are assigned to and may also hear the confessions of outsiders who frequent Opus Dei houses or apostolates. Opus Dei priests can also hear confessions in those public churches to which they are assigned and which belong to the institution. When there are no Opus Dei women's houses in a given city, Opus Dei priests may also hear confession in a church foreign to Opus Dei, at the request of his regional vicar to the bishop of that diocese. This happens mainly when Opus Dei is preparing for the arrival of women numeraries.

A numerary priest who has heard a nonmember's confession in a church or chapel foreign to Opus Dei is morally compelled, if requested by an Opus Dei priest superior, to report the fact and also reveal the name of the person if he is asked to. As a personal experience, I can well remember that when I was no longer a member of Opus Dei I once went to confession to an Opus Dei priest and since I am "persona non-grata" to Opus Dei, this priest felt morally obliged to report the confession to his superiors. He was severely punished. He was restricted from his ministerial duties and given a "canonical admonition," warning him that at the third infraction he would be out. In short, the most frightening aspect of freedom in Opus Dei, or rather the lack of it, is that it is taking place within an institution of the Roman Catholic Church. Neither the Holy Father John Paul II nor any other Pope has ever known the negative side of Opus Dei "freedom." I would say that political, social, or professional freedom doesn't matter. What does matter is the narrow-mindedness of Opus Dei superiors with respect to their subordinates and the brainwashing that goes on under the guise of "good spirit" or "formation" (indoctrination). This brainwashing, even if we acknowledge the good intention of most Opus Dei superiors, is the result of their reprehensible psychological ignorance that, when

---

1. *Code of Canon Law*, p. 360, no. 983, 1.

applied, creates a "guilty conscience," enabling these members to be turned into virtual robots in the hands of their superiors.

A final note regarding freedom of confession: I personally heard Monsignor Escrivá saying to members of the central government in Rome: "I would prefer a million times that a daughter of mine die without the Last Sacraments than that they be administered to her by a Jesuit."

As to outward appearance, Opus Dei men could dress like any young professionals, but the women had to observe a dress code that was different from that of other women. Around 1949 and 1950 numeraries in Opus Dei had to wear their hair in a kind of "chignon," since long, loose hair was discouraged. I had long hair and was told to tie my hair in a knot. I asked why, and was told that women in Opus Dei should not appear attractive to men. I well remember that this was my first act of obedience.

Nowadays, female numeraries may have short hair but not too long. Oddly, Monsignor Escrivá used to encourage Opus Dei women whose hair was turning gray to dye it in order to look younger.

Another struggle in the women's dress code was to gain authorization for short sleeves; mandatory long sleeves were unbearable in warm climates. I told several directresses very bluntly that by following Opus Dei dress codes we looked more like nun-servants than like lay women.

I talked to Father Panikker about this, and he seemed to understand. His only advice, however, was to obey, to be patient, and to wait for a time when I would be able to bring my own style to Opus Dei. I could not see at that time how I was ever going to have an influence on the rules of the institution. Years later, however, I was able to change many things. As a local or national directress, I always encouraged concern for good manners or, more precisely, I maintained the standards I had learned from my own family. I was able to allow Opus Dei women to have a comfortable yet fashionable style of dress. On this point my interpretation of Opus Dei Constitutions prevailed.

The first official change in the dress code of the numeraries took place in 1956 when I arrived in Venezuela. I could not understand how having been told in Rome, again and again, that Opus Dei numeraries were lay people and that, as such, we should never look like "the Theresians of Father Poveda" (a lay association recognized as a secular institution after Opus Dei and whose women-members did not then dress fashionably), we female numeraries had our own external sign: the use of long sleeves in the summer or in a tropical climate. We had repeatedly been told by Opus Dei superiors that we "must externally be as everybody and internally as everybody must be." To gain insight into this seeming incoherence, I asked the counselor of Venezuela, nowadays called regional vicar, to lend me a copy of Opus Dei Constitutions for a few days. The only volume existing in every country was always kept (then as well as nowadays) by the regional vicar. Specifically I must state that women's regional government was not allowed to have a copy of this document.

In part IV, no. 439, regarding women, it reads: "Given that women in Opus Dei are not 'religious,' they do not bring a dowry nor use a religious dress or habit. Rather, in everything common to lay women, that does not depart from the state of perfection, they behave, dress, and act as any other women at their same social level."[1] However, to avoid misinterpretations on whether Opus Dei numeraries should or should not use short sleeves, the matter was brought to the scheduled meeting of the regional advisory (the women's regional government), and it was decided that the question be submitted to the central government in Rome, or, in fact, to Monsignor Escrivá. We soon received their approval; that is, Monsignor Escrivá approved our suggestion. From that very moment, not only in Venezuela, but in the Opus Dei the world over, all women were allowed to use short sleeves. Perhaps this seems trivial but it was a positive step that relieved daily tensions in the lives of Opus Dei women.

Now women are even allowed to use eye shadow which was totally forbidden until the late 1960s.

Another matter of concern for Opus Dei was sports: skiing and horseback riding were not considered appropriate sports for women numeraries, since they required slacks and female numeraries were not allowed to wear pants. It is interesting that in 1993, after the first Spanish edition of this book, Opus Dei modified its dress code and, on special occasions, numeraries may even wear jeans.

Until 1966 Opus Dei numeraries could go to the beach, wearing a modest swimsuit. But, by the end of that year, numeraries were forbidden to attend a public beach. Now numeraries are allowed to swim only in the pools of their own residences. The swimsuit code for numeraries still requires a short skirt.

When I joined Opus Dei as a numerary, I had to quit smoking altogether. However, men in Opus Dei smoked as much as they wanted. Women smokers reveal a lack of femininity, while for men it is a sign of masculinity. Monsignor Alvaro del Portillo, then procurator general of Opus Dei (second in rank in the entire organization), was granted the "privilege" by Monsignor Escrivá to smoke even in the presence of Opus Dei women superiors. Del Portillo smoked cigarettes, using an ivory cigarette holder.

---

1. "Cum sodales non sint religiosae, dotem non afferent, neque religiosa veste seu habitu religioso utuntur, sed externe in omnibus, quae sacularibus communia sunt et a statu perfectionis non aliena, ut aliae mulieres propriae condicionis, se gerunt, vestiunt, vitam ducunt." *Codex Iuris particularis Operis Dei*, Rome, November 1982, n. 439 (Madrid: Ediciones Tiempo, 1986).

Escrivá often used to remark on this privilege that he had granted to Alvaro del Portillo.

At the beginning of my vocation in Opus Dei I lacked the perspective to see the differences between Opus Dei men and women. I came to realize that such differences were expressions of the macho behavior that always existed and still does in Opus Dei as a reflection of Monsignor Escrivá's sexual obsession.

While still living with my parents at home I felt trapped by Opus Dei demands. On one hand, I had to behave normally with my family; on the other, in my daily visits to Zurbarán I was required to recruit people among my young women friends. The truth of the matter was that many of my friends were already married or about to get married, and I had lost touch with others while I was engaged. It happened, however, that Françoise du Chatenet, a friend of mine from Paris was staying at my parents home for a year. One day I mentioned her name at Zurbarán and they immediately started to ask me to bring my friend to the Opus Dei residence under the pretext that she play the piano. I also had to ask her to go to confession to Father Hernández-Garnica under the most ridiculous pretense: he wanted to check with her about the Parisian university students because Opus Dei women were soon going to Paris. I was repeatedly told that "she could be the first French numerary." In fact, I was very reluctant to bring Françoise to Zurbarán and found the situation embarrassing. She was an old classmate from my French school in Paris, and I never considered that she might have a vocation in Opus Dei. Françoise was not only intelligent and gifted but also very attractive. She was blond, elegant, not very tall; she possessed a great sense of humor. Her family was from the French aristocracy. It is easy to understand why she was good "prey" for Opus Dei. After hours of conversation at home, I convinced her to come to Zurbarán and to speak with Father Hernández-Garnica in the confessional.

As a result of this episode Françoise never again wanted to hear about Opus Dei. Throughout the years we maintained a deep friendship. Her mother used to say that our friendship was "la fidelité de l'amitié" (the loyalty of friendship). Whenever Opus Dei is mentioned in conversations, Françoise du Chatenet (since years now, Madame de Tailly) reminds me with a laugh that she was able "to escape the claws of Opus Dei" in spite of my insistence.

My personal inclination was to be sincere with Opus Dei superiors and to tell them what I thought about particular matters. This brought me more harm than good, since on more than one occasion my way of thinking was diametrically opposed to Monsignor Escrivá's. Guadalupe used to say that proselytizing was like the lock nut ("contratuerca") that fastened our vocation. The first woman who, after speaking with me, asked for admission as an Opus Dei numerary was Pilar Salcedo whose spiritual adviser was also Father Panikkar.

Pilar was from Jaén and in personal appearance a typical Andalusian woman: tall, thin, black eyes and black hair, with an ironic wit. While finishing her studies in philosophy she lived in Madrid in another residence for students. Years later she became a journalist. She was also a major superior in the first central women's government named by Monsignor Escrivá in 1953. Later she was sent to Colombia as the women's directress of that country. She left Opus Dei after I did. We have kept a warm friendship but I do not understand why, being a journalist, she has remained silent regarding facts she knows very well about Opus Dei and Escrivá.

In 1949 one of the tests I had to undergo was to switch from making my "fraternal chat" with Guadalupe to making it with María Esther, whose last name I have forgotten. She was a recent numerary from Barcelona who came as the vice-directress of Zurbarán. María Esther had just graduated in philosophy. She was about my age, extremely self-sufficient, and literal-minded regarding the application of Opus Dei doctrine. She arrived with the tablets of the law in her hands and looked down on new vocations; in my case, she discounted anything I said. She had belonged to Opus Dei for only a few years. The first thing she asked of me was to give up my confessor, Father Panikkar, for Father Hernández-Garnica.

I simply refused. I spoke with Guadalupe and she understood my reaction, telling María Esther that I should continue to confess to Father Panikkar. So, for several more months I did not change my spiritual adviser. However, in July 1949, we were told that Father Panikkar had received a different assignment in Opus Dei. Since he would no longer come to Zurbarán, I would have to change my confessor.

Because of his new assignment in Opus Dei, Doctor Panikkar was also absent from the Council of Scientific Research where we had just started to edit the Proceedings of the International Congress of Philosophy that took place the previous year in Barcelona. He practically disappeared. He did not explain his absence to anybody nor did anyone know when he would return. People wondered whether he might be ill. When people asked me about the reason for his absence, I could say nothing, except perhaps that he might be traveling. The situation was rather confusing due to his position as general secretary to the congress. But I could not repeat what I had heard at Zurbarán about his new assignment in Opus Dei.

After several weeks, Father Hernández phoned me to say that all correspondence addressed to Father Panikkar as general secretary to the International Congress of Philosophy should be forwarded to Diego de León,

14, address of Opus Dei's headquarters in Madrid, from where, he added, it would be forwarded to Father Panikkar.

I asked Father Hernández-Garnica about Father Panikkar's health. His reply was that he was not ill. I also asked for an address or phone number where he could be reached. Father Hernández-Garnica did not reply but repeated that I must follow his orders. The situation in fact could not have been more bizarre!

So I was left alone to face the preparation of three volumes of the Proceedings of the International Congress of Philosophy. Given the bulk of work involved, Father Todolí as well as Roberto Saumells and Anton Wurster helped me very much.

Around Christmas 1949 I received a phone call from Rosario de Orbegozo, the central directress of Opus Dei women. She told me that the procurator general of Opus Dei, Father Alvaro del Portillo, known as "Don Alvaro," had just arrived from Rome and wished to speak with me that afternoon at 4:00 P.M. I should go to the Opus Dei men's headquarters on Diego de León, 14.

Father del Portillo was kind and let me know that the Father was very pleased with my letters and my behavior and I had his permission to attend the course of formation for numeraries to take place in January 1950 at Los Rosales, the center of studies for numeraries in Villaviciosa de Odón, near Madrid.

I told Don Alvaro of my obligations at the CSIC and that, because of Father Panikkar's absence, I did not see how I could possibly leave. Don Alvaro said not to worry about it and that everything would be all right. He also mentioned to me that, on behalf of Monsignor Escrivá, he had brought from Rome the wooden cross (a small dark wooden cross— around 6" × 3"—that Opus Dei gives to the first vocation of each country) for Father Panikkar, since he was the first British numerary in Opus Dei.

One afternoon before Christmas of 1949, a few days after this conversation took place, Father Panikkar showed up in the office. I was shocked and happy at the same time. Roberto Saumells and I could not believe it! We looked at him as if he were a ghost, still unable to believe that Father Panikkar was truly there. Father Panikkar seemed happy and was looking around in the two-room office, speaking with Roberto Saumells and me while opening drawers, looking at notes, smiling at rediscovering his office. My questions came as a torrent: What happened to you? Why did you disappear? Why did you not even telephone any of us? Father Panikkar smiled but did not answer our questions. When Roberto Saumells left, after having briefed Father Panikkar for a couple of hours on what had happened in his absence, Father Panikkar and I had a long conversation in his office, the last one before I moved to Los Rosales.

Father Panikkar was very calm. He told me that he had already been informed by Alvaro del Portillo that I would be going to attend the center of studies at Los Rosales the following month. Nevertheless, he was very vague about his months of absence but, although unsaid, I guessed at months of suffering. Many, many years later, when neither of us were members of Opus Dei, Father Panikkar said that he was punished by Opus Dei and secluded in Molinoviejo. With the hindsight of many years and knowing Opus Dei's obsessive suspicion regarding relationships between men and women, it is possible that my unwillingness to change confessor, added to my reluctance not to miss the International Congress of Philosophy in Barcelona, might have been one of the reasons for the punishment of Father Panikkar.

During this long conversation Father Panikkar reassured me that he was convinced that I would personally be happy in Opus Dei, although a different kind of happiness than the one expected in married life. In Opus Dei I would experience the joy of giving my youth to God for the conversion of the world.

It was a serious conversation. While we spoke I felt happy and grateful to God for having allowed me to speak with my spiritual adviser before going to Opus Dei's center of studies. Yet, I felt sadness because I knew that I would never again speak with Father Panikkar, unless, by coincidence, he might be appointed as ordinary confessor of the house where I might be posted.

As if understanding all my fears, Father Panikkar encouraged me to have a fruitful apostolate and said that I would never feel alone if I had a true life of prayer. He also promised to pray for me and reminded me that God was above everything and everybody.

He also recommended great patience on material issues which he knew annoyed me while insisting I could bring my joy and style into Opus Dei. He blessed me and went away.

I do not remember for how long I remained in that office. I do remember well, however, that when I stirred, the room was as dark as my fears. I was truly grateful for Father Panikkar's understanding and kindness and I promised God in that office that I would always follow Father Panikkar's advice regarding my vocation in Opus Dei.

Leaving My Parents' House

Since Opus Dei is a secular institute I had to be twenty-five years old before I could move into an Opus Dei house. Under Spanish law at that time, you came of age at twenty-three. Once you had attained your majority, you could enter a convent or marry without parental permission and either state implied a new juridical status. However, since Opus Dei was a secular institute, it could not confer a new juridical status. Hence, to leave home for Opus Dei before twenty-five years of age without parental permission implied *abandoning the parental home,* and parents would then have the right to claim their children from any place, including Opus Dei houses.

In the fall of 1949 the situation at my home was extremely tense. My father begged me to seek counsel about my vocation either from a Jesuit or a Dominican or some friends who were splendid Catholic intellectuals. My answer was always negative, because I had been told by Opus Dei superiors that I should never discuss my vocation with anybody under any circumstance, except with an Opus Dei priest. I had already assimilated the first part of Opus Dei indoctrination. For Opus Dei members only Opus Dei superiors and Opus Dei priests were "good shepherds"; the rest were mercenaries and "bad shepherds."

I had serious arguments with my mother. My father's silence devastated me. He could not understand why I refused to consult about my vocation with another priest.

As a result, the atmosphere at home was tense, and especially unpleasant at meals. My mother cried. My brothers remained silent. I was deeply saddened and tried to understand my parents' feelings, although I was convinced that Opus Dei superiors knew my situation better than my own parents. It is important, in my view, to note that once an Opus Dei member has arrived at this state of mind, he or she has already taken a first step toward fanaticism.

My paternal grandmother was a relief and a comfort to me. She could not stand my suffering and, at the same time, tried to make my parents cope with the situation. My parents gave up hope when they realized that they could not take any legal action since my twenty-fifth birthday was in March.

In January of 1950, for the first time in Opus Dei history, a course of formation for numeraries was going to take place in the winter and last for six months. Formerly these courses were held during the summer, for just one month. The reason for this special course was that Opus Dei superiors decided to gather several numeraries who, for different reasons, had been unable to take the course at an earlier date.

In mid-January of 1950 I quit my job at the CSIC and left my parents' home without their blessing and with their strong opposition to my decision to enter Opus Dei. I was cut off from my entire family. The ostracism lasted eighteen years, exactly the time of my stay in Opus Dei. In those eighteen years I met my mother just once in 1953 for scarcely a couple of hours, while I was stationed in Rome. I never received a letter from her during my entire time in Opus Dei.

I did not wish to make a scene when leaving my parents' home. For that reason over several days I gradually moved books and other objects to the Opus Dei house. On two consecutive days I packed my wardrobe in a couple of suitcases which I brought to Juan Bravo, 20, headquarters of the Opus Dei women's house in Madrid. I had to use the early hours of the morning when everybody was still asleep. Even my dog seemed aware of my situation and kept following me; when he saw me leave with my suitcases he wanted to come along. I well remember that one of those mornings I was saying in the elevator: "Good Lord, I even had to kick the dog to leave my parents' home!" It was not exactly joy that I felt on those cold winter mornings. My soul was frozen but I had the idea in my mind that in spite of everything I was doing God's will.

The evening I left my parents' home, they decided to remain in their room. My brothers were sent to the movies. I wrote a note to my parents telling them how sorry I was to leave home without embracing them, and I departed for good accompanied by a recently married cousin, Carmen Fullea Carlos-Roca, and her husband, Antonio Carrera. They were so deeply sad about the family situation that even at risk of losing my parents' friendship, they decided not to let me leave alone. They came with me to the door of the Opus Dei women's headquarters.

My reception at the Opus Dei house was utterly cold. Nobody, absolutely nobody, expressed any affection, understanding, or warmth. What to me was the most serious step I had taken in my life was for Opus Dei superiors almost a routine matter. In retrospect, the superiors were insensitive since they were well aware of the turmoil I had gone through with my family to come to live at the Opus Dei house. Nobody acknowledged it, nobody spoke privately to me either. I had also given up a job that was important to me, but this matter was not even touched on. I was only informed that since there were not enough beds in the house, I would have to sleep on the floor. It was, by the way, the first time in my life I slept on a parquet floor. This experience helped me, years later, to be very warm and understanding when a new numerary arrived at a house where I was assigned and much more so when I was the directress of a country. That is, I always tried to spare other numeraries the unpleasantness I had experienced.

Since my stay in Juan Bravo was going to be very short, I did not receive any specific assignment. I was simply asked to do the errands for the house. Close relatives of mine were living in the same building; I asked permission to visit them but permission was denied, although they told me to greet them if by chance we met in the elevator.

Los Rosales—Course of Studies

After a couple of days I left Madrid with Chelo Castañeda, a numerary who had just arrived from Santander to go to Los Rosales in Villaviciosa de Odón, around 55 miles from Madrid.

Before leaving Madrid, Rosario de Orbegozo, the central directress of Opus Dei women, asked me to take good care of Chelo Castañeda because she was a brand-new vocation.

I always remember with terrible anguish that cold winter evening in Madrid going to the bus station. I felt lost, lonely, tense, totally abandoned by everybody, and leaving everything behind that I had loved my entire life. I put myself in God's hands, thinking that I was doing his will. I am unable to explain the tremendous effort I made to overcome my inner emotions and pay attention only to my travel companion who was crying.

When we arrived in Villaviciosa de Odón it was pitch black. At the bus station Mary Tere Echeverría, the directress of Los Rosales, and María Teresa Zumalde, a numerary from Bilbao, were waiting. Since the bus station was fairly close to the house, we carried our own suitcases, and crossed a few village streets and the almost deserted main square with its Town Hall to arrive at Los Rosales. Crossing the plaza I would never have guessed that the Town Hall's bells were going to run my life for the next six months! Even now I am able to recall their ring.

On arrival at Los Rosales, the directress took us to the oratory. She opened the door to greet the Lord, as is customary when you enter and leave Opus Dei houses.

She then took us upstairs, where the bedrooms were located. The directress assigned us our beds. On that floor there were three bedrooms: one with three beds, another with six, and the largest with twelve beds. Initially I was assigned to the six-bed room, but a few days later I was moved to the twelve-bed room for my entire stay at Los Rosales. We were informed that the beds consisted of wooden planks without a mattress. For the first time in my life I slept on a wooden bed. The wood was covered with a light blanket. For the rest, it was made up and looked like any other bed. There were sheets, blankets, one pillow, and a nice printed bedspread.

In Opus Dei only female numeraries sleep on wooden planks. Everybody else, from the Opus Dei prelate to the priests, men and auxiliary numeraries, all sleep in regular beds with mattresses. We were told that the reason why female numeraries have to sleep on wooden beds is because women are more sensual than men. I heard Monsignor Escrivá more than once explain that he adopted this custom for Opus Dei women from some cloistered nuns in the Argüelles neighborhood of Madrid.

Wooden planks are hard but you get accustomed to them. What is really dreadful is the cold. In a house like Los Rosales, located in the heart of Castille, in the winter, without heat, the cold was so unbearable that we kept our coats on indoors. The heating system could not be turned on because coal was very expensive and the budget of the house was very low. I was so cold at night that I dreamt about hearing the six o'clock bells from the Town Hall, time when the directress's alarm woke up the entire house.

The half of the armoire I was assigned to share with Anina Mouriz was in the hall of the upper floor and it was so small that I had to give the directress those clothes I did not use daily. Members of Opus Dei can only keep in storage summer clothes during winter and winter clothes during summer. Nothing else. Clothes not used on a daily basis are handed over to the directress and not returned.

The bedrooms were poorly lit. To read in bed was forbidden and the lights had to be turned off 30 minutes after the last prayers were recited in the oratory, when the major silence started, ending the next day after Mass.

Los Rosales was a typical Spanish-style house. On the ground floor, the main entrance opened to a central hall. All the rooms had a door to the hall: the oratory, the dining room, an auxiliary bath, and the directress's quarters.

A staircase from the main hall led down to a small corridor with a bathroom and a lavatory. At the end of the corridor were the pantry, kitchen, and family room, which doubled as dining room or work room, as the occasion demanded. The decor was dark, majestic, and unattractive. A garden surrounded the house and a wall enclosed the entire property.

The first Opus Dei Constitutions read: "Opus Dei members live full evangelical perfection under a perpetual and definitive surrender to the service of Christ Our Lord. However, the Institute does not have in its houses any sign 'smelling' of religious houses." There are always mirrors in Opus Dei women's houses over bathroom sinks and in places where you can glance at yourself before leaving the house.

At present Opus Dei centers of study are in specially designed houses. They are well appointed and have all kinds of facilities including special quarters for the administration. There is enough grounds for a tennis court and swimming pool. This allows the numeraries doing internal studies to practice sports. In addition each numerary has her own independent bedroom and closet. Showers and toilets are well distributed in accordance with the number of rooms in any given area. There are also bedrooms complete with bath, reserved for Opus Dei major superiors. Interestingly, the first Opus Dei Constitutions read: "Let us not waste our time building houses; let us use those already built."[1]

1. *Constitutions*, 1950, pp. 102–3, n. 227.

Our course of studies at Los Rosales was truly spartan: to the best of my recollection, the last one of this kind in the history of Opus Dei Women's Branch. Besides two daily classes in the morning and sometimes another one in the afternoon, we had to run the house ourselves by turns: cooking, cleaning, preparing the oratory, doing laundry. One of the participants was in charge of the chickens and the pigs with scant help from a young village boy. After lunch we had only a daily half-hour get-together except on Sundays when it would last for over an hour.

Sunday mornings we used to do the so-called Sunday work which meant repairing what did not work properly, reorganizing drawers, or doing special cleaning of doors and radiators, removing finger prints or hidden dust. When the work was done, if it was not raining or too cold, we would all go out for a walk to a nearby castle or to the countryside.

Our studies started officially on February 2, 1950. The schedule was so tight we could hardly pause for breath. This is a key tactic for sectarian indoctrination: not to allow members free time to think and reflect. Every hour of the day was planned.

In the morning when the alarm rang from the directress's quarters, we instantly got out of bed to kiss the floor saying, *Serviam!* (I will serve [you, Lord]). Immediately afterwards, usually on our knees, we offered up the day's work, each in our own way. We rose at 6:00 A.M., still keeping the major silence which ended after Mass. The major silence means, as in a religious order, that you may not speak under any circumstance. The intention was to spend the time in prayer. As always our minds were controlled by Opus Dei rules, regulating how our silence should be used. In other words, we were not free to think on our own. The major silence is practiced in every Opus Dei house all over the world by both men and women.

During the major silence and from 6:00 A.M. to 7:00 A.M., the schedule allowed enough time for a shower, for making our beds, and doing little personal tasks. It was a hectic hour since there were only three bathrooms, with one reserved for the directress, and three lavatories for more than twenty persons. We had less than five minutes to take a cold shower and use the lavatory.

This practice of using only cold water lasted for many, many years in Opus Dei. About 1965 the cold-water policy was changed and we could use hot water. Most probably this change was due to many cases of rheumatism, bad backs, and gynecological problems often requiring surgery.

At 7:00 A.M. in the oratory, we sang Prime in Gregorian chant. For decades Opus Dei centers of study and annual courses have observed the custom of reciting Prime before morning meditation and Compline before going to bed. The first Opus Dei Constitutions mentions the recitation of Prime and Compline (respectively, the first and the last canonical hours of the Roman breviary, usually sung in the choir of religious orders). This custom was banned in Opus Dei about 1965.

Apparently all of us, one by one, told the directress about our surprise at the use of Gregorian chant at Prime. Mary Tere Echevarría, the directress of the course of studies, said that this custom was common in many places that were not religious such as the Castillo de la Mota, where girls from Falange, the only political party during Franco's rule, used to gather to recite the canonical hours under the direction of Friar Justo Pérez de Urbel. I could not verify the truth of this statement, but what I well remember was my surprise at this custom that was not exactly "secular." The directress also said that the Father wanted this custom to be practiced in Opus Dei centers of study and during formation periods such as annual courses.

The recitation of Prime provoked general criticism by all of us in the course. For this we were severely reprimanded and told that anything said or written by the Father could not be subject to comment or criticism among us. This would show a lack of "good spirit," a lack of unity, and *unity* in Opus Dei was sacred.[1] Anything said by the Father had to be accepted without comment, discussion, or criticism, since he knew what God wanted for Opus Dei. In a word: criticism was totally forbidden in Opus Dei.

The absence of criticism in Opus Dei was the very first point about which we were clearly indoctrinated. This antagonism to criticism is justified by the spirit of *unity* which is instilled in all Opus Dei members as essential. Monsignor Escrivá says: "To love Opus Dei *unity* means to feel like part of its body, where we are called to be. We do not care whether we are hand or foot, tongue or heart because we all belong as parts of that body, since we are one by the charity of Christ which unites us all.[2] I would like to make you feel as members of just one body. *Unum corpus multi sumus.* We are all just one body, and this is manifested in unity of goals, in unity of apostolate, in unity of sacrifice, in unity of hearts, in the charity with which we treat one another, in the smile before the Cross and on the Cross itself. To feel, to vibrate, all of us in unison!" (*Cuadernos-3*, chap. 7, p. 58) The same chapter stresses that *unity* is "one of the three dominant passions that every member of Opus Dei must acquire."

In hindsight, I see clearly that one of the devices by which Opus Dei eases its members toward fanaticism is to banish from their minds, under

1. See *Cuadernos-3*, p. 57, and especially chapter 7, pp. 52–59, in the paragraph entitled "Love for Unity."

2. These sentences are a reinterpretation of 1 Corinthians 10:7: "Because there is one bread, we who are many are one body, for we all partake of the one bread."

the pretense of formation, the slightest hint of criticism of the institution. Opus Dei superiors would not tolerate any criticism of its doctrine, customs, or spirit, because this might tarnish the image of the Founder. The center of studies is structured to set you on the path to fanaticism, on which I was already fully embarked.

Part of the routine at the center of studies was to begin the day with a half-an-hour meditation in the morning and half-an-hour meditation in the afternoon. In the morning, Father Hernández-Garnica was usually there. When he could not come, Father José López-Navarro replaced him. The priest led us in meditation before Mass. The custom of keeping the oratories totally dark during the meditation has been adopted worldwide in Opus Dei. In addition to the light of the tabernacle, there is only a reading lamp on the small table behind which the priest seats and speaks. The table, placed near the altar, is covered with a felt cloth, either dark red or dark green. An explanation of the practice of keeping the oratory dark is that it helps the "recollection."

Preaching differs from priest to priest. Father Hernández-Garnica was not a gifted speaker, and his meditations were monotonous, but the meditations delivered by Father José López-Navarro were, on the contrary, quite lively. Typically, the meditations are addressed in a very personal and direct form. For instance, instead of saying "humility is needed in a true spiritual life," a priest will say, "*You* have to be humble, if *you* want to have a spiritual life." The direct address in meditations was constantly used. At the center of studies as in Opus Dei houses, it was common to read paragraphs from any chapter of Monsignor Escrivá's *The Way* to stress a particular point related to our formation. At times, the Gospel of the day was employed but mostly the topics for meditation were related either to our formation or to proselytizing.

Recently, Opus Dei mainly uses, as material for meditations, texts from *Cuadernos,* a series of several volumes that mix phrases from Monsignor Escrivá with a commentary presumably by an anonymous Opus Dei priest. The *Cuadernos* series was printed at Opus Dei's Roma headquarters. To begin the meditation[1] or to end it,[2] a formula by Monsignor Escrivá is always used.

After the meditation our daily plan of life mandated the holy Mass and Communion, with ten minutes of personal thanksgiving after the Mass

1. "My Lord and my God, I firmly believe that you are here, that you see me, that you hear me; I adore you with profound reverence, ask your pardon for all my sins, and grace to make this time of prayer fruitful. Mother Immaculate, St. Joseph, my father and lord, my Guardian Angel, intercede for me."

2. "I thank you, O Lord, for all the good resolutions, inspirations, and affections you have granted me during this time of prayer. I ask your help to put them into practice. Mother Immaculate, St. Joseph, my father and lord, my Guardian Angel, intercede for me."

and the recitation of *Trium Puerorum* (the Hymn of Prophet Azariah sung by three young men going to be sacrificed in the fiery furnace).[1] The major silence ended after Mass.

After breakfast we had two consecutive classes: one on the Opus Dei Catechism. The second class alternated between moral theology, dogma, liturgy, and Opus Dei praxis. We were told not to ask questions nor to take notes. If we had any questions, they should be submitted to the directress later on.

An important document for study was the Opus Dei Catechism that, we were told, contained the entire doctrine of Opus Dei. We were informed that Monsignor Escrivá required that all members learn the Catechism by heart. The directress said that the Catechism was an internal document and, given its importance, she warned us never to show it nor to speak of its existence to outsiders.

We were also told that a member of the local council would distribute a copy of the Catechism to each of us. We were to keep it for an hour to memorize points assigned by the priest. Afterwards, the book had to be returned to the directress's office.

The Opus Dei priest celebrating Mass was the one who taught this class. He expected us to recite by heart the points he assigned the day before, and no excuses were accepted for not having learned the answers perfectly.

The Catechism was supposed to contain questions that an Opus Dei member might be asked by outsiders, along with the exact replies. It was said that we should never speculate about any of the questions in the Catechism. By way of example, here is a typical question and answer:

Q.: "What should we reply to a person who asks how many vocations there are in Opus Dei?"

A.: "To a person who asks how many vocations there are in Opus Dei, we should reply that there are enough, as many as God wishes; we are not concerned about their number since we are not interested in statistics."

The Introduction to the Catechism, written by Monsignor Escrivá, also had to be learned by heart and read as follows:

> In this small book
> is written the reason
> for your life as a child of God.
> Read it with love,

1. See the Book of Daniel 3:51–90.

be eager to know it,
learn it by heart,
for it should always be in your mind,
in your heart,
and in your way,
clear ideas.
Then, pray,
work,
and rejoice.
With the joy
of those who know to be chosen
by their Father in Heaven
to build Opus Dei on earth
being yourself Opus Dei.

While memorizing the Catechism, we learned about much that we did not know before, such as the different kinds of members existing in Opus Dei. *Numeraries* have full commitment and take vows of poverty, chastity, and obedience; among them, those who hold the positions of directress or major superiors are designated *inscribed* (members for life). Among the *inscribed* members, the president general, now prelate, may designate *electresses.* This designation is also for life, and they have a *passive voice* in the election of the Opus Dei prelate. That is to say, when the prelate is chosen by deliberative vote of the general council (Opus Dei men's central government), they have to take into consideration in the final ballot the opinion of the Opus Dei women.

Next, there are the *numerary servants.* Literally, the Catechism reads: "There are other numeraries who do the menial and housekeeping work in Opus Dei houses who are called *servants.*" In 1965, Monsignor Escrivá changed the generic term *servants* to that of *numerary auxiliaries.* In daily life, inside Opus Dei houses, they are simply called auxiliaries. Their mission is to work as maids, but only in Opus Dei houses. A select few help on Opus Dei farms, in the printing press at Opus Dei's headquarters, or in some other work.

Other members are the *associates* (*agregados* in Spanish) called *oblates* in the first Catechism. In 1950 there were still none. These members have the same commitments to Opus Dei as the *numeraries* with full vows of poverty, chastity, and obedience. The main difference is that they cannot live in Opus Dei houses; they always live with their families, and they come from all walks of life. They are only allowed to stay in Opus Dei houses for short periods, usually during retreats or periods of formation. They cannot be *inscribed* nor *electresses.*

The *supernumeraries* are yet another type of Opus Dei member. When I arrived at the center of studies, I still had hazy ideas about this classification, since in 1950 there were no female *supernumeraries*. More than once the superiors told us that we would eventually be informed about these members. *Supernumeraries* may be married or single and have a partial commitment to Opus Dei in accordance with their civil and social status, as in fact their vows state. To a married *supernumerary* her vow of chastity will lead her to have as many children as God wishes; exclusively with permission of her Opus Dei confessor, she may use the birth control known as Ogino or the rhythm method. Her obedience to Opus Dei is only related to her spiritual life. Regarding poverty the *supernumeraries* must channel any kind of alms through Opus Dei: each month she will give a fixed sum equal to what she formerly donated to her parish church or any other group that, from the very instant she asked for admission in Opus Dei, she stopped helping. The truth is that supernumeraries are and have always been the financial backbone of Opus Dei. I remember hearing Monsignor Escrivá speaking in general about the supernumeraries as well as about the housekeeping work in Opus Dei: "... they are the Opus Dei skeleton; without it, my daughters, the Work would collapse."

In many English-speaking countries the *cooperators* are called "Opus Dei auxiliaries." They are a special group of women who, without being members of Opus Dei and without any spiritual commitment, assist the prelature with their alms, prayers, and, where appropriate, with professional or social work. Interestingly, *cooperators* can include Catholics as well as members of other religious denominations. People not in full communion with the Catholic Church, a divorcee for instance, may still be a *cooperator*. Here is the basis for the Opus Dei claim that Monsignor Escrivá and Opus Dei were ecumenical in spirit before Vatican II, which is totally untrue. Cooperators were essentially economic assets. They supported schools for servants, peasants, even raising money for scholarships for university students attending Opus Dei centers. In exchange, and regardless of their religious background, they would receive spiritual blessings.

Thus, recalling the words of 1 Peter 4:8: "Love covers a multitude of sins," Opus Dei obtains obtaining financial help, even in those countries where the majority is not Roman Catholic. On the one hand, the *cooperators* raise money for Opus Dei, while, on the other hand, Opus Dei is credited for caring for nonbelievers or nonpractitioners in the eyes of the Roman Catholic Church.

To come back to the Catechism: since Opus Dei places this book among those documents called *ad usum nostrorum* (for our own use), it cannot be found in the official archives of the Roman Catholic Church and much less in any bookstore. The copies of the Opus Dei Catechism are numbered.

The text of the Catechism was formed with a selection of basic points from the Constitutions.

As a security measure, all volumes of the Catechism are kept in the archives of the regional headquarters in each country.

What Monsignor Escrivá could not prevent, ironically, is that as a result of his emphasis on learning the Catechism by heart, one retained it so well that years after having left Opus Dei, one is able to retrieve it literally point by point.

At one stage, Opus Dei's Rome headquarters ordered that all existing volumes of the Catechism be withdrawn. From 1964 to 1975 no edition of the Catechism existed. The 1975 edition was revised by Monsignor Escrivá himself. Since Opus Dei changed its official status in 1982, that 1975 edition became obsolete and a new edition may be out.

At Los Rosales, once classes were over, we attended to tasks assigned by the directress. The directress, Mary Tere Echevarría, was assisted by a vice-directress and a secretary. Mary Tere Echevarría was my age. She was tall with dark hair, the only daughter of a well-off Basque family from San Sebastián. She was exquisitely courteous and kind, perhaps, rather naive. Her numerary brother, Ignacio, later became a priest and one of the group that opened the Opus Dei foundation in Argentina. He had introduced his sister to Monsignor Escrivá when she was only 15. Her whole world was Opus Dei and its Founder. She felt very insecure with many of us in the formation course, especially in the presence of those who had worked and had had an independent social life. Mary Tere was a good person who became an Opus Dei fanatic.

Nisa González Guzmán, the vice-directress, had a real personality. Petite, slim, with grayish hair, you could tell that she always felt secure in any situation. Intelligent and at times very rigid, but not cold, she knew how to teach. She had an innate authority. She was not an Opus Dei fanatic and perhaps for this reason Monsignor Escrivá did not want her near him. I remember well that Monsignor Escrivá once said about Nisa: "She is very efficient but I don't want her here." However, he was convinced of her deep commitment to Opus Dei and sent her to open the Opus Dei Women's Branch in the United States with a house in Chicago, the administration of Woodlawn, the Opus Dei men's residence. At the writing of this book Nisa resides in Valencia, Spain. Her assignment is to write about Opus Dei's early days.

At Los Rosales I knew the local council secretary, Lourdes Toranzo very well. We requested admission into Opus Dei at about the same time. I never trusted her, because I discovered that she was two-faced. On one hand, she was kind to everybody, but, on the other, she reported everything to the members of the local council. In the Spanish idiom, "she could throw a stone and hide her hand."

The center of studies gave special emphasis to the spiritual plan of life of all numeraries. "It fits the hand like a glove" was Monsignor Escrivá's description of the spiritual plan of life.

According to the liturgical calendar, all Opus Dei members should recite the *Angelus* or the *Regina Coeli* at noon. In the Women's Branch the directress ends any common act with the ejaculatory prayer, *Sancta Maria, Spes nostra, Ancilla Domini* (Holy Mary, Our Hope, Handmaiden of the Lord) to which the others present respond *Ora pro nobis* (pray for us). In the Men's Branch the ejaculatory prayer is *Sancta Maria, Spes Nostra, Sedes Sapientiae* (Holy Mary, Our Hope, Source of Wisdom). The answer is again *Ora pro nobis* (pray for us). It is interesting that even in these short prayers established by Monsignor Escrivá, there was a machist note: for the women the designation of the Madonna is a "slave," while for the men it is "wisdom."

It was recommended that we read the Gospels for not less than several minutes each day and from a devotional book not less than 15 minutes. The books were selected by the directress to whom we could also suggest a title during the weekly chat. Opus Dei exercized strict censorship of spiritual books. We were not allowed to read books by authors with a marked contemplative style. For instance, from St. Teresa, we were assigned *The Foundations.* St. John of the Cross was not recommended at all. What is more, for years we were not allowed to read the Old Testament but only the New. Regarding text books for internal studies, Opus Dei censorship was even more severe than the Roman Catholic Church before Vatican II.

The Opus Dei *Preces* is the official prayer to which I alluded previously. To start this prayer, we kissed the floor saying, *Serviam!* (I will serve).

The examination of conscience takes place twice a day: one, usually before lunch right after the recitation of the *Preces.* The other time is at night, as a final act in the oratory, before going to bed.

Ordinarily after lunch, a visit is made to the Blessed Sacrament in all Opus Dei houses. Afterwards, the get-together is held, usually in the living room or garden. All Opus Dei members living in that particular house are obliged to attend. If a member is sick, the directress dispatches two numeraries to the patient's room for a half hour get-together there.

When Rosario de Orbegozo visited the center of studies as central directress, we would sing folk songs or songs related to Opus Dei which we were supposed to learn by heart and to consider in our private meditation since their topic was recruitment or personal dedication.

For a couple of days María Sofía Pacheo, the first Portuguese numerary, and I read the newspaper during the get-together. I was reprimanded through a fraternal correction because I was told that "get-togethers were to make life enjoyable for our sisters, not to get involved in our own preferences." We could not read the paper during the rest of the day either, nor any other book.

During the formation period at Los Rosales we could not make any telephone calls. However, we were allowed to write letters to our families on Sundays. The families were allowed to visit their daughters only once a month except during Lent.

On Sundays a couple of numeraries would sometimes play the piano while we were writing to family and friends. Correspondence was our only contact with the outside world except on those Sundays when Mrs. Mouriz used to come to visit her daughters Anina and Loli.

One spring Sunday afternoon, I had the great joy of meeting my youngest brother. Only twelve years old, he managed to convince the family housekeeper to accompany him in order to visit me. I was with him in the garden. Rosario de Orbegozo was so touched to see the youngster that she told me to prepare him some lemonade. This was the only visit I received from my family during the six months I was at Los Rosales.

Until 1966 all members in Opus Dei had to recite the three parts of the Rosary: one "in family," usually before dinner and whenever possible in the oratory; the other two parts were recited individually while performing ordinary tasks.

On Saturday evenings, in all Opus Dei oratories, the Benediction with the Blessed Sacrament is held[1] and the Gregorian "Hail Holy Queen" is sung.

On Saturdays, as a general mortification in all Opus Dei houses the tea time snack is suppressed. This same day all members use the discipline individually: thirty-three blows on the buttocks. We were told that when using the disciplines, the blows should be delivered with energy and vigor. With the directress's permission one could use the discipline on other days as well. For the mortification everybody uses her own room.

We were required to use the cilice daily for not less than two hours, except on holy days and Sundays. You had to tie it around the thigh as tightly as possible. In addition to these two daily hours, the cilice was also worn while teaching a class or directing a circle of studies, for instance.

Needless to say, when leaving Opus Dei, you throw away these instruments of torture. Life brings enough mortification by itself without the need for this additional flagellation.

---

1. Liturgical ceremony when the tabernacle is open and the priest blesses the congregation with the ciborium or monstrance containing the consecrated host.

At night, after the recitation of Compline and before the private examination of conscience, a designated numerary read a brief commentary on the Gospel of the day—previously submitted to the directress of the house.

Just before getting in bed, everybody knelt and with outstretched arms, individually and in a low voice, prayed three Hail Marys, asking for purity. For the same purpose, a few drops of Holy Water were sprinkled on the bed. Everyone kept a small bottle with Holy Water on their night stand.

Everybody individually prayed the Memorare for the person in Opus Dei who needed it most. I always liked this prayer very much before I joined Opus Dei. It was my father who taught me this prayer when I was only four years old, while playing with me during the summer at siesta time. At my early age that prayer sounded to me like a game: I repeated after my father, sentence by sentence, but at ". . . under the weight of our sins . . .," I was laughing heartily because to my mind the meaning of that sentence was "under a scale, under a bunch of fish . . ." (This was an unintentional Spanish pun, because *sins* is "pecados" and *fish*, "pescados." In addition, *weight* in Spanish is "peso" and "weight of a scale" is also "peso.") So, my understanding was that a bunch of fish were under a scale and from there my amusement. As a child four years old, I knew no other word for "weight" than the one of "scale" that I used to see when shopping with my mother. And of course, I could not imagine fish under a scale but on a scale. . .

Ordinarily before tea time, Opus Dei members devote half an hour to personal meditation. On Opus Dei and church feast days, the meditation is customarily guided by an Opus Dei priest.

The Opus Dei plan of life has weekly norms such as confession, fraternal chat with the directress, circle of studies, and recitation of Psalm 2 on Tuesdays. Monthly all the members have to attend a day of recollection and yearly a spiritual retreat of several days besides the so-called annual course of studies which lasts around three to four weeks.

Once classes were over, each of us had to undertake the task assigned by the local council for that particular week. At Los Rosales we had no appliances of any kind. All work was done by hand.

At Los Rosales there were two non-Opus Dei maids who did not live in the house. One was in charge of washing our clothes and the other served us at table and did the dishes. The rest of the house work was done by us.

The chores were rotated. The hardest, for me, was the laundry, because I was unable to keep the charcoal furnace burning. Every time that I tried to start it, it went out. We ironed with irons heated on the stove, implements that are now considered antiques. The numerary in charge of the laundry had to collect all the bags that the numeraries had previously prepared, including a small paper with names and contents, and to bring them to the laundry room. There, the numerary in charge had personally to open each bag, to check each piece in accordance with the sheet enclosed. If one of the pieces lacked its owner's initials, it had to be marked.

Ironing was the sole responsibility of the numerary in charge of the laundry; indeed to iron the clothes of more than twenty persons was no small task.

Oratory was the lightest task. The numerary in charge had to clean it, prepare the vessels for Mass the next day, and wash and iron the altar linens. She also had to make Communion hosts for the entire week.

The numerary in charge of the kitchen had to prepare the meals for the entire house. In the morning you had to light the coal stove, a bit complicated for those who had been accustomed to gas stoves. We had to build a fire using paper, wood chips, and coal to get the stove going and to maintain the fire till night. During classes, the directress used to help in the kitchen to keep the fire going and to prevent the food from being burned.

The numerary in charge of the pantry had to set the tables and prepare the desserts and bake cakes for breakfast or tea. Since there were no Saturday teas, that time was devoted to making the desserts for Sunday lunch.

During house work Opus Dei numeraries wear a white gown over their ordinary dress. This gown, buttoned either in the front or in the back, had to be kept immaculate always. A numerary changed this gown twice a week. However, the numeraries in charge of the kitchen or the pantry had to change their white gowns daily. To wear a soiled white gown was a matter for fraternal correction.

Numeraries who had no special tasks in the house or those whose tasks allowed them some free time had to go to the dining room, converted between meals into a sewing room for liturgical vestments and altar linens that were sold to Opus Dei houses or to a member to be ordained in the near future. With the income of these sales we supported the house; the majority of the numeraries at Los Rosales could not bring the stipulated two years' stipend, for the time considered by Opus Dei as formative period. Many of the families of those taking this course of studies opposed our vocation and did not give us any money. In a subtle way, the superiors stressed the kindness of Opus Dei that allowed us to study here without payment.

The two years' stipend is a contribution from the female numerary's family or from her own professional work. It is not technically a dowry because a dowry is brought to a marriage or to a convent. The stipend was equivalent to the room and board paid by any student living at any

Opus Dei residence. In my case and in that of several others in the course, it was an absurd issue, since we had to quit our job and give up our salary in order to attend the study course at Los Rosales.

However, Opus Dei claims that ". . . it is an indispensable condition for lay members, in order to be consistent to their own vocation, that they be engaged in a constant practice of civil work or a professional job like any other lay citizen . . ."[1] But this is not always the case. The general rule is not always applicable, because those members, male and female, attending the Roman colleges of the prelature as well as those primarily assigned to "internal work in Opus Dei," either formative or governmental, must quit their professional work.

At Los Rosales we were totally isolated from the external world. This is one of the characteristics of a sect.[2] Communication with our families and friends was exclusively by letter, with the sole exception of the Mouriz sisters, whose mother and sisters used to visit them almost every Sunday. I learned some time later that the visits were connected with the proselytizing in process of two other sisters: one of them a medical doctor, Angelita, for many years at the University of Navarra, while Carmen, after some time at Rome headquarters, was sent as regional directress to Germany.

Outgoing letters had to be given open to the directress to be censored. Incoming letters were similarly opened and read by the directress. This was standard procedure in all Opus Dei houses. Only those older numeraries who have already made perpetual vows (*fidelity*) are given their letters unopened with the recommendation that "if anything is important in them to inform the directress." Even priests and especially those of them who, for whatever reason, are under surveillance by Opus Dei superiors have their correspondence opened. There are even cases when a numerary was told that a letter had arrived for her, but was not given to her because "it was not convenient for your soul." Or the superiors say nothing and do not deliver the letter to the numerary. This is how they manipulate the minds of the members for the sake of indoctrination and acquisition of "good spirit."

My father wrote me from time to time but so briefly that his letters looked like telegrams. I wrote him the permitted two letters a month. We were told that in Lent we should not write our families, except in unusual

---

1. Rocca, *L'Opus Dei*, p. 193: "Transformazione dell'Opus Dei in Prelatura Personale," *T. Caratteristiche specifiche e realtà sociale dell'Opus Dei*, 1, para. 3.
2. "Insulation consists of behavioural rules calculated to protect sect values by reducing the influence of the external world where contact necessarily occurs. Of course, insulation may be a latent function of the moral demands of sect teaching." Wilson, *Patterns of Sectarianism*, p. 37.

circumstances, and the same policy was followed during Advent. However, they did give us the letters that arrived during these periods of the year. It was a matter for fraternal correction to read a letter during the minor silence.

The structure of life at Los Rosales was designed gradually to convert us into true Opus Dei fanatics:

· Total detachment from our families and friends
· Importance of life in a group
· No free time
· Excessive workload
· Daily meditation and mortification
· Opus Dei and the Father are central topics and only goals
· Our only family is Opus Dei
· All female members of Opus Dei are our sisters
· We must love the Father more than our own parents
· No outside influences, such as music or movies
· No radio, newspaper, or magazine

Although the Council of Scientific Research sent me its publication, *Arbor,* the superiors did not allow me to read it. I was told it was of no importance now to think of philosophy, but to learn instead how to administer the house.

One facet of Opus Dei's brainwashing was to make its members believe that Opus Dei is perfect because it came from God and that every pronouncement by its Founder was by God's divine inspiration. This was emphasized from the start at the center of studies and in the courses of formation. As in a musical theme, the note was given by the first violin, Monsignor Escrivá; repeated immediately by the second violins, the Opus Dei superiors; and followed by the string and percussion instruments, called fraternal chat, circles of study, days of recollection, spiritual retreats, fraternal correction, and so through all forms of indoctrination that Opus Dei has at its disposal.

The indoctrination we received did not allow us to reflect analytically on anything that we were unable to understand. Any critical thought was an indication of lack of unity and lack of "good spirit," which we had to report in our weekly chat as a negative moment in our spiritual life.

As women who had requested admission into Opus Dei, were we fools or so naive as to be manipulated like puppets? No! We had simply entered Opus Dei with the intention of doing God's will. We were innocent and fully believed that Opus Dei superiors represented God's voice. With total good faith we were convinced that to live this new secular path of apostolate, intellectual apostolate, we had to surrender ourselves into God's hands, believing that Opus Dei doctrine came from God. At the same time, we considered that if we were unable to understand something, it was obviously due to our spiritual ignorance.

Opus Dei has not yet come to terms with criticism, especially self-criticism within the institution, or criticism of sayings by Monsignor Escrivá or of customs established by him, which is precisely what makes Opus Dei a sect.[1]

There were many things which I could not understand, but Opus Dei superiors kept insisting that I should ask God to grant me the "good spirit" preached by the Father as they cited *The Way*, No. 684, on self-sacrifice.[2]

My inner conviction was that I must leave in Christ's hands anything of intrinsic value I had and that my sacrifice, through the communion of saints, would remedy some need of the church. I did not lose my optimism or my joy, because I learned how to survive in this atmosphere, which, as I was told, was not that of ordinary Opus Dei houses. To me, life with more than twenty women was impossible since I never had a herd mentality. I was assured during my weekly chat that the center of studies was only a necessary phase in our spiritual formation to adjust our souls and minds to Opus Dei spirit. Further, the sooner and more faithfully I absorbed Opus Dei doctrine, the happier I would be, and my apostolate would be more efficient. They induced me to distinguish Opus Dei spirit from the atmosphere I was living in. Accordingly, I resolved to assimilate everything in Opus Dei's doctrine to the best of my abilities.

My superiors were very astute; their indoctrination was to make me surrender entirely to God's supposed will. They utilized my sincere religious faith as a fertile ground to sow Opus Dei doctrine. They won! They made of me a perfect fanatic, a most efficient tool inside the sect named Opus Dei.

Córdoba: La Alcazaba

The course at the center of studies ended after six months. For weeks we speculated about where we might be stationed. We felt an urge to leave

---

1. See Wilson, *Patterns of Sectarianism*, pp. 23–36, where we can find the following definition: "Typically a *sect* may be identified by the following characteristics: it is a voluntary association; membership is by proof to sect authorities of some claim of personal merit. . . . exclusiveness is emphasised, and expulsion exercised against those who contravene doctrinal, moral or organisational precepts. . . . they [sects] dictate the member's ideological orientation to secular society or they rigorously specify the necessary stands of moral rectitude."

2. "So your talents, your personality, your qualities are being wasted. So you are not allowed to take full advantage of them. Meditate well on these words by a spiritual writer: 'The incense offered to God is not wasted. Our Lord is more honored by the immolation of your talents than by their vain use."

Los Rosales to carry forth the "good spirit" that the superiors had imbued in us during those six months of indoctrination.

Rosario de Orbegozo, the central directress, informed us where we would be posted. I was sent with Piedad García, to Córdoba, the city where my mother was born and where her whole family still lived. We would be responsible for the housekeeping of La Alcazaba, a male students' residence.

I knew Córdoba well, since I had stayed there with my mother's family. The last time I was there, my relatives invited me in May for the typical Andalusian feasts. I had a wonderful time and I was treated like a queen.

I left Los Rosales without any regret since I had minded intensely the cloistered months there and disliked life in a large group. Besides, I was looking forward to put into practice what I had learned and especially to do apostolate. I was full of desire to imprint Opus Dei spirit in souls and also afraid of the unknown: about the direct administrative assignment as housekeeper of a male students' residence.

As soon as I knew that I was sent to Córdoba, the central directress advised me to phone my father, the only time in my stay at the center of studies, in order to ask him for a round-trip train ticket Madrid-Córdoba, which my father sent by return mail. Since my father was one of the directors of the Spanish National Railroads, I was entitled to a free ticket in luxury class or sleeping car. The ticket I received from my father permitted either possibility.

Piedad's parents lived in Salamanca, and they sent her enough money to buy any ticket she might want. So, with her money and my ticket, we arrived at the women's headquarters at Juan Bravo, 20, Madrid.

Rosario de Orbegozo gave us a scolding and accused us of "lack of poverty" when she learned that we were planning to travel first class or luxury class. She ordered me to go to the railroad office and to exchange my ticket for a third-class one. I went, but that exchange was prohibited by the railroad rules. So, with Piedad's money for a first-class ticket, we bought two third-class train tickets.

Rosario de Orbegozo did not allow me to visit my father or my brothers. She simply told me that I could phone my father and inform him about the time of the train departure, in case he would like to go to the railroad station. I phoned my father and gave him the information. This saddened me and seemed to me unfair, for want of a better word, since I had not seen my father for six months. Looking back I realize how cruel this was to families like mine, as well as bad tactics because it aggravated our families' hostility toward Opus Dei.

At the railroad station I could not find my father. I was concerned because I really wanted to see him. I had even hoped that my brothers might come. Since I could not see him, and the train was about to leave, we took our places. At that time third-class compartments had wooden seats, were full of soldiers, people with baskets of chickens or packages. From the window I searched the crowded platform for my father; Piedad tried to help by matching my description of faces in the crowd.

Suddenly I discovered Antonio Mellado, the son of a friend of my father's, shouting at me: "What the hell are you doing here, in a third-class wagon when your father and I could not find you in the sleeping car or in first class? Your father is desperate."

My father arrived, a minute before the train left, in anguish because he could not find me and said: "How can they possibly allow two young women to travel by night in this atmosphere?"

He was infuriated. In the stupidity of my brand new indoctrination, I replied: "Dad, we have to live in poverty and offer up all this unpleasantness for souls."

The train left at that moment, and I could see my tearful father gesticulate and hear my enraged friend shouting at me: "Tell all of them on my behalf that they are fanatics with no heart!"

In this way I left Madrid for Córdoba. I felt badly for my father. I did not know how to manage to patch things up with my family and to live the spirit of Opus Dei at the same time. Piedad was very understanding during the trip and, as if thinking aloud, she said, "I am glad that my parents are in Salamanca and did not come to see me."

At 6 o'clock A.M., the train chugged into Córdoba. Digna Margarit, one of the oldest numeraries in Opus Dei, was waiting for us at the railroad station. She said we did not need a cab because the house was very close to the station.

On the way to the house, she informed us that, unfortunately, the residence was located in a bad neighborhood, that she would leave that very afternoon for Madrid to participate in the annual course of studies, and that the directress of the house, Sabina Alandes, was quite ill. Sabina had had an accident a few days earlier when a pan of boiling oil fell on one leg.

So, carrying our suitcases we arrived at the administration of La Alcazaba. My dreams of an Andalusian-style residence like my family's houses were shattered when we arrived at an ugly, recently constructed, six-story building. We went up the steps to the first floor, where the administration was located. The rest of the floors did not belong to the residence: they were occupied by regular tenants.

Sabina, whom I had met in Zurbarán   aited at the door. She welcomed us warmly. Entering the flat I could see that the vestibule was decorated in good taste. To the left was a three-bed bedroom and bath for the three maids. Next to it was the laundry. And the last door gave access to a pleasant living room, decorated in a vaguely British style. At the right of the vestibule was a short corridor. Two doors on its left led to the kitchen and to the storage room for provisions. A bedroom for the numeraries assigned to the house was at the end of this corridor. The room was very small. It could hold only two beds. A couch under the window was the third bed. We were assigned a bed, and Sabina got the couch. Needless to say the beds were wooden. There was a tiny bathroom and the secretary's work room that had access to the oratory. The directress had an old armoire with a mirror in a corner of the corridor. Piedad and I shared a closet in the middle of the same corridor.

Administrations

Since Digna was leaving that day, instructions about the house were given before we unpacked. La Alcazaba was a residence mainly for veterinary students, who were not Opus Dei members except the three Opus Dei numeraries on the local council.

The residence had two apartments on the first floor but in an adjacent building with the entrance on a different street. The rest of that building was occupied by regular tenants. Since both residence and administration were on the same level, it was possible to communicate from the residence to the administration through a door in the dining room, in accordance with Opus Dei's *Internal Rules for Administrations.*

As mandated by the rules, the door had two different locks. The director kept one key and the other one, different, was kept by the directress. The door had to be locked with the two keys, from the time of the examination of conscience at night till morning prayer. During the day, the doors of communication are always locked on the administration side.[1] The internal communication is made ordinarily through the sacristy and the dining room which are treated as part of the administration zone except when in use. When the chaplain has to enter the sacristy to vest for Mass or when men have to enter the dining room, the directress then opens the door with her key and notifies the director by internal telephone. I would like here to clarify that this document of *Internal Rules for Administrations* was revised and corrected by Monsignor Escrivá about 1954. In fact, it was the first task I performed as directress of the printing press at Opus Dei's Rome headquarters. For this reason I talked frequently with Monsignor Escrivá. Alvaro del Portillo corrected the galley proofs of this document.

1. See *Reglamento interno de administraciones* (Grottaferratta: Scuola Tipografica Italo-Orientale, 1947), 9; in Rocca, *L'Opus Dei,* pp. 163–65.

This document is absolutely not at the disposal of whomever wishes to read it. Indeed, the 1985 book by G. Rocca, which I cite, includes only a brief first version of those *Internal Rules for Administrations.*

Our first act in the administration was to go to the oratory to greet the Lord. I was surprised that the oratory, a small room with space for only four chairs, had a lattice facing the altar. The *Internal Rules for Administrations* state that when there is no separate oratory "female numeraries attend liturgical acts behind a lattice like those used by cloistered nuns when their churches are open to the public."[1] During the day a heavy red velvet curtain covered the lattice, with a small opening so that the tabernacle could be seen from our side. I used to say that we attended a needle-point Mass.

As soon as Digna left that afternoon, Sabina asked to speak with Piedad, and when she emerged, she was laughing heartily and said to me: "What a number I have done on you!" Sabina had asked her who of the two of us was the better cook and Piedad said that I was.

Overnight I was in charge of the kitchen and cooking for about 25 people. My only cooking experience was what I had observed at my family's home and my week at Los Rosales. I had to go to the market every day and quite frequently ran errands during hours that did not conflict with my cooking chores. Early in the morning I went to a market, located far from our house. A custom of the Andalusian vendors surprised me: they made the sign of the cross with the money received from the first purchase of the day. After several weeks of going to the market, I began to meet my uncle Ramón Jiménez, my maternal grandmother's brother, a lawyer on his daily trip to court. He was very dear to me. He was a generous man, and every time we met, he always told me that if I needed money or anything else to ask him or his wife, aunt Aurora. He was upset to see me going to the market and to learn of the neighborhood where I lived. Especially in Andalusia it was not customary then for a girl or a lady to go to the market and much less alone. When an exception was necessary, the lady was always accompanied by a maid.

Piedad was responsible for the cleaning of the residence and the administration, plus the laundry. She noticed that the maid could not do all the work, so she also ironed the residents' laundry. She was also in charge of the pantry and of the spiritual education of the maids.

Just two days after our arrival from Los Rosales Piedad and I had taken over the administration of the residence. We tried not to nag Sabina with questions, because she was still quite sick and in great pain because of the burn on her leg. I used to change the bandages daily but I was shocked

---

1. See Rocca, *L'Opus Dei,* p. 164.

to learn that she had not yet seen a doctor, because she did not know a single soul in the city. I asked permission to visit my family to ask for a good doctor. She told me to phone them but since we had no telephone in the administration, I had to call them from a grocery store. My family, with whom I had stayed before entering Opus Dei, had not the slightest idea that I was living in Córdoba. I had not yet met my uncle. My family invited me for lunch but I declined their invitation and explained that I was in charge of the kitchen and could not leave the house. They gave me the name of an excellent physician to whom I took Sabina. He was astonished that Sabina had not received any medical assistance. Her healing and recuperation took around three months.

During that period Piedad and I enjoyed ourselves immensely. We laughed a lot at our inexperience and took the housekeeping work as an amusing experience. However, the work for the residence went well and nobody learned of our inexperience. Since Sabina was incapacitated, Piedad and I would tell her that the residence was clean, the residents well fed, and the laundry delivered with punctuality. I must say that Sabina tried to help us as much as she was able to. As directress of the administration, she maintained communication with the director of the residence through the internal telephone, as regulated by the *Internal Rules for Administrations,* which stated that between the administration and the residence there may be no relations of any kind. Opus Dei men never visit the houses of female numeraries. The residence and administration only communicate by internal telephones, one of which is in the director's office and the other one in a visible spot such as a corridor or a hall in the administration, never in the directress's room. The internal telephones are used by the director or the directress to pass on information. At the beginning or end of the telephone call, the word *Pax* is said, to which is replied *In aeternum.*

The *Pax* and the reply *In aeternum* are used by all members of Opus Dei. Its recitation gains five hundred days' indulgence by the Roman Catholic Church. But it cannot be used in front of outsiders. Even when a member kneels at the confessional for the sacrament of penance, he or she must always say to the Opus Dei priest *"Pax"* to which the priest answers *"In aeternum."*

Conversations with the residence director were extremely brief. For instance, at night, usually after supper, the residence director would call the administration to inform about the number of people for breakfast, lunch, tea, and supper. The directress then conveyed the information to the numerary in charge of the kitchen and also to the numerary in charge of the pantry to set the exact number of places.

To give notification of any delay in serving meals, I informed the directress. She would then phone the director alerting him to keep the residents from entering the dining room at the scheduled time. The same system was observed to send messages related to housecleaning or laundry.

Summer in Córdoba is renowned for its heat. Typical Andalusian houses have a central court, generally with a fountain, palm trees, and geraniums. An awning covering the patio at sunny hours makes these houses not only comfortable but also fresh. By contrast, in a small apartment like ours in a so-called modern building (at a time when Spanish builders considered not climate but only profit), summer was truly infernal. We had no fan in the house and no money to buy one. Furthermore, we were required to wear long-sleeved dresses. Even the nights were so hot that I used to wake up on the floor without realizing when I had slipped out of bed.

The change was enormous from an earlier stay in Córdoba at my relatives' comfortable Andalusian-style home to being an Opus Dei house-keeper in charge of the kitchen.

My year in Córdoba within Opus Dei was my first experience with Opus Dei housekeeping. It was a kind of challenge, and as I met each difficulty, I offered it to God with joy applying my effort toward proselytism with girls and also for my parents.

I believed that Opus Dei's so-called humble labor of housekeeping was a silent and efficacious contemplative activity. Monsignor Escrivá used to say, "The perfect administration is not seen and not heard." He also said: "Without the administrations, Opus Dei would collapse, since they are the skeleton supporting all Opus Dei works." I was convinced I was doing something of great importance.

Looking back now the housekeeping performed by Opus Dei women was an obvious manifestation of the institution's rampant machismo. As a woman, you had to serve the males of the institution. Even if Monsignor Escrivá used to praise this kind of work in front of everybody and stressed that for a few female numeraries and for all the maids, it was their professional work, at rock bottom it was a way to guarantee a life style in Opus Dei houses equivalent to that of a luxury hotel. This activity provides cheap labor that when performed with "good spirits" may imply sanctity for many souls.

Many Opus Dei women were expected to give up their professions permanently to devote themselves to administration. It is important to stress that the Opus Dei numerary who does not joyfully abandon her profession for as long as needed, or even for good, to do housekeeping is considered to have "bad spirit."

I was vigilant about my spiritual life. The plan of life was now carried out in accordance with the work assigned to each of us. We attended Mass at the house whenever there was a visiting Opus Dei priest at the residence. We usually went to a public church. Mental prayer was my time of close intimacy with God. Other persons, whose names came to mind, I brought them all into his presence.

I always offered up for our proselytism my spiritual mortification as well as the use of the cilice and discipline. Although I was generous in the use of the discipline, it always cost me a considerable effort. Besides, its use in Córdoba was something of an "art," since the only adequate place was the bathroom, which was so small that one had to be very skilled not to give the blows to the door instead of to the buttocks.

My spirit of poverty was focused on cooking, since this was my assignment.

Shopping was part of the job. With no refrigerator, we had to measure the amount of food to be consumed each day exactly to avoid waste. Calculating the milk to be consumed each day was impossible. If any milk was left over, it soured within minutes. So, in my examination of conscience as a way of living the spirit of poverty, I carefully noted the food wasted.

La Alcazaba was a residence without a permanent Opus Dei priest and jokingly we used to say that the motto of the house was "not to sin" because we could only go to confession when an Opus Dei priest was in residence, ordinarily every month or month-and-a-half. Meanwhile, we could not confess to any other priest except in a dire emergency, but never to a Jesuit.

During one of my first confessions after nearly two months in Córdoba, something funny happened. In the confessional I was reading my list of sins; among them were infractions against poverty such as having wasted 50 liters of milk. The Opus Dei priest, Juan Antonio G. Lobato, asked me with a great sense of humor: "What did you do, daughter, did you bathe in milk like Popea?"

I explained that we had no refrigerator, and he could not believe it. Opus Dei men, including priests, were ignorant of the housekeeping by Opus Dei women.

Sabina was a very good directress and a joyful person. She taught me how to cook. However, she was very strict regarding family relations, so she allowed me to visit my family only twice during the year I lived in Córdoba. Indeed, one of the visits was occasioned by her need for legal advice for her family and she knew that my uncle was an attorney. On a visit, my aunt looked at me with her mocking smile and remarked, referring to Opus Dei: "That is not for you, darling. It is very strange."

Relations among the three of us in the administration were pleasant. Spiritual life was not easy, however, since we had no priest and all spiritual questions had to be raised with the directress instead. Sabina reprimanded me quite often. Her reprimands usually had to do with perfection in our work, in my case perfecting my cooking skills. I always accepted her reprimands well because they were kind, clear, and direct. More than once Sabina called me after a reprimand to tell me that she was very sorry, because she had been unduly harsh, which I appreciated. In my opinion Sabina was a humble person.

I did not like the oratory in this administration, since the lattice made me feel cloistered. During our personal meditation, we had to keep the oratory dark in order not to be seen from the men's side. If we wished to read, we had to draw the velvet drape covering the lattice and then turn on a tiny light on our chair.

When an Opus Dei priest visited the residence, we too were able to attend Mass from our oratory, which was kept dark so that it would not be visible to the residents. We received communion after the residents. Then the priest approached a small window within the lattice, which was opened only at that moment by the directress. During the rest of the time, this window was always locked and the key held by the directress of the administration.

Work of St. Raphael

A few days after my arrival in Córdoba, the Opus Dei central advisory, still in Madrid, communicated that Piedad García would be subdirectress of the local council and I the secretary. I was also put in charge of the external apostolate with the girls of St. Raphael. That is, I had to give the so-called circles of study that I had previously received at Zurbarán. The circles of study were based on outlines several pages long that the directress provided to help us prepare the talk. The outlines were mass-produced for all Opus Dei houses.

When we came to Córdoba there was not a single vocation nor any girls who came to the house. The directress told me that the time had come to offer up my work, the heat, and any shortcoming of the house—we had no radio, telephone, record player, nor any possibility of entertainment—to recruit vocations among the girls that I had known through my family before belonging to Opus Dei.

I thought that the moment had arrived, of which Father Panikkar had spoken so much, namely, to put my talents and all my charm to work. I try to see some of the girls I had known earlier and explain not only my new way of life but also what Opus Dei was and encourage them to make confession to the Opus Dei priest on his next visit to Córdoba.

I became a great Opus Dei proselytizer, because I was convinced that everything the superiors had told us was true: Opus Dei equaled sanctity in the world through interior life. It also helped me to recall all the advice

Father Panikkar had given me, although in accordance with the system of Opus Dei, I had never heard anything further about him.

To these young girls, I enthusiastically explained the urgent need to put all the good things they enjoyed in life at the feet of the Virgin and become apostles of Christ in the army called Opus Dei. That many of these girls, and their families as well, knew me before I belonged to Opus Dei greatly facilitated obtaining the first numerary vocations in Córdoba. If anyone raised any objections to joining.Opus Dei, the directress told me to use my own life as an example, as one who had sacrificed both fiancé and family.

On his visit to Córdoba, I briefed Father Juan Antonio G. Lobato in the confessional about the girls who were ready to "whistle" (to request admission into Opus Dei). The priest's evaluation was necessary for a more balanced opinion of the potential candidates. Loli Serrano, whose brother was an Opus Dei numerary, was the first female vocation in Córdoba. She was not typical of woman from Córdoba since she was blond, with smiling clear eyes. Her joyfulness was almost contagious. Elena Serrano, on the contrary, was truly representative of Cordoban women. She could have stepped out of a painting by Romero de Torres. She had all the beauty of an Andalusian woman and all the naiveté of a sixteen-year-old young girl. She was a delightful girl who brought to Opus Dei her friends and introduced us to many old families in Córdoba.

The objective for Córdoba was to form a select group of numeraries from élite old families. I made it possible with all my proselytizing zeal and absolute dedication to Opus Dei. I had met several girls previously in Madrid at the Mellado's home whose family was from Córdoba. One of the girls, Luchy Fernández de Mesa, however, never became a numerary. Opus Dei superiors told me that she was not "numerary material" and for this reason never allowed me to continue any further contact with her when I left town.

In any city where I lived as an Opus Dei member, the girls with whom I dealt became true friends and by talking to them convinced them to consecrate their lives to God in Opus Dei.

Once a person who had been in charge of the girls moved to another city, all contact with the girls ceased.

Approval of Opus Dei
as a Secular Institute

In Córdoba, on July 15, 1950, the director of the men's residence notified us by intercom of an extraordinary development. Opus Dei's Constitutions had won final approval by the church in Rome as "holy, perpetual, and inviolable." For the first time in the history of the church this took place within the lifetime of the founder of an institution. Accordingly, Monsignor Escrivá had ordered that the event be marked by extraordinary celebration within the family on the day the news arrived at each house, although the official recognition had been granted on June 16, 1950.

Naturally, the celebration would involve a thanksgiving meditation in the oratory and a special meal.

Through this news we discovered what had been the "special intention of the Father" for which we had been asked so insistently to pray at Los Rosales.

A very important event in my life took place in Córdoba; on December 8, 1950, I received permission from the superiors to make the *oblation*, that is, to take my first temporary vows until the next Feast of St. Joseph. Since the priest would not arrive until December 10, I had to wait for that day to make my first vows.

The ceremony took place in our tiny oratory with the door open to the pre-oratory space where we placed the regulation chair for the priest. Kneeling in front of the priest with the wooden cross on the left side of the oratory, I sustained the dialogue with the priest mandated by the ceremonial book. As witnesses Sabina and Piedad were there. It is customary in Opus Dei to be embraced by the persons who attend the ceremony, but there is no celebration of any kind nor special communication to anybody. However, Sabina authorized me to tell Loli and Elena, the first two Opus Dei numerary vocations in Córdoba.

My life was full of activity between my work in the kitchen, trips to the market, and, above all, my conversations with the girls of St. Raphael. When they came to the house, I brought them to the kitchen to help while we chatted about everything on heaven and earth. I tried to copy what I had seen done at Zurbarán where I had begun to attend a residence. Whenever I had to run an errand, I tried to call some St. Raphael girl or one of the recent vocations to invite them to accompany me so that we could continue to talk about Opus Dei and especially about the Father.

On my outings I would go into bookstores and savor titles that I was not allowed to read. One day returning to the house I met my cousin Rafael in Las Tendillas, one of the main streets. My cousin gave me a hug, and offered his condolences on the death of my uncle.

"My uncle?" I asked embarrassed.

"Your uncle, Dr. Tapia," he answered. "How could you not have found out about his death, when the news has been in all the newspapers?"

I was extremely fond of my uncle Antonio García-Tapia for many reasons. He was my godfather, he was my father's age, and he had had

THE MAKING OF A FANATIC · 71

great affection for my paternal grandfather, whom I had never known, so Doctor García-Tapia had been like a grandfather to me. My cousin, who knew all this, was astonished that I did know anything and that she should be the one to give me the news.

When I returned to the house, I told the directress that I wanted to call my family, but I was not allowed to do so. Sabina only told me to offer my grief to God. Nothing else.

Next day Sabina called me to talk to her and I told her of my frustrations. I told her that added to the hurt I felt, I was angry that we were kept in the dark about everything that happened. We read no newspapers and were kept from the real world inside our little universe. Sabina seemed sympathetic, but told me to offer God this sacrifice for our work of proselytism and for the Father.

The arrival from Madrid of María Jesús Hereza, then an Opus Dei superior, gave me peace again. She said that my uncle had been her professor at the Faculty of Medicine, that she held him in great esteem, and understood my sorrow. She added that we lived in exceptional times, the foundational period of Opus Dei, and that these sorrows and hurts were the deep foundation of a fruitful apostolate. As if to change the subject, she told me to accompany her to Seville, where there were plans to begin Opus Dei activities. She wanted me to meet some girls there.

The trip to Seville was quick, one day, but we had time to meet a very pleasant group of girls. I recall that we had just enough money for lunch, but María Jesús decided not to eat but to buy instead some San Leandro pastries, a typical Seville desert, for Aunt Carmen, Monsignor Escrivá's sister. I had met Aunt Carmen briefly during a visit she made to Los Rosales. One of the "devotions" that Monsignor Escrivá instilled in Opus Dei members was veneration for his relatives.

Another of my jobs in the Córdoba administration, as secretary of the local council, was to keep the house accounts. This required care because we were a very poor house and it was necessary to walk a tightrope to be able to afford food. Theoretically, the administration received a salary from the residence, but in fact, I do not remember that the residence in Córdoba paid us any salary. Piedad's family sent her money, which went totally to the administration funds, and Sabina also received something. My family did not send me anything at all except an old piece of jewelry from my paternal grandmother which was sent immediately to the Opus Dei central government, which in turn sent it to Rome.

Afternoons, after helping the maid to pick up the kitchen, I would go to the hall, called the secretary's office to tend to the accounts.

I remember that when I worked on them, I had the window open onto a patio and could hear someone on an upper floor play the music from

The Third Man, which was then very popular. I knew the tune well without knowing that it was from a movie.

María Casal: Conversion

The most important apostolic memory of my life from Córdoba was María Casal's conversion to Catholicism. She became the first Swiss female numerary.

On one of his visits, Father Juan Antonio G. Lobato told me that he had met a girl in Seville whose name was María Casal, who like her fiancé was a medical student. The fiancé had left María to join Opus Dei as a numerary.[1] She was furious. Hence, she had come to see Father Lobato. And now he asked me to start writing her.

I thought long about how to write the first letter but finally resolved to write it with great frankness, expressing my understanding and sympathy for her pain. Thus began my correspondence with María Casal. She informed me that she was a Protestant and could not understand the idea of "sacrifice or happiness on the cross" about which Catholics spoke.

Many more topics followed. A real and deep friendship began. Finally, after months of correspondence and chats with Father Lobato, she wanted to come to Córdoba so that we might get to know each other.

By arrangement with Sabina, who stayed with Piedad that Sunday and took over my obligations in the house, I went to the station to meet María Casal, who was arriving on the first train. Interestingly, we recognized each other immediately though we had never met.

María was a mix of the organized Swiss mind and the joyful Andalusian spirit. Her accent was fully Andalusian.

While talking, we walked around the beautiful city of Córdoba. We entered the Mosque, went through the old-city Jewish ghetto, crossed the bridge of St. Raphael, and went to the Shrine of St. Raphael, patron saint of Córdoba and also of Opus Dei's apostolate with young people.

María Casal said that our correspondence and her conversations with the Opus Dei priest had made her interested in Opus Dei. I encouraged her to write to Monsignor Escrivá mentioning that interest, even though she was not yet a Catholic. I recall that letter well.

Then we discussed her conversion to Catholicism. We talked in depth. I was very aware of helping to solidify in her soul the knowledge of Catholicism and the attraction, doubtless, to Opus Dei.

María had to inform her parents about her wish to become a Catholic. Her father, a Swiss engineer, an executive at an electric company in Gauzín,

---

1. The fiancé, Diego Diaz, eventually became a numerary priest. He spent many years in Ecuador. Years ago he left Opus Dei and married.

Seville province, did not want to hear about it. Her mother was more understanding but unenthusiastic. Her siblings did not even want to discuss the subject.

We got to the La Alcazaba administration at lunchtime. María met Sabina and Piedad, and I recommended that it would be a good idea for Marìa to talk to Sabina as directress of the house.

When she returned to Seville, María wrote to say that she was happy to have met us and that she had decided to be baptized as a Catholic. After several months of required instruction, she was baptized in a little chapel in Gauzín in May 1951, on the feast of the Sacred Heart of Mary. She asked me to attend her baptism. Needless to say I wanted very much to be present at the ceremonies before and during the baptism, but my superiors did not allow me to attend the ceremony "because we should not participate in these acts." I could not understand the rationale behind this decision and deeply regretted not being able to attend the baptism. However, I was allowed to send her the crucifix that I had as a memento of her baptism.

After her baptism, María Casal again insisted that she wanted to be an Opus Dei numerary. However, an unforeseen disappointment was in store for the group in Córdoba. The superiors of the central advisory informed us that María Casal could not become an Opus Dei numerary because she had been a Protestant. They reminded us that the questionnaire that the girls of St. Raphael had to fill out in Zurbarán contained the question: "Religious background: For how many generations has your family been Catholic?"

When we informed the priest on his next visit, he was stunned and furious and told us to ask the superiors again, because the rule did not hold true in the Men's Branch of Opus Dei. Finally, on our insistence, the superiors relented and told us that María Casal could write Monsignor Escrivá requesting admission as an Opus Dei numerary. For the first time in the history of the Opus Dei Women's Branch, it was clear that a woman with a Protestant background could indeed be admitted into Opus Dei as a numerary.

From the very moment that María Casal sought admission into Opus Dei, we could never again write to each other or speak as friends. According to Opus Dei terminology, we were "sisters." Her contact with Opus Dei had to be channeled through the directress of the house, not through any other individual numerary.

This case reveals that authentic friendships between Opus Dei members and young girls were not allowed by the superiors for two reasons, as I understand it. The first is the sexual obsession enunciated in the prohibition of "particular friendship." The second is the typical discipline within a sect.[1]

María Casal went on to obtain her medical degree and worked at Opus Dei's University of Navarra for several years and was one of the prime movers in founding its Nursing School.

A few years ago, visiting Switzerland I learned that María Casal lived in the Opus Dei women's house in Zurich and that María had the reputation of being a hard liner, even on general church questions. I decided to phone her. She was happy to hear from me, so much so that I wondered if she knew I had not belonged to Opus Dei for some considerable time. I mentioned it and she said she knew. Her living outside of Zurich and my flight leaving for London the next day made it impossible to meet. We talked about things in general, and I asked María if she was working as a physician. She answered that she had left her profession for God and Opus Dei, although at times "she attended our own women who were sick."

Knowing how much she loved her profession, I asked as gently as possible: "But is it not through one's own profession that people become saints in Opus Dei?"

"The Father knows best what is the most suitable thing for me," was her response.

"But María, don't you realize that Opus Dei is using you to proselytize, since you are the first Swiss numerary, and that for the Work, recruitment is more important than your professional vocation.

As expected, she said that we would probably never agree on that point because she was convinced that she had to follow the guidance and suggestions of her superiors.

Our conversation ended but I could sense, on the one hand, her affection for me and, on the other, her stereotyped responses were the same that I too would have given years earlier.

The following day, on a short flight to London, I reflected on Opus Dei's sectarian character, and on the need to reveal that other side of the coin to the church.

At the end of May 1951, the major superiors announced that I would make my annual course of studies in Molinoviejo, in Ortigosa del Monte, province of Segovia, which meant I was leaving Córdoba permanently. It saddened me to leave that tiny house and the girls I had met, but above all, it saddened me to leave Sabina and Piedad. Family life had been tranquil in La Alcazaba.

---

1. "Fellowship is an important value for all members: fellow-members are 'brethren'. . . . The individual is a sect-member, before he is anything else, he is expected to find his friends within the group." Wilson, *Patterns of Sectarianism*, p. 43.

Furthermore, I had the sensation of starting over by attending another course, at whose end God only knew where they would send me. Changes never have appealed to me, because they mean constant starting from scratch. But in Opus Dei, constant changes uproot individuals, making them lose friendships and attachments and converting them into interchangeable parts at the total disposition of the institution.

My stay in Córdoba was another step toward becoming a full-fledged Opus Dei fanatic. My life was happy in Opus Dei style, because I accepted anything I was told without hesitation. I felt separated and different from everyone else. Unlike nuns, the absence of a habit made us look like normal people, but over the years I came to realize that a discalced Carmelite nun understands more about life than an Opus Dei woman.

Sometimes I felt terribly lonely in Córdoba, because I only received scant news of my family through my father's letters. They did not allow me to visit my relatives who resided in the city.

Was it the same person going to Molinoviejo, I asked myself, as had arrived in Córdoba a year earlier? The answer was "No!" The first year of Opus Dei experience had taught me many of the rules of the game, what the Work considered "good spirit." I felt more serious, less spontaneous, with a clear idea: the only important thing for me was Opus Dei.

In Córdoba I learned to rid myself of attachments, not only to relatives but even to those from the apostolate, to have the prudence to listen, and the wisdom to accept whatever I was told. In other words, Opus Dei fanaticism was slowly becoming part of my very flesh and spirit.

Although I never would have labeled any of this fanaticism then, I turned over all these ideas, while the click clack of the train lulled me to sleep, carrying me from Córdoba toward Madrid.

Molinoviejo

On arrival in Madrid, I was informed that we would leave for Molinoviejo in the afternoon. I was allowed to telephone my family. The maid said that my parents were in England, but I spoke to my brother Javier and said that I would like to come home for lunch. To my great dismay, he responded that he had given our mother his word of honor not to allow me to set foot in the house. My father had proposed that he invite me to a restaurant for lunch, so that the three children could be together.

The hope that my parents might understand my vocation again ran aground. Still, the three of us did have lunch together in a restaurant.

That evening I left for Ortigosa del Monte by train with several numeraries who had also just arrived in Madrid to have their annual course in

Molinoviejo. Almost all of us had already met, either at Los Rosales or at Zurbarán.

Molinoviejo was Opus Dei's first retreat house anywhere in the world. The house had the special aura of having been purchased and remodeled under orders from Monsignor Escrivá, who had stayed there quite often. The administration consisted of several numeraries, who were also in charge of the center of studies for servant numeraries. Hence, the retreat house was well attended. On the grounds was a little farm that the servants ran under the supervision of numeraries.

Molinoviejo was a pleasant, well-built, comfortable house, in modern Castillian style.

This annual course was the first time that Opus Dei women numeraries would live in a house as residents without being part of the administration at all.

There were individual rooms, and all had a normal bed with box spring and mattress, since the house was used for retreats to outsiders. The rooms were comfortable, had a closet, sink, and a window. However, like Opus Dei men, who always sleep in ordinary beds, every week we had what was known as "the watch day." This meant that you were supposed to be spiritually on guard so that the schedule for common activities like prayer and get-together was followed and that you should be particularly diligent in your fraternal corrections. Furthermore, on the eve of the watch day, since the bedrooms had tile floors, we had to sleep on the floor of the only room with a parquet floor. We brought our sheets and blankets but not a pillow. This was part of the watch-day mortification. Needless to say, discipline and cilice were faithfully employed by each of us according to regulations.

Apart from the peculiar charism of Molinoviejo within Opus Dei, the most important thing about the premises is the shrine dedicated to Our Lady, Mother of Fair Love. We were told that in that shrine, Monsignor Escrivá had found the way to guarantee "the continuity of the spirit of the Work"; in other words, that God had made the Father see that Opus Dei would always be the same as on the day of its foundation; that in Opus Dei there would never be either reforms or reformers; that all this rested on fraternal correction, on living the spirit of unity, and on avoiding any murmuring whatsoever. This implied that the slightest criticism within the institution was forbidden—another sectarian trait. The rejection of criticism, even with the most honest intention, has precisely been the rope that has strangled the majority of those members who abandoned or were dismissed from Opus Dei, one more trait that makes Opus Dei a sect within the Roman Catholic Church.

Whatever occurred in the shrine with regard to Monsignor Escrivá or the beginning of Opus Dei was not explained to us clearly and openly. One of the first numeraries intimated that something "extraordinary" had occurred in the shrine without specifying exactly what. We surmised that Monsignor Escrivá, Alvaro del Portillo, José Maria Hernández-Garnica, and some other early male numeraries had made the promissory oaths there, which later became part of the *fidelity* (perpetual vows), and had nominated the first *inscribed* members (those with positions in the regional and central Opus Dei government or in charge of the formation of other members). These oaths bound the members a) "to avoid any statement or action that in any way might affect the spiritual, moral, or legal unity of the institution . . .; b) carefully to avoid any murmuring on your own part and reject that of others, that might undermine the reputation of the superiors or diminish their authority . . .; c) to exercise fraternal correction with an immediate superior according to the spirit of Opus Dei, if having reflected in the presence of God, it appears that the fraternal correction contributes to the good of the institution . . .; d) always consult an immediate superior or the highest major superior, according to the seriousness of any case, on professional, social, or other matters, even when they do not constitute direct material of obedience."[1]

Years later in Rome, Monsignor Escrivá himself told us that in the shrine of Molinoviejo he resolved a point of great concern for the unity of Opus Dei: how to combine the priests, the laymen, and the women as members of the same institution. He also told us on another occasion, and speaking also about the juridical structure of Opus Dei, that he had once thought about leaving Opus Dei to dedicate himself to the priests alone. But, once more, Alvaro del Portillo helped him resolve the dilemma.

We arrived at Molinoviejo on May 30, 1951, and were informed that on the following day, May 31, the feast of Our Lady of Fair Love, we would make our pilgrimage to the shrine.

The May pilgrimage is an Opus Dei custom, much like the ancient Christian practice of visiting a sanctuary of Our Lady during May. In Opus Dei you pray five decades of the rosary on the way to the shrine, another five inside the shrine, and the third part on the way back. I made my pilgrimage devoutly having always had a great love for the Virgin, and I felt the emotion of being allowed to enter the inner sanctum of Opus Dei.

Annual courses usually last a month. We had the obligatory Opus Dei Catechism class. As at Los Rosales, the class was taught by an Opus Dei priest and again we had to learn the Catechism by heart. This time we were instructed to study chapters, rather than points, because it was taken

---

1. *Constitutions*, 1950, p. 44.

for granted that we knew the text by heart and that we would not need so much time to review the points. The fundamental difference between this annual class and that during the formation course was its openness: we now could pose questions to the priest, when there was something we did not understand. We also attended a daily class on dogma, also given by an Opus Dei priest, an elementary course on the history of Catholic dogma without philosophical or theological depth. As at Los Rosales, we were not permitted to take notes in class. A senior woman numerary gave a daily class on praxis (an explanation of the regulations of ordinary life in Opus Dei houses and activities). Opus Dei women had as activities at that time only the following: Zurbarán as a residence for students and Los Rosales as a center of studies, and Juan Bravo where the women of the central advisory lived. Women numeraries were in charge of the administrations of Molinoviejo, a retreat house, and of men's residences: La Moncloa in Madrid, El Albayzin in Granada, La Alcazaba in Córdoba, Abando in Bilbao, Monterols in Barcelona, and Lagasca, Opus Dei male headquarters, then in Madrid. The Opus Dei women foundations of England, Portugal, and Mexico had been opened quite recently: London as an administration for a male students' residence, and in Mexico City and Lisbon as residences for women students.

Getting back to the classes in the annual course: direct questions were not allowed in the praxis class but we could submit questions in writing to the annual course directress. They advised us not to take notes supposedly because we would find the so-called notes of experience in the houses where we were assigned. These cards on regulation octavo size (about 6 by 4 inches) sheets were left by each of us in the house where we worked for the numerary who succeeded us in that assignment. A copy was submitted to the administration directress. If she approved, the card remained as basic information for those who followed in the task.

In a separate wing of Molinoviejo there were rooms reserved for the Opus Dei priest who directed the annual course. He said daily Mass and gave us a meditation besides the dogma and Opus Dei Cathechism classes. The priest was ordinarily José Maria Hernández-Garnica, called "ours" within the Opus Dei's Women's Branch, because he was the central priest secretary for Opus Dei women worldwide. He knew each and every Opus Dei woman numerary, there being less than sixty of us at the time.

Father Hernández-Garnica was very monotonous, and it took great effort not to doze off during his meditations. On weekends another priest, obviously also from Opus Dei, substituted for him, usually Father José López-Navarro, who at the same time was the priest in charge of the Opus Dei Women's Branch in Spain.

Sunday was devoted to long walks or an excursion; once we went to Segovia. On Sundays we wrote letters to family and friends, during which, if we wanted, we could play a record. It was a great surprise to us that we could listen to music in the get-together and on Sundays. Compared to Los Rosales life here was luxurious.

One weekend, on our return from the long walk, to everyone's great joy, we saw Opus Dei general secretary, Father Antonio Pérez, second in command after Monsignor Escrivá. Don Antonio had come to substitute for Father José María Hernández-Garnica. Jokingly, Don Antonio told us that he had made Father Hernández-Garnica an offer: "I will swap my visit to this bishop for Molinoviejo," so he spent the weekend with us in Molinoviejo. Father Pérez-Tenessa was handsome, attractive, and elegant; his cassock was always impeccable and he was almost majestic in his movements. He had a remarkable British sense of humor.

On entering the house we heard music from the living room. When we came into the living room we discovered that it was Don Antonio who had put on the music. He greeted us cordially and told us in his natural way, "Without music, I cannot work." Father Antonio Pérez assured us that music was a very important element in our spiritual and even material life. (However, this was not always so in the Opus Dei Women's Branch.)

Don Antonio invited us to sit down and asked us about the course, about our work in the houses where we had lived, and so forth. It was a simple but very human exchange that pleased us all. We loved Father Antonio Pérez in the Women's Branch, because he was very good to us; he was a kind man who treated us as equals. He never used his position of authority to rise above people, but made the servants and the rest of us at ease, so that our encounters were pleasant and comfortable. This was the only time he came to our course.

To describe what has happened between that weekend at Molinoviejo and the present, a whole book on Antonio Pérez-Tenessa would be required. By way of introduction, let me say that he thought out, worked on, and accomplished everything really important in Opus Dei, from the creation of the University of Navarra in Pamplona, to writing the speech for Monsignor Escrivá when he was named grand chancellor. At a handsome price and on very dubious grounds Antonio Pérez-Tenessa obtained for Monsignor Escrivá the much desired title of Marquis of Peralta. Don Antonio was the brain behind one of Franco's cabinets, that of the "technocrats," and he played a role in the restoration of the monarchy in Spain. Antonio Pérez-Tenessa left Opus Dei years later, because his personal integrity and good faith would no longer allow him to endure that pile of lies dressed up in different ways to suit the occasion. Naturally, many of his erstwhile Opus Dei brothers made his life quite bitter and very difficult when he returned to Spain after a long stay in Mexico.

Personally, I found the annual course restful. Knowing all the numeraries made it pleasant, and there were certainly advantages of being a resident rather than in the administration.

I used to do my spiritual reading in the garden and was glad to see the sky and breathe fresh air. The choice of spiritual books was limited. St. Theresa of Avila's *Foundations* was among the most frequently read. St. Francis de Sales and the Rialp series published by members of Opus Dei constituted the tiny spiritual reading library. Before reading any book, you always had to consult the directress who received your confidence. Jesús Urteaga's *Man the Saint*[1] was devoured. Father Urteaga was then a very recently ordained numerary priest. He had no contact with Opus Dei women. But we all knew that he was a Basque and of quite brusque demeanor. Besides assigned books, the New Testament was also read for seven to ten minutes a day.

We all had a little task in the house like closing windows at sunset before turning on the lights, writing the course diary, reminding people of the watch days, blessing the table, collecting the Catechisms and so forth.

One day the directress told us to go over to the administration quarters to visit the servant numeraries who were attending their formation course and also tended the farm.

We had a get-together with the numerary servants. Then, they took us to see the farm. One servant said that she had been told that the boots she wore to work in the henhouse had been my ski boots. In truth, I felt a little quiver inside: the boots were Norwegian; I had saved up from my earnings to buy them and now they were used in the henhouse . . . Another servant told me to look at the curtains they had made for the administration out of one of my evening dresses . . . The visit to the administration made me angry. I did not understand how they could use such good boots for the henhouse. The use of the evening dress for curtains made sense. When I spoke to the directress, she told me I was still attached to material things. In fact, she must have been right: those little things ought not to have bothered me.

What was very clear to me then and is even more so now is that the goal of that course was to learn—I would call it indoctrination—to identify ourselves with the personality of Monsignor Escrivá, the Father. First, they emphasized that all Opus Dei priests were addressed as "Don" plus their first name, because "Father" was reserved for Monsignor Escrivá

---

1. Jesús Urteaga, *Man the Saint* (Chicago: Scepter, 1959), translated from the Spanish *El valor divino de lo humano.*

alone. For many years this was the ordinary rule in Opus Dei, but about 1965, and after realizing that the title of "Don" sounded very Spanish, we were told in North and South America to call Opus Dei priests "Father" followed by their last name.

In Molinoviejo and on every possible occasion the superiors spoke of Monsignor Escrivá, his habits, his demands on the administration "based on the love of God that moved him," and his demands for perfection. To forget something, to make a mistake, were imperfections, and in the last analysis a lack of love for God. They spoke to us about the responsibility of having come to Opus Dei during his lifetime and thus being "cofounders." They also spoke to us about Rome, where Monsignor Escrivá now resided permanently, and told us that all the numeraries who lived in the Father's house were "edifying."

In Molinoviejo there are rooms called "The Father's quarters," set aside exclusively for Monsignor Escrivá.

We were told that we would be shown these rooms in groups of three to four. They proceeded to exhibit the quarters which consisted of a bedroom, a sitting room, and a bathroom. Although nothing special was in the rooms, we visited them with mythical reverence, respect, and devotion. We could not touch anything, we spoke in low tones; we walked through the rooms and the superiors explained that the directress of the administration, a numerary, and two long-time Opus Dei servants were always in charge of cleaning the Father's quarters.

While showing us the Father's quarters, the directress said that eventually in each country and even in more than one city per country, there would be rooms and an oratory set aside for the Father, so that on his visits to different places, he might rest perfectly. The most frequent question in the annual course was, "Have you seen the Father's rooms yet?" It was a great experience.

I had met Monsignor Escrivá at a meditation that he gave in the little oratory of Lagasca for a group of new vocations, when I still lived with my parents. His meditation touched me, but I could not say exactly how. I do remember that his shrill voice struck me as odd in a man, as did his frequent hand gestures and movements while he spoke. The reason for his hand gestures, we were told, was due to "living in Rome and having become very Italian," a remark that I personally do not consider very accurate after having lived in Rome for several years. And Monsignor Escriva's language would have been appropriate for little children.

My first impression of Monsignor Escrivá did not square with the strong and manly person they depicted in the course. Because he was the Founder of Opus Dei, I asked God with all my heart to make me grasp

Monsignor Escrivá's sanctity, since those who knew him well said he was so holy.

Remembering all these things now after so many years, I realize with great sorrow that the basic indoctrination I received about the sanctity of Opus Dei's Founder continues to be given to new vocations today. I, too, employed the same terms that they used on me. Then, I was perhaps as naive as the new Opus Dei vocations today.

It is obvious that from the time I came to Opus Dei, respect for the Founder amounted to a personality cult, enunciated doctrinally: the Father was more important than the Pope, at least the current Pope, at that time His Holiness Pius XII, and needless to say, more important than our parents. Worthy of investigation today is the conditions applied in Monsignor Escrivá's beatification process. In fact, the previously initiated beatification processes for Opus Dei members who died many years before Monsignor Escrivá, like Isidoro Zorzano and Montserrat Grasses, were derailed to leave the way clear for the Father's process. Now that Monsignor Escrivá has been beatified, Opus Dei states that the biographies of these two members, whose cause of canonization is on its way, have been published."

Naturally the superiors spoke to us about proselytism; we all knew the numeraries who had just founded the Opus Dei Women's Branch in Mexico: Guadalupe Ortiz de Landázuri, María Esther Ciancas, and Manolita Ortiz; Rosario Morán (Piquiqui), who was in the course with us, was completing legal arrangements to go to Mexico as well.

A new Women's Branch was about to open in Chicago. Nisa Gonzílez Guzmán, Emilia Riesgo, and Blanca Dorda were going there, and they expected the arrival at a later stage of Marga Barturen. Consequently, the invariable topic for get-togethers was the beginning of apostolate in these two countries. Don Pedro Casciaro was the counselor in Mexico and Don José Luis Múzquiz in Chicago.

A new topic of conversation in the get-togethers was Monsignor Escrivá's request of his numerary daughters to go to new foundations and new countries. In South America foundations were planned in Chile, Colombia, and Venezuela as well as in Argentina. In addition, England was on the verge of receiving a group of numeraries already gathered in Ireland by the proselytizing spirit of Teddy Burke, the first Irish female numerary, sister of Cormac Burke, a numerary who was later ordained a priest and sent to the United States.

A few days before the four-week course ended, Rosario de Orbegozo, the central directress read to us the new assignments: I was to go to Barcelona to be part of the administration at Monterols, as the men's students residence was called.

Four weeks went by quickly and I was now enthusiastic about going to Barcelona. When I was ten, my parents took me to visit Barcelona for having passed the secondary school entrance exam. I had also been there a number of times subsequently with my parents, and I liked the city.

The fact of going to another administration did not frighten me much, because I now had the experience from Córdoba. Furthermore, numeraries familiar with the Monterols administration said that the house was very pleasant.

Rosario de Orbegozo told me that I was going to devote myself primarily to the work of St. Raphael because it was necessary to "raise the social status of the numeraries who might seek admission to Opus Dei from now on."

Personally, I had a faint uneasiness, which was that some major superior might have the idea of sending me to Rome. The image of Monsignor Escrivá that the superiors presented to us frightened me.

The Molinoviejo annual course marked a new step toward my Opus Dei fanaticism, because it meant accepting the person of the Founder of Opus Dei as an acknowledged saint, for whom our love had to be greater than any human love, for he had "engendered us in the Lord."

Curiously, this idea has been literally set forth for future generations: ". . . God will call you to account for having been with that poor priest who was with you and who loved you so much, so much, more than your own mothers!" "I will pass away and those who come afterwards will look on you with envy, as if you were a relic; not for me, for I am—I insist—a poor man, a sinner, who loves Jesus Christ madly, but because you have learned the spirit of the Work from its Founder's lips."[1]

Barcelona: Monterols

I arrived in Barcelona on a splendid June morning. I caught a taxi from the France railway station to the Monterols administration.

My life in the Monterols administration will reflect the perspective of a numerary who is no longer a newcomer to the institution. She encounters persons and tasks with which she is familiar. There are few surprises, although expectations continue to be centered on proselytism.

The directress of the Monterols administration was Maruja Jiménez, one of the first Opus Dei female numeraries. I had not met her previously because she was always assigned to administrations outside Madrid. She

---

1. *Cuadernos-3,* "Vivir en Cristo," p. 86.

was motherly and all the numeraries were very fond of her. When I arrived at Monterols, I was delighted to find Anina Mouriz whom I had not seen since Los Rosales. Anina was a perfectionist in her work but was pleasant to live with. I knew the remaining numeraries of the house only by name.

The Monterols administration had eight numeraries. The house was very large and the administration was enormous. There were large individual rooms with closet, shower, and sink.

Monterols was the first newly constructed building for an Opus Dei residence. The Monterols experience in Opus Dei allowed for corrections in the design of subsequent residences. But after the administrations I had known, it was a joy to be able to live in this house that even had a good-sized terrace next to the living room.

Although the establishment purported to be an ordinary students' residence, in reality, it was a center of studies for Opus Dei men. Because it was summer and most were attending annual courses, the administered house was almost empty, but it was still necessary to clean it.

As promised, they put me in charge of the work of St. Raphael as well as of cleaning the residence.

The first person to whom I was introduced in Barcelona was Mrs. Mercedes Roig, who had a numerary son, Barto Roig. He had just gone to the Opus Dei residence in Bilbao, Abando, as a member of the local council there. Barto Roig was an industrial engineer who later spent many years in Caracas. He died in Pamplona in 1995.

Mercedes Roig also had two daughters, one with some sort of handicap and the youngest one, known as Merceditas in the Work, who was also a numerary. Mercedes Roig was a charming woman, quiet and discreet, and elegant in appearance; a youngish widow, she came every day to the administration to help in any way she could. The directress told me that Monsignor Escrivá was very fond of her because she had always been very generous to Opus Dei. I was surprised that she recited the *Preces,* the official Opus Dei prayer mentioned above, with us. Maruja Jiménez said that, if the Father consented, Mercedes Roig could be the first Opus Dei supernumerary in Barcelona and possibly the first in Spain.

It was then that I first connected the Opus Dei Catechism theory about supernumeraries with a person. The directress explained to me that the case of Mercedes Roig was unique, since her status as widow and mother of two numeraries gave her greater freedom to help the Work.

Since it was summer, there were no talks to the girls of St. Raphael, but there were get-togethers for some university students of Father Francisco Botella's, one of the first numerary priests and professor of mathematics at the University of Barcelona. They were agreeable girls, although very different in temperament and style from Madrid university students. Roser

Torrens at the ripe age of fifteen had just requested admission as a numerary. She was pretty and full of energy. I went out several times with her and I found her to be a sensitive, intelligent, and mature person at such a young age. Her parents were happy with her vocation. Her father would drop her off and pick her up at the residence. I was astonished that they would allow her to become a numerary at such a young age. Years later, Opus Dei sent Roser to Colombia, where we met again. I had also the joy of seeing her parents in Caracas.

Concha Campá was one of the numeraries who requested admission while I was in Barcelona. She was also very young, joyful, with great artistic talents. She, too, was assigned years later to Colombia, where eventually I saw her again.

The major superiors in Madrid gave me a few specific tasks while in Barcelona. One of them pleased me very much since it meant going to Montjuich to copy Romanesque designs in the museum for chasubles to be produced at Los Rosales. So, I had reason to visit that extraordinarily beautiful museum several times.

After the cleaning of the residence, I would frequently meet the girls recently admitted to Opus Dei or future vocations and ramble around Barcelona. Let it be clear that when I say "ramble," I mean precisely that, visit the city on foot. As numerary of Opus Dei we could not have lunch or take a snack at any cafeteria, nor could Opus Dei numeraries attend any form of public entertainment.

One of the girls who came almost daily to the Monterols administration was María Josefa Planell. She was very pretty but had a spinal problem that caused her great pain and required a great deal of rest. We got along very well. She had two male numerary brothers; one of them Quico who was part of the Monterols local council at the time. Years later he was ordained an Opus Dei priest and works at the film archives of the Vatican. María Josefa used to go to San Quirico, a little village in the mountains, and had met Monsignor Escrivá and his sister Carmen there at some point.

I had hoped that María Josefa Planell might become a numerary, but I was told by the directress that her health was too precarious, but in time she would become an Opus Dei oblate. I had also learned about the term *oblate*—now called "associates"—in the Opus Dei Catechism but I lacked any clear notion of what these members would be like in real life. I think that she finally did seek admission as an oblate, but I am not sure of that, since I left Barcelona after a short time. What I do know, through one of my sisters-in-law, a relative of the Planells, is that a few years ago, under the pressure of a depression, she committed suicide.

In 1951 Barcelona and all Catalonia were in an upheaval because Franco would not allow Catalonian to be considered an official language in Spain, but rather a dialect. Although Franco died in 1975, and Catalonian is now legally recognized as a language, there remains a conflict between Catalonians and non-Catalonians. I attempted to learn as much Catalonian as I could and Roser Torrens corrected me and was enthusiastic about my fondness for Catalonian.

With regard to the early days of Opus Dei in Barcelona around 1940, we heard about the "Palace," *Palau* in Catalonian, a somewhat pretentious name for a little apartment that the few men who then belonged to Opus Dei had rented. The anecdotes about that Palau had even reached the ears of the Women's Branch. As an interesting footnote, I learned a few months ago that Father Panikkar had been one of the directors there, if not the first, when he was still a layman.

Speaking of those early days, both superiors and Opus Dei priests, always stressed that Monsignor Escrivá suffered a great deal in Barcelona because one of the attacks by government officials against the nascent Opus Dei had occurred there, and that one of the most sceptical persons was the Abbot of Montserrat, then the Most Reverend José María Escarré. Although the official Opus Dei biographies of Escrivá do not state clearly that the Jesuits were the most energetic enemies of Opus Dei, within the houses of the Work everyone knew this to be true.

I also learned in Barcelona that because of all the "contradiction" suffered in this city, Monsignor Escrivá had said that he would not return to Barcelona for many years until the city would receive him as he deserved. What exactly had occurred was a particularly obscure point that I never managed to clarify during my stay in Barcelona.

Superiors in Opus Dei also reported, most secretly, that in June 1946 on his trip to Rome on the *J. J. Sister,* when Monsignor Escrivá embarked "the devil nearly made him suffer a shipwreck, because he did not want him to go to Rome." It impressed me personally that Monsignor Escrivá should have traveled to Genoa on that ship, because my father made the return trip Genoa-Barcelona immediately following Monsignor Escrivá's arrival in Genoa. I had gone with my mother and my youngest brother to meet my father and indeed had taken a snapshot of the boat. When I had left Opus Dei, I asked my father about "the terrible storm" that fell on the *J. J. Sister* on her trip to Genoa and my father said that no one on the ship had spoken of it as unusual, but as the most ordinary thing for that time of year. When this boat was decommissioned and sold for scrap, Opus Dei superiors bought parts of it as relics.

Monsignor Escrivá publicly returned to Barcelona in 1964, when the mayor, who was very close to Opus Dei, officially named him "adoptive son of Barcelona."[1]

---

1. See Andrés Vázquez de Prada, *El Fundador del Opus Dei* (Madrid: Rialp, 1983), p. 356.

Although life in the Barcelona administration was pleasant, the plan of life was as rigid as anywhere else, and the practices of not leaving us time to read or of not allowing us to read the newspaper were the same as in the previous houses where I had lived.

In Barcelona there was talk of a future Opus Dei apostolate in which the women would open a school of art and home economics, where there would be classes of cooking, ceramics, painting, and so forth, for girls who were not university students, but specially designed for married women who could visit us and would participate in these classes. It would be the beginning of proselytizing married women as Opus Dei supernumeraries. Opus Dei superiors were also interested in Barcelona as a city of great financial resources that could contribute to the development of future activities of the Work.

During my stay in Barcelona, it was demonstrated once again that our apostolate had nothing to do with the poor, although we told the girls of St. Raphael to visit the poor, usually on Saturdays. On the occasions I had spoken to the directress about the apostolate with the poor, she had said that the direct apostolate with the poor was the main goal for other religious congregations but that "our task" was to do apostolate "among intellectuals," that is to say, among leaders in society. Years later, I also heard Monsignor Escrivá say this, although he insistently recommended that the girls who frequented our houses should make visits to the poor, accompanied by a recent numerary vocation, in order to draw them near to Opus Dei. That is to say; visits to the poor were one more occasion for recruitment rather than a genuine apostolate to people in need.

Also, more than once I repeated in my confidence to the directress that our lack of real contact with what went on in the city, in the nation, in the world, not even reading the local newspaper, made us live, as a friend of mine would say today, "in a bubble," isolated.

Toward September, the directress told me that she had been told by the advisory central in Madrid that I was to leave Barcelona because I had been "permanently" assigned to Bilbao and the administration of the Abando men's residence where I would stay without further moves. I would also take over the work of St. Raphael there. The superiors specified that it was necessary to "raise the social level of the vocations of numeraries in that city because it is presently very low."

When changes were announced in Opus Dei, you are on your way to a new post three days later.

After a few months in Barcelona this new assignment is another brush stroke in the portrait of my life in Opus Dei: I had to accept that there would never be anything permanent in my life. I used to say that "you knew where you got up, but never where you would go to sleep."

My stay in Barcelona made me get a glimpse of the new supernumerary and oblate members of Opus Dei, but above all it made me see very clearly that there would no longer be anything permanent in my life, and I realized that as soon as I got used to a place, I would receive an order to change. Because juridically our life in Opus Dei as a secular institute was so different from that of nuns in orders and religious congregations, I never thought that in the matter of "reassignments," it was almost identical. And this was my new point of dedication to Opus Dei and toward fanaticism in my life within the institution: I would be ready to change residence as often as the good of the Work and the apostolate would require it without considering my inner feelings.

I departed from Barcelona, leaving behind a small but very select group of new numeraries, with whom, I would not be able to maintain the slightest friendship.

The numeraries in the administration of Monterols did not envy me my new assignment.

Bilbao: Abando and Gaztelueta

There were no startling events in my stay in Bilbao. Mine was the life of a woman Opus Dei numerary in the administration of a male students' residence. The account is one of constant work and a routine, obscure, hidden life, alien to the vicissitudes of any ordinary Christian. It was the final point of the transformation of a woman of character and personality, as I believe I was, into one more piece in that puzzle called Opus Dei, a fanatic who like a puppet moved at the tug of a string.

From the Bilbao railway station, I took a taxi to the Abando residence administration. I was unfamiliar with Bilbao, but had heard that it was very gray in winter and quite humid in summer.

On my arrival, the administration directress, Dorita Calvo, received me. Her kind smile was an encouraging welcome. She was the kind of person who did not impose her authority, but her wisdom was so obvious that you followed her blindly. We had a natural relationship.

Mercedes Morado was the subdirectress and Tere Morán, secretary. They were waiting for me to come so that Dorita and Tere could attend their annual course, which was held right there in the Abando residence, usually occupied by men.

We were left alone in the administration for three weeks: Mercedes Morado as directress, Loli Mouriz, and I. Loli, had also been at the Los Rosales formation course.

The central and regional Opus Dei women major superiors and some directresses of Opus Dei women's houses were at this annual course.

Opus Dei has a kind of military hierarchical mentality. That is to say, annual formation courses or spiritual exercises are organized so that the numerary participants are homogeneous. Hence, mixtures are avoided at all cost.

Monsignor Escrivá, on his visits to Bilbao in the early days of Opus Dei, fell in love with the house, the customs, the style, and the elegance of an aristocratic lady, Carito Mac Mahon. He tried to duplicate them in Opus Dei from the uniforms of the servants to the manner of waiting on table.

Loli Mouriz was in charge of the kitchen, and I was responsible for the laundry, cleaning of the entire house, and the pantry. I always got along well with Loli in Bilbao. She was younger than I and I always accepted her strong personality as she did mine. Like her sister Anina she was very well-mannered and cultured and had a very ironical sense of humor. My conversations with Loli dealt with work. She was frank and direct.

By contrast, Mercedes Morado, the subdirectress was not open. It always seemed that she was waiting for a mistake to be made so that she could correct someone, not with affection but as a disciplinarian. She was not very attractive: she had a round face with bulky eyes and protruding teeth. When speaking you felt she did not believe you. I knew her not only from Zurbarán, where she attended the same spiritual retreat as I did, but also from my work in the Council for Scientific Research with Dr. Panikkar. She went to talk to him frequently while she was a student of pedagogy. I also knew Mercedes from Segovia, where our families were friends. So, I was delighted to see her as directress and thought everything would go well because we were within the same "spirit."

During the weeks that Mercedes substituted for the Abando directress, I realized that she was very rigid: if a day passed without my making a fraternal correction to Loli, she would do a fraternal correction to me for insensitivity in not noticing this or that detail. This became oppressive, because we were always told in our classes that fraternal corrections ought to be aimed at some error in conduct or in spirit but not at being a policeman. I always had the impression that Mercedes Morado might have felt inferior to me, perhaps because we came from different social levels. She knew that my family was prominent in Spain, just as I knew that hers was not. Unquestionably this created a kind of tension in her. I always had the impression that she used her rank as directress to keep me from skipping any rung on the ladder. My dealings with Mercedes were strictly formal.

Mercedes Morado became the directress of the central advisory, and I met her in Rome during my last stage in Opus Dei.

There was no conversation during the day except for the half-hour lunch and dinner and the half-hour get-together. Otherwise, each person had her little patch to cultivate in the administration, and we worked physically separated.

As an administration we functioned with complete independence from the residence or administered house. However, I recall a very kind gesture by María Jesús Hereza, major superior at the time. One day she came over to the administration so that I could teach her to make Swiss rolls, a favorite ingredient of the Spanish *meriendas* or afternoon snack. With this excuse, she spent time chatting with Loli and myself in the kitchen, giving us several pleasant hours.

By contrast, I recall what to me was negative behavior on the part of María Teresa Arnáu, regional directress of the Spanish regional advisory. While I was cleaning the administered house with the maids, she summoned me to her office and told me to write to *Arbor,* the CSIC's journal, to tell them to stop sending me the journal, because my life was now involved in other activities and I had no time to read it.

I was completely absorbed in cleaning the house and with the clothes in the laundry room, besides attending the pantry. My only outing in several weeks was to accompany a group of the numeraries from the annual course to the shrine of Our Lady of Begoña on the outskirts of Bilbao. On the way I got a panoramic look at the city, which I personally did not like. It was very gray and well nicknamed "the hole" because it is sunk in a river valley. It was covered with smoke from blast furnaces and its humid summer heat was very unpleasant. Furthermore, DDT did not yet exist, and fleas were endemic, however clean you kept a house.

When the numeraries' annual course ended, Dorita returned to the administration as directress. Mercedes went back as subdirectress, and Tere as secretary. Tere Morán was an exquisite person.

The Abando administration followed classic Opus Dei asceticism. We had no distractions. Of course we read neither the newspaper nor any book other than the spiritual reading which was designated for each of us. We hardly went out. Only Tere, in charge of errands, went out each day.

Our servants did not belong to Opus Dei, and they went out on Sunday afternoons and sometimes on a weekday if they had to go shopping.

The Abando administration house was pretty and pleasant. Not large, but decorated with good taste. We were told that Father Pedro Casciaro, the Opus Dei numerary priest who was already counselor in México, had decorated it. The visitors' parlor was on the first floor and the dormitory-office of the directress on the second floor as were the rooms of the numeraries; individual rooms, with closet and sink. We had only one bathroom, so Tere or I took turns using the servants' shower and never spent more than half an hour getting washed and dressed so as to arrive at the morning meditation punctually.

The windows in the administration bedrooms were half blocked, because they opened onto a patio which the residents' windows also overlooked.

As usual, the administration oratory was behind a lattice. In order to let the other numeraries attend the Mass in the house and to prepare breakfast for the residents while they were in the oratory, one of us would take turns going with some of the servants to Mass in a public church.

In Abando there were around ten servants. Each had her individual cubicle, *camarilla*, in Opus Dei jargon, with a sink and small closet. These cubicles were in the cellar of the house. In the same area there was a bathroom with several showers.

The kitchen was also in the cellar of the house and had very poor ventilation. It was large and old-fashioned. A kind of nook within the kitchen was called the pantry. The numerary in charge of the pantry in Opus Dei administrations is responsible for having the tables perfectly set and the servants ready in their uniforms inside the dining room when the students arrived. The ratio between the number of maids to serve at table and the number of students to be served was ordinarily one maid to every eight residents. From the pantry the numerary watched the servants doing their job, handing them the trays to be served through a special window between the pantry and the dining room. It is customary in Opus Dei houses and residences that meals last for thirty minutes only, except on Sundays and festivities when they last for forty-five minutes. During the meals silence in the administration was rigorous. We spoke when absolutely necessary and in a whisper.

The laundry area consisted of two large rooms. In the inner room, without windows or ventilation of any kind, there was an ancient washing machine and two stone sinks where the servants washed clothes by hand. In the outer room there were two large ironing tables. Most of the irons were old-fashioned. We had a hot plate for them. There were also a couple of electric irons for the oratory linens and the residents' white shirts and suits. There were numbered cubbyholes for each resident. The ironing room was small and claustrophobic. Not only was it in the cellar, but the windows were blocked almost to the ceiling. Since it rained and there was a great deal of humidity most days, we also had clothes lines inside the two laundry rooms, where we always left clothing to dry during the night and quite often during the day.

As I was in charge of the laundry, at the end of housecleaning, we collected the residents' bags of dirty clothes on Mondays and made a pile in the ironing room. I was the only person who could open each bag and check that each piece of dirty clothing coincided with the number of the paper that was inside of the bag. The residents never numbered less than seventy.

Usually there were six servants in the laundry rooms, two washing and four ironing. As the numerary in charge of the laundry, my mission also included responsibility for the servants in regard to the care of their uniforms, their personal hygiene, and their spiritual life. My task was to entertain them, to lighten their work. We would sing sometimes, at other times I would tell them about some other country, about customs of some Spanish region, and also about the spirit of Opus Dei. Each day, I prayed the rosary with them in the ironing room, and I also made some commentary on the gospel or a spiritual topic, while they had their snack. Needless to say, my chief mission was to win their confidence, help them, and especially to find out if anyone of them could become an Opus Dei numerary servant.

In general, servants in Opus Dei houses wore a colored cotton uniform, and a white apron for heavy work. At that time they also wore white caps covering their hair. The servants who waited on table wore black uniforms with white aprons and a white headdress. On feast days they served table with white gloves. In the laundry they all were in blue cotton uniforms and white aprons.

Within the ironing area was a bell panel. There were also intercoms in the directress's room, the kitchen, the laundry room, and the secretary's room.

Many hours of my life were spent in the Abando laundry area. Friday was especially busy, because I had to distribute clothing by cubbyhole and check that each ironed piece corresponded to the number of the cubbyhole. Usually, the directress came down to the ironing area on Fridays to find out how things were going.

Saturday evenings, while the residents had supper, I would enter the residence with two servants to distribute the bags of clean clothing in accordance with the paper enclosed in the dirty clothes bag.

An odd detail that was hard for me in Bilbao was waxing the floors. All of the floors of the residence and of the administration were parquet. There were no electrical machines to polish the floor. With brushes tied to our feet with leather belts and then felt rags on each foot we had to brush and dance the wax. It was brutal work. This caused many numeraries in the course of time to develop uterine problems that sometimes required surgery, as in my own case.

After I had been in Bilbao for a short time, we were told that a boys school called "Gaztelueta" would open in Las Arenas but that this school was to be an exception in Opus Dei, since our mission was not to have schools like other religious congregations, Monsignor Escrivá said. We knew that Father Antonio Pérez-Tenessa, as Opus Dei secretary general, was the person primarily responsible for this project.

Since the school was about to open and the Opus Dei male numeraries on the Gaztelueta local council would move to the house before Christmas, the superiors in Madrid informed us that an administration would also be opened there. No external activity would be carried on from that administration. Mercedes Morado was appointed directress, María Ampuero, who had arrived recently from Madrid, subdirectress, and Pina Revilla, who had come to live at Abando weeks before, secretary. María was open and kind, extremely modern and elegant. Pina Revilla was very kind, efficient, and intelligent.

The shifts to Gaztelueta required reshuffling the local council of the Abando administration. Dorita Calvo continued as directress, Tere became the subdirectress, and I secretary.

The change involved a new room for me. The secretary's room was somewhat larger than the others, with a small desk where all the ledgers and the house money were kept. This room was next to the oratory.

Around November 1951, I was told to take charge of the work of St. Raphael. When I had to give the circle of St. Raphael and talk with the girls, Tere replaced me in the ironing room.

The work of St. Raphael was well organized. There was a file for each girl who had come to the house, with details about her life and personality, besides her telephone number and address.

We had a telephone in the administration, which facilitated contact with the girls. I found myself among a group of wonderful girls again.

When I was in Bilbao, Begoña Elejalde, then very young, requested admission as a numerary. Years later, Begoña was one of the founders of the Opus Dei Women's Branch in Venezuela. I encouraged her very much to be totally generous and try to proselytize her sisters. I tried to be affectionate and understanding to make her interior life easy so that things would not be as hard for her as they had been for me. Begoña was intelligent and a very good artist; she painted very well and had a tremendous avant-garde style. She had a natural instinct for decoration. In fact, in Venezuela she gave classes in arts and crafts at the Etame School of Art and Home Economics, and left her mark as an artist on Opus Dei houses in Caracas.

These girls talked to me with great confidence. They explained what they had done recently and how they were preparing their families for the news that they wanted to come to live in Opus Dei as soon as possible.

Before coming to live permanently in the Work, they had to resolve the financial problem of obtaining the tuition stipulated by the Opus Dei for the first two years of formation.

María Josefa (Mirufa) Zuloaga also requested admission as a numerary. Mirufa's family members were almost all well-renowed artists, and oddly, I knew one of her uncles, a well-known Spanish painter, who was a friend of my family's. These connections seem silly, but in the atmosphere of proselytism in Opus Dei they are still very important. Years later, Mirufa was in Rome when I lived there. When she returned to Spain she became a journalist. She contributed for many years to the magazine *Telva,* and later to *Ama,* both entrusted to Opus Dei women.

Tere González was another girl who requested admission as a numerary during this period. Tere was pure goodness, open and sincere. She managed to come almost every day to Abando.

Mirufa Zuloaga, Begoña Elejalde, and Tere González asked me about the Work and the Father. I had identified myself with Opus Dei to such a degree that I spoke to these new vocations with the great ease of "the first" (as the first women numeraries in Opus Dei were called) about the "mission God had given to the Father" and about "the happiness of renouncing everything without receiving anything in exchange." The strange thing is that when you become a complete fanatic, you exercise a certain magnetism that can attract even very strong personalities. This is the terrible power of sectarian fanaticism. Outsiders cannot explain how a person can change so much so quickly. The faith that these three girls had put in me was infinite. I realized, furthermore, my responsibility as "an instrument in the hands of God for his Work.

The Bilbao girls were different from those of Córdoba. Within Spain Bilbao society and Andalusian society are remarkably different, not that one is better, just distinct.

I hardly set foot outside, but these girls came almost every afternoon and stayed a bit longer each day. I was notified when the girls arrived and I would go up to the visitors' parlor to talk to different girls about spiritual and material life, and the problems they might encounter. My mission was to encourage them to get through the period of separation from their families and to throw themselves into Opus Dei without the slightest doubt, and with the energy and enthusiasm of youth. The St. Raphael girls in Abando were not allowed to enter the working areas of the administration.

My life in the Abando administration was very professional. Dorita Calvo, the directress was understanding, courteous, and open. She had the charisma of having spent the very first years of the Work in Rome in Monsignor Escrivá's house. We asked her to tell us about him. Now, I realize years later that what Dorita used to recall were rather pleasant anecdotes about family life in the Opus Dei house, but nothing especially related to Monsignor Escrivá's personal characteristics. She only repeated to us that "The Father likes things well done."

My confidences with Dorita Calvo were very sincere. The three basic points of any confidence were faith, purity, and vocation. In my case, thank God, I never had doubts about faith, and my confidence in God always was and is infinite. Regarding purity, you had to explain in detail any personal impulse whatsoever that you might have felt and explain how you had overcome it. Regarding "the way," that is, vocation, I also had no doubts.

As an example of any confidence in Opus Dei, one of my Bilbao confidences may serve: using the Luxindex weekly planners (manufactured by one of the many companies headed by Opus Dei people and which in the last analysis belong to Opus Dei) I would religiously jot down the points, i.e., failures, to be discussed. I would begin to speak about the fulfillment of norms of the plan of life. For instance, if I had felt lazy about getting up or if I had hesitated an instant before jumping out of bed to kiss the floor saying, *Serviam!;* if my spiritual reading had applied to my own life; if I had been distracted or sleepy in the meditation; if I had prayed the three parts of the holy rosary meaningfully or routinely; whether I had been generous in my corporal mortification (this meant whether I had worn the cilice as tightly as possible and if I had applied the discipline with energy or sparingly).

In all these points the directress would make me see clearly how "feeling" was not important. The advice was ascetically sound and directed to form an iron will, like a suit of armor that would completely banish sentimentality. Strictly speaking, everything so far is correct Christian asceticism. I would call this part "A" of the confidence, and you cover the same ground as in your weekly confession but in greater detail. What I would call part "B" is manipulative when the directress would utilize my confidence to add that whatever work I might have done, whatever development had taken place in my interior life, everything had to be channeled toward Monsignor Escrivá. Between Opus Dei and Monsignor Escrivá there were no boundaries. They were the same, since the Father "engendered" Opus Dei. They did not ask us in the confidence about our love for the Pope, the church, the poor, but about our "love for the Father."

We were made to feel veneration for him similar to worship, all your prayer and all your mortification were oriented toward "the things the Father had in mind over and above any church or personal thought." The Opus Dei dictum "we are not preoccupied but we occupy ourselves with things" has the exact sense that absolutely nothing in our lives had the slightest importance. Only the Father was important and consequently we had to consider the Father's things above all else. It must be remembered that numeraries have to write Monsignor Escrivá, the Father, "at least once a month." Failing to write showed "bad spirit" or "lack of the spirit of filiation." However, not to write to our families once a month did not have the slightest importance. The directress—Opus Dei in essence— employed the confidence to indoctrinate, affirm, and insist on certain points in a numerary's life in order to make her identify with Opus Dei doctrine. The confidence exercises control over the members and is a very real kind of brain washing under cover of "good spirit" or "formation."

At that period, we also had to make index cards with the names of persons who might be able to contribute financially to the construction of the Roman College of the Holy Cross. Obviously, how you carried out proselytism was another topic. I gave a detailed report on each and every girl of St. Raphael, of their problems, and their confidences. Many times the directress indicated what I ought to say to the girls or if I should correct anything that was not quite right concerning the spirit of the Work. Today, I understand that in these confidences the souls of other persons were pawed over, since what the St. Raphael girls had said to me in trust and confidence was reported to the directress, to a major superior, or to any other person whose position in Opus Dei entitled her to ask about the girls. I must make my own act of contrition here, because I acted the same way when I occupied positions in Opus Dei government, particularly in Rome. That is to say, the most important thing in the confidence was to relate how you had lived the spirit of Opus Dei and specifically "the love for the Father."

By the time I reached Dorita's hands, many other superiors had manipulated my conscience and my soul.

It is worth noting here that according to canon law, members of religious institutions "are to approach superiors with trust, to whom they can express their minds freely and willingly. However, superiors are forbidden to induce their subjects in any way whatever to make a manifestation of conscience to them."[1] So, there is not, according to canon law, any clause *that obliges and considers it a duty,* a basic rule of life, to lay bare your conscience to the superior. By contrast, Opus Dei, which is not a religious institution obliges you to speak with your directress each week, "the fraternal talk," formerly called "confidence." Monsignor Escrivá stressed that in your confidence you must speak with even greater clarity and

---

1. *Code of Canon Law,* p. 237, canon 630, 5.

detail than with the priest in confession. For Monsignor Escrivá the "confidence" was fundamentally more important than confession.[1]

Whatever Opus Dei ordered me to do I did and this became proof—according to the spirit of the institution—that I had fulfilled the will of God and that God, in consequence, was happy with me.

In Opus Dei faith is cultivated through piety. I mean by this that piety is cultivated so that members do not formulate any kind of question whose resolution would take them toward true faith. Simply put, in Opus Dei, people are made childish, not more mature.

This childishness and abandonment into the hands of superiors is nothing but an escape from the daily life of ordinary Christians. My own development had reached the point where I coldly accepted anything at all without allowing it to make waves in my spiritual life. I was a faithful instrument in the hands of the superiors. I was a perfect fanatic within Opus Dei and consequently a numerary without problems. Therefore, I had the happiness that you can have in a life of dedication in the Work. The person of the Father and proselytism were the first things for me.

The numeraries who went to Gaztelueta lived in Abando, but at Christmas 1951, they had permanent quarters at the administration of Gaztelueta.

It was difficult to reach the Gaztelueta administration because the route was circuitous and the door bell could not be heard anywhere in the house but just in the hall. On Christmas Day, Dorita told me to come and have lunch with them, so they would not be alone.

My temper surfaced for the first time in a long while. Walking from Las Arenas on a cold and rainy winter day, I had trouble finding the administration entrance. I rang the door bell for more than forty minutes but nobody heard the door bell so I had to walk back downtown again and call them to open the door.

Although there were no classes during Christmas vacation, the administration still made the rounds. The Gaztelueta administration directress, Mercedes Morado, invited me to put on a white house gown to accompany them to see the boys' school.

Gaztelueta began to function as a school in 1951. It was the fruit of the efforts by Father Antonio Pérez Tenessa. Tomas Alvira had assisted him, and was a member of Opus Dei who had participated actively in the Instituto Escuela, the Institución Libre de Enseñanza's chief educational activity.

Since the Instituto Escuela had been my first school, and I was one of the pupils who had inaugurated the newly constructed building on Serrano Street in Madrid, in 1931, it is impossible to express my astonishment on

1. See "La Charla Fraterna," *Cuadernos-3*, 17, pp. 142–48.

visiting Gaztelueta that late afternoon. Before my eyes appeared a copy—a bad copy—down to minute details like the shape of the cubbyholes for the pupils, little tables instead of desks, the number of pupils per class, even the colors of the little tables and the blackboards. It disturbed me that Gaztelueta had copied the Instituto Escuela's material layout, while the Las Arenas upper crust were led to believe that the Opus Dei school was "original."

Back in Bilbao that night I reflected on why I had been angry to see Gaztelueta copy the Instituto Escuela. Years later, I now believe that my displeasure was so great because the Instituto Escuela had a special charisma. It is well-known in Spain that this school—in a very positive way—forms your character. It had been my first school and any student from the "insti," as we called it, felt proud to be part of it. A burst of light suddenly brought a ghost from my very happy childhood. I saw Gaztelueta as something degenerate, without any sign of the spirit which animated the Instituto Escuela. Opus Dei had copied the shell but they could not grasp the spirit: the freedom we enjoyed in the Instituto Escuela, a mixed school for girls and boys. None of that could be implemented in Gaztelueta, which was only a school for rich boys, located in a chalet which had belonged to a wealthy family, where there was even a sedan chair in the vestibule as decoration. Over the marble staircase there was a large ornamental hanging with the school motto: "May your yes be yes, your no, no."

In the Instituto Escuela, telling the truth was so much instilled in every student that we did not need an ornamental cloth to remind us that truth is precious.

When I speak about Monsignor Escrivá, I will explain in detail his great dream of transforming the Institución Libre de Enseñanza for Christ, making its ideas and ideals his. Now I see beyond doubt that this was always Opus Dei's tactic under Monsignor Escrivá's thought: copy and adapt. If you dig into Monsignor Escrivá's thought, you do not find many great original ideas. His enthusiasm for replicating all sorts of things was notorious. The decorations of Opus Dei houses, much of their architecture, oratories, galleries, and living rooms, headquarters in Rome, were copied from chapels, palaces, villages; the furniture he had seen some place he had visited and ordered a copy made by an Opus Dei architect. When he saw a movie in the aula magna, when some feature of the decoration interested him, he had not the slightest hesitation to have that part of the picture cut out—from that rented movie—and subsequently enlarged the photo to copy whatever it was.

After my visit to Gaztelueta, I spoke to my directress who gave me, of course, the universal answer. If Monsignor Escrivá did something, it was by divine inspiration. She made it very plain that I should never doubt that inspiration.

Relations with my family continued unchanged. There were no confrontations but no improvements.

I had my twenty-seventh birthday in March in the Abando administration, but there was no celebration of any kind. A few days into early April, Rosario de Orbegozo, the central directress, announced that she would visit Bilbao. We were all looking forward to seeing her on her return from Rome and she had said that she had many things to tell us about the Father. She arrived and summoned me to a private conversation where she told me that Monsignor Escrivá had said that he wanted me to come to Rome to serve as his private secretary for the Women's Branch worldwide. María Luisa Moreno de Vega, a major superior, had also been selected to go to Rome and to be secretary to the Father. She also had worked for the Council of Scientific Research in Madrid.

I was so affected that I did not react. Rosario very gravely asked me whether I did not want to go or did not realize the privilege involved in the Father's call.

I told her that I understood the enormous privilege of going to work directly with the Father in Rome, but I was somewhat apprehensive, not knowing exactly how the Father was. Rosario did not like my reaction.

Rosario also told me that although it was Lent, when we did not write nor have any contact with our families, I should telephone my father to announce my trip to Rome and ask him to give me a ticket Madrid-Barcelona-Rome.

We obviously never did anything without an ulterior motive. Our sole contact with our families was to request something or other: from a ticket to an overcoat, a dress, or money. We were told in Opus Dei that we always had to make our parents give us things because that way they would be united to the Work. Also we were advised that when visiting our families we had to take something from the house always: from an ashtray to a porcelain vase. What is easy to see is that our families were not given the slightest consideration but were used and manipulated. The interesting thing is that nowadays I have also heard some families with children in Opus Dei say that if they give things to their children, the Work esteems them more highly.

Rosario Orbegozo told me María Luisa Moreno de Vega would go by airplane, because she was a major superior, but that I would go by train with an Opus Dei numerary servant, along with the trunk of clothes and other things needed by the house in Rome plus our own personal luggage.

I went to the oratory to thank God for choosing me to go to Rome to work for the Father, and I also asked God with all my heart for his help, because I was afraid of the unknown.

When I asked Dorita: "What is the Father really like, you who know him?" she laughed and said to me: "To live near the Father is hard because he is very demanding."

I had to leave Bilbao April 8 or 9, I do not recall exactly which date, arriving in Madrid the next day to apply for my Italian visa; my passport was valid.

Looking back, the moment at which my departure for Rome was announced, I realized that I was an Opus Dei numerary more than a normal person. With this I mean I was ready for anything as long as it fulfilled not just God's will, but "the Father's will." This is what happens when you become an Opus Dei fanatic: the will of God no longer counts as much because what counts is "the will of the Father," what "the Father says," what "gives joy to the Father." It is as if the adoration owed God is exchanged for "the will of Monsignor Escrivá," in whom the "good spirit of Opus Dei" is acquired. The Father is turned into the likeness of God. This cult to the Founder is so ingrained in the numeraries with "good spirit" so as to form the essence of their interior life. To please the Father, pleases God, and not the reverse.

This is the tragedy of Opus Dei. Whereas sects like that of the Reverend Sun Myung Moon or of the Bhagwan Rajneesh are considered small barren islands isolated from world religions and not belonging to any one in particular, Opus Dei, which is no less a sect, is part of our holy mother the Catholic church. Yet, the fact that Opus Dei has received all the church's approvals, first as secular institute, February 24, 1947,[1] then with the perpetual ratification of its Constitutions, June 16, 1950,[2] and on November 29, 1981, with the juridical change from secular institute to personal prelature, does not detract at all from its thoroughly sectarian character.[3]

---

1. See "*Decretum laudis* de la Sociedad Sacerdotal de la Santa Cruz y Opus Dei como Instituto Secular de derecho Pontificio," 24 February 1947, in de Fuenmayor et al., *El itinerario jurídico del Opus Dei,* pp. 532–35.

2. See "*Decretum Primum Inter,* de aprobación definitiva del Opus Dei y sus Constituciones como instituto secular de derecho pontificio," 16 June 1950, in de Fuenmayor et al., *El itinerario jurídico del Opus Dei,* pp. 544–63.

3. See "Constitución Apostolica *Ut sit,* de Su Santidad Juan Pablo II, relativa a la erección del Opus Dei en Prelatura personal de ámbito internacional," 28 November 1982, in de Fuenmayor et al., *El itinerario jurídico del Opus Dei,* pp. 622–23.

4

THE TRIP
TO ROME

When I arrived in Madrid from Bilbao I went to live at 20, Juan Bravo Street, headquarters of the Opus Dei women's central advisory, still based in Spain. Every day I went to Lagasca to try to help assemble the items I was supposed to take to Rome.

The Juan Bravo and Lagasca houses were close to each other and equidistant from my parents' home. The short walk brought back a flood of old memories. Madrid has always been dear to me. I spent the first twenty-four years of my life there. Now, after several years away, first in Villaviciosa de Odón making my formation course, then in administrations of Opus Dei residences in Córdoba, Barcelona, and Bilbao, to return to Madrid was to relive my whole life. I knew every inch of the Salamanca neighborhood. I recalled my early childhood, schooldays, student years in the Escuela de Comercio, my first dates, my fiancé. As I walked the streets, I tried to put all this out of my mind, because the memories seemed to interfere with my dedication according to the spirit of Opus Dei. I realized that a numerary with good spirit had to "detach" herself from everything that stirred up emotional currents in her mind and heart. I was in Madrid only in order to gather the material I was supposed to take to Italy, where I would work close to the Father.

At Lagasca I met María Luisa Moreno de Vega, a major superior in the Women's Branch central government. She was coming to work with me as one of Monsignor Escriva's two personal secretaries for matters related to the Women's Branch of Opus Dei worldwide. María Luisa had been José María Albareda's secretary at the Council of Scientific Research, when I was there as Dr. Panikkar's secretary. María Luisa was to go to Rome at the beginning of April. As a major superior she would fly. Since I had no government status in Opus Dei, I would go by train with Tasia, a servant numerary who was assigned to Villa Sacchetti. I would also take the heavy luggage such as a trunk and our suitcases.

The post of "personal secretary to the Father" was not a government position. It was created by the Father to assist him in material things, as did the male secretaries he already had.

The day María Luisa Moreno de Vega left for Rome, Rosario de Orbegozo asked me to accompany her and María Luisa to the airport. María Luisa was elegantly dressed for the trip and wore a very pretty, stylish hat. Since the Women's Branch had no cars in those days, Father José María Hernández-Garnica arranged for a male numerary to drive us to the airport in a car belonging to the Men's Branch. In her rush, María Luisa forgot her passport and only noticed it was missing when we were near the airport. When Rosario heard María Luisa say she had left her passport, she panicked because it meant that María Luisa was going to miss the flight to Rome. Furiously, she began to strike out, crushing María Luisa's hat and grumbling that María Luisa should have been more concerned about remembering her passport than about getting a hat for the trip. The scene was absolutely comic. The male numerary could not help hearing the heated conversation in the back seat. María Luisa was distraught, but a nervous reaction made her laugh, and I found it difficult not to join her. The numerary chauffeur, who had maintained the most absolute silence until then, intervened: "We are going back, no?"

We all assented at the same time. We returned to Lagasca. Rosario went on scolding María Luisa for having missed the weekly plane from Madrid to Rome. The following week, María Luisa's departure went smoothly. I accompanied her in a taxi, as ordered, to the Iberia bus terminal, from which passengers were transported to the airport.

Since I was probably leaving Spain forever, the directress told me I could see my father every day. Going to my family home was unthinkable because my mother refused to see me as long as I remained in Opus Dei. My father and I met daily for about an hour at the Hotel Emperatriz cafeteria, which was very close to my family home. After a while, however, the directress of Juan Bravo announced that since it was Lent, it would be better if I met my father only every three to four days. I hardly saw my brothers because of the conflict between their class schedules and my free time in the afternoon; besides, they knew my mother did not want them to visit me. The family's reaction to my vocation deteriorated further with the news of my imminent departure for Rome.

Conversations with my father were painful for both of us. He saw that my mother was suffering and realized that I was hurt by her attitude. My father loved me deeply; we were very much alike in much of our thinking, and I was the only daughter and the oldest child.

Every time we met, my father repeated that if I had any problem in Rome, I should go to the Spanish Ambassador to the Vatican, whom he knew fairly well, and that I should not hesitate to write home to him for anything I might need. Of course, he repeated as well that if I were not happy, I should come back home, where he and my mother would receive me with open arms.

One day my father told me of the audience my mother and he had had with the Pope in October 1950; they both got the impression that Pius XII had no sympathy for Opus Dei. There was another couple with them at the audience, who told the Holy Father that their son was a Jesuit. Pius XII spoke enthusiastically about the Society of Jesus and gave them a special blessing for their Jesuit son. My mother, who was very moved by the audience, began to weep. Pius XII then asked my father if they had any children and if they had problems with them. My father answered that they had no problems with their sons because they were very good. "The problem," my mother stammered between sobs, "is my daughter." Again, Pius XII addressed my father to ask what the problem was with the daughter. My mother said, "She has gone off to Opus Dei." Pius XII responded with a certain coldness. "Yes," he said tersely, "it is a recently approved secular institute." He did not say anything else. However, he was extraordinarily affectionate to my mother, and he gave both my parents his blessing while he gently caressed my mother's head.

My father said that my mother remained opposed to Opus Dei because it was neither fish nor fowl. I listened but believed that my parents were twisting things in their anxiety to have me return home. An Opus Dei refrain was engraved in my mind: "Parents can sometimes be the greatest enemies of our vocation." Years later I realized the correctness of their instinctive evaluation of Opus Dei.

The directress told me that, since the majority of my friends were married, it was not worth the trouble to see them in the few days I had left in Madrid. I should not even call them, advice I found difficult to accept. It would be better simply to leave notes with their names so that some other numerary could telephone them later to invite them to days of recollection. Meanwhile at the Madrid Opus Dei houses, people kept telling me how lucky I was to go to the Father's house in Rome. I must have special "connections" to have gotten such an assignment.

My three weeks in Madrid were drawing to a close; my trip was scheduled for April 22, Madrid-Barcelona-Rome. My father, resigned to what was then Opus Dei practice, got me a third-class train ticket. He could not go to the station with me this time, because he had to go to London on business; he took my mother with him to lessen the tension of my departure.

Father José María Hernández-Garnica gave Tasia and me a blessing for the trip, an Opus Dei custom, and handed me some personal mail for Monsignor Escrivá. I was to give it to Don Alvaro immediately on arrival. Just as we were about to leave for the station, Rosario de Orbegozo called me aside. To my astonishment she told me to lift up my skirt, because she had to attach a pouch to my waist. She told me not to ask questions and did not give the slightest explanation about the content of the pouch. She instructed me not to remove it for any reason, nor speak of it to Tasia or anyone else, but to hand it over personally to Don Alvaro del Portillo on arrival in Rome. She recommended special care at the Italian and French borders. In case they wanted to search me at any border, I should demand that international law prohibited body searches, except by female officers wearing uniform and white gloves.

At first I thought that the content of that pouch would surely be some very important document of the Work, but in the excitement of departure I almost forgot about it. After checking the trunk and the suitcases through to Rome, it was a relief to get to our compartment, which we shared with an elderly French lady and a young, well-dressed Italian man, who had lived in Spain for several years and spoke Spanish fluently.

Since the Madrid-Barcelona portion of the trip was at night, Tasia and I tried to sleep as much as we could. I did not sleep well, because I thought that I was probably leaving Spain for good. Once again, I was leaving my whole life behind and, this time, also my country. Still, I thought that God asked me to offer anew my life and future to him. It was like cutting the umbilical cord.

I could look forward to working with the Father and be grateful for the charism of having been chosen along with María Luisa Moreno de Vega for this sensitive work as his secretary.

Our papers were in order, and we crossed France with no problems. I remembered the pouch, but nobody thought of searching us. The coast from Spain through France to the Italian border is so beautiful that we were absorbed in looking at the Riviera and Monaco. For many years I had a dream in my heart that if I ever left Spain, it would be because the Work sent me to France. I had shared this with Monsignor Escrivá in more than one of my personal letters.

In Madrid they had prepared sandwiches and fruit for our trip, but no water, because they told us we could drink at fountains at the stations where the train stopped. The fact was that the train only paused briefly at these stations, allowing us no time to get off and look for a fountain. I always drink a lot of water and was very thirsty, but since they had given us no money for the trip, we could not purchase any of the soft drinks offered by the vendors who came to the windows when the train stopped.

Seeing two young, pleasant-looking women, our companion must have expected that he would have a fine trip in our company. What he did not know is that Opus Dei numeraries never socialize with men, and that in situations like travel, they do not reveal their membership in Opus Dei, which frequently, as on this trip, creates confusion and embarrassment. As a normally dressed woman just past her twenty-seventh birthday, I looked like a graduate student who was going abroad. Tasia was also normally dressed. Despite her attire, it was observable that her manners and look were a bit rough. The Italian gentleman wanted to begin a conversation at all costs. I answered his questions politely. He kept trying to break the ice, but Tasia and I were trying to live up to the rules of Opus Dei, spending long intervals in the corridor of the car, and when we came back to the compartment we pretended to fall asleep.

At Ventimiglia Italian police and customs agents got on board the train to check our passports and luggage. I was relaxed because we had checked the trunk and two suitcases through to Rome, so that we did not have much luggage in the compartment. Once the Italian police and customs officials got off the train, Tasia and I stayed in the corridor looking out the window at the hustle and bustle of that border station. We saw how our suitcases were loaded onto the baggage car headed for Rome, but suddenly we realized that our trunk had been set aside in the middle of the platform where the customs agents check the luggage, without the slightest appearance of being loaded onto the train. There were some ten minutes left for the train to begin when we noticed this. I did not think twice. I gave Tasia her ticket and passport and asked the Italian gentleman please to look after her during the trip; and especially in Rome where our friends would be waiting.

I got off the train and flew to customs. For about three minutes, I ran between the counters of the French and Italian customs trying to discover the reason why they had not put the trunk back on the train for Rome. The response was that I would have to leave the trunk at the border and could then send for it via a customs agency, unless I immediately paid in liras or French francs an amount equivalent to some thirty American dollars. Besides, they doubted there was time to load the trunk onto the train.

To my horror, I realized that since I had no foreign currency, the trunk would probably be lost or that it would be very complicated to send for it from Rome; furthermore the superiors in Madrid had instructed me that the trunk was to arrive in Rome with me. Suddenly, I thought of the pouch and wondered if it might hold some money. Rosario de Orbegozo's strict order not to undo or touch that pouch flashed through my mind, but at the same time the biblical passage of the consecrated loaves of offering came to mind and I ducked into a filthy bathroom and ripped open the pouch. To my amazement, it contained thousands and thousands of American dollars. Trembling, I took out only fifty dollars not wanting to know what an enormous quantity of money I carried. So I paid the Franco-Italian customs and insisted that the customs agents put the trunk on the train.

I ran across the tracks and headed toward the train which was just beginning to move. Tasia wept, thinking she had been left alone because I would not be able to get on the moving train. In fact, I reached the stairs to the door of one of the last cars. Meanwhile the Italian gentleman had witnessed the scene and ran down the corridor of the train toward the door I was trying to reach and with all his strength helped me get on board the train, which by then was moving quite fast. I thanked him cordially and a friendly conversation followed.

Besides being out of breath after sprinting for the train, I was upset at having opened the pouch and wondered what Don Alvaro would say when he realized I had found out that I was carrying so much money.

When I think back today and realize that I had crossed the boundaries of three countries with that package of money, I am horrified that Opus Dei dared utilize its members, exposing them to violations of international law. How could any police officer believe that I did not know that I carried foreign currency? As someone who had attained her majority, I would personally have suffered any penalty that might have been imposed in Spain for exporting money without permission or in France and Italy for not declaring it.

Monsignor Escrivá with some important member of Opus Dei— we never knew who—went to visit Franco during this period. In the course of the conversation, he let slip that they were building the Roman College of the Holy Cross in Rome and that they would need to bring funds from Spain for the construction. Franco, a native from the northwestern region of Galicia, whose inhabitants are legendary for their astuteness, simply ignored the hint. Following the old Spanish saying, "he who warns does not betray" (Quien avisa no es traidor), Monsignor Escrivá then requested Opus Dei major superiors in Spain to send him large-scale financial assistance so that he could meet his obligations to outsiders. Opus Dei in Spain was bled to help Rome. Since there were no official channels to transmit this money openly, given the Franco regime's monetary policy, "discreet" methods were used including the diplomatic pouch or some similar method. In Rome we all knew that there was a weekly mail delivery from Spain, that is to say, someone brought confidential papers. Today I have no doubt that such persons illegally or ignorantly as in my case may have also brought some quantity of foreign currency.

As we came closer to Rome, the Italian gentleman asked questions such as—"What do you plan to do in Italy?" My logical answer was, "To study Italian." I tried to be as vague as possible, but the questions continued: "Where in Italy?" "In Rome." "Where will you live in Rome?" "In a students' residence." "What is its name?" "I don't know," I answered. "My friends will tell me when they come for me tonight at the station.

Questions and evasions continued. Naturally, I didn't give him any address. I limited myself to explaining, in order not to appear too odd, that I believed the residence was in the Parioli, but that since I was unfamiliar with Rome, I might be confused.

Realizing it was not very easy to have a conversation with me, he kindly offered me some Italian magazines he had brought, for we also lacked any reading material. I accepted them courteously.

What this man could not even conceive is that they were the first magazines that fell into my hands since 1950. I had great curiosity and interest to leaf through them, especially because they were Italian. They were illustrated magazines, not pornographic in the slightest, which did not mean that there was not an occasional more or less suggestive photograph. I took extra care so that Tasia would not see those photographs, and I spent some minutes trying to find out if I could understand written Italian. With the excuse of our going out to the corridor, I left the magazines on the seat. The hours went by and we arrived at Stazione Termine in Rome. It was eleven o'clock P.M., April 23, 1952.

Waiting for us on the platform were Iciar Zumalde who had done the Los Rosales formation course with me, and Mary Carmen Sánchez-Merino from Granada, whom I did not know. It struck me that Stazione Termine was not as noisy as Spanish stations, and they pointed out that the phenomenon was a result of the material used for the floor. We got a taxi for ourselves and all our luggage, trunk included. Rome seemed attractively lit to me, but I was so tired and thirsty that the only thing I desired was to get to the house and drink water. After some twenty minutes, we arrived in front of the house that seemed small to me, because from the threshold, one could only see three windows and a kind of little roof. It was Via di Villa Sacchetti, 36, the headquarters of the Opus Dei Women's Branch in Rome.

5

ROME I: THE GOLDEN CAGE

Antonina, one of the Work's first numerary servants, who had been in Rome for many years, opened the door for us. Encarnita Ortega, then directress of the Villa Sacchetti administration and Mary Altozano, a numerary from Jaén, who was the subdirectress of the house, were waiting with her along with María Luisa Moreno de Vega. After warm greetings from each of them, we went up some granite steps to the Gallery of the Madonna, and thence by another stairway to the oratory of the Immaculate Heart of Mary to greet the Lord.

I asked Encarnita Ortega if I could have a glass of water because I had not had anything to drink for nearly forty-eight hours. I will always remember that she looked at her watch and said: "It is after midnight. If you drink water now, you will not be able to go to communion tomorrow. How nice," she added, "the first thing you are going to offer up in Rome for the Father." Of course, I didn't drink water.

My first impression upon crossing that threshold was of entering a medieval castle. I observed there was a great deal of stone, red tile, and iron in the construction. There was little furniture, but heavy inside shutters.

They turned on the lights in the Gallery of the Madonna, named after a stained-glass window at the end so that I could see it better. On the other side of the Gallery is the ironing room, and when its lights are on, light shines in the Gallery as well. The Gallery is very pretty. Because of the number of different levels that exist in these buildings, the Gallery of the Madonna is in a cellar which has excellent natural light from a skylight in the ceiling. The floor is of red tile arranged in a zig-zag pattern with a border of soft white stone, and set off against the grey granite molding at the bottom of the wall. There is a fountain against one of the walls, made out of a genuine Roman sarcophagus. Drops of water always fall from a hippogriff's mouth, which creates a quiet, recollected atmosphere. Instructions for the house in Rome mandate permanent minor silence in the Gallery, which means that one must speak as little as possible and in a very low voice because of the proximity of the oratories. At the time I arrived, there was only one oratory for the administration, the Immaculate Heart of Mary.

Antonina, Mary Carmen Sánchez Merino, and Iciar brought Tasia, the servant who came with me, to her compartment (*camarilla*). Encarnita Ortega and María Luisa Moreno de Vega brought me to my room.

Climbing the steps of red tile trimmed in wood, toward the first floor of the sleeping quarters, we stopped on a big landing where there was a living room or *soggiorno,* whose door of iron and glass allows you to see the whole room from the outside. The room was large, with the furniture in several groupings, and very attractive. It struck me as well furnished. Encarnita pointed out a series of trompe-l'oeil drawings which decorated the walls and created optical illusions. The room had three windows to the street, which I had just seen from below.

From there, they took me to my room, which was on the first floor, showing me where the showers and toilets were. María Luisa Moreno de Vega had her room very near mine.

Our rooms formed a block of two floors whose windows opened onto a terrace, planted with several cypresses.

Of course, Encarnita repeated that I had "pull" because I had come to the Father's house and what a responsibility it would be to work directly with him as one of his two female personal secretaries.

Encarnita asked if I had brought anything for the Father and I said I had. I handed over the mail that Father José María Hernández-Garnica had given me and also the money belt, explaining what had occurred in Ventimiglia. She said that I should explain everything to Don Alvaro del Portillo, when I saw him the following day.

When I closed the door of my room, I saw that it was mid-sized with a greenish-black iron bed and a very pleasant flowery covering over the planks. During the next few days I realized that all the bedrooms were laid out and furnished in exactly the same way. There were two doors, one to a sink with a large mirror and light, and the other to the closet. My window was closed. I didn't know at first where it faced, but the next day, on opening it, I realized it overlooked the terrace of the cypresses. There was a niche in the wall for books, but no books, and a picture of Our Lady painted on the wall. A very simple desk and chair rounded out the decoration of the room. The floor was of red mosaic. The room was pleasant but its austerity chilled me a little.

I got up when the bell rang and following the rules of all Opus Dei houses was dressed and had my bed made in thirty minutes. The light poured in when I opened the window, and it was as if that sun had filled me with optimism. Encarnita came to take me to the oratory, because the house was so big that it was easy to get lost.

First there was meditation, as in every house of the Work, and then Mass. The oratory of the Immaculate Heart of Mary was very different from those I had known in Spain. It seemed rather large. There were choir seats for the numeraries and in the middle of the oratory pews on either side of the central aisle for the servant numeraries with a small organ in the middle.

At the end of Mass I went to greet the numeraries and servants who lived in the house, some of them old acquaintances and others not, who waited for us in the Gallery of the Madonna. These greetings are usually very noisy, with big hugs, but Opus Dei numeraries never kiss each other. We immediately went to have breakfast. At that time the male numeraries' dining room was not yet finished, so they used ours. Because of the conflict, and in order to maintain the rule for administrations, we had breakfast in the ironing room, on a table, usually used for sewing. We used our own dining room for lunch and dinner only, because there were several turns for meals in the house. This went on for almost two years until part of the construction was complete and we could also have breakfast in the dining room intended for the administration.

There were not many numeraries at Villa Sacchetti when I arrived. The local council was formed by Encarnita Ortega as directress, Mary Altozano as subdirectress, and Mary Carmen Sánchez Merino as secretary. María Luisa Moreno de Vega and I were informed that we would primarily work in cleaning the administration section and, then, as the Father's secretaries we would carry out the duties assigned us.

At breakfast they explained that more numeraries had previously lived in Villa Sacchetti, but that the Father had just organized the Italian region of the Women's Branch, with headquarters in Rome, in a house called Marcello Prestinari after the name of the street where the apartment was located. Pilarín Navarro Rubio, one of the first members of the Women's Branch was regional secretary. Also assigned to the region of Italy were Enrica Botella, Victoria López Amo, Consi Pérez, Chelo Salafranca, and Maria Teresa Longo, the first Italian woman numerary. Except for Chelo whom I knew from Zurbarán, I did not know any of the others.

The Father's Secretary

As soon as we had finished breakfast, Encarnita arranged the things that I had brought for the Father on a silver tray and told Tasia and me to get ready because the Father was going to come to the Gallery of the Madonna to meet us. We asked how to greet him and were told that we should kiss his hand, if he offered it. Tasia and I were with Encarnita in the gallery when we heard the Father's voice as he approached through the Gallery of the Birds, so called because the walls and ceiling are decorated with birds. He and Don Alvaro paused with their backs to the stained-glass window of the Gallery of the Madonna, and he said to us with a big smile: "*Pax*, daughters!" We answered filled with emotion: "*In aeternum*, Father!" We kissed his hand, when he offered it. Don Alvaro also said *Pax* to us with a big smile, and again we answered, *In aeternum*.

I had not seen Don Alvaro since the afternoon when they told me to visit him at Diego de León in Madrid toward the end of 1949. Although I had seen Monsignor Escrivá once before in 1949, when he gave a meditation to new numeraries in the Lagasca administration in Madrid, this was the first time he spoke to me directly or personally.

The Father asked us if we had had a good trip and if we had slept well. We told him we had. Addressing Tasia, he said that there was a lot of work in the house and that he hoped she would always be joyful. Then with a "God bless you, daughter!," he dismissed the servant. After she left, he looked me in the eye and said: "How little did you imagine, Carmen, daughter, that you were coming to Rome!" I answered: "Truly, Father." Monsignor Escrivá went on: "Do you see the Lord's plans, daughter?" "Yes, Father." He said that there was a lot of work to do and that we would talk. He asked me if I had seen Rome, and I told him I had not. Then he said to Encarnita that someone should take me to St. Peter's and show me around. He added: "It's necessary to learn Italian!" "Of course, Father."

The Father inquired whether I had brought mail for Don Alvaro, and I said I had. Encarnita opened the ironing room door, and Rosalía López, one of the first servant numeraries, came out with the tray with the mail and pouch. The Father indicated that they should leave it in his dining room in the Villa Vecchia. I took advantage of the Father's silence to try to tell Don Alvaro why I had had to open the money belt, but the latter did not let me continue. He made a gesture with his hand as if to tell me not to worry.

The Father called for María Luisa. Encarnita had told her to stay in the ironing room in case the Father wanted her. She came out immediately.

The Father, quite affably, told us that we would work closely with him (*muy cerquica*) on secretarial matters related to the Opus Dei Women's Branch worldwide. It should be clear to us that our secretarial work did not involve membership in the government, "although," he added, "María does belong to the government as a major superior, but you don't," he said to me. During the following days he repeated that so often, that I used to say to María Luisa in jest: "The Father will tell me again when he comes that you have a role in the government and I don't."

We agreed that we would meet him in the secretary's office the next day after the cleaning. This very small, triangular office was the house secretary's room on the first floor of Villa Sacchetti. They assigned María Luisa and me this room as the most suitable place. The room had an Italian-style desk, a closet, just enough space for a couple of extra chairs. It was a room full of light near the terrace onto which our bedrooms faced. It had a little cabinet, resembling a safe, set in the wall and covered with a painting, where we kept confidential documents, duplicates of the keys to the house, especially the duplicate to the mail box. The mailman could slip letters into this box from the street. The inside box was located at the delivery entrance, and had a small metal door on the inside which could only be opened with the key which was kept in the house secretary's desk, whose duplicate was placed in the cabinet set in the wall. Our only equipment was a portable typewriter.

I was very pleased with this assignment in Rome. Everything seemed like a dream, as if I had died and gone to heaven. With all respect to Muslims, I felt as though I had arrived in Mecca. I could not believe that there could be greater happiness on earth for a member of Opus Dei. The Father had spoken to me, knew who I was, and had announced that I was going to work with him. Isn't this the greatest thing to which a completely fanaticized member of Opus Dei, as I was, whose star and guide was none other than Opus Dei and Monsignor Escrivá, could aspire? What I could not even have conceived of were the undercurrents that existed between people in the house and the Father and between the Father and the Holy See.

If I remember correctly the subdirector Mary Altozano accompanied me to St. Peter's. She had been in Rome for more than a year, and her Italian was very good. She was very young and had entered Opus Dei almost as a child. She had an older brother who was a numerary. By chance, I had been a good friend of a cousin of hers, who was a naval doctor and whom I had met in Cartagena.

We went by the *circolare* (trolley) to the stop closest to St. Peter's, and she pointed out the building in the Città Leonina where the Father had lived when he arrived in Rome. From there we crossed the Colonnata, and for the first time I saw the vast Basilica of St. Peter's. I had the sense of being at the heart of the church. When we arrived at the altar of the confession, Mary said that the Father liked us to say the Creed there and we did. I soaked up everything she told me, and the grandeur of St. Peter's overwhelmed me. Mary said Pius XII used to give his blessing after the Angelus at noon, but we had to return before then so as not to be late for the Father's lunch hour, since he might have some work for me. So, we did not stay for the Pope's blessing. This strange detail reveals that under Pius XII, John XXIII, and Paul VI it was a manifestation of "good spirit" for the numerary who arrived in Rome not to insist on staying to receive the Pope's blessing but to go back to Via di Villa Sacchetti so that she would be there, if the Father called.

On the *circolare,* I could sense how big Rome was and realized that I could not understand a word of Italian.

In sum, the first day in Rome was full of varied impressions. One memory from the first day was that I kept getting lost in the house and had to wait for someone to come down the gallery to seek directions to the oratory, my room, or the dining room.

Normal life, so to speak, began the second day of my stay in Rome. Encarnita was showing me the kitchen, when Antonina, the servant who usually answered the phone, approached Encarnita and whispered something. With an air of annoyance, Encarnita asked me: "To whom have you given our telephone number?" "To nobody," I answered truthfully. "We'll see who that man is who is calling you."

I couldn't imagine who it could be, because I hadn't given my father or the Italian gentleman on the train any phone number, and I did not know anybody in Rome.

The telephone was in the ironing room. To my great surprise, I heard the voice of the Italian gentleman from the train, delighted because he had located my telephone number and address. He wanted to come by to show me around Rome. My answer was brusque, rude, and sharp. I told him not to bother me again and hung up. I went back to Encarnita and said that it was a gentleman who was in our compartment on the train from Madrid, and I would explain everything later. The expression on her face made me think she was going to scold me.

As the directress of the house, Encarnita received all the confidences of numeraries and servant numeraries, so that she had complete control of each and every one of us.

Encarnita used to receive the confidences of the servants in a part of the ironing room that was on a different level, while she was sewing. Later in the ironing room, I saw that Tasia was talking to her, and I guessed that what Tasia said might give Encarnita a reason to speak to me.

I did not have to wait long. Next day, without even listening to me, Encarnita launched into a great oration, saying what a bad example I had been to the servant during the trip; I had not only continually flirted with the Italian on the train, but had allowed him to take me by the arm to get me on board, and had read the pornographic magazines he had loaned me, although I knew that numeraries could not read any magazine without permission. The worst thing was that since she said everything as a fraternal correction, I could not defend myself and had to accept it all without a whimper. Naturally, I was angry that the servant had been so stupidly scandalized and had indulged in such misinterpretations.

What I did not know on arrival at Villa Sacchetti was that Encarnita was the thermometer of "good spirit" in the Work, and reported everything, absolutely everything to the Father or Don Alvaro. Furthermore, since Encarnita fully shared the Father's notion that the servant numeraries were like little children, anything said by them had greater weight than anything we might say. In her correction/scolding, Encarnita said that I had barely arrived in Rome when I was already failing the Father and that she preferred not even to think of how upset the Father would be, if he knew of my behavior during the trip.

When it was my turn to make my confidence, I gave my version of the trip, but I remained convinced that my truth did not change her opinion in the slightest. Instinctively, I realized that Encarnita did not totally trust me, although I did everything possible to gain her trust.

Over the years I came to realize that Encarnita tended to be jealous of anyone who could overshadow her in relation to the Father. She managed to have Pilarín Navarro sent to the region of Italy as directress, so that she became the senior person in Villa Sacchetti, and the one who knew the Father best. However, since María Luisa and I arrived, she was no longer the only woman who saw the Father in confidence. She was no more than the directress of the house, and was not privy to the confidential matters of the secretarial office, something that she clearly disliked.

The following day, María Luisa and I waited in the secretarial office at the time set by the Father. We prepared two chairs for him and Don Alvaro. When we heard them arrive, we stood up and the Father told us to be seated.

Basically, he told us we would be in charge of writing weekly letters to the regional directresses in the countries where there were Opus Dei women. Matters of government could not be part of these letters. We should only write about the headquarters in Rome, anecdotes about the servants, and what we had heard from the Father. If any of the incoming letters dealt in any way with government, we were to let him know so he could give an appropriate response. I was assigned to write to Nisa, who was in the administration of the men's residence in Chicago; and also to Guadalupe, who was in Mexico. María Luisa was assigned to write to England, where Carmen Ríos was regional directress, and to Spain. María Luisa and I wrote by turns to Chile, Argentina, Colombia, and Venezuela. Moreover, María Luisa wrote to Germany, where there was no Opus Dei house, although Marianne Isenberg, the first German woman numerary, and Valerie Jung lived in Bonn. Both left Opus Dei a number of years later, due mainly to the lack of tact shown by Opus Dei priests and superiors, as I will explain below. I used to write to Teddy Burke, the first Irish numerary, who had gathered several more numeraries around her in Dublin. In the first letter we had to explain our mission in Rome. The reaction of all the regional directresses was very positive, because they knew María Luisa and me personally.

Monsignor Escrivá warned us that our mission imposed the "silence of office," which meant that we could never speak to anyone about anything that we had dealt with in the secretarial room, and that consequently our work was not a topic for our weekly confidence. He also said that we would have to keep informed about everything that happened in the secretarial office, and that we both had to read all the mail, including personal letters that were directed to him, and that only when there was something out of the ordinary should we give him those letters, but otherwise, we should file them.

Letters to the Father

The letters to the Father deserve special mention. From the time you wrote "the letter" to Monsignor Escrivá as president general requesting admission to Opus Dei, the superiors told us that it was good spirit and "the Father saw with pleasure as a manifestation of spirit of filiation" that we write him as least once a month. We had to give this letter to the directress of the house who was obligated to forward it to Monsignor Escrivá through the superiors of that country without reading it. We were also told that we could write to the Father in a sealed envelope whenever we wished.

When María Luisa Moreno de Vega and I began to read the letters to the Father from all Opus Dei women of all countries where we worked at that time, I remember perfectly that we did so with the greatest respect and we never allowed ourselves the slightest commentary about any of them. Needless to say, we handed over the letters that came in sealed envelopes—one arrived now and then—directly and immediately to Monsignor Escrivá, who often told us to read them ourselves afterwards.

Letters from the numeraries to the Father were ordinarily brief. Their contents varied but were usually speaking about the work in a new country, frequently about their interior life, about proselytism. Generally the numeraries who were superiors in a country spoke about the financial difficulties of getting started, of some misunderstanding or disagreement with the counselor of the country, or some problem of perseverance, or the difficulty in finding the first vocations. These were almost constant topics in the letters to the Father.

What shone through in these letters was the degree of maturity of the numerary who wrote them. For example, when the directress of the United States wrote to the Father, she opened new horizons for us, because she made us understand how she confronted a totally new panorama of manners, customs, and lifestyles, how she had to deal with the problem of Spanish numeraries who wanted to study when they arrived in the United States as they tried to adapt to the life of a normal girl in that country. We could even feel the difficulty of the language and the distances in traveling to do apostolate. I remember the case of a numerary who became seriously ill, so that the directress had to spend hours on the train to visit her frequently in the hospital.

There was a notable difference in the letters from the fanatical numeraries and those who tried to adapt quickly to the new country.

My personal letters to Monsignor Escrivá years later when I was in Venezuela almost always spoke of our activities in that country, of progress in apostolate, of new vocations. Other times, I spoke about the possibility and desire to have a center of studies as soon as possible, and in the last period of my stay in Venezuela about lack of support from the counselor when we dealt with the topic of the administrations.

When the number of vocations began to increase in Opus Dei, the members were assured that the Father read absolutely all the letters as his principal work. It was difficult for many people to believe this, but it was our obligation to assure them. When the central government of the Women's Branch began to function in 1953, each of the assessors read the letters to the Father from the members of the region assigned to her; afterwards these letters were read by the central directress and the Women's Branch government secretary. It was a matter of their judgment and discretion whether or not to give the letter to the Father. In this first Opus Dei Women's Branch government in Rome there were some very young immature numeraries, who on occasion made fun of what a numerary wrote to the Father, which personally infuriated me.

However, when I was no longer in Rome it was difficult to write the Father with spontaneity and confidentiality, and I used a sealed envelope a number of times, when I did not want my letter to be the subject of interpretation by the assessor.

In reality, saying that the Father read the letters from the members was a lie that they were resolved to maintain. Monsignor Escrivá and Alvaro del Portillo knew that as did all of us who had been in Rome as numeraries in the central government, including me. As a major superior, I affirmed the statement, knowing that it was a lie, a "lie required" by my superiors, including the Father.

María Luisa Moreno de Vega and I, as the Father's secretaries, executed every instruction received from him with complete responsibility. This was a full-time job, except for some time in the morning spent cleaning the Villa Sacchetti administration, or at the end of the afternoon when the numeraries of the house went into the Villa Vecchia to clean the rooms for the Father and Don Alvaro and the vestibule which was the size of a small bull ring. We were generally absorbed in this work until the Father went to supper.

Mariá Luisa and I worked well together. The fact that we had been coworkers before, helped us to work as a team. Beside, María Luisa was a very good person, sensitive and well educated. She had attended the German School in Madrid and had complete mastery of German. My education in a French school similarly equipped me with a good command of French. We both could understand and write English. Monsignor Escrivá appreciated all this. We both took learning Italian very seriously, something that our linguistic talent and strenuous effort let us accomplish in a few months without a single grammar class.

In our personal relations or in our work, it never mattered that María Luisa was a major superior and I was not. She was very sensible and never said anything that could remotely amount to asserting her authority.

There were few days on which we did not see the Father and Don Alvaro. Both came to the secretarial room or called us after lunch to go up to the Villa to go over something or other. In fact, while the Father and Don Alvaro had lunch, María Luisa and I would go to the kitchen so as not to make the Father wait in case he called us. At lunch and supper time, Encarnita was also in the kitchen, since she took care of the Father's meals.

The Father's meals were brought up to his dining room, measured and weighed according to instructions from a physician, transmitted via Don Alvaro. We knew the Father had a special diet, but no one spoke openly of what was wrong. Unquestionably, he had diabetes, as one of Monsignor's official biographers confirmed after his death.[1]

---

1. Vázquez de Prada, *El fundador del Opus Dei,* pp. 253–54.

While we waited in case the Father called, we helped the numeraries in charge of the kitchen prepare the teatime snacks for the whole house.

Many mornings when the Father arrived in the secretarial room, he spoke to us about future plans for the Opus Dei Women's Branch. More than once, he showed his discontent with the church, and criticized Pope Pius XII. I remember him say: "Daughters, you don't realize what is happening around you; my hands and feet are tied. This man [i.e., Pius XII] doesn't understand us; he doesn't let me move; I'm cooped up here." He gestured with his hands as if to say, "This is incomprehensible." More than once I heard Monsignor Escrivá say in slightly different words that the Pope didn't let him leave Rome.

One day Monsignor Escrivá said to me that, in time, he would send me to France because he knew I loved that country. And, in fact, in the Villa dining room, he introduced us to Father Fernando Maycas, who was going to France as counselor, and to Father Alfonso Par, who was going to Germany as counselor, telling them that very possibly I would go as directress to France and María Luisa to Germany in some government role.

Monsignor Escrivá assigned me to take charge of the passports and residence permits for all the numeraries who lived in Villa Sacchetti. My responsibility would be to make sure that both were valid. Don Alvaro would tell me what I had to do about the residence permits. This became one of my regular duties during my stay in Rome and obliged me to go out frequently to the Roman police headquarters (*Questura romana*). Our residence permits in Italy were very peculiar, because, although members of a secular institute, we availed ourselves of a law designed for members of religious congregations residing in Italy. We had to fill in a form that had previously been validated by a Vatican agency, located outside Vatican City. I prepared the forms for each case, and Don Alvaro signed them for submission to the Vatican agency. I would then bring the forms and the passports to police headquarters. The Father stressed how lucky we were not to be like "those little nuns" who had to go one by one, all confused, to arrange for their residence permits. After a few years I got to know the staff at the Questura romana, and they knew me. Once they even remarked that, given the time I had been in Italy, they could easily arrange for me to acquire Italian citizenship. I did not accept. Why would I want to be Italian, if I lived in Villa Sacchetti, the Father's house . . . ?

Speaking of passports, I recall two things vividly: first, immediately on arrival, the numeraries had to hand over their passports, which they did not see again until the day they left Rome or when it was necessary to renew them, and they went with me to the respective consulate. Second, there was a rather young police officer who periodically came to Villa Sacchetti to revise passports and residence permits. We had hundreds of foreigners and it was logical they they should check their information. I was in charge of meeting and speaking with him. When I told the Father about the police officer, he suggested that we should always have a bottle of Spanish brandy ready to give to that officer.

On another occasion, in the secretarial room, Monsignor Escrivá instructed us to take note of the things he said as we went along, "because they would be for posterity." I paid attention to what he had to say during my time in Rome. I regarded it as a special sign of trust. It never crossed my mind that this was Monsignor Escriva's campaign to start constructing his own altar.

When María Luisa and I arrived in Rome, Encarnita Ortega was in charge of the diary of Villa Sacchetti. Shortly thereafter she passed it on to me. In all the houses of Opus Dei the custom is to keep a diary, but the diary of the house in Rome had greater significance within Opus Dei because it reflected many daily events in the life of the Founder. Encarnita instructed me that when I noticed that the Father showed obvious anger, I had to use a phrase such as "Today the Father was displeased because we did not put enough love of God in such and such task." I wrote this diary for a number of years. If, for some reason, I was not going to be able to do it on a given day, I had to notify the directress, so she could write it or assign someone else to do so.

The first part of my stay in Rome was one of my most interesting periods in Opus Dei. Out of blindness, or fanaticism, I was changing into such an automaton that nothing and nobody had importance in my life except that house, the Father, Encarnita. Everything revolved around Monsignor Escrivá, whom we usually saw several times a day. Looking back, I perceive perfectly the essence of Opus Dei's sectarian character. We were absolutely overwhelmed by different types of physical work; if there was a free moment, it was to accomplish the plan of spiritual norms of life. Everything was sprinkled with the presence and indoctrination of the Founder. There was not the slightest relaxation except for a daily half hour get-together with the servants, either playing ball in the Cortile del Cipresso, a very small patio with a cypress in the middle, in summer or, in winter, chatting or singing in the ironing room, the very place where we spent the greater part of our day. We had no music and needless to say we did not listen to the radio. Villa Sacchetti was and continues to be an island in the great city of Rome, whose life is only the Work and its Founder. Everything else has no importance. If we went out, we obviously saw people and the city, but the occasions to go out were exclusively to make necessary purchases, for the house, our work, or something like shoes. It was as if we were in our own world, passing next to but without mixing with any other.

I thought then I was free, because we were allowed a freedom within well defined limits. But it was not genuine Christian freedom which allows you to exercise free choice on the basis of familiarity with a situation without the bridle of "good" or "bad" spirit. Opus Dei members have only the freedom which "the good spirit of the Work" permits after consultation with their superiors, even on professional, political, and social questions. It would be interesting to know what an organization like Amnesty International would make of Opus Dei if it had the necessary access to sufficient information to make an objective analysis.

We did not do any direct apostolate. That was entrusted to the Italian region. Our work was totally internal: the administration of the Father's house or Villa Vecchia and of the incipient Roman College of the Holy Cross whose construction had just started. When I arrived in Rome, the male numeraries who were students at the Roman College of the Holy Cross still lived in what was called the Pensionato.[1] Their meals were served in the administration's dining room.

One day in the ironing room we heard great shouting and screams from the Father. Frightened, I thought that something very serious was happening and he was calling us. I was about to open the door from the ironing room onto the Gallery of the Madonna, when one of the senior numeraries in the house warned me quietly: "Don't go out. The Father must be correcting the architect." In fact, I heard Monsignor Escrivá shout at the architect many times. First, Fernando de La Puente, and later, when he was sent back to Spain because of illness, a rather young man named Jesús Gazapo who took Fernando's job. On another occasion I witnessed the very unpleasant scene of the Father scolding Encarnita because she was nearsighted and did not want to wear glasses. Encarnita blushed to the roots of her hair and her chronic headache was worse that day.

It was easy to pick out those whom the Father scolded. The kitchen often triggered Monsignor Escrivá's bad temper. One of the numeraries who worked there would open the window, and odors would waft up to Villa Vecchia. The Villa Sacchetti kitchen is located in the bowels of the building. Although the architects experimented with different exhaust systems, there were always cooking odors. This exasperated Monsignor Escrivá to a degree that it is difficult to describe. I saw him on occasion enter the kitchen, go straight to the open window, and slam it shut. Strangely, he did not understand that the heat in the kitchen made it unbearable, unless the windows could be open.

---

1. This building was the servants' quarters when the Villa Tevere was purchased in 1947. It previously housed the Embassy of Hungary to the Vatican.

As directress of the house, Encarnita was on the receiving end of most of his scoldings. For example, when one of the servants or one of us had forgotten a dust cloth or a rag to wax the floor in the administrated house. For whatever reason, the target of the Father's ire was ordinarily Encarnita. I always admired the manner in which Encarnita accepted abuses as "good spirit," but I realize today that rather than good spirit, Encarnita really had a morbid love for the Father. She must have considered the scoldings a sign of predilection. In fact, there was a phrase repeated among the numeraries of many countries: "Blessed are they who receive the Father's scoldings," because they were a sign that they were close to him. Monsignor Escrivá certainly did not have a mild manner.

Encarnita had quite a different relationship with Don Alvaro del Portillo. Alvaro was a person with whom Encarnita could speak about anything and in fact took advantage of all sorts of circumstances to do so. She would tell him that we needed money or mention the Father's health or meals, or inform him about a serious problem of some numerary or servant. How could Encarnita speak to Don Alvaro if the separation between the Men's and Women's Branches of Opus Dei is total? For instance, if he came down to the dining room for supper alone, while we cleaned the Villa Vecchia vestibule, Encarnita could speak to him for a few minutes. Other times from the directress's room by intercom, and sometimes, when the Father was leaving the Villa dining room, if Don Alvaro fell back a little, Encarnita took advantage of a few minutes to ask him or consult him about something.

Monsignor Escrivá had given Encarnita permission to use the familiar Spanish "tú" instead of the formal "usted," when addressing priests of the Work.

The Father's tantrums terrified me, because I did not know how I might react if he were to scold me. Until now I had heard only what he had said to others.

At that time, Monsignor Escrivá and Don Alvaro del Portillo used to come to the ironing room after their supper. Since they came almost daily, we used to have two chairs ready for them. The numeraries who worked in the sewing section were at the front. Sometimes the servants who did ironing were on the side which faced the Cypress Courtyard, or those who were in the laundry room continued ironing and washing unless the Father specifically told them to join the group.

Entering the ironing room the Father would always say *Pax* loud enough for all of us to hear him, and he would repeat it several times. He would enter with a characteristic gesture of his hands, a little thrust out and hanging.

When he was seated, he usually crossed his hands and rested them on his lap, but he would never cross his legs, at least not in our presence. If he wore the clerical cape (*manteo*) he would wrap it around himself, while he looked over us saying, "Let's see. What can you tell me today, daughters?" Often there was a profound silence. Nobody dared to speak. Then he would say, "Well, if you don't have anything to tell me, I will leave." A murmur of protest would follow: "No Father, no."

Unless Encarnita threw out a topic for the Father or instructed some servant to do so, the Father would address Julia, one of the first numerary servants, a Basque, who was older than most, and would say: "Well, Julia, you say something, daughter."

Julia was intelligent and knew how to pick a subject that might interest Monsignor Escrivá.

On one of his visits to the ironing room, Monsignor Escrivá announced that for the first time in the Work Mexican numerary servants were going to come to Rome. Then, addressing María Luisa Moreno de Vega and me, he asked us jokingly, "How come you haven't told your sisters who is going to come from Mexico?" We smiled in silence. "Daughters, your sisters have not told you because they are obliged to keep the silence of office. But, let's see, speak up! Who is coming?"

María Luisa and I responded: "Constantina, Chabela, and Pelancho, Gabríela Duclos, Mago, and Marta, a Mexican architect; all numeraries."

So, Monsignor Escrivá spoke about Mexico, about the work Opus Dei was doing there, and that an estate in Montefalco had just been donated to the Work, where, "if we remain faithful," an agricultural school and farm would be started for peasant girls.

At other times, Monsignor Escrivá spoke to us about the progress of the construction of the Roman College of the Holy Cross and asked us to pray for Don Alvaro, who was responsible for the finances and each Saturday had to pay the workers.

Many other times the conversation turned to how "smart we had to be in life"; he "did not want stupid daughters." He added: "Daughters, don't be silly like nuns." When he said this he would change his voice and with his hands pressed to his face mimic a fatuous person, which provoked great laughter among the servant numeraries and unfortunately among many ordinary numeraries as well.

On one occasion, someone said that she had been to Ciampino, the international airport in Rome, and had seen a large group of Spanish nuns waiting for their mother general. When they saw her descend the steps of the plane, they began jumping up and down and shouting: "Our mother, Our mother! Here comes our mother!"

Monsignor Escrivá roared with laughter, saying: "how amusing, but how amusing!"

As the years went by, Monsignor Escrivá was received much the same way.

In this regard, Monsignor Escrivá told us that "nuns are stupid," adding that the only nun he visited was Sor Lucia in Portugal, "not because she had seen Our Lady, but because she loves us [Opus Dei] very much." He generally added: "She is somewhat silly although a good woman."

One of those evenings Monsignor Escrivá also reported that Sor Lucia in Portugal once had said: "Don José María, you in your place and I in mine, we can also go to hell."

As I mentioned above, we did not do direct apostolate in Villa Sacchetti. However, Encarnita Ortega used to go once a week to the house of the Italian region to speak to married women and do apostolate with them. That also gave the numeraries who were there the chance to speak to her and provided Encarnita the opportunity to find out what was going on in the Italian region, information she passed on to the Father or Don Alvaro.

One day I asked Encarnita about the numeraries in the Italian region, especially Pilarín Navarro, who was the regional directress and one of the first women in the Work. She spoke quite harshly of Pilarín Navarro Rubio. They were from the same city, she said; Pilarín had a lot of relatives in Opus Dei; especially her brothers Emilio, a numerary who years later was ordained a priest, and Mariano, one of the first supernumeraries, who would eventually be a member of Franco's cabinet. Encarnita said that Pilarín was very proud and had had differences with the Father, because she did not have affection for him. Encarnita added bluntly that the Father did not trust Pilarín, because there was "something" about her that he did not like, and Encarnita hinted at something very serious. The Father was apprehensive during the meals that Pilarin prepared for him when she was in the kitchen, because he did not feel sure of her. Encarnita Ortega also added that the Italian region had very serious financial problems because "they had no idea of doing any apostolate" and that Maria Teresa Longo, the first Italian vocation, whose brother was also a numerary did not seem a very secure vocation. She liked Chelo Salafranca and said that she was a numerary who loved the Father very much and that she was great at doing proselytism. Oddly enough, years later Chelo Salafranca staged a rather spectacular escape from Opus Dei.

Some afternoons the first two Italian supernumeraries, Mrs. Lantini and Mrs. Marchesini, would visit. They would be brought up to the ironing room where they would help us. Both had numerary sons. Mrs. Lantini was charming, wore glasses and was quite deaf. She must have been very pretty at one time. Mrs. Marchesini was cheerful, very pleasant, with hair dyed blond, chatty, and had a somewhat shrill voice. When she came on

Saturdays and sang the Salve Regina with little trills, she provoked great hilarity amongst us.

One day, Mrs. Marchesini commented that King George VI of England had died. All of us were more or less startled to hear the news and said: "The King of England has died?" The lady was astonished that we didn't know this. "But how could you not know? He died several days ago." Encarnita responded smartly: "I knew, but I didn't want to upset them."

We did not laugh at her response until after the lady had departed. Naturally Encarnita confessed after Mrs. Marchesini left that she did not have the slightest idea that the King of England had died.

That afternoon, when Monsignor Escrivá and Don Alvaro came to the ironing room, we told them about the visits by Mrs. Lantini and Mrs. Marchesini, and especially about Encarnita's response concerning the death of the King of England.

At that point, I am not sure which of the numeraries remarked: "So, Father, now Princess Elizabeth, who is so young, will be Queen of England."

The person had not finished her sentence, when Monsignor Escrivá rose violently from his chair, gathered up his cape, headed for the middle of the ironing room, shouting at the top of his lungs: "Don't speak to me about that woman! I don't want to hear you talk about her! She is the devil! The devil! Don't talk to me again about her! Understood? Well, now you know!"

Slamming the ironing room door shut, he went out toward the Gallery of the Madonna. We were all still stupefied, when he returned to stick his head through the door without coming in, to repeat again: "Understood? Do not speak to me ever again about that woman!"

Before he slammed the door for the second time, Don Alvaro, with his usual affability and smile, probably trying to smooth things over, looked at us and said, *Pax*, also departing toward the Gallery of the Madonna.

Encarnita immediately told us that we should return to our work and that we should not talk about the matter. She instructed me personally not to write anything about this in the house diary.

I kept wondering why Princess Elizabeth would be the devil. The explanation for what I did not understand and what impressed us all so much then became very clear to me when I left Opus Dei: Monsignor Escrivá had no grasp of ecumenical spirit, contrary to what Peter Berglar (an Opus Dei supernumerary and one of Monsignor Escrivá's official biographers) tries to demonstrate.[1] Monsignor Escrivá's remark to His

---

1. Peter Berglar, *Opus Dei: Vida y obra del fundador José María Escrivá de Balaguer* (Madrid: Rialp, 1987), p. 246: "Monsignor Escrivá commented how he had said to Pope John XXIII during an audience: 'In our Work, everyone, Catholic or not, has always found a cordial place; I have not learned ecumenism from Your Holiness.'"

Holiness John XXIII, as reported by Berglar, is in my judgment disrespectful, to say the least. That a monarch and, to make matters worse, a woman,
was head of the Church of England must have aroused indignation in
Monsignor Escrivá. Given this view, years later, but still during Monsignor
Escrivá's lifetime, Opus Dei had the cynicism to invite the Queen Mother
to inaugurate Netherhall House, the Opus Dei residence in London. When
I found out, I thought it would have been interesting to know the reaction
of the Queen Mother and the Court of St. James if it had become known
that the Founder of the group whose residence she had been invited to
inaugurate had called her daughter, the Queen, a "devil" with such passion
and conviction.

Monsignor Escrivá's reaction on this matter will never be erased from
my memory. I am, therefore, astonished when Opus Dei claims that its
Founder had ecumenical spirit. He did not have it ever, as can be seen in
the first edition of his book, *Camino (The Way)*, where this spirit is
fundamentally absent.[1]

Cleaning and Miscellaneous Jobs

Cleaning was a major part of our life during this period in Rome. It is
always important in every Opus Dei house, since along with cooking it
is the essential part of the activities of administration. Monsignor called
the work of administration "the apostolate of apostolates." He also used
to add that it was like the skeleton upon which absolutely all the houses
of women and men rested and that "without the women the Work would
suffer an authentic collapse."

When I arrived in Rome the cleaning was murder. First, every morning
a group of numeraries and servants went to the *Pensionato*. About sixty
Opus Dei male numeraries lived there. Some numeraries went to the
Lateran and others to the Angelicum to do their theses in philosophy,
theology, and canon law, while some stayed at the house "watching construction workers." By express order of Monsignor Escrivá the workers
were "never to be left alone." Since the financial situation was very shaky
in those years, many of the numeraries walked to save money on transportation, and the Father used to tell us that smokers should cut their cigarettes
in half so that they would last longer.

We had very little time to clean the *Pensionato*. It was like a military
operation. While the numeraries made beds, the servants did bathrooms.

---

1. José María Escrivá, *Camino*, no. 115: "Minutes of silence. Leave them to atheists, masons,
and Protestants who have their hearts dry. Catholics, sons of God, speak to Our Father who is
in heaven." The Father had all copies of the first edition of *Camino* in Opus Dei houses burned.
Subsequent editions modify nos. 115 and 145.

Although there were few bedrooms, there were many three-tiered bunks, so that making the beds was quite an operation. We could often see the Father and Don Alvaro get in or come out of Monsignor Escrivá's car. His chauffeur, who also washed the Father's car, was the first Portuguese numerary. We could also see the comings and goings of male numeraries in the garden, while they waited for us to finish cleaning their living room.

The printing press, which male numeraries ran, was in the *Pensionato*. It was located in the two smallest rooms, and we had specific instructions not to touch anything, except to empty the waste paper baskets. The cleaning of the *Pensionato* took place in the morning and very rapidly.

Then there was the cleaning of our house by sections: the bedrooms, bathrooms, the stairs, the *soggiorno,* and the galleries, the servant responsible for the oratory, the sacristy, and the visitors' parlor, the servants' compartments or *camarillas,* the ironing and laundry rooms. Julia, the older servant, was in charge of the gardens with Chabela, the Mexican.

Big cleaning projects were shared by all, such as putting red wax on the tiles of the Gallery of the Madonna, the floors of Villa Sacchetti, the stairs, the servants' compartments. The difficulty about applying the red wax was not to stain the white sandstone border and to make the tiles shine by buffing with your feet or on your knees.

Every afternoon as soon as the workers left, we entered Villa Vecchia where Monsignor Escrivá had his provisional rooms, his oratory, and his work space. Encarnita or, in her absence, Mary Altozano made Monsignor Escrivá and Don Alvaro's beds and cleaned their rooms with another numerary and two servants. The rest of the numeraries remained in the Villa vestibule, which had a newly finished wooden floor. The wood was completely dry and rather dirty. Cleaning that floor meant applying turpentine with stiff brushes to remove all stains. The liquid had to be removed and then the wax was applied. The vestibule was immense. Finally, we all tried to put a bit of shine on the floor by buffing it with our feet. So it went afternoon after afternoon, month after month.

On Sundays we had so-called extraordinary cleaning of the Retreat House, the first location of Opus Dei's Roman College of the Holy Cross at Viale Bruno Buozzi, 73. The construction workers were finishing, and it was necessary to clean everything. The main thing was to remove drops of paint and cement using razor blades discarded by the male numeraries. To get more use out of the blades, we would divide them in two. Our hands were full of cuts, because all this was done without gloves.

The *Procura Generalizia* was finished, and this was another cleaning project done frequently but not daily. The main entrance to the *Procura Generalizia* is in Via di Villa Sacchetti, 30. It was built as the reception area for visitors to the president general. The *Procura Generalizia* consisted of a vestibule, a visitors' parlor, a small bath, an oratory, and a dining room for twelve. The French-style furniture was so delicate that we had to use white cotton gloves to dust it.

Monsignor Escrivá was accustomed to invite people he considered important to lunch in this dining room. He dined there several times with his physician, Dr. Carlo Faelli, and his wife. At other times, it was a cardinal or a bishop. The instructions regarding guests were clear and specific, as was also the rule that nobody should be served before the Father. Because of this, two maids attended the dining room, simultaneously serving the Father and the guest of honor.

When there were guests for lunch, I used to assist Encarnita in preparing the table and the floral centerpiece, and stay with her in the pantry while the meal lasted.

So, I played a fairly prominent role on many occasions. It seems that I was very efficient in matters relating to guests and in settling questions of etiquette, particularly in relation to embassies and consulates.

Inconceivable as it now seems to me, this made me aware of the great confidence that Monsignor Escrivá and Encarnita had in me and made me very happy. What I did not realize then was that they were using me. Not until I was out of Opus Dei, did I notice how, under the guise of "good spirit," "love of the Father and the Work," Opus Dei exploits all its members. The Father's opinion and keeping the Father happy mattered more than God.

On Sundays we usually did not clean the administration to increase the numbers of those who could go over to the Retreat House or to wherever the workers might have finished.

Evidently, those cleaning sessions were traced for us the previous day by Don Alvaro. Neither Monsignor Escrivá nor Don Alvaro ever put in an appearance where we were cleaning. Until the Father's meal time, Encarnita put her shoulder to the wheel with the best of us.

With this exercise, those of us who lived in Villa Sacchetti were thin as toothpicks, although we ate well. Encarnita, by contrast, barely ate.

After the day's work, we ended up in the ironing room, where the servants ironed and went over clothing, and the numeraries did many other things.

Since we were unable to cope with all the cleaning, Monsignor Escrivá ordered that several more numeraries should come to the Rome administration. The Father wanted some Women's Branch central government major superiors. He requested that some of those who held positions of authority in the government should come to Rome, not as major superiors but simply as numeraries to help in the administration. The first persons to arrive were Marisa Sánchez de Movellán, Lourdes Toranzo, Pilar Salcedo, and others who had no government position in Spain, like Cathérine Bardinet, María José Monterde, and Begoña Mujica.

In his biography of Monsignor Escrivá, Peter Berglar reports a conversation between the Founder and Pilar Salcedo in 1968, when she was still an Opus Dei numerary, in which he is quoted as follows: "For me the work of a daughter who is a domestic servant is as important as the work of a daughter who has a title in the nobility."[1] That claim is false. Without involving the aristocracy, which will eventually come up, let us use one example of wealth. When Cathérine Bardinet, the first French numerary, was sent to Rome, there was no other French woman. Cathérine requested admission very young and her parents, owners of Bardinet liqueurs in France, were less than enthusiastic about their daughter's vocation. Cathérine's contact with her family was mainly through her mother. Without wanting a complete break, her father maintained a hostile attitude. The couple wrote their daughter Cathérine telling her they were going on a cruise around the Mediterranean and that they would like her to accompany them. When Cathérine told us, we began to joke with her, and each time we had a heavy cleaning project, we said we were going on a cruise. Then, Encarnita explained the situation to the Father and said that when the Bardinets came to visit their daughter, they wanted to greet him.

One day Encarnita announced that Cathérine's parents had arrived. To our astonishment she also said that the Father would come down to our parlor to greet the Bardinets. Beyond question, "it was suitable to win over" these people, given their supposed wealth.

The Father came down to the parlor with Don Alvaro and without any kind of introduction approached Monsieur Bardinet, saying—"Another fat person like me! How could we not get along well?"

He gave him a warm embrace. Needless to say, Cathérine Bardinet went on the cruise around the Mediterranean with her parents.

Such treatment was unheard of, given the restrictions placed on dealings with our families. Not only to see them, but to go on a cruise![2]

So, respectfully I regret that I have to contradict Dr. Peter Berglar, who as a male never lived in any Opus Dei women's house. Nor, it would appear from his book, did he ever speak with any female numerary, but limited himself to information on the Women's Branch and Monsignor Escrivá presented by Encarnita Ortega in Monsignor Escrivá's beatification process. Berglar notwithstanding, not all numeraries were the same to Monsignor Escrivá.

---

1. Berglar, *Opus Dei*, pp. 212–13.
2. Cathérine Bardinet and Encarnite Ortega, both present at the encounter, told us about it.

Tapestries and Rugs

For a number of months in 1952–53 we repaired a tapestry that the architect or some other male numerary had found in an antique shop. The tapestry was handed over to us to be washed. It was an enormous pile of rubbish, all torn, and we could not even tell what it was supposed to represent. They told us to wash it well with soap and water, and several of us set to work assisted by some of the servants. The first step was to remove a red backing, which attached to the tapestry, so that the color would not run during washing. When this was done, we found the seal of authentication. When they gave us the tapestry, they had informed us that it was attributed to Michelangelo, but until we found the seal, there was no certainty about this. There was indeed great rejoicing at our find. Because it was too big to hang in the laundry, several of us carried it out to be hung on the wall of the Cypress Courtyard. As it was drying—a process that took several days—we tried to guess what the picture in the tapestry might be. It was so deteriorated that nothing was clear. One very imaginative person claimed to see a little girl at the bottom of the tapestry. I only saw an arm. Meanwhile, Monsignor Escrivá directed Mercedes Anglés, a numerary who was extraordinarily gifted in embroidery, to devote all her time to restoring the tapestry and to tell him when she expected to be able to finish.

When Mercedes began the project, she announced it would take several months. That seemed to us all like an eternity, but she was right. Mary Carmen Sánchez Merino began to help in the restoration, and eventually we all did. An enormous frame was set up in the ironing room, so that eight of us could work on the tapestry from both sides. One day, Monsignor Escrivá came into the ironing room and asked Mary Carmen how the tapestry was coming. With her charming Andalusian accent, she responded: "Father, I'm still on the little rolls (*panesillos*)."

After several months of hard work, the tapestry was finally finished and hung for posterity on the Villa Vecchia staircase wall. Then a painter touched it up. In effect, a prophet handing bread to a youth turned out to be the central figure of the tapestry. Perhaps it was based on some biblical passage; the sketch was attributed to Michelangelo.

Since there was not an instant during the day to work on these things, we worked at night until after 2 A.M. To fight drowsiness, we told jokes, made up stories, and exhausted our repertories of songs. Thus, between humor and real life, song and song, at the sacrifice of our sleep and rest, we hand wove all of the knotted rugs in the buildings. The rug we made for the dining room of the *Procura Generaliza* seemed to me like the physical embodiment of infinity. Gray, without design, it went on indefinitely. It totally covered the room.

Since we worked until late at night, we were all drowsy, and for months we all confessed to the same mistake. "I fell asleep during the priest's meditation." There were so many priests in Rome during this period, that each afternoon a different one gave us the meditation, and it was easy to notice us dropping off to sleep. I remember María Luisa Moreno de Vega saying, "For Heaven's sake, let's wake each other up, because otherwise, one of these days, the priest is going to tiptoe out of the oratory in order not to wake us up."

After more than a year, the news that we were falling asleep reached Monsignor Escrivá, who, to our great surprise, instructed us to sleep eight hours a night. It is hard to understand why he had been unaware of our situation, because a normal workday did not suffice for all the tasks assigned to us.

Get-togethers

Our get-together or period of rest was only a half hour daily and an hour on Sunday. The female numeraries had only one get-together a day, whereas the male numeraries had two.

Our get-togethers included the numerary servants. Occasionally, on Sundays some of the numeraries from the Italian region would come with two or three of the numerary servants assigned to Italy. As I have mentioned, in summer we would play some kind of basketball without a basket with the servants. Other times we chatted and told them anecdotes about some house or other. Preferred topics were events from the early days of the Work, things the Father had said, or something that had happened while we were out on errands. We never discussed current events, world politics, or anything similar. The "world" for us consisted of those countries where Opus Dei had been founded. As a special treat for those Sunday get-togethers, a selected letter from the numeraries or servant numeraries in Mexico or Chicago might be read. This was the world for Opus Dei numeraries in the central house in Rome.

Matters related to poverty or world hunger, basic human social problems in other words, were never even raised. We were told more than once that such matters were the concern of religious associations. From Chicago Nisa Guzmán began to send issues of *Vogue, Harper's Bazaar* and similar magazines from time to time, but some puritanical numerary told Encarnita that many of the models who appeared in those magazines looked like loose women. Consequently, those magazines ceased to circulate in get-togethers. By exception we were allowed to look at dresses in those magazines, if we were going to make one, but only when a number of pages had been prudently torn out.

Although I tried to participate in these get-togethers, I found them quite dull. When I said this in my confidence, I was accused of being bored with the servants, of having "bad spirit." I really loved the servant numeraries, but that type of get-together did not relax me at all. They also told me that the get-together was not a time of rest, but for charity. Other times, if we were in the ironing room as usually happened in the winter, we sang songs of the Work, and it was almost a ritual that volunteers would perform some kind of regional dance. María José Monterde, who was from Zaragoza and executed the Aragonese *jota* very well, performed the dance for the Father several times. Monsignor Escrivá was very fond of her. Fortunately, when the Mexican servants arrived, the *chapaneca* and the *bamba* were also added, which were at least entertaining because of the new rhythms.

The arrival of Mexicans broadened the very limited horizon of that house as well, because new customs, other names, previously unknown events began to be mentioned. However, some of the events narrated by the Mexican servants brought fraternal corrections on the numeraries in that country, and in many instances a request for clarifications of matters that the servants had described.

Servant Numeraries

"Servant numeraries" was how Opus Dei initially denominated that class of members who devoted themselves to manual labor or domestic service in houses of the Work.[1] A rescript from Rome was dispatched to all regions in 1965 saying that the Father had ordered that henceforth the term *servant numeraries* should be replaced by that of *auxiliary numeraries* to designate Opus Dei servants. Accordingly, since that date, the term "servant" has been suppressed, and the usual designation within Opus Dei houses is "auxiliaries."

Opus Dei numerary auxiliaries have the same obligations in their spiritual life as the numeraries as regards norms of plan of life, corporal mortification, poverty, chastity, and obedience. Just like regular members, they took cold showers each morning. The servants who waited on table were required to take a shower before putting on their black uniforms.

Fundamental distinctions exist, however. Servants can never occupy positions of authority, they cannot belong to the category of inscribed members, nor work outside Opus Dei houses. Furthermore, like the male numeraries, but unlike the ordinary female numeraries, the servants sleep in regular beds with springs and mattresses.

---

1. *Constitutions*, 1950, p. 172, no. 440.

Opus Dei servants wear whatever is customary garb in the country where they live, usually a white apron over a colored uniform. When waiting on table, they put on a black uniform with white cuffs, a small white apron, and a headpiece. In some countries like Venezuela there were slight modifications: the uniform, for example, had short instead of long sleeves, and the dining room uniform, which did have long sleeves, was dark green. In Rome, on feast days or when there were guests, they usually waited on table with white gloves. In the afternoon, the servant who is concierge wears the same black uniform with cuffs and black satin apron.

When the servants go out, they do not wear uniforms but dress as any other women of their social level. They usually dress well, may use makeup, and can dye their hair. They do not use makeup when they clean and very little when they wait on table.

Opus Dei servants sleep in tiny individual rooms called *camarillas,* which have a bed, a closet, sink, and sometimes a chair. There is usually a window or half window and a picture of Our Lady. These compartments tend to be larger in buildings recently constructed by Opus Dei. In Rome, the servants' compartments formed a special block. As additions were built onto the Women's compound, the number of *camarillas* also increased. However, the servants' rooms are never mixed with the rooms of numeraries. Everything is smaller and separate. The auxiliaries also have dining rooms separate from the numeraries, but the food is identical to that of the rest of the house.

In Rome, and some Opus Dei houses the bedding, table cloths, and towels are set off and stamped with the word *servicio* (servants).

Like delivery people Opus Dei servants regularly enter houses of the Work by the servants' entrance. Rarely do they use the main entrance. Therefore, every Opus Dei house has its special servants' entrance, and some large houses such as the one in Rome have an additional special entrance for deliveries. Not that delivery people enter Opus Dei houses, they merely have access to a small room or counter where they leave merchandise and are usually paid. A delivery person never enters the kitchen, for example, of any Opus Dei house.

The servants are never alone. "They can never be alone," according to the Founder's dictum. "They are like little children," the Founder repeated more than once, and indeed he called them "his little daughters." "Don't ever leave them alone on me!," he shouted at us at other times. "They have their mentality, and it is the only one they can have." Nevertheless, Monsignor Escrivá claimed that many Opus Dei servants have better theological training than many priests and certainly better than the majority of nuns.

Opus Dei servants do not go out alone ever, but in pairs, always accompanied by a numerary. This last rule can be dispensed with when they are older and have been in the Work for many years.

Monsignor Escrivá's obsession with never leaving the servants alone, became a torment for us. They couldn't be alone in the ironing room for five minutes. One of us always had to be with them. So, if a numerary was in the ironing room with the servants and had to go to the oratory to do her mental prayer, she notified the directress in order that another numerary, or failing that, the directress herself might come to the ironing room, while the first numerary was in the oratory. We were always with them in the house work, on excursions, and at every instant.

Even during the half hour of prayer every afternoon, a numerary always had to be with the auxiliaries. They could not go to the oratory alone as we did. We read the book for their spiritual reading out loud while they worked. They did absolutely everything with us. You were required to declare in your weekly chat with the directress if you had left the servants alone for five minutes.

The priests did not deliver special meditations for the servants. We had the same meditations and the same spiritual retreat as well.

We were with the servants all day and did the same work except for washing and ironing clothes from the men's residence, which only they did. The essential difference was in personal relations. Both sides had to address the other with the formal "usted" instead of the familiar "tú," and they addressed us as "Miss" (Señorita) plus our first name, while we called them by their first name.

The schooling of the servants was very limited. They knew how to read and write, but not much more, with the exception of Dora and Julia, the first two Opus Dei numerary servants, who were very intelligent and had worked in families of some social standing which had rubbed off enough on them to distinguish them from the rest.

Curiously, the secularity which Opus Dei claimed to pioneer did not lead it to impart any general culture to its female members, whether ordinary numeraries or servants. The servants in Rome had no classes of any kind. Many desired to learn Italian but had to be content with the little we could teach them. In later years, there were "schools for domestic servants" in some countries. Also, about 1970 in Venezuela, for example, classes for auxiliary numeraries were begun, which were equivalent to elementary education. In the special centers of study for auxiliary numeraries, they received a very basic religious instruction: apologetics, liturgy, carefully adapted to their mentality.

Monsignor Escrivá treated them like little girls and encouraged childishness. They knew they were "the Father's little daughters" and behaved as such to the point that the immaturity of the servants in the Rome house was deplorable. It was pathetic to see how adult women acted like thirteen-year-olds as a result of their indoctrination.

Needless to say, if the numeraries always were accompanied by another numerary to go to the dentist or any physician, much more so the servants. This regulation was extended to all countries where the Opus Dei has been founded.

We could never reprimand auxiliaries nor could we give them fraternal corrections directly. If we saw that one of them had done something out of order, we were to tell the directress so that another servant or the directress herself could correct her in the confidence. Nor could they make fraternal corrections to us. If we did something wrong, they went to the directress, who took charge of making the appropriate correction.

The Opus Dei servants in Rome at that time were all Spaniards and had the typical Spanish rural mentality of the time. Some of them with a more refined demeanor had been maids or nannies in upper middle-class households.

Auxiliaries also help in farmwork or in the press, but they never abandon their household chores. According to the Founder an auxiliary could never aspire to be more than a good servant.

The mentality of the Spanish auxiliaries of that period tended toward servility and was aggravated in Rome because of their childish fanaticism. If for the numeraries the whole of life revolved around Monsignor Escrivá, for the servants there was no other goal nor God than "the Father."

One servant who merits a few lines of her own is Rosalía López. She was from a town in Castille. She was thin, a bit taller than average, with dark hair and sharp features, very small twinkling eyes, certainly not beautiful, but clean-looking. Besides being childish, she could only absorb what physically related to the Father. She had no capacity to grasp anything else. If she wanted something, she pleaded like a child. If something didn't please her, she would put on a dour face and lapse into deep silence. In many ways she considered herself the Father's "defender." She knew she was the only servant Monsignor Escrivá allowed to wait on his dinner table, to which Salvador Canals Navarrete, an Opus Dei numerary priest, was invited with some frequency because he worked within the Vatican.

Rosalía was so convinced that she was indispensable to the Father that she dared confront any numerary, whether the central directress or the directress of the house administration.

Everyone in the house knew that Rosalía reported anything done or said to Monsignor Escrivá. It would be equally true to say that Monsignor Escrivá obviously utilized her to learn what visitors arrived, who went out, and so forth.

To my astonishment I recall one day when Monsignor Escrivá asked me about the priest who had come to visit me. As it happened, Father Rambla had come to see what could be done to establish better relations between me and my mother. Although the directress obviously knew I had had this visit, she had not said anything to Monsignor Escrivá, because there was no reason to do so. Rosalía's exchanges with Monsignor Escrivá were pure gossip, prompted by Monsignor Escrivá himself.

The game was unbelievable: there were numeraries who danced to Rosalía's tune in the hope that their name would be mentioned to the Father. By contrast, I have seen Rosalía frequently come down to the kitchen while waiting on Monsignor Escrivá with crocodile tears confronting the director and even Encarnita, while she protested: "You people are going to kill the Father. You've given him oily food, and he has not been able to eat today." With a gesture of displeasure she would exhibit the little tray prepared for Monsignor Escrivá as she deposited it on the kitchen table. This was after the directress or the person in charge of the kitchen or both had measured with a dropper the oil to be used in the Father's meal.

Other times, Rosalía came down to the kitchen giving orders: "The Father wants to have coffee served today in the Roman College dining room." If anyone dared to ask, "Why?" she answered completely scandalized: "Miss, the Father has said so."

Monsignor Escrivá frequently had her sit down at his table after lunch or dinner and tell him things. It is unnecessary to add that "the things" were always administration gossip. Rosalía like to humiliate numeraries insinuating "her sources." For instance, the last time I was in Rome during 1965–66, Rosalía said to me one night: "You, Miss, forget about going back to your country. Whether you like it or not, you are going to stay in Rome."

Since I had known her for years and realized that my reaction was going to be relayed to Monsignor Escrivá, I simply gave her a lesson in good spirit, telling her: "Rosalía, if you know that because you heard the Father say so, never forget that what you hear while you wait on table ought not to be repeated in the administration."

When Rosalía attended her annual formation course, the directress of the administration and the central women's directress had to figure out what servant "would please the Father" at meals. During the three-week courses Tasia waited on his table.

Serving in the Father's dining room was the maximum privilege among auxiliaries.

When houses were founded in the United States and England, Spanish servants were imported. Naturally, in the United States, they soon realized that the Spanish regime could not be followed, and observed that the ladies who frequented the house made presents to Pilar and Francisca, believing they were doing these two servants a favor. All this provoked a crisis in the lives of these two auxiliaries, with the result that they had to return to Rome. Pilar stayed in Villa Sacchetti, but Francisca had to go to the region of Italy because she was Rosalía's sister, and two sisters can never reside in the same Opus Dei house.

Subsequently, Monsignor Escrivá sent a note to the countries where live-in maids were not common: "In those countries where it is not the custom to have live-in maids, they should exist but not be obvious." This meant that the servants did not always wear their uniform. They were pushed behind the scenes. Because of the failure of the Spanish numerary servants in the United States, Monsignor Escrivá arranged with Father Casciaro, counselor of Mexico, to have Mexican numerary servants sent to the United States.

In countries where numeraries and servants perform housekeeping in centers of male members of the prelature, they receive a salary, though a very low one, but no social security. On the principle of poverty, these salaries go directly to the coffers of the house where the servants live. The servants do not receive any money. It is supposed that the numeraries who accompany them will pay for whatever purchases are made. Naturally, when they need clothes or shoes, they get them, but they do not handle any money.

If a family needs financial help, the Work might send a check for a ridiculously small amount, but by virtue of their vow of poverty, the servants cannot dispose of any money.

There are natives of almost all the countries where Opus Dei is established who are numerary servants, but just as Spain has provided domestic servants to the Opus Dei houses in Europe, Mexico has supplied servants to the regions of the Americas.

The social structure of the world is changing rapidly, and work as a domestic servant is no longer attractive except when it is well paid and by the hour, but Opus Dei continues maintaining the old ways that benefit the institution, but which do not correspond either to Christianity or social reality.

The servants and numeraries of the central house in Rome did not get any salary. Money transmitted to us through Don Alvaro as procurator general at the time paid for food and cleaning products for Opus Dei men's quarters and food for us. That was all. There existed no kinds of insurance policies in Opus Dei, which thrust any auxiliary numerary who, for any reason, left Opus Dei into grave difficulties.

Annual Courses: Castelgandolfo, Villa delle Rose

Annual courses are periods of formation required for all members of the Opus Dei prelature. They last from three weeks to a month.

When I arrived in Rome, our annual courses took place in Castelgandolfo together with the numeraries of the region of Italy.

Pius XII gave Opus Dei a little villa with a good piece of land in Castelgandolfo. It was said that the Women's Branch center of formation would be built there. When I came to Rome, there was no sign of such a building, but thirteen years later it became a reality: Villa delle Rose, the Roman College of Santa Maria, housed for many years Opus Dei vocations from around the world who came there to finish Opus Dei internal studies of philosophy and theology, and sometimes, since it was a branch of the University of Navarra in Spain, to do studies of pedagogy. Recently, the Roman College of Santa Maria is located near the Opus Dei women's headquarters in Rome at Via di Villa Sacchetti. Villa delle Rose remains as the center for pedagogical studies.

Villa delle Rose was the name of the Castelgandolfo house from the beginning. It was old, ugly, and uncomfortable. The women numeraries had to sleep on the dining-room floor. I still remember that when the trolley passed, the floor vibrated. The best and most comfortable part of the house was occupied by the Men's Branch. There was usually a priest with several male numeraries, and sometimes, Monsignor Escrivá came to visit.

We had been told in Villa Sacchetti that we would go to Castelgandolfo by turns to do our annual course. Two weeks before I was supposed to leave, one day after the midday meal Encarnita told me that I had to go to Castelgandolfo immediately. Pilarín Navarro knew already and was waiting for me. She gave me no reason for the hurry but warned me that I had to try not to miss the bus and said that the other people would complete their course later.

I went alone. When I arrived, Pilarín Navarro, directress of the region of Italy and of the special course for new Italian vocations was surprised to see me and asked: "What did you come for?" The truth is that I didn't know, and I said so.

I began to wonder whether Encarnita had not told me the truth, because Pilarín Navarro had no idea I was coming. Why would she send me to Castelgandolfo so many days before the actual beginning of the annual course. Why was my departure so rushed?

Always wanting to find a reason, I wondered whether I had done anything wrong and she had sent me to give me time to realize my mistakes. Yet I remembered Encarnita all smiles when she spoke to me. The whole range of possibilities passed through my mind. In the end, none seemed reasonable, so I decided to say nothing about it at all until Encarnita (due to arrive for the course for the Italian girls two days later) could explain things to me.

Encarnita arrived and left on the run. I managed to reach her and ask: "What is going on? Why did you send me here?"

Not only did she not answer but she said she had to leave immediately not to miss the bus in order to be on time for the Father's supper.

Her smile irritated me even more. It was as if she mocked me.

I was extraordinarily irritated, and so angry, realizing Opus Dei's murkiness, that the thought passed through my mind to toss everything overboard and leave Opus Dei. Consequently, the next day I wrote a letter to Monsignor Escrivá seeking authorization to leave Opus Dei. I gave the sealed letter to Pilarín Navarro, who was going to Villa Sacchetti, asking her to give it to Monsignor Escrivá or to Don Alvaro.

That afternoon, when Father Salvador Canals came, we all passed through the confessional, and I explained what had happened and what I had done. Father Salvador, who was a very good, calm man, put me at ease and told me to rush to the phone to call Pilarín to tell her not to give my letter to anyone. That same evening, on her return from Rome, Pilarín returned my letter.

Though I did not send the letter, as a result of my irritation I retreated into almost complete silence without being rude until that blessed course ended and I returned to Rome. Moreover, logically, everything was in Italian. It was still a great effort for me to speak Italian all day long, so that life was not easy on that score either.

On August 15, 1952, we learned that Monsignor Escrivá had consecrated Opus Dei to the Immaculate Heart of Mary in the shrine at Loreto. This consecration took place that year for the first time in all Opus Dei houses and is annually renewed on August 15. The words of the consecration are read by the director of each house in the oratory.

I intended to speak to Monsignor Escrivá to ask the reason that impelled Encarnita to act as she had, but I did not have time. On one occasion, when I crossed paths with Don Alvaro, he said, without further ado: "You behaved like an animal in Castelgandolfo, giving such bad example."

Two days after that, the Father called me in front of Don Alvaro and María Luisa Moreno de Vega and gave me the biggest scolding that I can recall.

As always, he shouted. He said he had found out from Encarnita how badly I had behaved on the trip from Spain, flirting with the Italian gentleman. (The kind man had helped me climb aboard the train in Ventiemiglia on my way to Rome months earlier.) I had given him the house telephone number. I had scandalized, "scandalized!" he shouted at me, that "poor servant" who was with me on the train by reading those disgusting magazines. Above all, in Castelgandolfo, I could not have given a worse example, as one of his secretaries, submerging myself in silence.

María Luisa Moreno de Vega had no idea about my trip nor about what the servant said, nor about anything. The poor woman was dejected and serious. She suffered visibly.

As the Father shouted furiously at me, Don Alvaro tried to calm him, saying: "Father, I have already told her that she behaved like an animal." "Worse than an animal!" shouted the Father. "Giving bad example to all the new vocations, she, who is one of my secretaries."

When Don Alvaro tried again to soften the scolding, saying, "Father, these are already things from the day before yesterday," trying to stress how much time had elapsed, Monsignor Escrivá responded: "Not at all the day before yesterday!" he shouted. "Things of yesterday."

To impress on me how badly I had behaved, he said in conclusion: "And now you know. I don't intend to speak to you for two months."

From there, in complete silence, María Luisa and I went to the secretarial room, after stopping in the oratory for a moment.

On the grounds that María Luisa Moreno de Vega was a major superior, in which capacity an ordinary numerary like myself could speak confidently on occasions, I explained what had occurred on the train. She listened very attentively; I am convinced she believed me; and she said I ought to speak to Encarnita again to assure her that everything I had previously explained to her was true. I was really crushed and the Father spoke not a word to me for two months.

Those two months seemed like an eternity. In front of everyone, Monsignor Escrivá made it known that he was not speaking to me. That punishment truly caused me to shed more than one tear in my prayers.

More than two months went by when, one fine day, he began to speak to me with the greatest ease, as if nothing had happened. Remembering these events nowadays, I confess my astonishment at the capacity for suffering that a person endures when he or she follows a leader blindly. I also wonder what kind of sentiments could be in Monsignor Escrivá's heart when he permitted himself to play with our feelings so insensitively.

Terracina: Salto di Fondi

One day Monsignor Escrivá called us to say that there was a house in Terracina that met the basic needs of the students of the Roman College of Holy Cross during the summer vacation where they could be close to the beach. He told us there was a small administration but that, unfortunately, it was not suitable (*no conviene*) that we go swimming, although we could go for walks and "wet our feet." We should offer it up to God for the Work that our brothers might be holy.

There was not to be a regular administration in Terracina for the moment. Accordingly, the Father had resolved that his sister Carmen who was going to Rome could be in Terracina with one of us, for example, Enrica Botella, until the house that Opus Dei had acquired for Carmen and their brother Santiago was ready. He added that eventually the house would be for the Work. He told us that it was necessary to begin to clean that house even before the workers entered, because it was very dirty. He had decided that Encarnita and I accompanied by Dora and Rosalía should go, but that absolutely nobody in the house had to know about it.

Tía Carmen

We were delighted at this sign of confidence from Monsignor Escrivá, since nobody knew that Tía (aunt) Carmen[1] was coming to live in Rome and absolutely nobody was aware that a house was being readied for her and Santiago. The house was on the Via degli Scipioni.

At noon Don Alvaro and the Father called to tell us which afternoons we could go. The house was a villa in a lovely residential area, and we all thought that once clean, it would be very pretty. There were four of us and each one of us attacked one sector. It was quite a battle. The house was so filthy that I remember perfectly how I had to grasp a kitchen knife with both hands to scrape the tiles of the walls of a bathroom. There was a laminated layer of grime. It was unbelievable. Several months were spent on this initial cleaning, until the workers began to come. So, we went to clean Sunday mornings. I recall that one Sunday morning Monsignor Escrivá and Don Alvaro came to see us and brought assorted pastries and snacks. Obviously the Father had purchased them in a bakery. Our jubilation was extreme, naturally. From time to time we saw Javi, an extremely young numerary, gilding ceilings. Javi customarily accompanied the workers to our house and was characteristically unpleasant. Years later, this youth became the Father's secretary and *custos*.[2] On August 7, 1955, he was ordained a priest. When Monsignor Escrivá gave us the news, I remember we made a gesture almost of repugnance. Monsignor Escrivá

---

1. Monsignor Escrivá established the custom for us to call his mother "la Abuela" (grandmother) and his siblings Carmen and Santiago "tíos" (aunt and uncle), but since Santiago was so young, we seldom called him "uncle."

2. The Father has two *custodes* (plural of *custos*, guardian) "to watch over the spiritual and material good of the Father, who do not belong to the General Council of Opus Dei in virtue of this post. They are appointed to a five-year term by the Father himself among nine inscribed members presented to the Father by the General Council. They have their family life with the Father." This means that they accompany the Father wherever he goes. They are responsible for fraternal correction of the Father, one in regard to spiritual matters, the other in regard to material issues. See *Constitutions*, 1950, p. 132, no. 333.

knew through Rosalía that Javi was not well regarded by any of the women numeraries. Shortly after his ordination, Monsignor informed us that that afternoon "Don Javier" would direct our meditation. This priest was Father Javier Echevarría. He was named vicar general of the Opus Dei Prelature in 1982 and elected prelate of Opus Dei on April 21, 1994, after Bishop del Portillo's death on March 23, 1994.

Tía Carmen was in Terracina for several months during which a number of numeraries accompanied her. Encarnita spent more than a month there. When Tía Carmen's house was finally remodeled and redecorated, they brought her and Santiago to live in Rome. They had two servants recruited by the region of Italy and a dog named El Chato.

Once Tía Carmen was installed in Rome, the Father designated a few female numeraries to visit her, so that she would always have company every afternoon. Only Encarnita Ortega and María José Monterde went from Villa Sacchetti. From the Italian region Mary Altozano, Mary Carmen Sánchez Marino, and another person whom I no longer recall, usually went. It surprised me that I could not go to her house after having struggled with all the cleaning. It surprised her, too. One day she asked me: "Tell me why you can't come to my house." I answered honestly: "Tía Carmen, they haven't told me to go." When I asked if I could go, they said that the Father hadn't said anything. She made a gesture as if to say "What a bother!" and added: "I don't understand it, after you suffered through the cleaning." I laughed and let the matter die.

Tía Carmen and I got along very well. When she came to our house for lunch from time to time, she seemed smothered by people who kept kissing her and taking her by the arm. I always believed that this obsequiousness annoyed her. She and I had simple, short conversations. She felt very uncomfortable outside Spain. Although her house was very pretty, at rock bottom it was like being in a gilded cage. She could not do what she wanted, because her whole life was directly or indirectly mapped out by the Father. Yet, Monsignor Escrivá did not go to see her very often, and when he went, conversation was not easy. Encarnita, who was present at more than one of these visits, told us that it was very uncomfortable to witness the silences that prevailed between Tía Carmen and the Father.

Commenting about one of these visits, Monsignor Escrivá told us that one day when he went to see her, Carmen was fairly disagreeable and he remarked:

"Well, to everybody I am the Founder and president general of Opus Dei, and for you, who am I? Some nut?"[1] Tía Carmen retorted aggressively:

---

1. In Spanish, "un cuerno," a coloquial expression; literally a "horn."

"That's right, some nut." Monsignor Escrivá recounted this with amusement, even laughing.

I had not known Tía Carmen in the early days of Diego de León. I only met her in Lagasca after making my admission. Since Carmen and Santiago had no house of their own, for a long time they lived at Diego de León, where there were a couple of rooms for them. There are former Opus Dei male numeraries who do not have fond memories of Carmen's stay at Diego de León in the sense that they were all in some degree obliged to court her as the Father's sister.

I saw Santiago a couple of times in Villa Sacchetti at lunch, because it must have been the Father's birthday or some festivity, but I do remember him from our brief conversations as a very different personality from Monsignor Escrivá in the sense that he seemed much more straightforward to me.

Personally, I always felt sorry for Carmen and Santiago because it seemed to me that they lived in a fish bowl. They didn't belong to Opus Dei and yet their lives depended on the Work. On the one hand, Monsignor Escrivá made a show of being distant toward his siblings. On the other, on the grounds that they gave him all they owned to start Opus Dei— something of which I have never seen proof and which was never explained in detail to us—he gave them the royal treatment. Monsignor Escrivá provided them with a splendid house under the pretext that when they left Rome or died the house would be turned over to the Work. He established the tradition that on Carmen's and Santiago's saints days, birthdays, Christmas, and so forth, all the regions would send them presents, which were not mere trifles. We gave with pleasure, but they got exceptional treatment solely by dint of being the Founder's sister and brother. Thus, we were greatly surprised in Venezuela, when a note arrived saying that henceforth no more presents would be sent to Santiago. (Tía Carmen had already died.) Later we found out that Santiago was about to get married.

What is not true is what Andrés Vázquez de Prada, one of the official Opus Dei biographers of José María Escrivá, narrates about Tía Carmen in his book, when he describes how the Father's siblings went to live in Rome: "Santiago had been working in the legal profession for some time. Nor did Carmen change her occupation. She was available to help at times in matters that were not especially pleasant. When bank negotiations had to be undertaken, the Founder's sister got up her courage; she put on her finest apparel and went to get loans. The truth is that without much collateral, they greeted her with courtesy to be sure, with a 'Come in, countess.' And she overcame the obstacles."[1] If Tía Carmen were alive,

---

1. Vázquez de Prada, *El fundador del Opus Dei*, p. 262.

she would say to Andrés Vázquez de Prada with all the frankness that characterized her, that he was inventing a fairy tale, and would laugh in his face. That description is false, first, because neither Carmen nor Santiago were involved in financial affairs of the Work. Second, because Carmen did not speak Italian nor did she know any banker. Third, because although I truly loved her, I cannot say she "looked like a countess."

What Carmen did do was to embroider blouses for some of us. She embroidered very well and she enjoyed it. Like any woman her age, she also liked to chat and not be left alone. She very much liked plants and had a green thumb. I would joke with her saying that she could get a flower from a dry stick, because sometimes walking along the street, she would cut a twig that protruded from a grill, plant it in her house, and get flourishing growth.

More than once some of us would go with Tía Carmen to have an iced coffee. She loved to invite us or accede to our request that she invite us to a coffee shop.

She didn't like changes. She hated to see new faces.

In 1956, when I told her that the Father had said I was going to Venezuela, she came to lunch, and gripping my arm, said to me in a low voice: "But where is my brother's head? Now that you manage everything that has to do with the press and all is going so well, he sends you to Venezuela. He's crazy!" "Don't say that, Tía Carmen," I pleaded. "It's hard for me to go, but the Father has his reasons."

She would shake her head without being convinced.

When a numerary from the Women's Branch central advisory would leave for another country, it was the custom to have her picture taken to be left at the house.

Since I disliked going to the photographer, I asked Tía Carmen to accompany me. She agreed. As we talked along by the *Tritone* she asked me what I wanted her to give me as a souvenir. "Two things," I said. "First the rosary you use every day, second, that you have a picture taken too, and give it to me."

She looked at me with a very peculiar smile and said: "All right. But it will have to be taken now, just the way I am, because I'm not coming another day."

At the house, I had been given the address of a photographer in that very street, but when I arrived it seemed to me that it was not the sort of place to bring Tía Carmen, so I decided on the spot to go to Luxardo nearby, a very good photographer, who took good pictures of both of us. One of my pictures stayed in Rome, and they told me to take two copies to Venezuela. Oddly, these pictures of Tía Carmen are those that remained officially in Opus Dei for posterity, since she died the following year, on June 20, 1957, and I am speaking of an episode at the end of September 1956.

She forgot to give me the rosary, but assured me that she would send it before I left Rome. She did. It was a very pretty rosary with silver filigree. For the sake of clarification, I should mention that the only gifts a member of Opus Dei can keep forever, for which no superior can ever ask, are those given by the Father or by Tía Carmen. However, Mercedes Morado, in a fit of rage, took it from me in May 1966, and never returned it.

I was deeply affected by Tía Carmen's death. We knew she was seriously ill, because they informed all the regions that she had cancer. When I returned to Rome in October 1965, I went to visit her grave, which, by the way, could not be in a more inconvenient spot. I questioned Lourdes Toranzo, who had been with her in her last illness. Lourdes told me that Tía Carmen said again and again that she wanted to die in Spain, but that Monsignor Escrivá would not permit it, and—Lourdes went on—they kept telling her she would stay in Rome and that she should offer it up for the Father and for the Work. Finally after much insistence, she agreed.

"It was horrible," Lourdes told me, "because she did not want to stay and it was terribly difficult to convince her."

The scenes that Lourdes Toranzo described in Rome with such naturalness remained etched in my mind. It made me wonder why Monsignor Escrivá had been so stubborn. Why did he want to rule even over the life of his family and even refuse the wishes of a dying person. I could never understand that cruelty and over the years I still do not understand. Does this not contradict what Vázquez de Prada assures us that Monsignor repeated[1] and that I too heard him say insistently: "I am a friend of freedom because it is a gift of God, because it is a right of the human person . . . ?" Carmen did not deserve to be kept from dying where she wished.

Women's Branch Central Government

The Opus Dei Women's Branch central government is called the *Asesoría*, a term translated into English as *advisory*, and its members *advisors*. This central government was initially headquartered in an apartment at 20, Juan Bravo Street in Madrid.

In 1953 Monsignor Escrivá was deeply alarmed because he sensed that the central secretary, Rosario de Orbegozo, was deforming the spirit of Opus Dei, and that the young Opus Dei numerary women who composed the central government, under her sway, were acquiring a deformed spirit, especially in regard to the *unity* of Opus Dei. This danger he saw not only

---

1. Vázquez de Prada, *El fundador del Opus Dei*, p. 291.

in the central government where the assessors dealt with the ecclesiastical assistants for the Women's Branch, the general secretary, and the central priest secretary, but also in the regional Spanish government, whose directress at that time was María Teresa Arnau.

It is important to keep in mind that Monsignor Escrivá's understanding of unity was monolithic. No divergence from his opinion was allowed. Dialogue does not exist in Opus Dei. You do things because they are done "just so." "Just so" means that everything is carried out according to rescripts, notes, and instructions sent by the Father. No one with "good spirit" dares to deviate a fraction of an inch when the Father gives suggestions. The problem is not exactly fear of disobedience, but a lack of unity. Everything is always based on the claim that "God wants things thus." This monolithic spirit was so imbued in every member that not to live in the Work conforming to the manner indicated by the Father would have been a serious breach against unity.

To strengthen this unity, therefore, Monsignor Escrivá decided that some members of the women's government, including Marisa Sánchez de Movellán, María Teresa Arnau, Lourdes Toranzo, and Pilar Salcedo, come to Rome as simple numeraries. As those in positions of authorities were transferred, the vacant positions were filled with others whom the Father carefully selected.

Every time one of these numeraries arrived, she had a private conversation with Encarnita Ortega by order of Monsignor Escrivá. The session lasted for hours and sometimes for days. We would have had to be deaf and blind to not hear the newly arrived person sob and then see her with red eyes. Frequently, she was requested to write down the matters where she did not measure up to the unity of the Work.

Although we did not know the topic of these conversations, months later, we found out, because Encarnita herself commented on them to those of us who formed the central advisory, explaining that "it was providential" that those numeraries had come to Rome and that the scoldings were necessary "to cut off the evil at the root." By evil, of course, is understood "lack of unity."

We must have repressed any questions we had about this procedure, reassuring ourselves that it was necessary to preserve unity. Today I am forced to recognize that it has an alarming resemblance to Stalin's tactics when he required party members to confess errors of "wrong interpretations" of Communist dogma. Making those persons feel guilty created a kind of dependence on the source of truth—in our case, Encarnita and Monsignor Escrivá.

One could fill books on the topic of Opus Dei *unity*. In Opus Dei the theme of unity is relevant under any heading. It is discussed so frequently because it is considered the treasure of the Work. The chapter entitled "To Love Unity" in the Opus Dei book *Cuadernos*[1] hammers away insistently in every paragraph. "We must love the Work with passion. One of the clearest indications of this affection is to love its unity, which is its very life. Because where there is no unity, there is decomposition and death." You must "care for, watch over the *unity* of the Work, and be ready to defend it from any attack, if that should occur." One could never criticize, much less contradict, Monsignor Escrivá, because that would have meant lack of *unity*. The same doctrine is applied to the counselors in the countries where Opus Dei operates. The regional directress, in principle, ought to accept the approach expressed by any of the ecclesiastical assistants, either counselor or regional priest secretary, lest she be on the brink of a fault against unity.

Clearly, Encarnita was the woman numerary "with the best spirit" in the Work and, further, the one who "enjoyed the Father's complete confidence." There was a halo of sainthood around Monsignor Escrivá. All his old articles of clothing from handkerchiefs to underwear were kept, and it was "an enormous piece of luck" for one of us to get anything that the Founder had used. For example, I still have a pair of very unusual desk scissors that he used until one of the points broke. Curiously, out of habit, I had them in my study until one day, a Dominican friend, Friar José Ramón López de la Osa, who was spending some time in Santa Barbara, criticized those scissors. I said to him reproachfully: "Don't insult the scissors that used to belong to Monsignor Escrivá." No more than three days had elapsed when he appeared at my house and deposited genuine paper scissors on my desk saying, "You can throw out the 'blessed' [he used a different word] scissors of the Founder."

Toward the end of the summer of 1953, Monsignor Escrivá called all the numerary women including the auxiliaries to the kitchen of Villa Sacchetti. Don Alvaro del Portillo was with him. When he was assured that absolutely everyone who lived in the house was there, he said he had a very important announcement to make. It was so silent you could have heard a needle drop.

Monsignor Escrivá informed us that he had been planning for a long time to have the Women's Branch central government "close by" (*cerquica*) to be able to govern in a coordinated fashion. Accordingly, in agreement with Don Alvaro, they had decided that from that day on the Women's Branch central advisory would be established in Rome. He was going to tell us who the new superiors were. The list was as follows:

---

1. *Cuadernos-3*, p. 57.

Directress of Central Government—Encarnita Ortega
Secretary of the Central Government—Marisa Sánchez de Movellan
Vice Secretary of St. Michael—María del Carmen Tapia
Vice Secretary of St. Gabriel—María José Monterde
Vice Secretary of St. Raphael—Lourdes Toranzo
Prefect of Studies—Pilar Salcedo
Prefect of Servants—Gabriela Duclaud
Delegate for Spain—María Luisa Moreno de Vega
Delegate for Italy—María del Carmen Tapia
Procurator—Cathérine Bardinet

The surprise was indescribable. None of us expected this. He said to me personally:

"We are giving you two jobs so that you can carry the weight better like a good little donkey."

He also announced that as Encarnita would now be the central directress, Begoña Mújica, a numerary from Bilbao who had been in the central government in Spain and had arrived a few months earlier at the Villa Sacchetti administration, would now direct that administration. The directress of the region of Spain would be Crucita Taberner.

This central advisory, together with Monsignor Escrivá, the Father, Father Antonio Pérez-Tenessa as the priest secretary general, Don Alvaro del Portillo as procurator general, Father José María Hernández-Garnica as priest central secretary, formed the worldwide central government for the Opus Dei Women's Branch.

Both Monsignor Escrivá (who also belonged to the general council or Men's Branch central government) and the other priests who were part of the central advisory all had a full vote and some of them a veto. The only one of them who resided in Rome, besides Monsignor Escrivá, was Alvaro del Portillo. The others continued in Spain where the general council for the Opus Dei Men's Branch was still located.

According to Opus Dei's Constitutions, responsibilities of these posts are as follows: the central advisory directress under the guidance of the president general and the central priest secretary devotes her efforts to the overall leadership of the Women's Branch.

The secretary of the central advisory distributes tasks among the vice secretaries and other government members and supervises the faithful fulfillment of their obligations. She replaces the central secretary (or directress) in case of absence or incapacity, and prepares the official minutes of the central advisory meetings.

The vice secretary of St. Michael has responsibility for the formation of all Opus Dei female numeraries and associates in any country where there are members of the Work as well as to further any activity related to these members.

The vice secretary of St. Gabriel has responsibility for everything that concerns supernumeraries and cooperators worldwide, both their formation and activities.

The vice secretary of St. Raphael has as her charge the apostolate and proselytism of young people in all Opus Dei houses worldwide as well as to further any kind of activity that leads to an increase in vocations or work with youth.

The prefect of studies has charge of all those matters that refer to education, whether spiritual or intellectual, of ordinary numerary women.

The prefect of servants has charge of the religious and professional formation of servant numeraries.

The delegates' mission is to study problems of their respective regions. They represent the country within the central advisory and in the regional governments they rank immediately after the regional directress and have a vote and veto power in the respective women's regional advisory.

Every five years, the central procurator must inspect the account books of every region herself or by representative, in order to correct any defects and faithfully implement norms set out by the institute's general administration. Each quarter she will receive from the regional procurators statements of accounts, which must be submitted to the scrutiny of the central directress and the advisory. The term of these positions is five years.

To facilitate understanding of the government of Opus Dei, I include a diagram on the following page.

During all the years in which I was part of the Opus Dei government, it was officially collegial but in practice acted at the pleasure of the Founder. To put it more politely, the government was a "directed democracy." Let me give an example: Monsignor Escrivá decided that it was necessary to give major impetus to the region of Colombia and that it would be good to send one of the numeraries then on the central advisory. Summoning Encarnita and myself, he asked us how we felt about assigning Pilar Salcedo to Colombia as regional directress to replace Josefina de Miguel, who had begun the foundation of Opus Dei women in that country. Although Pilar Salcedo then held the position of prefect of studies on the central advisory, we immediately answered that it seemed a very good idea to us.

On the spot Monsignor Escrivá had us call Pilar to the Villa dining room. When Pilar appeared, the Father spoke to her very affectionately, saying that he wanted her to take on the important task of regional directress for Colombia, but that it was up to her to decide. He overwhelmed her with all kinds of flattery: "You know, daughter, what confidence I have in you," "I know you will do good work there, because you

OPUS DEI CENTRAL, REGIONAL, AND LOCAL GOVERNMENTS

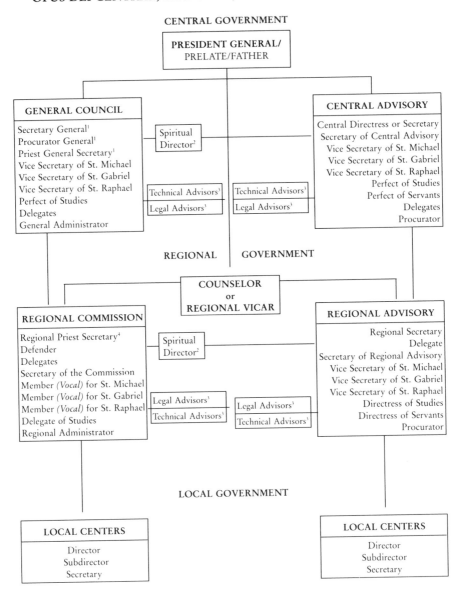

CENTRAL GOVERNMENT

PRESIDENT GENERAL/
PRELATE/FATHER

GENERAL COUNCIL

Secretary General[1]
Procurator General[1]
Priest General Secretary[1]
Vice Secretary of St. Michael
Vice Secretary of St. Gabriel
Vice Secretary of St. Raphael
Perfect of Studies
Delegates
General Administrator

Spiritual Director[2]

Technical Advisors[3]
Legal Advisors[3]

Technical Advisors[3]
Legal Advisors[3]

CENTRAL ADVISORY

Central Directress or Secretary
Secretary of Central Advisory
Vice Secretary of St. Michael
Vice Secretary of St. Gabriel
Vice Secretary of St. Raphael
Perfect of Studies
Perfect of Servants
Delegates
Procurator

REGIONAL GOVERNMENT

COUNSELOR
or
REGIONAL VICAR

REGIONAL COMMISSION

Regional Priest Secretary[4]
Defender
Delegates
Secretary of the Commission
Member *(Vocal)* for St. Michael
Member *(Vocal)* for St. Gabriel
Member *(Vocal)* for St. Raphael
Delegate of Studies
Regional Administrator

Spiritual Director[2]

Legal Advisors[3]
Technical Advisors[3]

Legal Advisors[3]
Technical Advisors[3]

REGIONAL ADVISORY

Regional Secretary
Delegate
Secretary of Regional Advisory
Vice Secretary of St. Michael
Vice Secretary of St. Gabriel
Vice Secretary of St. Raphael
Directress of Studies
Directress of Servants
Procurator

LOCAL GOVERNMENT

LOCAL CENTERS

Director
Subdirector
Secretary

LOCAL CENTERS

Director
Subdirector
Secretary

1. Belong to both General Counsel and Central Advisory
2. Has voice but no vote in
3. Advisory groups to Central and Regional Governments
4. Like the Counselor is also a Regional Advisor

have spent time close to me and know how deeply the Father loves his daughters." Pilar turned red at the news, but was deeply moved by "the confidence the Father was placing in her." Naturally, she agreed to go to Colombia. Monsignor Escrivá immediately called a meeting of the central advisory for that afternoon "to tell the others." When the whole central government gathered with Monsignor Escrivá and Don Alvaro del Portillo in the Villa Vecchia dining room, the Father said that he had called us together to let us know that Pilar Salcedo would leave for Colombia in a few days. Praising that country, Monsignor Escrivá pronounced a sentence that became famous within Opus Dei over the years: "Colombia, my daughter, is the country of emeralds. But the best emeralds are my daughters, if they are faithful to me" (si me son fieles). It is worth stressing that when Monsignor Escrivá spoke about fidelity, he frequently used sentences such as "If you are faithful to me," "Be faithful to me." That is to say, I never heard him say, "Be faithful to the church." He always seemed to be more concerned with fidelity to himself than what was due God.

Returning to the story of Pilar Salcedo's departure for Colombia, Monsignor Escrivá added jokingly that he wanted an emerald "to use as a paperweight," and he suggested how large a stone he would like by a gesture of his hand. If my memory serves me, I believe I heard that years later they sent him the desired gem from Colombia.

Obviously, the government was not authentically collegial. In a collegial system, Monsignor Escrivá would have proposed that a numerary from the central government be sent to another country, giving an opportunity for everyone to ponder the pros and cons. Since Opus Dei claims that its members have the freedom to accept or refuse to go to a country which is not their own, he would have given the interested party at least a week to reflect on the proposed new assignment. A subsequent full meeting of the advisory ought to have had at least a consultative vote to express their judgment. But that is not how things were done in this case, nor when the Father sent María José Monterde as directress to Mexico, Gabriela Duclaud as directress to the United States, Lourdes Toranzo as directress to Italy, or myself as directress to Venezuela.

Government at the Father's pleasure is based on number 328 of Opus Dei's Constitutions. "The Father has power over all the regions, centers, and each member and possession of the institute, which power is to be exercised according to the Constitutions."[1] Before meetings we were alerted to those matters in which Monsignor Escrivá had a preference. There was voting, of course, but mostly on the issue of the permanent incorporation of a member, whether numerary or auxiliary; votes were

1. *Constitutions*, 1950, p. 130, no. 328.

taken on very few other issues. While a member of the central advisory, I never witnessed a single case of disagreement with the Father; I wonder what would have happened if someone had said "no" to one of his suggestions. The truth is that we spontaneously repressed possible questions, because we believed that raising an objection would have been a fault against unity.

Since the advisors' house was not completed, the government meetings took place in the Villa Vecchia dining room. This dining room was familiarly called "the Father's dining room." It was never remodeled and retained the style of the original villa. It had two large windows that opened onto the garden, called Garden of the Villa Vecchia, and two doors, one of black wood which opened on to the villa vestibule, and the other, upholstered to muffle sounds, led to the administration pantry. In the center was a refectory table which could seat fourteen or fifteen persons, two armchairs and a number of high-backed chairs similarly upholstered in "cardinal" red velvet.

There were no drapes or curtains on the Villa Vecchia windows, because the windows were mostly of leaded glass. The small pieces of glass cast pretty refractions into the rooms.

Until the Montagnola, as the central assessors' house was called, was finished, the new assessors continued to live in rooms in Villa Sacchetti. Our cleaning duties were unaltered. The only novelty is that we spent less time in the ironing room and instead worked on what María Luisa Moreno de Vega and I previously had done and which was now divided among all of us as a function of government, since we were all major superiors.

For many months we had two rooms in Villa Sacchetti for our work as assessors. One was the same secretarial room that María Luisa Moreno de Vega and I had used and that Encarnita Ortega and Marisa Sánchez de Movellán now used. The other was opposite the secretarial room and had been the bedroom of a numerary. There were two tables in the room where most of us worked. One was of normal height and the other very low. The only other furnishing was some chairs. It was uncomfortable to work at the tables because we all had to share them, but we made no mention of our discomfort.

Every morning, once Encarnita and Marisa had read the mail from abroad, they gave each of us the letters from the country that corresponded with her, plus a note to guide us in our response. Included, naturally, were the letters directed personally to the Father.

Encarnita frequently entered our room when she needed to comment on something, ask our opinion, or give us instructions.

Monsignor Escrivá frequently came to this work room with Don Alvaro and would talk to us about the spirit of Opus Dei. His greatest concern was to impart the spirit of unity as an indispensable foundation for "good spirit." This refrain may fatigue the reader, but it was the nucleus of Monsignor Escrivá's doctrine regarding the internal functioning of Opus Dei. He spoke about apostolate in very general terms: "We have to carry our salt and our light to all souls." He mentioned Jesus Christ, but as preamble to speaking about Opus Dei. On the few occasions he spoke about the church, he mentioned the work Alvaro del Portillo or Salvador Canals did for the church, but he frequently conveyed the impression of the Vatican's lack of comprehension of Opus Dei. If he spoke of the Society of Jesus for any reason, he always referred to the Jesuits as "the usual ones" (*los de siempre*). When Monsignor Escrivá was photographed with the Jesuit General Father Arrupe, the picture appeared in the Madrid daily *ABC* with the cupola of St. Peters in the background. Monsignor Escrivá was not openly pleased, except that it showed that the Jesuits had to take Opus Dei seriously. Those were not his words, but the context made it plain.[1]

On one of those visits to the office, he remarked: "I prefer a thousand times that one of my daughters should die without receiving the sacraments, rather than that they should be administered to her by a Jesuit."

Frequently he talked to us about cleaning and especially about cleaning his room. He insisted that his room was simply a kind of corridor, which was true in a way. His office, however, was not simply a corridor, nor was the room where he ordered that special glass cases be constructed to keep all the donkeys and at a later stage ducks that men and women numeraries from all over the world sent him as presents. The collection was picturesque and varied. It was based on the story that one day he prayed to the Lord: "I am a poor mangy donkey" and heard an answer from heaven saying, "A donkey was my throne in Jerusalem." Hence, on occasion when he gave someone his photograph, he would inscribe "Ut iumentum" (Like a donkey). During the time that Alvaro del Portillo was Opus Dei prelate he continued the practice. There is no word yet on what the current prelate, Javier Echevarría, will do. Ducks were collected on the basis of Escrivá's saying that as ducks plunge their ducklings into the water to make them learn how to swim, he sent his daughters and sons to do things they had never done before.

---

1. See Juan Arias, *Un Dios para el Papa: Juan Pablo II y la Iglesia del Milenio* (Madrid: Grijalbo, 1996): ". . . at that time [Father Arrupe remembered] the Founder of Opus Dei thought that the Jesuits did not like him, and he used to invite himself for lunch at the General House [of the Jesuits] in Rome, near the Vatican. During those meals, he [Escrivá] would suddenly start crying, embracing, and kissing us" (p. 127).

With one expression or another, he implied very clearly that the church was indispensable, but inefficacious. He was absolutely convinced that Opus Dei was above the church, in sanctity, in doctrinal preparation, and in everything. When he spoke to us about the priests of Opus Dei, he would tell us they were "his crown."

During these visits, he would leave us with the essential points of Opus Dei doctrine and repeated to us many times: "The women who come after you will envy your having known me."

Opus Dei regulations clearly establish that women do not maintain friendship with any priest. However, when it was useful for public relations, he would make exceptions. For example, with relative frequency he used to send María José Monterde, who was from Zaragoza, to visit Monsignor Pedro Altabella, also from Zaragoza, who lived in Rome and had a position in the Vatican. Not only did she go to see him, but each month she took a copy of the Women's Branch internal publication called *Noticias.* The strange thing was that these inconsistencies seemed natural to us because they came from the Father and nobody dared to contradict him.

Monsignor Escrivá's many and often conflicting demands made it difficult to live in his house. A more serious inconsistency had to do with his attitude toward the servant numeraries. On the one hand, he required that we treat "our little sisters, the servants" with special care and to never leave them alone. Yet, on the other hand, he never gave them more than a few minutes of his time when visiting the ironing room, and always in the form of teaching doctrine. Whereas he loved to have get-togethers with the students of the Roman College of the Holy Cross, I never remember Monsignor Escrivá coming on a regular basis to have get-togethers with the servants, quite possibly because he was bored and didn't know how to speak with them. So, I am astonished when Opus Dei biographers praise Monsignor Escrivá's dealings with people of modest station in life, stressing his occasional visits to the favelas on his trips to Latin American countries.

Monsignor Escrivá established a protocol on how to receive visits to the house in Rome, how meals should be served and so forth. The goal was to impress the guests and encourage their future activity in Opus Dei in their country. On the occasion of the visit by a bishop, the Father told Encarnita and me that we should prepare a good meal because the bishop enjoyed eating very much. The Father's exact phrase was, "Daughters, give him enough to eat until he can touch the food with his fingers," and saying this he opened his mouth, inserting his fingers.

Unquestionably, Monsignor Escrivá wanted Opus Dei to be viewed as universal, but all its vocations were Spaniards except in Mexico and a little group in Ireland, without counting one Frenchwoman who was in Rome, and one Japanese woman who spent a short time in Villa Sacchetti, but who abandoned Opus Dei after having lived in an Opus Dei administration in Spain. To demonstrate this universality to bishops who visited the house, the administration would be notified that no Spaniard should be in the Gallery of the Madonna through which the visitor was to pass with Monsignor Escrivá. They would station the few available non-Spanish women in strategic places, so that when the Father came by with that dignitary, Monsignor Escrivá would introduce them saying, "This daughter is French. Cathérine, my daughter, may God bless you." Or, "this other daughter is Mexican. Gabriela, God bless you," and so forth.

Monsignor Escrivá wanted a Mexican, Gabriela Duclos, and a French-woman, Cathérine Bardinet, on the central advisory, simply to give the group a bit of color, but never assigned them any responsible work nor did he consult them. He had innate suspicion of anything that was not Spanish, and therefore surrounded himself with Spaniards in key posts. That was obvious. Even nowadays the majority of Opus Dei key government positions are held by Spaniards.

Encarnita had to make a trip to visit the European countries where the Work existed. Of course, she took the Mexican Gabriela Duclos to demonstrate in Europe and especially in Spain the Work's universality, despite the extremely expensive visa fee that Mexicans then had to pay to visit Spain. Besides, Gabriela was very docile toward her and was not going to cause any difficulties on the trip.

The Opus Dei secretary general, Antonio Pérez-Tenessa, had told Escrivá that the Spanish region would meet the payments due for the construction in Rome, and he never failed for many years. However, at some point during 1954–56, the financial problem of the Villa Tevere construction was resolved thanks to the contractor Castelli, a friend of Don Alvaro. In some way that was never explained to us, Castelli arranged things so that Don Alvaro did not always have to be preoccupied with the construction. In fact, thanks to this gentleman the construction was brought to completion. Naturally, Opus Dei reciprocated to this person who had behaved so well toward Don Alvaro. We only found out about this when a son of the Castelli family made his first communion. Don Alvaro celebrated the Mass in the Opus Dei central house. Monsignor Escrivá requested that the women prepare a sumptuous breakfast in the new dining room at the Roman College of the Holy Cross. The maids appeared in impeccable black uniforms with white gloves. The breakfast was served on the best silver. We supervised every minute detail. "That man deserves everything," the Father insisted, referring to Castelli the contractor.

These stories show that my stay in Rome coincided with the foundational period of Opus Dei. I experienced the entire government reorganization, was present as the buildings grew day by day, and heard the Father instruct us as the first female numeraries under his wing. I witnessed unique events in the life of Opus Dei: the arrival at the Rome headquarters of the first numeraries and numerary servants from Mexico, the United States, Ireland, Argentina, Uruguay, and so forth; the Opus Dei silver jubilee; the foundation of the Roman College of Santa Maria; the establishment of the printing press; and almost daily contact with the Founder, Monsignor Escrivá.

Our government activity, consequently, was not just to legislate but to clear the ground for future numeraries.

Monsignor Escrivá used to call us many Sunday mornings, when there were no workers, to visit the construction site of the Retreat House with him and Don Alvaro. The Retreat House was to be the provisional site of the Roman College of the Holy Cross. I recall that on a few Sundays we went with Monsignor Escrivá alone. Since we were generally cleaning at that time and we wore the required white house coats, he told us to take them off out of discretion, so as not to attract the attention of neighbors who might see us.

We were able to get to know the new buildings that later on we would have to clean.

There are many stories from our visits to the construction site. I will limit myself to a few. One of them concerned the water. Apparently, the neighbors registered formal complaints to municipal authorities, because our house with so many residents had a water consumption superior to that allotted per dwelling in the neighborhood.

I do not know how they solved the problem, but years later I found out that the Roman College of the Holy Cross or more exactly the Retreat House, where the students of the Roman College of the Holy Cross lived, had its own unregistered well.

On another occasion and in relation to the same construction, Monsignor Escrivá told us in confidence that Opus Dei was about to recover the down payment for Villa Tevere. The Father told us that along with the only money he had, the former owners were given "a handful of coins" that came from his mother, with the request that the coins be kept. I subsequently heard from a very reliable source that: "One day in the Roman College of the Holy Cross, Monsignor Escrivá brought out a number of ten-dollar gold pieces called eagles, which have the approximate size of dimes. Naturally, they are now worth much more than ten dollars. They were inside a cloth bag, and there is no doubt about their existence, because we touched them under the watchful eye of one of the priests who was with Monsignor Escrivá. Monsignor Escrivá told us that there were ten thousand dollars, that is, a thousand eagles (although he did not mention the name of the coin). He explained that they had served as a kind of security for the loan for the purchase of the villa and the land. He also said they were his mother's dowry. They had managed to pay the debt and had recovered the coins."

The story does not square with Monsignor Escrivá's tale of how his family had given to Opus Dei their entire fortune, nor how those golden coins were kept throughout the Spanish Civil War.

On other occasions Monsignor Escrivá used our visits to tell us about the Work. More than once he remarked about women's lack of sincerity and complained about how complicated they are: "You are like onions. However many layers they take away from you, there is always another one." Referring to the foundation of the Women's Branch, he used to tell us that he had not wanted women in Opus Dei and that in some very early Opus Dei document he had written: "a difference between Opus Dei and other forms of life of dedication is that it will not have women." He would add to this: "I didn't want you. I didn't want women in the Work. You can truly say it was from God." He would continue: "I began the Mass without knowing anything, and I ended by knowing everything."

Truly the zenith of my fanaticism in Opus Dei was during my stay in Rome and as a member of the central government of the Women's Branch.

On one hand, I undertook my duties with a deep sense of responsibility. On the other, I was very drastic in my first years in the government and very harsh in my judgments, especially toward the numeraries and superiors of the region of Italy.

Region of Italy

At this point, I must make a public *mea culpa* for my harshness toward the superiors of the Italian regional advisory, especially Pilarín Navarro Rubio, who was then regional directress. I appeared on the scene with the sword of unity unsheathed and the letter of "good spirit" and "love of the Father" on my tongue.

In my fanaticism, I concluded that bad spirit prevailed, because in the get-togethers they spoke of public events like elections or about the families of numeraries instead of the Father. I was also scandalized because Pilarín Navarro argued that the maids, as they existed in Opus Dei, should be replaced by a responsible and well-remunerated staff. I passed on this information to the central advisory, which naturally scolded the superiors of the region. Pilarín Navarro was regional directress and María Teresa Arnau secretary of the regional advisors. The latter was one of those whom Monsignor Escrivá did not want to have close to him. Why? Most probably, because she was not an attractive woman, although intelligent and dedicated. After several years in Italy as a regional advisor, she was ordered without the slightest explanation to return to Spain. Instructions were given to the Opus Dei superiors to send her to her family home. Her parents were dead, and her family was undergoing a period of financial hardship. The superiors in Spain were willing to accept her request to return to houses of the Work there, but Monsignor Escrivá said this was impossible. With typical inconsistency, however, when he met her on one of his trips to Spain, he acted affectionately toward her.

The two ecclesiastical assistants for the region of Italy were Father Salvador Moret as counselor and Father Salvador Canals as priest secretary.

The region of Italy was very difficult and very hard. There was no money and no solidly established external apostolate. There was a house in Milan and one in Naples. I visited the women numeraries in Naples. The directress was Victoria López Amo, whose goodness I remember well. In Rome there was only the apartment on Marcello Prestinari street, where the regional advisory lived. The Women's Branch was also in charge of the administration of the regional commission and Villa delle Rose in Castelgandolfo.

Many married women frequented Marcello Prestinari, however, and the apostolate with them went well. The work of St. Raphael was very difficult. It had produced one vocation, Gabriella Filippone, who belonged to a prominent Abruzzi family, although they lived in Rome. The family was also wealthy. Encarnita Ortega was delighted with Gabriella, so much so that she did not rest until she brought her to the central house; she certainly was a lovely person.

We discussed the possibility of a students' residence, which later became the very successful Villa delle Palme, but at the time the apostolic horizon was very cloudy. There were also two German vocations, one of them Christa, who left Opus Dei three years later, and the other was Marga, who had organized a kind of day-care center. This required special permission from the Father, because women numeraries could not hold a child, let alone hug or kiss one, because such acts stir maternal feelings which might undermine our commitment to chastity. Notwithstanding, Opus Dei publishes bulletins on the life of Monsignor Escrivá, where he is shown holding children and even kissing them.

At the height of my fanaticism, whatever the Father did seemed perfect to me. What Encarnita did made less sense to me.

Personal relations among the advisors were good. What was clear is that Encarnita was completely in charge. She and Marisa presented us with government matters already half digested. That is, they made us see that what they suggested was better than what we thought, so we had very little independence. Encarnita had her fixations, and one of them was

Pilarín Nararro. She lost no opportunity to censure Pilarín's lack of "love for the Father," sometimes subtly and at other times directly. She also stressed that Monsignor Escrivá had no confidence in Pilarín.

Encarnita Ortega's "reign" in Rome ended around 1965 as a consequence of the scandal provoked by her brother Gregorio.[1] Gregorio Ortega arrived in Venezuela October 16, 1965, and was deported the following November 12, after having been detained in the suite which he occupied in the Hotel Tamanaco in Caracas. Unquestionably, Monsignor Escrivá was not interested in keeping the sister of the numerary who had caused the Work so many problems. Many years later, Opus Dei sent him to Argentina as a supernumerary; he married there and died a few years ago.

Encarnita was told to go to Spain to speak to her brother. Once there, they made her stay in Barcelona for several years. Then, they sent her to houses of less importance, Oviedo and Valladolid, where she recently died of cancer.

The Father's trips date from this period. We did not know his whereabouts, but assumed that he might be away for a month. During the summer he vacationed in the north of Italy or sometimes in Switzerland. Many times, two numeraries and two servants were taken to attend the house where he was resting. Meanwhile, the male numeraries were at Terracina, the Opus Dei house in Salto di Fondi, and the women numeraries used the "vacations" to do special cleaning, especially in Monsignor Escrivá's room.

The Roman College of Santa Maria

The year 1953 was important in Opus Dei history: it marked the establishment of the women's central government in Rome; it also was Opus Dei's silver jubilee. On September 8, 1953, Monsignor Escrivá wrote a letter from Rome to all members on the occasion of the twenty-fifth anniversary of the foundation of Opus Dei. He celebrated in Molinoviejo.

Two events changed the established routine of the central advisory: the Roman College of Santa Maria was created by Monsignor Escrivá on December 12, 1953; and the Women's Branch took over the press in Rome.

Some of the first vocations from almost all countries came to the Roman College of Santa Maria (*Collegium Romanum Sanctae Mariae*). Teddy Burke from Ireland and Pat Lind from the United States caused great sensation, because Teddy was the first Irish and Pat the first North American numerary. Pat arrived with Theresa Wilson, who was also assigned to the Roman College.

---

1. See p. 2 of this work.

In 1954 the central advisory's house was finished and turned over to us, and so we went to live there and work in the advisory offices. I designed the archives for almost all the offices; work was pleasant, we had splendid light, and there is doubt that the physical comfort brought a more relaxed atmosphere.

The so-called visitors' parlor and the oratory, which was not yet finished, were on the first floor. The *soggiorno* (living room) and a block of rooms for the assessors were on the second floor. On the third floor was the central directress's suite as well as several more rooms for advisors. The central advisory offices were on the fourth floor. All the rooms were well equipped with closets and showers in addition to a sink; the central directress's suite had a bedroom, full bathroom, and a rather large sitting room. There was an intercom in the central directress's room and the intercom was in the hall on the other floors.

Classes for the Roman College of Santa Maria were given in La Montagnola *soggiorno*. A priest came after lunch to give classes in dogmatics and moral theology. There were no books, but we could take notes. It was recommended that advisors who had the time should attend classes. Then, there were classes on the spirit of the Work, its Catechism, and on administration, which the advisors taught by turns, but the greatest burden was carried by Pilar Salcedo and Lourdes Toranzo.

As the number of students in the Roman College of Santa Maria increased, it became necessary to construct the buildings in Castelgandolfo at Villa delle Rose.

Monsignor Escrivá used to come to the Montagnola to speak to the students at the Roman College. At one of these encounters in the Montagnola living room he addressed Pat Lind, the first American female numerary, who could speak Spanish fairly well, and said: "Pat, I have just spoken to your cousin Dick."

Here Monsignor Escrivá explained that Dick was Pat's cousin, who had grown up with her like a brother, and who was the first male numerary from the United States and who, God willing, would be a priest. He went on to say: "He [Dick] says that he has never read that St. Thomas says that blacks have souls. What do you think?"

Pat, with a smile of amusement, answered: "If my cousin says so . . ."

Monsignor Escrivá took this answer with great guffaws, while he repeated: "How amusing! How amusing!"

The truth is that in spite of being such a fanatic, I mentioned this in my confidence as a lack of charity and universality. I was rather indignant at his comments. Naturally, they told me the fault was Pat's, not the Father's.

The students at the Roman College of Santa Maria worked part time on house cleaning, as their class schedule permitted. They had their get-together with the central advisory. The advisors, from the time the Roman College of Santa Maria began to function, ceased to have get-togethers with the administration of the house and the servants.

The Press I: Beginnings

The press, like the Roman College of Santa Maria, was a factor that greatly contributed to change the advisors' work.

Toward the end of 1953 Monsignor Escrivá informed us that just as "our brothers" published an internal magazine called *Crónica,* we had to prepare an internal magazine for the Women's Branch. He suggested as a title *Noticias.* Apparently this was the name of a bulletin that the first Opus Dei members put together to keep members abreast of developments.

Monsignor Escrivá spoke to us often and with great emphasis about work in journalism. He said "We have to cover the world with printed paper." He explained that Opus Dei journalists (men and women) could avoid erroneous information about Opus Dei. He also spoke to us about schools of journalism all over the world and that, in time, there would be one at the University of Navarra where "our people" (*los nuestros*), Opus Dei women and men, could study journalism. He then told us that a miniature press already existed in Rome, run by Opus Dei male numeraries, and that we would have to take it over very soon. Not only would internal magazines be printed there but all kinds of documents and informative material, which "there was no reason to give to outsiders." Here he explained that the men were also planning another magazine that could be given to many people who did not belong to the Work, called *Obras* (Works). He told us that it was practically ready.

As a result of all this, he instructed us to write to the regions requesting contributions for our magazine so we could begin to prepare the first issue of *Noticias.*

He also said the male numeraries would turn over to us a Vary-Typer so that we could learn to use it. When Monsignor Escrivá asked who could assume responsibility for finding a machine for our press, almost in unison everyone answered that I could.

The next day I went out with Gabriella Filippone to look for "a machine for the press."

Exactly what sort of machine? Ah! We didn't know and nobody told us. We began to look for good mimeograph machines, but all of them seemed very expensive to me. We made a summary of those that seemed best, and that night when the Father called me after his supper, I went up with Encarnita to the Villa dining room. Monsignor Escrivá began to ask about the machines we had seen. All my life I will remember that I gave him the most stupid answer conceivable. To his question: "Did you see anything useful that you liked?"

I answered: "Yes Father, I saw a green mimeograph machine."

I spoke with utter assurance.

Monsignor Escrivá's expression was ineffable. When he was able to speak, he shouted at me: "Green! Green! Well buy it, if it serves."

I bought it. The green machine arrived at the advisors' offices, still in Villa Sacchetti. When we began to use it, for weeks our voices could be heard in the corridors as we gazed at the machine: "Bad, bad, bad, bad, good!!"

When Monsignor Escrivá arrived and contemplated "our work of art," he asked: "How many copies does it make per minute?"

We all looked at each other in defeat, and I dared to say: "Father, I don't think this is what you want," showing him the big pile of bad copies and the little pile of good ones.

Monsignor Escrivá looked at Don Alvaro and said to us: "We are going to put a cassock on one of your brothers so he can teach you how the press works."

Directing himself to me, he instructed me, with a certain understandable annoyance, to have the green machine sent back the next day, and that within a very few days, they would turn over to us all the machinery in the Pensionato so that we could run the press by ourselves.

The Father told me specifically that I would be in charge of these machines and that I should look for other numeraries to help me. He also left us an issue of *Crónica* to read.

We began to ask ourselves what numeraries would work on the press. None of the advisors wanted to get involved. They preferred to edit the articles. In sum, they told me to propose numeraries from the administration who seemed best for this type of work. I thought of two who were extraordinarily meticulous, Elena Serrano, whom I knew well from Córdoba, and was very good at photographs, and the other Blanca Nieto, who had learned book binding in Spain. There was another numerary, María, a Catalonian from Vic, enthusiastic and good, whom Encarnita told me to incorporate into our group, which we did.

Telephone Switchboards

While we were making plans to take over the press, Don Alvaro del Portillo had told us a few days earlier that, since I spoke Italian, I would take over the telephone switchboards of the Opus Dei *Procura Generalizia* and the Roman College of the Holy Cross; the job was to be shared with another numerary for whom I was to search within the administration. I selected Julia Vázquez, who was on the local council of Villa Sacchetti as one of the vice directresses of the administration. Julia knew Italian fairly well, because she was in charge of house errands.

The telephone switchboards and the printing press were located in the same area, at the end of the Galleria delle Anfore, so named because its walls were decorated with authentic Roman amphoras unearthed on the Opus Dei property in Terracina. Monsignor Escrivá told us that many Roman amphoras along with other Roman artifacts were discovered on the property, but that they were not going to inform the Italian government about the find. Indeed, I remember seeing many amphoras at Opus Dei headquarters, when they were brought from Terracina.

The gallery opened onto a large area, a kind of irregular great hall. Entering the area one encountered the telephone booths to the right and on the left a small room whose window was totally blocked, because it opened onto the men's house. The room contained an ugly, old sink where we could get water for the press operation and to wash our hands. The main offset press was at the center of this small room. Opus Dei men had already christened the machine "Catalina."

There was a stairway which led to a visitors' dining room next to the entrance of the men's house at Viale Bruno Buozzi, 73. This door at the end of the stairs was one of the "communication doors," subject to the internal regulations for administrations, of which I have already spoken. Shipments of paper were left in the dining room that we had to carry to the press. There were some twenty-five steps to the press room and I hurt my back carrying heavy piles of paper. The back pain periodically recurs to this day.

The windows in this large area were of translucent glass, facing on to Viale Bruno Buozzi. Since they faced the mezzanine floor of the men's house, they could only be opened to an angle of about fifteen degrees, to avoid our being seen from outside.

Don Alvaro and the Father gave me instructions on how to answer outside calls and how to make the connections to the telephones of the persons whom they called. Except certain persons specified by Monsignor Escrivá or Don Alvaro, when someone asked for the Father, we were always to say that he was out of Rome.

Similarly, they gave us a number of printed sheets to record absolutely all the calls we received. The sheets were kept in a folder and given to Don Alvaro del Portillo after lunch and supper by the maid Rosalía López, and to the rector of the Roman College of the Holy Cross, who was Father José Luis Massot at that time, also via the maid who waited on his table at supper. In other words, the rector kept absolute track of all the calls that any person in his house had received, whether or not the call had actually reached the person.

They gave me the names of all the men who lived in the Retreat House so that I could make an alphabetical list to be kept always in the telephone booths. I prepared these lists on the Vary-Typer offset machine at the press. Consequently, both Julia Vázquez and I were informed, first, of the first and last names of all the men in the Roman College of the Holy Cross, and second, of who called Don Alvaro or Monsignor Escrivá. Of course, the silence of office prevented us from speaking about anything that happened in the *cabinas* (Spanish for booths) or in our weekly confidence. Moreover, nobody could enter the cabinas, except the persons who did their fraternal talk with Julia or with me.

Julia and I spoke Italian and we had firm orders both from Monsignor Escrivá and Don Alavaro del Portillo not to answer or speak in Spanish *under any circumstances.* We fulfilled this order rigorously.

I began work at eight in the morning and Julia relieved me after lunch around two to two-thirty in the afternoon. Meanwhile, I performed all the press work right there. During the afternoons, Julia received the confidences of the servants in her charge.

We frequently spoke with the Father or with Don Alvaro for a variety of reasons. I remember one day Monsignor Escrivá called at noon. He began to pray the Angelus with me on the phone, and at the end, when he should have said the ejaculatory prayer, "Sancta Maria, Spes Nostra, Sedes Sapientiae"—since he was in the presence of men—he stopped and said "Sancta Maria, Spes Nostra, Ancilla Domini." When I said "Ora pro nobis," he added laughing, "let them suffer" (*que se aguanten*). Obviously, this was a gesture of preferential treatment for the Women's Branch in the presence of men.

There were no Saturdays, Sundays, feast days, or extraordinary meditations during this work in the telephone booths. They functioned until after eight at night and the installations could not be left alone.

My happiest times in Rome were in the *cabinas* and the press. From Madrid, intelligent, with sparkling black eyes, Julia possessed an excellent sense of humor mixed with an infinite goodness and warmth. She was truly attractive, always impeccably dressed. Her fragile, slender appearance, black hair hid a very mature person. She had a kind word for everybody. You could confide in her without fear that she would report anything afterwards. She was a person of integrity.

The telephones made me concentrate on something different and were a healthy escape from the rest of the house, from the tension of not knowing whether the Father would summon you or not, from the opinions of the different advisors. It isn't that I wasn't happy in Villa Sacchetti, but there were so many people that I felt suffocated. I am not comfortable in crowds and never was. The booths were an oasis of peace. I felt happy every time I closed the door and left the noise out.

A very important milestone in my personal life occurred in 1954. Those of us who had not made our perpetual vows, called the "fidelity," petitioned the Father to waive the time that remained for the required five years and requested that he preside at the ceremony. (According to the Opus Dei Constitutions, all numeraries who are part of the central government, not only have to have made the fidelity, but also have to be inscribed members.)[1] To our great joy, Monsignor Escrivá agreed to this. They notified us that he would wear full regalia of a domestic prelate for the fidelity of some servants who were going to take perpetual vows at about the same time, but would preside at our ceremony "wearing his old shoes." In effect, November 24, 1954, saint's day of Cathérine Bardinet, Monsignor Escrivá received our fidelity in Villa Sacchetti in the oratory of the Immaculate Heart of Mary.

The ceremony of the fidelity involves perpetual vows of poverty, chastity, and obedience for one's whole life, according to the spirit of Opus Dei. After kissing the wooden cross and responding to the prayers set out in the book of rituals, the rings are blessed by the priest and given to the person. Monsignor Escrivá told us that this blessing virtually duplicated the blessing of the rings in the marriage ceremony. The ring belongs to the member already. Mine was the first piece of jewelry I received at fifteen. It was a present from my aunt and uncle in Córdoba. It was a ring that I liked very much because they told me that it was the first present that my uncle gave to my aunt when they were engaged. I still have it. Once the ring is blessed, the priest gives it back to the person. The ceremony ends with *Preces* or official Opus Dei prayers.

At the end Monsignor Escrivá said: "I do not want to end this ceremony without saying a few words" (*unas palabricas*). After this he added that it filled him with emotion to think we had come to Opus Dei in "this first foundational hour." He then spoke of the importance of our fidelity to Opus Dei and that we should conserve the spirit of unity, fundamental for our perseverance in the Work of God. And he blessed us.

The next step was to take the promissory oaths. Days before, Father Manuel Moreno, who was the spiritual director of the Roman College of

---

1. Inscribed members are designated by the Father. They occupy positions of authority or have tasks of formation within Opus Dei. Being an inscribed member involves promisory oaths, which are made by touching the gospels and invoking the name of Christ, swearing solemnly (1) to maintain the practice of fraternal correction, (2) not to desire positions of authority or desire to retain them, and (3) to live the virtue of poverty as in the foundational period. *Constitutions*, 1950, p. 26, no. 20.

the Holy Cross, prepared us for them.[1] These oaths are taken separately and after the ceremony of fidelity. We took the oaths in the Villa Sacchetti *soggiorno*. As a consequence of this perpetual commitment, the oaths involve: 1) *In regard to the institute* sincerely to avoid anything in deed and word which might go against the spiritual, moral, or legal unity of the institute, and to that end, exercise fraternal correction whenever necessary; 2) *In regard to each and everyone of the institute's superiors* a) to avoid saying anything that might diminish their reputation or detract from their authority; and similarly to repress murmuring on the part of other members; b) to exercise fraternal correction with our immediate superior. If after a prudent lapse of time, such correction has been in vain, the matter should be fully communicated to the next highest major superior or to the Father and left fully in their hands; 3) *With regard to oneself* always to consult with the immediate or highest major superior depending on the gravity of the case or the security or efficacy of the decision, any question—whether professional, social or of an other kind—even when they do not constitute direct matter of the vow of obedience, without pretending to transfer any obligation for this to one's superior.

Freedom is *always diminished* by these oaths under penalty of perjury. Although as a prelature, Opus Dei now claims not to have vows, but commitments or contracts with the prelature, the essence is the same: only the names are different.

Days later, Monsignor Escrivá announced that all the advisors except María Luisa Moreno de Vega and myself had been named electors.[2] This omission did not bother but surprised me. I am certain that Encarnita had an important part in the decision, because she never fully trusted me.

The Press II: Projects

Monsignor Escrivá informed us that they had already ordained Fernando Bayo a deacon. Fernando Bayo a painter, now became "Don Fernando." Monsignor Escrivá repeated that they had ordained him a deacon in order to let him wear the cassock so that he could come and teach us in the press. This event was an exception in Opus Dei, because there would be

---

1. Father Manuel Moreno was one of the many Opus Dei priests who left the priesthood. This was arranged quietly years ago. Eventually he married and became a supernumerary member.

2. Female electors have a "passive voice" in the election of the president general. They must already be inscribed members, at least thirty years of age, be in the Work and have made the fidelity at least nine years, be a proven member, have solid piety besides having performed services for the institute, have solid religious and professional culture. All of this is recorded in secret reports, given under oath as to their truth and sincerity, by the regional counselor and the local director. Naturally, Monsignor Escrivá disregarded those rules when he felt like it, which is what he did on this occasion.

no deacons in the future. Monsignor Escrivá further told us that an Opus Dei numerary, Remigio Abad, a student at the Roman College, "on whom we are going to put a cassock soon" (indicating that he was to be ordained a priest shortly) would come to the press to teach Blanca Nieto and two servants all about binding. We chose two numerary servants. Carmen was from the Spanish region of Galicia, and Constantina was Mexican. Both of them were extraordinarily good with their hands.

The machines arrived. They were installed when we were away. Next morning we were like children with new toys.

Monsignor Escrivá came with "Don Fernando," repeated all the earlier statements about his ordination as a deacon, and naturally he told us to pay close attention and that we would soon learn.

When we were alone with Don Fernando, who is Basque, he looked at us gripping his cassock, and said: "They've just dressed me in these skirts to teach you, so come on, learn quickly. This is what I needed in life: to leave my artist's study in Madrid to a person who doesn't know how to hold a brush and wear a cassock to work in the press with women."

I laughed and said: "We are not so bad, even if we are women! For your information, I wouldn't have cared if you came without a cassock to show us how the press works."

The truth is that Fernando Bayo was like an older brother. He was kind, pleasant, good-humored, with admirable practical and pedagogical talent. We all got along very well with him, and he not only taught us to master the printing presses but to love the work and take an interest in it.

The work at the press delighted me. When we received the material from the men for *Crónica* and *Obras,* beyond basic, indispensable instructions, they left it up to our judgment how or where to edit the magazine. However, when we edited *Noticias,* the women's magazine, we had to adjust it to the taste of the central directress, in content, titles, fonts, page layout, and photographs. Encarnita came to the press and would give us orders. All of the instructions were inspired by a magazine to which my friend Françoise de Tailly subscribed for me, *Plaisir de France.* Encarnita wanted *Noticias* to imitate different page layouts in that magazine. This was no easy task, and Fernando Bayo got so sick of it that he told Encarnita off in front of us and said that by agreement with the Father he gave orders in the press and nobody else. When Encarnita left we said to him: "This is going to cost the rest of us dearly."

But we were mistaken. Fernando Bayo told the Father he would not continue to work, if the women at the press could not be autonomous. Monsignor Escrivá paid serious attention. One day he called us and said that he already knew that Don Fernando had scolded Encarnita. But he also said that an independent local council was to be named for the press.

It was made up of me as director, Blanca Nieto as subdirector, and Elena Serrano as secretary.

Although I argued with Elena in the photography laboratory, I was very fond of her because she had all the patience in the world and put up with just about anything. She knew I was fond of her, admired her, and we got along well. The three of us loved the work and put all our effort into it.

There was a sense of satisfaction in this job, but some things surprised me even at the time. For example, one day Don Alvaro came and told us that, at the Father's order, it was necessary to change the punctuation and a few words on a page in the volume of the Constitutions, approved in perpetuity by the Holy See and printed in Grottaferratta. We had to find the same type of paper, color of ink, and bind the volume in exactly the same way, so that the replacement of page and the other changes would not be noticed. I wondered whether the Holy See knew about this, but assured myself that it must. Today, I am convinced that the Holy See was totally ignorant of the fact that the Constitutions that had been approved as "holy, perpetual, and inviolable" had undergone changes. Of course, I kept no record of those changes and cannot say what they were.

Another strange practice was doing over pages of *Noticias* that had already been mailed to the various countries where we had members. Generally, the reason for this was that we wanted to touch up a photograph, perhaps someone in the photo. If the person's name appeared in the text, it was deleted and a few lines were reprinted. The corrected pages were distributed to the countries with a covering note from the central advisory simply saying, "Please, destroy such and such pages and replace them with the pages enclosed. Inform us when you have carried this out."

Obviously, this is the way Opus Dei erases from its archives any *persona non grata*, who no longer belongs to the Work. Therefore it can be said later that "there are no records of that person in its archives." Such procedures duplicate the practices of totalitarian security forces. The difference is that Opus Dei is supposed to be an institution within the church.

While I was at the press, many Opus Dei instructions *ad usum nostrorum* (for internal use) were printed, as were the first volumes of *Construcciones* (Constructions), the regulations sent from the central governments in Rome to be followed in building or remodeling Opus Dei properties. The instructions had to be followed, or one had to explain why they could not be followed.

Similarly, documents like special letters were prepared to be presented to the Pope.

The servants who worked in the bindery were delighted. For the first time in their lives, they did something other than cleaning. The truth is that the group assigned to the press was wonderful.

Since we were in ink all day up to our ears, they made blue coveralls for us, which we found very funny since they certainly were a departure from the customary white housecoat. Don Fernando painted an image of Our Lady on the wall that was a copy of a Ghirlandaio. We began to criticize it one day. He got angry and despite our insistence did not finish it. He treated us all very well and was happy, because they had told him that as soon as he passed a few remaining courses in theology, he would be ordained a priest and would leave the press forever. We joked with him, asking whom we were going to consult if he went away. He always pointed his finger at me.

During the summer of 1956 the central advisory with the approval of Monsignor Escrivá organized a series of annual formation courses which were held in Villa Sacchetti. As the vice secretary of St. Michael I contributed to these courses, giving classes on the spirit of the Work that the central director assigned to me.

One of the numeraries who came from Argentina to these courses was Sabina Alandes, regional directress in that country, and my old directress in Córdoba. One day as I left the press, I met her in a gallery and she said she wanted to talk to me. I stopped to chat. With all the vigor that characterized her passionate temperament she said: "I hope to God they send you away from here. You have become a lamb in this house. You don't know what goes on in the world. You need to get some fresh air, live in the real world. You're dry. I love you very much, and I don't care a bit that you're a major superior and that you riddle me with corrections. You need to know firsthand what is going on in a country and not be satisfied with all the folderol of notes and rescripts."

I knew Sabina cared about me and kept what she said in the back of my mind. I never told anyone about it, because I knew she would be scolded for giving such advice.

Not long afterwards, one evening Monsignor Escrivá called me to come up to the Villa dining room after supper. He looked tired, but he told me he was very happy with the press and added: "Carmen, we will leave you here seven more years. But we won't keep you any longer. Then we will send you out there to work."

Needless to say I went out bubbling over with happiness, and I told the story to all the women at the press. This meant the world to me, a complete Opus Dei fanatic, with extraordinary love for Monsignor Escrivá, happy in my work and knowing that the Father in person had told me that I would be in Rome for seven more years.

Since there is neither good nor evil that lasts a hundred years, according to a Spanish saying, my happiness hardly lasted twenty-four hours. Next day's mail brought news from the region of Venezuela, saying that after

Opus Dei women had had a house there for some time, there was only one vocation, and that financial matters were shaky. Besides, Marichu Arellano, one of the first women in the Work, who was regional directress of Venezuela, was somewhat identified with Rosario de Orbebozo's "crowd."

By then Monsignor Escrivá had already dispatched numeraries formed by him. In Colombia, Pilar Salcedo (who was already in the country) replaced Josefina de Miguel. María José Monterde replaced Guadalupe Ortiz de Landázuri in Mexico. Gabriela Duclaud went to the United States instead of Nisa Guzmán. Marisa Sánchez de Movellán was delegate in Spain. Lourdes Toranzo was regional secretary for Italy. The central advisory had practically disappeared, so much so that Monsignor Escrivá asked us for a person of some stature whom he could bring from Spain to be secretary of the central advisory. As vice secretary of St. Michael, I strongly recommended Mercedes Morado, who was vice secretary of St. Gabriel in Spain. They followed my advice and Mercedes Morado came to Rome without knowing that she came to be secretary of the central advisory. The news had to be given by the Father in person.

I received Mercedes well. I even told Encarnita to give her my room, which had a shower, for the duration of the annual course. Certainly, she did not treat me in the same way when I returned to Rome a decade later.

That morning the mail from Venezuela made me apprehensive. I thought, the only person left is me. But then I told myself that it was foolish to worry, the Father had personally assured me the night before that I would stay in Rome seven more years.

The letter from Venezuela was sent that morning to Monsignor Escrivá's dining room, and I was summoned that very day. I went up with Encarnita. The Father said to me: "Look, daughter, how far was I from imagining last night that this letter was going to arrive today? But, daughter, I have no choice but to think of you for Venezuela. You know well that I wanted to leave you here, and that it causes enormous inconvenience if you should go. Think it over, daughter, and tell me tomorrow."

I was troubled, but said I would think it over. When I got to the kitchen, I said to Encarnita: "I'm not going. I don't want to go to South America. France yes, but not Venezuela."

I could not concentrate on anything for the rest of the day, and that night I dreamt that the whole map from Canada to Patagonia fell on top of me. The fright woke me up.

During Mass and communion I thought about it seriously and made the comparison that if I had been married and my husband had had to go to any country in the world, I would have gone with him. Naturally, Encarnita followed me like a shadow, telling me not to fail the Father because of the trust he had put in me. I should realize that it was God who again asked something different in my life. Finally, after lunch, I went up to the Villa dining room and told the Father that I would go to Venezuela. Then and there the Father told Encarnita that that very afternoon Dr. Odón Moles, counselor in Venezuela, would come with Father Severino Monzó, central priest secretary, to the Villa dining room to meet us and to speak to me.

First of all, I went to the press and told the local council. Never in my life had I seen sadder people. They were very fond of me. Elena Serrano was devastated. But it was most difficult to tell Fernando Bayo. That afternoon he came to solve a few problems. I told him while he watched the pages fall from "Catalina."

Hearing my news, he abruptly turned off the machine.

"You're not going," he shouted, "because I say so and that's it." "Don Fernando," I said, "it isn't Encarnita, it's the Father who has asked me." "Well, people can say no! How can you leave now that you've mastered everything, and I am going to be ordained in a few months? You can't leave; this is crazy!" He was furious and said he would speak to the Father immediately.

The next two days he didn't appear at the press. When I called to say that we needed help, he said: "Call your directress and let her straighten things out."

Finally one day he came, still angry with me. I said to him: "Look, don't take it out on me, because I'm not to blame. It's hard enough for me to leave. Please help the women who are staying."

I was on the verge of tears, and he realized it. It was the last day I saw him. I called the rector of the Roman College of the Holy Cross a few days afterwards, and I said that I was going to Venezuela and wanted to say goodbye to Don Fernando. He replied that he knew I was leaving and that Don Fernando was so furious that they had sent him to Terracina to stop him from protesting.

I was encouraged, however, by my meeting with Dr. Moles in the Villa dining room. He made a marvelous impression on me. His training as a psychiatrist helped him put me at ease, and his evident love for Venezuela was contagious.

Monsignor Escrivá told me I would not go to Venezuela alone but that I should select a numerary I wanted to help me. I chose Lola de la Rica, a Spanish numerary from Las Arenas near Bilbao, who was attending one of the annual courses of formation in Villa Sacchetti. She was in her mid-twenties, petite, slim with black hair and piercing dark eyes. She had a good education, particularly in medicine, for she was a midwife. Mature and serious with a delightful sense of humor, she had great *savoir faire*, perhaps as a result of her comfortable family background. From our first encounter in Rome, we felt at ease with one another. When I proposed that she go to Venezuela, she was surprised but liked the idea.

With the official documents that we received from Venezuela, we arranged for our visas in Rome. Though our papers stated that Lola would teach first aid and I Italian at the Opus Dei's Etame Art and Home Economics School in Caracas, she was to be a member of the Venezuela regional advisory, and I was the new Venezuela regional directress of Opus Dei women.

On September 23, 1956, we left Rome with the blessings of Monsignor Escrivá and Don Alvaro. My heart was full of affection, confidence, and fidelity toward the Father and toward Opus Dei in general. I parted from Rome with all of the tablets of the law memorized, ready to fight for the unity of the Work with all my strength. Apart from this, though, the great force in my soul and bulwark of my hope was the security that come what might, the Father would always believe in me.

María del Carmen Tapia in 1947 when she first encountered
Opus Dei

The statue of the Madonna on the wall of Opus Dei headquarters in Rome separates the women's house from the men's, symbol of the union/separation of the two.

The *Procura Generalizia*, Via del Villa Sacchetti, 30

Barred window on the ground floor of Opus Dei headquarters in Rome

Overview of Opus Dei headquarters in Rome and the Cypress Courtyard

María del Carmen Tapia in Casavieja, Caracas, in 1957

Group of Venezuelan numeraries. *From left to right:*
Mercedes Mujica, Eva Josefina Utzcátegui, Alida Franceschi,
Josefina de Miguel, Carmen Gómez del Moral, and
Maricucha (a numerary from Peru). *In front:* María
Margarita del Corral.

Ut iumentum!
Romae, 1977

LEFT: Monsignor José María Escrivá

RIGHT: Monsignor Alvaro del Portillo (*Ut iumentum!* "Like a donkey!")

Three generations of Opus Dei: José María Escrivá, Alvaro del Portillo, and Javier Echevarría. Photo: Europa Press

Opus Dei emblem: The cross in the circle of the world; the rose symbolizing Opus Dei women. The rose represents a gilded wooden rose that Monsignor Escrivá found on the grounds of a destroyed church during the Spanish Civil War while fleeing the Republican side. Monsignor Escrivá often said it was a sign sent by Virgin Mary that his escape was God's will.

6

VENEZUELA

⚜

Lola Rica and I left Rome on September 23, 1956, with Carmen Berrio, who was going to Colombia. Previously, we wrote to our families in Spain explaining our new assignments in Venezuela and Colombia.

The three of us arrived in Barcelona exactly on September 24, feast of Our Lady of Mercy, patron saint of Barcelona. It was a religious holiday. We went to the administration of Monterols, where years before I had spent several months. My first impression was that the house looked old. Perhaps it was the contrast with the Roman style to which I had grown accustomed. I knew some of the numeraries stationed there, but there were women I did not know, many of them recent vocations. I was delighted to see Mercedes Roig again. She told me that her numerary son, Barto Roig, was now also living in Venezuela, where he worked in the *Textilana* textile factory, which belonged to the family of another Catalonian numerary, who also had been assigned to Caracas.

Since our train arrived in mid-afternoon, they took us to Mass at a nearby public church. When we came back to the house after Mass, it was clear that everyone wanted to hear about the Father and about Rome—it was as if Lola, Carmen, and I had come from Mecca. We were too exhausted to say much, however, and we asked them to let us go to bed.

The next day, Lola de la Rica and Carmen Berrio left for Bilbao fairly early, since Lola's family lived in Las Arenas and Carmen's in Bilbao, and they had to make their farewells. Because my train did not depart until that night, I went to the sanctuary of Our Lady of Mercy before leaving for Madrid.

I recall asking Our Lady's help because I was frightened at the responsibility of becoming regional directress of a country with which

I was unfamiliar. Although I knew the country's basic geography, I had read very little of its history. I read the material Dr. Moles gave us in Rome but still had only vague notions about how the Etame Art and Home Economics School functioned. The students' names surprised me. In contrast with the Spanish custom of placing Our Lady's name, María, before any other: María Lourdes, María Pilar, for example, I saw Etame lists with names like Eva Josefina, Julia Josefina, and so forth. I also noticed that the questions put to the students on religion exams implied a very low level of Catholic education. One example: "If someone dies, what is better, light two candles to a saint or to have a Mass offered for his soul?" I felt very confused, even about the climate. I asked the Virgin to help and guide me.

On my arrival in Madrid, I went to stay in the headquarters of the Women's regional government for Spain, located in part of the building of the Montelar School of Art and Home Economics in Serrano Street, half a block from my family home.

I was warmly received by Crucita and María Sánchez de Movellán and particularly by María Ampuero. Their concerns ranged from reviewing my wardrobe and providing what they thought I might need, to giving me special permission to visit my family in whatever way I thought best. They knew that I had not seen my family for years and thought I ought to leave them and some of my friends with a good impression before leaving Spain. They told me simply to explain to the superiors where I intended to go each day. I was deeply appreciative, because this degree of autonomy was not at all frequent in Opus Dei.

The day after my arrival, Crucita Taberner, the regional directress for Spain, informed me that Father Antonio Pérez-Hernández[1] wanted to speak to me. Don Antonio Pérez was the priest secretary general, the superior immediately following Monsignor Escrivá in rank. Crucita and María told me that María Ampuero would accompany me on that visit. None of them knew why Father Antonio wanted to see me.

That afternoon we went to Lagasca and from the administration we went up to the dining room of the house at Diego de León, 14.

I had great respect and real affection for Father Antonio. He entered the dining room and told us to be seated. He was on one side of the large dining room table, and we were at the end near the window. After asking me about my trip and how the Father seemed, he went on immediately to the task at hand. His tone was serious but not angry. I recall his words clearly. "María del Carmen, a few days ago your

---

1. Years later he left Opus Dei while in Mexico and, because of Opus Dei pressure, was obliged to change his name to Antonio Pérez-Tenessa.

father came to see me. He told me you had written to let him know that you were going to Venezuela. Your mother apparently became ill on hearing the news, and as you are the only daughter and oldest child, your father too was extraordinarily saddened. He asked me if there wasn't some way that you might stay in Spain."

Don Antonio looked at me closely; his countenance was serious, but he did not seem angry. "I told him in so many words that if he did not want you to go to Venezuela, you should not go. He is your father and has the right to have you nearby. Besides, I told him," Father Antonio added, "that whenever you deserved it, he could give you a couple of slaps."

I listened to everything in complete silence. Knowing my father, I realized that Don Antonio's account was accurate. At this point Don Antonio added, accurately again, that I had not been affectionate to my parents, that I had seldom written them, and that I never gave them the kind of news that families like to get.

"But your father is a true gentleman. He came to see me again and said that he didn't want to do anything that you didn't want and much less spoil your career in Opus Dei."

I smiled at the last part, realizing that my father had thought of Opus Dei in professional terms. A minute later I was almost crying as Don Antonio reminded me of how much my father loved me and how little I had returned his love. I had to make an effort not to start crying, because I had always loved my father deeply and it was difficult for me to leave him once again.

Father Antonio explained that he wanted to tell me all this before I saw my father. The date must have been September 27, 1956, since a week later, on October 4, I was due to leave for Venezuela.

We returned to Montelar. I was truly repentant. I must say that all of the members of the regional advisory tried to help me, because they knew that, on the one hand, I had to obey Monsignor Escrivá and, on the other, Don Antonio was right about my obligations to my father and to my family.

In conversation with one of the advisors, I asked whether Don Antonio knew the list of restrictions imposed on numeraries regarding contact with their families. We thought that he must not know them, although this seemed incredible. To cheer me up Crucita and Marisa arranged for a special dinner that night and a get-together with the members of the regional advisory. They asked me how long it had been since I had seen a movie and were astonished when I told them that the last movie I saw was *Botón de ancla* in 1950 during the formation course at Los Rosales. They rented *Ana*, a fine film with Anna Magnani, a great hit at the moment, not only because of her performance, the *bayón* music and dance, but also because the central theme was the perseverance of a nun. The dinner, get-together, and movie were signs of affection and for a while made me forget the difficulties of the day and those that still lay ahead of me.

Although this diversion helped me forget my situation for a while, by the time I went to bed my inner conflict returned. I kept going over what Don Antonio had said, with his genuine sense of charity toward my family, but I could not ignore that Monsignor Escrivá's attitude was quite different, insisting that our family should not be our first concern. I could not help but be impressed with the relaxed, affectionate atmosphere of the numeraries in the Spanish regional advisory. Seeing the movie reminded me of the outside world from which I had been cut off.

Although I had not lived in Montelar enough time to make an objective judgment, and consequently my opinion was impressionistic and intuitive, Montelar and the Spanish regional advisory seemed to me at the time to be the embodiment of how government and family life should be lived within Opus Dei. It was certainly a striking contrast to the cold asceticism of Encarnita Ortega and the women's headquarters in Rome.

The following day, I saw my father at coffee after the midday meal and in the same place as on other occasions. I had not seen my father for more than three years when he came on a short two-day trip to Rome on business. At that time, I went to his hotel room and saw my mother for barely an hour. The situation was so tense and harsh, because my mother refused to speak to me.

Now, in Madrid, and with the permission from the Spanish regional advisory, I had freedom in regard to the number and lengths of visits with my family. I tried my best to be understanding and affectionate with my family. At the same time, though it was hard for me to leave them, my feelings were very different from theirs. For them, I was going away for an unforeseeable length of time. For me, it was the price I had to pay to fulfill the will of God in the mission with which Monsignor Escrivá had entrusted me.

Today, I understand my father's sadness more completely, because I have taken off the blindfold of fanaticism. I believe Opus Dei ought to have treated our families more humanely.

I also saw my brothers. I even went with my brother Javier to the Ybarra home to meet the girl to whom he was engaged. Her mother had just died. She was a delightful girl, who helped my brother enormously during his years in medical school.

I got to visit life-long friend Mary Mely Zoppetti and her husband, Santiago Terrer. During the week, I was with my father whenever he had time or with my brothers. My great regret was that I did not see my mother and did not know how many years it would be before I would see her. My father and brothers argued that it was preferable that I not go home to prevent a painful scene with my mother. Truly, it was an uncomfortable time.

Lola de la Rica and Carmen Berrio arrived in Madrid two days before our departure. On October 4 we left for Caracas with tickets purchased by the women's regional government of Venezuela and by that of Colombia in Carmen's case.

Climbing up the stairs of the three-engined Iberia plane, I said to Lola: "Today is October 4, the day we are supposed to do the *expolium*[1] and with the trip I completely forgot it." Lola de la Rica looked at me and said gravely: "Don't you think it's *expolium* enough to leave our country?"

She was right. One of the stewardesses, Cole Peña, I knew well. She took good care of us. For all three of us this was our baptism in the air, crossing the Atlantic. The first stop was at midnight on the Island of Santa María. The next stop was at San Juan in Puerto Rico. We were astounded by the beauty of Puerto Rico from the air: a blot of dark green against a deep blue sea. All the passengers were served breakfast in the San Juan airport cafeteria. I sat down in an empty seat, and when I looked at the woman across the table, she turned out to be Viruchy Bergamín who lived in Caracas and was returning from a visit to her sick son in Spain. Viruchy was the girl whose family took mine into their house in Madrid during the Civil War. Her father was the architect who built the residential zone El Viso and the Colonia de la Residencia. Viruchy talked enthusiastically about Caracas and described a number of buildings her father had constructed there. Naturally, she eventually asked me what I was going to do in Caracas. I said simply that I belonged to Opus Dei. She very courteously told me that we would doubtless not meet in the city because she did not approve of "those ideas." We never met again, which I regret.

The flight continued to Caracas where we arrived at noon on October 5, 1956. The heat and humidity was so oppressive at the Maiquetía Airport, that I sought shade under the airplane wing. Drops of oil splattered on my red dress, completely ruining it.

---

1. The *expolium* is an Opus Dei custom whose purpose is to provide another way of living poverty. On October 4, numeraries leave on the house director's desk personal items like a watch, necklace, pen, and so forth. The directress decides whether all or only some of these things should be returned.

We went through customs and picked up our luggage without incident. Nobody was at the airport to meet us, which did not surprise us since the mail functioned very poorly in Venezuela then, and we thought that our letter might not have arrived, which was indeed the case. So we took a taxi, or "carro libre" as they are called, and headed toward Caracas on the recently opened highway.

Our first impression of Venezuela was that a military coup might be under way. The highway was full of soldiers with rifles. We did not question the driver. We had no idea of distances, and the trip began to seem interminable after half an hour. Finally, we reached the city which we had to cross to get to the Altamira neighborhood. Our address was correct and we immediately recognized the house from the photographs we had seen in Rome. "Etame" appeared in handsome wrought-iron letters on the wall. It was the name of the School of Art and Home Economics.

A maid came to open the door, but everyone got up from the table when they heard us arrive—they were having lunch. I did not know Marichu, the regional directress, well, but I had seen her a few times. Of course I knew Begoña Elejalde from Bilbao, and it was a delight to meet her again. María Teresa Santamaría, whom I had known in Rome, was also there. I only knew Ana María Gibert indirectly, because her brother-in-law Alfredo Alaiz was a colleague of my father. Nor did I know Carmen Gómez del Moral or Marta Sepúlveda, a numerary from México who arrived a few months earlier to help in proselytism.

They opened the door of the oratory so that we could greet the Lord. I noticed its baroque style. We passed through the central patio. The house charmed me. It was lovely. I suppose I fell in love with Venezuela at first sight. It seemed as though I had known that house all my life, with its central patio, a palm tree in the middle, a fountain at the end, corridors all around with doors and windows to the different rooms. The house was permeated with light. The dining room was in a corner of the same corridor. This house resembled houses in Andalusia. I soon discovered that Caracas is called "the city of red roofs." From the central patio one can see the mountains. A garden of "grama" grass surrounded the house, and a white wall ran around the property. The climate was splendid. I remember how Carmen Berrio went over the doors with her eyes and her hands and repeated: "It's mahogany, all the doors are mahogany."

They brought me to the regional secretary's room, where I left my luggage. Lola and Carmen were given other rooms. That afternoon I met the first and only Venezuelan vocation: Julia Josefina Martínez Salazar. She was finishing economics at the university. Julia was about twenty-seven years old, laughed easily, was tall, dark, pretty, with beautiful black eyes, but was spoiled and tended to be childish. She was the youngest of several sisters, who may have babied her very much when their parents died. It would be unfair not to add here that Julia Martínez changed and matured astonishingly during the years I was in Venezuela. After finishing her university studies, she became a very successful economist. For me, though, Julia's best trait was her humility. Supernumeraries liked her very much. Julia accompanied me on a number of apostolic trips to Valencia and Maracaibo. Her enthusiasm was contagious. Her loyalty was even more so. I was very fond of her and came to admire her. I never saw her again after I left Venezuela and learned with deep sorrow that she had died of cancer on August 28, 1987. Years later, on one of my trips to Caracas, I brought flowers to her grave.

On arriving in Caracas I telephoned the counselor, Dr. Moles. I said that the house was charming. He answered: "It is good that you like your workplace." During our brief conversation, I realized that Dr. Moles did not pronounce his z's in the Spanish style but as s's like Andalusians. He also would frequently interject, "Aha! Aha!" which meant "Yes! Yes!" Both usages, I later found out, showed his attempt to adapt to the Venezuelan manner of speech.

That afternoon José María Peña, who was the regional priest secretary, came to hear confessions. Before he entered the confessional, Marichu introduced us.

Several married women including two older Venezuelan supernumeraries came for confession. When Marichu introduced me, they exclaimed: "You're so young, child, you're just a baby!"

I answered: "Unfortunately that will be cured in no time." I was only 31 and those women were easily twice my age.

I realized that they were upset about Marichu's departure and that I would take over as directress for the country. I realized that the road ahead would not be easy, but I was not particularly frightened or discouraged.

One reason for my confidence was that María Teresa Santamaría was going to direct the work of St. Gabriel with supernumeraries. I felt comfortable because María Teresa was accustomed to dealing with married women, she was intelligent and had been in Rome. Especially at the beginning, this was reassuring.

María Teresa was very efficient. She was the secretary of the regional advisory. We had different points of view, perhaps because I was more fanatic, but I always admired her deeply. She had been a student at the Instituto Escuela in Madrid, and a sister of hers, who died as a child, was my classmate. After a visit to Venezuela from Father José Luis Múzquiz, sent by the Father, it was decided that María Teresa should go to the region of Canada. When she left, Lola de la Rica became regional secretary.

My first encounter with the tropics took place in the middle of the first night when shivering I got up to get my raincoat to use as a blanket, and discovered a winged cockroach some two inches long on my nightgown. Holding my breath I went to the bathroom and grasping it with toilet paper flushed it away. I found out next day that flying cockroaches were not unusual, and flies and mosquitos began to devour my legs. So, I issued my first order in Venezuela to install screens in all the windows, which was common practice there.

Next day Dr. Moles came to celebrate Mass. After Mass, Marichu and I spoke to him briefly. Marichu was preparing to go to Rome that week and had to bring mail and $3,000.00 for Monsignor Escrivá, which in 1956 was a substantial amount.

In two to three days we completed the preparations for Carmen Berrio's trip to Colombia and Marichu's trip to Rome. Carmen Berrio was very attractive; intelligent and rational, she was unable to accept anything she did not understand. I had good conversations with her, and in fact, she returned from Colombia to stay in Venezuela for a while. She was not at all a fanatic.

Marichu did not speak much to me, but restricted herself to official matters. She explained that the Women's Branch paid a monthly rent for the house, which belonged to an auxiliary cultural association of the Men's Branch. I told her about Rome, about the Father, and about unity. I was so full of my Roman training that I simply forgot that Venezuela was not Rome. To make matters worse, I sent a letter to Rome speaking of Marichu's "bad spirit" because of the "deformation" she was causing in the first Venezuelan vocation, who had been spoiled and babied. Of course, I must have insisted that the spirit of unity was lived imperfectly, because of the comment that "The Father resembled Bolívar." It seemed offensive to me to compare Monsignor Escrivá to Bolívar, who was a political leader, while Monsignor Escrivá, by contrast, was a "saint." So I thought in my years as a fanatic in Opus Dei. However, if you can imagine a public opinion poll in Venezuela about who should be canonized, Bolívar or Monsignor Escrivá, it's clear who would win!

It also surprised me that coffee was served after the midday meal every day instead of on Sundays or major feast days as in Rome or Spain. Naturally, some days later, after constant headaches made me vomit several times a day, I understood that coffee is a necessity, not a luxury, in a tropical climate.

Marichu went to Rome, and I know that she was savagely scolded, which was 90 percent my fault. I have not had the opportunity to beg her pardon, as I want to do now. Nobody has the right to do what I did, to judge without knowing the background well. This was the first and last pejorative report that I sent to Rome regarding a member of the Work.

Years later I learned that Monsignor Escrivá gave lessons about things of which he was completely ignorant: how to deal with the customs of a country he had never visited, for instance. Those of us whom he sent to other countries as his puppets danced to the rhythm of the string that tied us to Rome.

Lola and I made our first sally into Caracas to a neighborhood called El Silencio in the center of the city. Despite its name, it is the noisiest part of the city. We had to visit the immigration authorities to arrange for a year's residence permit, according to the visa we had been issued by the Venezuelan consulate in Rome.

A few days later, a different Opus Dei priest, Father Rodrigo, who spent many years in Caracas, came to hear confessions. He had been a priest in the Roman College of the Holy Cross. He was adept at proselytism and acted as spiritual director to a select group of Caracas girls, many of whom belonged to a well-organized association devoted to helping the poor. The association was called "The Santa Teresita Committee," or just "The Committee." Among its leaders were María-Evita and María Teresa Vegas Sarmiento, María Elena Benzo, María Margarita del Corral, and Eva Josefina Uzcátegui. The soul and brains of the committee were the first two. These girls belonged to prominent families. They had begun by going to confession with Doctor Moles, had attended classes at Etame, and now that Doctor Moles confessed and directed mainly married women, Father Rodrigo was the spiritual director of most of them.

Excepting Dr. Moles, who had become a Venezuelan citizen, the other priests were still Spanish subjects. Years later, Father José María Peña also became a Venezuelan citizen.

The Opus Dei women in Venezuela were all Spaniards. Only Lola de la Rica and I became Venezuelan citizens four years later, as soon as it was permitted by Venezuelan law.

When I came to know these girls during the following days, they impressed me quite favorably.

I was soon to learn that Venezuelan women were pretty, refined, and had exquisite taste. This was contrary to the widely held belief in

Spain that South Americans were inferior to Spaniards. There was a refreshing openness between girls and their parents, especially their mothers. This early good opinion has been strengthened over the years; in my judgment, Venezuelan women are sincere, courageous, and capable of confronting almost any situation.

As I spoke with people, I realized that my Spanish sounded harsh and strong. In South America Spanish is much more gentle and musical. So I resolved to learn to speak it as the language is spoken in Venezuela, and acquire new terms, idioms, and expressions.

Caracas: Etame

Schools of art and home economics were preferred by Monsignor Escrivá as the apostolate of Opus Dei women in many countries. In Costa Rica, Venezuela, Colombia, Ecuador, Chile, and Peru, Opus Dei women were founding such schools. These schools were created by Opus Dei to provide girls who were not interested in going to the university with a general education. Until the 1960s, upper-class Spanish and South American families preferred to give girls what they called "cultura general" rather than university training. Hence, Monsignor Escrivá thought that these schools would be a great way to recruit girls from the upper classes.

More than once Opus Dei superiors and priests debated whether professional men felt more attracted by a woman's beauty or by her intellectual achievements. The Opus Dei apostolate in the schools of art and home economics might prepare women for a significant position in society in married life.

In Europe only Spain had these Opus Dei schools. Llar in Barcelona and Montelar in Madrid both recruited many vocations of numeraries and supernumeraries for Opus Dei.

In Madrid, Montelar began at the end of the 1950s. Located at Serrano, 130, in a residential area, on the same site where the house for the women's regional advisory was constructed, the school successfully attracted members of the Spanish élite. Classes were taught in ceramics, philosophy, languages, and cooking. The cooking class became the most popular, because Pilarín Navarro was a superb teacher. Renowned as one of the first Opus Dei numeraries, she was directress of the administration in Monsignor Escrivá's house in Rome and then regional directress of Italy for many years. Later, as the sister of the then Finance Minister in Franco's cabinet, Opus Dei used her to make an impact on Spanish society ladies who attended her classes.

I should add that Pilarín Navarro left Opus Dei a few years later, totally disillusioned about Monsignor Escrivá.

In Caracas, the classes at Etame were only held during the morning. In Ana María Gibert, who had a doctorate in philosophy from the University of Madrid and considerable teaching experience prior to entering Opus Dei as a numerary, we had an excellent philosophy teacher. Begoña Elejalde taught arts and crafts. A real artist, she painted a marvelous mural and exotic birds in the room set aside for these activities. She was the numerary who made all the artistic tapestries for all the houses—for both men and women—in Venezuela. One of her last masterpieces was a triptych for the oratory of Urupagua, the center of studies for female numeraries in Caracas.

Cooking was the domain of Carmen Gómez del Moral, a numerary from Catalonia. These three women and Marichu Arellano founded the Women's Branch of Opus Dei in Venezuela. Carmen Gómez del Moral headed the apostolate with supernumeraries as well as the sewing group, whose members included Opus Dei cooperators. These sewing groups made all the linens for the oratories of the Opus Dei houses in Venezuela according to the measurements given by Monsignor Escrivá through the women's central advisory. Since Rome revised these measurements quite frequently, oratory linens was turned over to poor parishes, and new linens made again for our own oratories.

When I arrived in Venezuela, I lived at Etame. The regional advisory also lived in this house and the advisors doubled as teachers in the school.

Etame was pretty and had all the charm of a colonial house. It was nicely decorated. Much of the credit should go to Dr. Odón Moles, then counselor, who made many suggestions. The classrooms became the numeraries' bedrooms at night. I lived in this charming house throughout my time in Venezuela; later we purchased a more appropriate building for the Etame school, leaving the original house, that we named "Casavieja," for the regional advisory living quarters and office space. This was the first real estate which the Opus Dei women had acquired on their own.

All of the Etame furniture was moved to the new house. Taking advantage of a visit of the architect Luis Borobio, a numerary who was living in Colombia, we requested through the counselor that he design the cover of the Etame brochure. This brochure was the first public-relations effort for a corporative activity of Opus Dei women. It served as a model for many subsequent brochures put out by Opus Dei.

For many years Casavieja preserved the historical roots of the foundation of the Opus Dei Women's Branch in Venezuela—the first vocations had lived there and some numeraries had died there. In late 1991, Opus Dei had the house demolished to sell the lot at a handsome profit. Opus Dei, which is so obsessed with conserving and filing everything that refers to the first times of the institution or prelature and inculcates the notion that "poverty ought to be lived as in the foundational period," has torn down the house where work with women originated in Venezuela, with the object of financial gain.

As mentioned above, Lola de la Rica and I also taught at Etame. An excellent native speaker of French had been hired to teach that language. She had no connection with Opus Dei. The students of Etame were girls between 14 and 18 years old, mostly members of socially prominent families. From my room I could see the girls sitting in the corridor around the patio between classes. On occasion the teachers came into my room to unburden themselves if their class had not gone well or when they were having trouble with one of their students. During class time I generally did not leave the house in case anybody needed me or parents wanted to speak to me.

Most of our recruiting effort was directed at the girls who came in the afternoon. Most of them went to confession to Father Rodrigo. I soon realized that we could not follow the style of proselytism cultivated in Spain, since the girls repeated everything we told them to their mothers. I made an extra effort to meet the families and talk with them, so that they would have a better idea of what their daughters might be getting involved in.

Recruitment during my first year in Venezuela was quite successful; Monsignor Escrivá and the central advisory in Rome were ecstatic with the progress of proselytism. After consulting Dr. Moles, I posed the possibility of a vocation to María Teresa Vegas, who became the second Venezuelan woman numerary. The third was Eva Josefina Uzcátegui, a girl who was well situated in Caracas social circles. The fourth, María Margarita del Corral, came to us after strong opposition from her family. Her mother's brother was at that time the Minister of Health under the Pérez Jiménez dictatorship, and his wife arranged for police surveillance of our house to see whether or not her niece came to visit. María Margarita's parents decided to take her away for several months on a trip abroad, but she came to stay with us on her return. She was an intelligent young woman who was excellent at recruiting and showed leadership qualities. Then Mercedes Mujica, nicknamed "Amapola," who had just turned sixteen and was finishing her secondary education in the Guadelupe School, requested admission. She always wanted to study sociology, but we eventually sent her to the Roman College of Santa Maria in Castelgandolfo, where she studied pedagogy.

The next numeraries were Elsa Anselmi, who was finishing her studies in pharmacy, and Sofía Pilo who was an architectural student. Without question it was a fine group which entered Opus Dei before the first anniversary of my arrival in Venezuela.

While Dr. Moles was still counselor in Caracas, we resolved to send four of the first vocations to study at the Roman College of Santa Maria. They were Julia Martínez, Eva Josefina Uzcátegui, Sofía Pilo, and María Teresa Vegas.

María Teresa was very intelligent, refined, and well read. She had been brought up in prosperous circumstances, which allowed her much travel. Her mother was a sweet woman; her father was very protective of his daughters and suspicious about Opus Dei. He openly and publicly treated me with hostility.

Eva Josefina Uzcátegui was a good, well-mannered girl. She had only a basic education without intellectual or artistic interests of any kind. She was well-placed socially and fond of attending all kinds of parties organized by well-known people. She was popular with men, although never engaged. Her family was not wealthy but, as the only girl in a family with two brothers, all her whims were heeded. She had considerable good will, but tended to be servile with Opus Dei superiors which left her open to manipulation.

Sofía Pilo was an absent-minded intellectual. Young and beautiful, she was a mixture of Jewish and Spanish blood. Though kind and sweet, she was very strong-willed and had difficulty combining her duties in Opus Dei with her studies to become an architect.

After preparations for the trip and explanations about the complexity of the central house in Rome, they all left with great anticipation for the Roman College of Santa Maria, still situated within the central house. I spoke to them of Monsignor Escrivá frequently and with great affection.

María Teresa was the only one who had problems. Her trip to Rome, or more precisely, her return from Rome, made me doubt for the first time the central government's sense of justice and charity and Monsignor Escrivá's love for his daughters. No clarification of exactly what happened in Rome was ever forthcoming; a telegram arrived saying that María Teresa was returning from Rome and that we should meet her flight and bring her to her parents' house because she no longer belonged to the Work.

I immediately informed the counselor who told me to go to Maiquetía.

When I met María Teresa at the airport, she seemed happy but disconnected. She still had her wonderful smile but was like someone out of touch with reality. She did not seem sad to leave Rome, and I asked her very little. On the way back I realized that María Teresa was sedated. At the moment, there was no time to consult anyone, and at the risk of being considered insubordinate, I took her to our house and put her to bed in the quietest and most out-of-the-way rooms of the house.

Dr. Moles came, and we explained María Teresa's situation. We did not know anything specific or if she had been sedated before departing from

Rome. I told him that it seemed inappropriate to bring her to her parents in that state. Dr. Moles agreed. For several days María Teresa got up for a while to eat and went to the oratory, and returned to bed. Meanwhile, we had not informed her family that she had returned from Rome, because of her condition.

After a week, she came to my office and asked what she was doing in Caracas. I told her that she had been ill and that the superiors had recommended her return. We were informed by Rome later that María Teresa had had a breakdown. I listened to everything she wanted to tell me, as did Dr. Moles in the confessional. She came back with an irrational fear of the Father and the superiors in Rome. When she seemed stable enough to return home, Dr. Moles broke the news to her father, who accepted his daughter's illness—assuming she had inherited it from her mother's side of the family. María Teresa made no objection about returning to her family, but there were painful scenes before we were able to explain to her that she was no longer a member of Opus Dei. Years ago, she married, has children, and is an Opus Dei supernumerary.

I tried not to dwell too much on this experience at the time, but it never completely left my mind, raising doubts about the central government's sense of charity and justice. How could they put a sedated person on a plane without telling anyone? They could have waited a few weeks for the crisis to pass, or one of the superiors could have accompanied her on the trip. I had always believed in Monsignor Escrivá's affection for his daughters, so it seemed cruel to let María Teresa travel alone in her condition without the least security. Was it a manifestation of paternal affection to abandon a daughter in that condition, to tell her that she was no longer part of Opus Dei because of a breakdown and to send her back to her family home in such a state? This incident was an alarm, so to speak, that began to awaken latent doubts.

Secretarial Schools

From 1964 Opus Dei began the transition from art and home economics schools to secretarial schools in several countries, including Venezuela. The only recognized school of secretarial studies that began as such was Kianda in Nairobi, Kenya. It opened at the social and political crossroads in the changing status of women in that country. Opus Dei started Kianda and obtained several vocations from it.

During recent years, given the vast changes in education of women all over the world, the secretarial schools as well as the schools of art and home economics have practically disappeared. In a sense, Opus Dei has changed the schools of art and home economics and secretarial schools into secondary schools. In many cases the previous buildings and names remain the same, but the activities are different.

Language School

The only language school for women officially founded by Opus Dei is Seido in Kyoto, Japan.

Casavieja: Women's Branch
Regional Government

When Etame moved, leaving Casavieja to the Women's Branch regional government, it took all the furniture. We refurnished the building little by little.

A supernumerary, Beatriz Roche de Imery, who came to Mass each morning contributed the gray marble floor and even paid for its installation. Luis Borobio designed the stained glass window with the three archangels, St. Michael, St. Gabriel, and St. Raphael, patrons of the different apostolates of Opus Dei. Don Luis de Roche, a cooperator, and Beatriz de Imery's mother gave generous contributions to make the stained glass window possible. Begoña Elejalde and I supervised the artisan's work. I was delighted with the oratory when it was finished: it was truly a thing of beauty.

Dora McGill de las Casas, the widow of the prominent Dr. Herman de las Casas and a supernumerary for many years, presented us with a marvelous polychromed wooden statue of Our Lady. It looked medieval. She was with me when I found it in an antique shop, and seeing that I wanted it for the oratory in Casavieja, she bought it for us. She also gave us the bronze light fixtures for the oratory and embroidered the Opus Dei seal in red velvet on the back of the pews. Dora also donated a delicate set of antique chairs for the visitors' parlor. They needed to be upholstered, which we did ourselves. We also upholstered a good deal of furniture for the Men's Branch, both for the residence and the counselor's house. Naturally, we did not receive the slightest remuneration for our time or work. It is assumed that the Women's Branch of Opus Dei should do things of a practical nature as a way of living unity.

Dora de las Casas, who had been so good to us, ceased to be a supernumerary, because the Opus Dei numeraries paid no attention to her after I left Venezuela. On my last visit to Caracas I went to visit her with my friend Mrs. Cecilia Mendoza de Gunz at the nursing home to which she had moved. She had lost her ability to speak, but her old smile remained.

We spoke to the nurse who cared for her, who said that beside some family members nobody came to see her. When we asked whether a priest visited her, they said no.

Once again I was jolted by the lack of charity—there is no other word for it—with which Opus Dei treats those who cease to be members of the prelature. This lady was extraordinarily generous: she gave scholarships for the Roman College of the Holy Cross and cooperated in every Opus Dei fundraising activity in Caracas, for whatever purpose. When Cecilia and I left her, we realized we were crying as we walked along the street. She died months ago, and I received the news with great sorrow, because I loved her like a sister and a close friend.

In Casavieja, each advisor had her room. I took personal charge of seeing that all the advisors lived comfortably and had what they needed for their work. Lola de la Rica, then secretary of the Women's Branch regional government, had the birds room, which Begoña had painted. Later Eva Josefina Uzcátegui would occupy the room, when she became secretary after Lola de la Rica went to Mexico. I never understood that turn of events. Lola de la Rica carried more than her share of responsibility as secretary of the regional advisory. In addition to our rigorous spiritual regime that included bodily mortification, she devoted considerable time to her classes at Etame School, while running one of the three houses we were directing and also developing the future structure of the Women's Branch in Venezuela. She was superb in every way. She helped me enormously on my arrival in Venezuela and put her shoulder to the wheel in the administrations along with the servants. The houses were large and the help was scarce and inefficient, mainly composed of 13 and 14 year-old girls. More than once Lola had to tell her charges a story to encourage them to work. At other times she had to confront more serious problems, as when she realized one of them was pregnant.

However much youthful vigor you have, it is exhausting to carry such a burden of responsibility every day, and Lola was very responsible. What finally exhausted her were the demands of Don Roberto Salvat Romero, the counselor who replaced Dr. Moles. The new counselor required perfection in the three administrations. Lola was completely open with me, but felt that making a complaint would show lack of unity.

With her consent, we first consulted the women's central advisory in Rome as to whether she could go to Mexico, where the work was more stable and she could rest for a couple of months. So, she went. I corresponded with María José Monterde, then regional directress of the Women's Branch in Mexico, who had been with me in the central government. She told me that Lola was getting better. When it was time for Lola de la Rica to return to Venezuela, I received a letter from María José Monterde notifying me that after consulting her the central advisory had decided to leave Lola de la Rica in Mexico. To be truthful, I was furious, because apart from my great personal esteem, Lola was the mainstay of our work in Venezuela. We did not receive any kind of explanation for this decision. Later I learned that Lola de la Rica had returned to Spain. In conformity with the spirit of Opus Dei, I could not ask anything about the reasons that had led to the decisions.

In the absence of Lola de la Rica, the Woman's Branch central government named Eva Josefina Uzcátegui Bruzual, secretary of the regional government. We got along well. Since she was the second in command in the regional government, I tried to teach her everything I knew, from how to type to write a note. I always kept her informed about everything, so that she could replace me at any moment. Her preparation, however, was very deficient, probably because she had never worked or studied. In all the government activities, I tried to give her and all the other advisors complete charge of their tasks. Personally, I got along well with all the members of the country's regional government, as well as with the directors of individual houses. I also learned in Venezuela to control my explosive temper. I can truly say that the person who arrived in Venezuela and the person who left that country ten years later were two different individuals. Venezuela changed me, thank God. All of the members in the country, especially the numeraries, knew that I loved all of them together and each one in particular with all my soul. That made them confide in me fully and correspond in my affection. They were certain, and rightly so, that I was not going to send a report about any of them to Rome without first having tried to correct whatever it was. My reasoning was very simple. If somebody does something wrong, she is corrected; she recognizes her fault and promises to change. If it is serious, she goes to confession, and that should be the end of it. Why send a report about that to Rome? Except for some extreme case, I wanted to make sure that no one's name would appear in central government records with negative comments. This does not mean that we ceased to inform about what was really important. What I always tried to avoid was to meddle with consciences and personalities. When I was in the central advisory, I saw how easily a person could be judged irresponsibly because of lack of perspective or ignorance often caused by distance and the peculiarities of a country or particular situation. Recognition of my own earlier errors in this regard taught me to act cautiously as directress of the Women's Branch in Venezuela.

Dealing with people, both girls and married women, always attracted my apostolic spirit. To be able to help and give them good advice, to bring their souls nearer to God, and to make their lives better, was always my north star. In addition to personal apostolate, proselytism was a major concern to me in Venezuela. My first year was exclusively devoted to the work of St. Raphael, to push these young girls to take the final step of giving themselves to God in Opus Dei. I was in charge of receiving the weekly confidences of these new vocations at the beginning, in addition to those of the older numeraries. Little by little, according to how they assimilated the customs and spirit of Opus Dei, I would leave those young souls in the hands of the other members of the regional government and of the directors of the different houses, and I gradually concentrated on the internal apostolate of the formation of numeraries and superiors.

Financial management occupied much of my time. It required seeing persons who might be able to help us. This endeavor brought many disappointments and much joy when things came out right.

I had realized from the beginning that it was necessary to acquire another house, since the Art and Home Economics School had to be separated from the living quarters of the members of the regional advisory. When I mentioned this to Dr. Moles, he suggested that I go to speak to Doña Cecilia González Eraso and ask her to donate her house. She lived in the Anauco Estate, which is now a museum and historic landmark.

"What if she says she lives in it?" I asked. "You might then mention," Dr. Moles countered, "that she has another house on El Bosque avenue." "If she says no?" "In that case, tell her to give you 40,000 bolívares [at that time equivalent to $20,000], enough for the down payment on a house."

A visit was arranged for four o'clock one afternoon, and Ana María Gibert accompanied me.

The house and garden captivated me. Mrs. Eraso was charming, and the conversation was easy. I did not know that she was the widow of a Spaniard, whom the communists killed in the Spanish Civil War. She was very pious, very intelligent, and a charming person. It turned out that the girlfriend of her only son was a student in Etame. Ana María talked to her about how good the girl was. Once the social part of the visit was over, I had to bring up the financial matter. With great calm, I explained that we needed a large house for Etame and thought she might want to give us her house. She began to laugh and jokingly said to me: "And where do you want me to go?" "Why not go to your house on El Bosque?" I suggested with aplomb.

She smiled but said no, and I relied on my fall-back position: "Do you think that you might give us 40,000 bolívares to buy a new house?" "Yes, I could," she said with a smile. "I will send the money with my chauffeur in two weeks."

We left with the same ease with which we had arrived.

When we got home, I called Dr. Moles and told him. He could not believe it. He thought we had misunderstood. But, in effect, two weeks later, the chauffeur arrived with a check for 40,000 bolívares. Dr. Moles told me later that he was convinced that I had realized that he was speaking in jest when he had mentioned the house and the request for money. He was surprised to learn of the results of the visit.

For the second major request I approached Napoleón Dupouy, whose daughter was one of our students. The amount was another 40,000 bolívares. We began house hunting in earnest.

Having raised 80,000 bolívares, I began to negotiate the first bank loan for the Women's Branch in Venezuela with the director of the Banco Mercantil y Agrícola.

Our main source of income were the supernumeries' contributions. Each month Beatriz Roche de Imery and her mother sent us some 3,000 bolívares with which we were able, on the one hand, to pay the rent for Casavieja and, on the other, send to Rome at least 1,000 bolívares for the construction of the Roman College of the Holy Cross. We also had to send $300 a month for scholarships for the men at the Roman College of the Holy Cross who were studying to become Opus Dei priests, and another $300 a month to pay for three scholarships at the Roman College of Santa María, whether or not we had students there. When it was all added up, we sent more money to Rome than we kept to live on.

As soon as money came in every month, we would get a check in dollars at our bank. (We had an account in the name of Ana María Gibert, Elsa Anselmi, and myself at the Bank of London and South America in Chacao.) We had been instructed by the Central Advisory that the check should be made out to "Alvaro del Portillo. For the Works of Religion" (Per le Opere di Religione). During the ten years I was in Venezuela we sent him checks of at least $10,000 a year, a considerable sum in those days.

What was more heroic, as I found out, was that as early as in the first three years of the foundation of the Women's Branch in Venezuela, while the numeraries used tooth paste that came as publicity samples to avoid purchases, they sent what for them were large amounts to Rome, even though the sums were less than we sent subsequently for the construction of the Roman College.

Ever since I joined Opus Dei, I had been told that, because we were poor, we could not give alms, but that superiors in Rome took the responsibility of doing so. This was one of many things that I believed with all my soul.

When I arrived in Venezuela and was told that we had to send all the money we could "for the Works of Religion," I was absolutely convinced that the funds were for vast charitable endeavors that Opus Dei would conduct from Rome. I left Opus Dei with that belief intact.

One New Year's Day, as a guest in the home of Dr. Mino Buonomini and his wife, Dr. Teresa Mennini, whom I met after leaving Opus Dei, I discovered that Teresa's father was a Vatican economist and that on Epiphany the whole family was accustomed to go to visit the Pope. Somehow they mentioned the name of the Bank for the Works of Religion (Banco per le Opere di Religione) as a financial institution. I was shocked. The money that we used to send from Venezuela to Rome had been deposited into the account in Don Alvaro's name that Opus Dei had in that bank.

I do not know whether a human being can become more deeply disillusioned than I was with Opus Dei when I made that discovery.

The amounts that arrive in Rome are quite out of proportion to the two or three social projects that Opus Dei has begun in Central America in the last few years; each country where there are such projects is responsible for financing them. The money sent to Rome is not earmarked for such activities; it is made possible by the generous efforts of Opus Dei members who believe in their superiors. Perhaps some will consider me naive, if at my age and at this late date, I still dare ask whether the church knows all this. How much money does Opus Dei receive in Rome and where does it go? What are the activities that Opus Dei sponsors on behalf of the poor, the homeless, and the unemployed?

Among the members of the Venezuela regional advisory relationships were good. Some of the numeraries, however, found it difficult to accept Eva Josefina Uzcátegui as a superior, partly because she had no higher education but also because she would sometimes innocently refer to having moved in the cream of Caracas society in addition to dropping subtle hints about her social successes with the young men of her generation. However, the members in the central advisory in Rome, particularly Mercedes Morado, then central directress, thought very highly of her. They considered that she had very good spirit because she addressed them with great deference and accepted whatever they said, no matter who suffered for it. A good demonstration of that was her appointment as delegate in Venezuela, ignoring the proposal that by request of the central advisory we had sent individually as inscribed members in Venezuela. We recommended Elsa Anselmi as a mature, serious person, with professional experience. (She was then the director of a toxicology laboratory.)

When word came from Rome that Eva Josefina Uzcátegui had been appointed delegate for Venezuela, second in command in the regional advisory, I was deeply concerned, since the country was now in the hands of an easily manipulated person. The position of delegate is very important. According to the Constitutions, she is the second in rank in the regional government. The delegate has a vote and a veto in the regional government and a vote in the central government. She represents the central government to the regional government and is the representative of a particular country, in this case Venezuela, to the central government. I was worried that her notion of "good spirit" meant yielding to the slightest hint from the counselor or the central advisory in Rome. Nevertheless, I knew the importance of unity and recalled Monsignor Escrivá saying: "In Opus Dei great brains are no use because they turn into swelled heads. Average minds, my daughters, are very useful, because they are docile and prepared to accept whatever is told them." Accordingly, I accepted the decision, and during the weeks that Eva Josefina spent in Rome at the gathering of delegates, I worked with Begoña Elejalde to prepare her room, have the furniture upholstered, and organize her closets and filing cabinets in agreement with the rescript sent by the central advisory, where it was specifically indicated how the delegates' rooms should be. We naturally left a bathroom and telephone line for her exclusive use. Her room turned out to be very pretty and quite functional.

What had been a noisy house when Etame shared the building was now quiet. We could hear the song of the "Cristo fue," a Venezuelan bird whose chirp seems to repeat "Cristo fue" (It was Christ), according to legend, a reward for the bird's having perched on the arm of the cross when Our Lord died.

The sessions room of the government was also decorated in colonial style. In it was the statue of Our Lady of Coromoto, patroness of Venezuela, prepared under the direction of Dr. Moles by a Basque sculptor, Ulibarrena, who lived in Caracas. Virgin and Child have the facial features of the Andes Indians. The statues were brought to Rome to be blessed by Monsignor Escrivá.

To let light into the advisory conference room we placed beautiful wrought-iron grills where there had previously been a wall, and the adjoining porch became the living room where get-togethers usually took place and where we watched TV. I tried to have everyone see the news each night and often pretended I did not notice when the allotted half hour had gone by if a good picture or a ballet was on. I wanted these periods to be occasions when everyone could be at ease, feeling that exact observance of a regulation was of less importance than genuinely Christian spirit. When the priests would tell me that I "ought to take care of my sisters," that was one of my applications, not just handing out aspirins for headaches.

Our apostolate was with married women of the upper levels of society, where wealth and power come together, women whose husbands or families were known and respected throughout the country. Our friendship with such persons separated us from the people, from the poor. I believed what Opus Dei told me: that apostolate with the poor was not our task but belonged to religious congregations. Opus Dei's statement of goals proclaims that it should "do apostolate among all social classes, especially among intellectuals." I would note that rather than among intellectuals who cultivate the humanities, who are not usually rich, Opus Dei concentrates its apostolate with technocrats, that is with intellectuals from the sciences, banking, and the law; in a word, with the groups who control the money and power in a country. Opus Dei women do apostolate with the wives of influential men. Yet, I had heard Monsignor Escrivá say frequently: "The poorest people are often the intellectuals, they are alienated from God and nobody cares for them."

It is a fact that Opus Dei houses are furbished according to the social status of the people with whom apostolate is done.

The numerary women dress well without being luxurious. This does not mean that our wardrobe was our own, because by virtue of the vow of poverty, we were always prepared to give up anything the instant a superior might indicate it should be given to another person who might need it for whatever reason. In other words, what I usually kept in my closet was what I used all week long. If a month went by and something was not actually being used, it was given to the person in the house who could best use it. In general Opus Dei numeraries dress better than many upper middle-class women, and Opus Dei houses generally have an atmosphere in which working-class women would feel completely out of place except as a servant. There are, to be sure, places explicitly devoted to apostolate with peasant women or servants.

The essence of poverty in Opus Dei is not "not possessing but being detached." This provokes many objections. I was indeed aware that we moved among upper classes and consequently moneyed people. More than once Monsignor Escrivá told us, women of the central advisory in Rome a propos of the house, "No husband would have given you what the Work has given you."

We had the newspaper delivered every day to all of the Women's Branch houses in Venezuela. Nobody was excused from reading the paper, because we had to be informed about what was going on. I did not want our people to live in the limbo in which I dwelled for so many years in the Work.

Similarly, in the Women's Branch regional government we agreed that we had to begin to read books. We decided to start with the best sellers that people who came to the house talked about. I recall that one of the first books we read was *Exodus*. Afterwards we would recommend the books to one or another numerary according to their interests. Our people began to get out of the dark tunnel in which we had lived for years.

Music also brought new dimensions to our lives. Children in Venezuela learn to play the *cuatro,* a little guitar with four strings, used as accompaniment for folk songs from Caribbean variety to the rhythmical melodies of the interior. Young people still get together nowadays to play the *cuatro.* Particularly during the Christmas season, the *cuatro* is an essential ingredient for the Christmas carols. By now, all our houses had record players that were either gifts or had been brought by the numeraries when they came to live permanently. We always played records on feast days and Sundays when you also have an aperitif.

Weekly outings were absolutely required, although not necessarily in groups. Everyone took advantage of her outing to do apostolate or proselytism. Frequently two of us would be interested in going to the same art exhibit, if we were free and had a car available.

When I arrived in Caracas, only Carmen and Begoña could drive the car, so I ordered all the numerary women to learn to drive and to get their driver's licenses.

I modified the regional secretary's room a little. I had a little closet made in the bathroom and devoted the large closet in the room to the government archives. There was also an IBM executive typewriter and, in a different place in the house, a copying machine and a paper shredder.

"Secure Places"

One constant problem was Opus Dei's obsessive concern for the safekeeping of documents. We received elaborate orders from Rome to have a "secure place" where duplicates of all personal records of numerary, supernumerary, oblate, and servant members might be filed. The originals had to be hand delivered to the central advisory in Rome. The personal sheets on members contained photographs and such standard information as the date of birth plus data concerning incorporation into Opus Dei; since the abbreviation for the Venezuelan Women's Branch was Vf, my record was filed under Vf-1/50. That meant I was the first person who had made the oblation in the year 1950.

These notes were kept in the secure place along with the wills of the numeraries, the Opus Dei Constitutions (on those days when the counselor lent them) and Monsignor Escrivá's *Instructions, Regulations,* and *Letters.* These were documents *ad usum nostrorum,* for internal use. Next to the secret place there was a bottle of gasoline to burn whatever was necessary, in case of emergency. In my own closet in Casavieja, for example, which was in the bathroom, Alicia Alamo, an architect, had dug a hole in the floor, lined it with cement and covered it with a wooden trap door. On top was a mosaic which hid the trap door and was removed to open it.

This device would never have been entrusted to an outside worker. Besides being an architect, Alicia Alamo was an Opus Dei numerary for many years. Subsequently, she became a supernumerary as she needed greater freedom of movement and was feeling suffocated as a numerary.

Codes

A code book was sent from Rome—naturally hand-delivered—to decipher reports. It was a small book entitled *San Gerolamo*, bound as an ordinary volume and to be placed among the other books of the regional director's bookcase. This volume consists of a series of chapters without explanation, simply followed by words. To be specific, there would be a Roman numeral as if starting a chapter, and then Arabic numerals followed by terms such as—

1. good spirit
2. bad spirit
3. orderly
4. respectful toward superiors
5. serious faults against unity
6. faults against poverty

Suppose, for example, that a regional assessor wants to send a report saying that a numerary, whom we may call Elizabeth Smith, has committed serious faults against unity. Then, on a four-by-two inch piece of paper, she would note the country code in the upper left with the number that identifies this note. In the center, she would put, Vf-3/53, which would correspond to Elizabeth Smith, and at the bottom of the paper, the date. On another paper, sent under separate cover, at the upper left the country code followed by the number that identifies this new note; at the right would be the reference (Ref.) to the previous note; in the center there would be only:

IV.1.5

When the notes come, someone opens *San Gerolamo* to chapter IV, section 1 and goes to number 5, where she reads "grave faults against unity." The interpretation is that Elizabeth Smith, the third numerary who made her oblation during 1953, has committed grave faults against unity.

Opus Dei produces mountains of rescripts, notifications, and notes. The curious thing is that the superiors in the central government recommended to numeraries in regional and local governments that these rescripts be used as spiritual reading and that they be taken as the topic for our personal mental prayer. Once more you can see how indoctrination in the spirit of Opus Dei is placed above Christian formation. Obviously, in the central house on the office floor, there was the required "secure place for documents." Once when I was with Monsignor Escrivá in his office and on another occasion as well, I heard him say that one of the walls of his room could be moved to permit entrance into Opus Dei's central secret archives. "It is not that we have anything to hide," he added, but they were family matters that were none of anybody's business.

All this was part of Monsignor Escrivá's obsession with security. He began with the oratories. He frequently stated verbally and left a good deal of written material repeating the idea that: "Our oratories ought to be secure places where no one can enter."

The security of the Opus Dei women's headquarters at Via di Villa Sacchetti, 36, is like a medieval fortress. The main door is armor-plated and has no lock on the outside. To open it from the inside, you must give five turns of the key, which is never left on a table or tray or in a drawer. The key always hangs at the belt of the concierge, that is to say the maid or other person responsible for opening the door. If someone wants to go out, she has to ring a bell next to the door and wait for the concierge to come to open the door. If you have been out, you press the door bell which registers on the bell panel located in the little room off the Gallery of the Madonna; two persons—two servants or one servant and a numerary— come to open the door. Nowadays there is also an intercom at the main door.

There is another entrance called the "service" or "delivery" entrance in the same area, whose street number is Via di Villa Sacchetti, 34. If someone calls at this door, the concierge first has to open the door that opens on the vestibule. Then she opens a door with a little window that opens onto the space next to the street. Then, after turning the key in the lock of the street door and removing the key, she gets behind the door with the little window, which has a large bolt. She slips this bolt and presses an electronic button which opens the door to the street at a distance. The system is evidently quite elaborate. There is a third door for merchants, which opens onto the other street. This part of the building was under construction when I left Rome and I am not familiar with the details of its functioning.

What I am trying to make clear is that nobody, absolutely nobody in Opus Dei women's headquarters in Roma can just open a door and go out.

By contrast in Venezuela, in Casavieja, since the staff was composed of a few, very young maids, who only helped with the kitchen and laundry, we installed an electronic device with an intercom, so that when somebody called I could identify the person and open the door from my desk without having to get up. When someone wanted to go out of the house, the only thing she had to do was to take the key which hung next to the door to open it. The door that opened onto the garden worked like any other door in the house.

During a period when the security in houses was a matter of great concern because of the danger of robbery or rape, I remember that the ecclesiastical assistants advised us to keep guns in the house. Those numeraries who had weapons in their family home brought four or five revolvers and ammunition. I kept them in a drawer of the bureau next to my desk and at night checked the guns. I have never used a revolver in my life, but Elsa Anselmi, daughter of a colonel, knew very well how to handle guns and apparently was a good shot. One day she wanted to know what she should do in case of an emergency, "aim to wound or to kill." I remember well Ana María Gibert saying: "Ay, not to kill, please." The truth is that I was puzzled and told her that it was better that we should ask the ecclesiastical assistants, which we did. The answer was very vague: "At such a moment, do what you can." The revolvers were still there when I left Venezuela.

Many years later, I was talking one day with Raimundo Panikkar and told him this story. He listened attentively and finally said, "The two things are not comparable! How can you compare the responsibility for killing someone with the personal trauma of a rape?"

Wills

Also kept in the secure places at the central or regional advisories are the wills that all members of the Work make when they make the perpetual commitment called the fidelity. On arrival in Venezuela, I mentioned that oddly enough I had not made my last will and testament. We did not write them when we made the fidelity in Rome. There were several others who had not made their wills either. We asked the counselor for a model to follow in making a will. I remember that we each wrote them out longhand. The opening, besides the usual formula identifying the writer, continued with an affirmation of having lived and wanting to die in the Catholic faith along with an explicit statement that the Father had instructed us to include: "I desire that I be wrapped for burial in a simple white sheet." We had to respect Venezuelan law which stipulated that if our parents were alive, they must receive a certain percentage of the deceased's property, the so-called *legítima*. All goods that we could freely dispose of were assigned to two Opus Dei members, whose names were left blank. When the Women's Branch got its own "auxiliary corporation,"

ASAC, about which I will speak below, the counselor told us to remake our wills and leave all our property, except the *legítima,* of course, to ASAC. Monsignor Escrivá repeatedly proclaimed that we had the freedom to leave our goods to whomever we pleased, but that logically it was absurd to leave them to anybody but the Work. The comparison was that a married woman leaves her property to husband and children, not to the husband and children of the neighbor across the street.

However, the comparison is fallacious, because "by the husband and children of the neighbor across the street" could well mean brothers and sisters or a family member who might really need what was ours. At that time I did not know that there are religious orders and congregations that stipulate that their members will their assets in favor of anyone but the order or congregation to which they belong. Monsignor Escrivá always cited as an example of "bad spirit" the case of a servant who had a donkey in her village and in her will left it to some relative. We never knew who the servant was nor what Opus Dei would have done with the burro! The copy of the testaments are sent to Rome and the originals stay in the secure place within the regional headquarters.

When an Opus Dei member leaves or is expelled, her will is not returned. It is hardly surprising, therefore, that one of the first steps that all of us took on leaving Opus Dei was to draw up a new will.

Internal Studies:
Records and Certificates

It is quite certain, and I bear personal witness to the fact, that also kept in the secure place and sometimes in the archives as well are copies of the original final exam grade sheets for each course in Opus Dei's internal studies of philosophy and theology. The original record goes to the central advisory in Rome. These records include the name of the course and the name of each numerary who took the exam with a column of grades from one to 20. At the end of the page the professor of the course signs first, then the regional director of studies, the regional counselor, the regional priest secretary, and the regional directress. Finally the act is stamped with the Opus Dei seal. The official seal to be stamped on those acts came from Rome; in Venezuela it read, as I recall, "Collegium Romanum Sanctae Mariae. Regionis Venezolanae."

In Venezuela we remarked on the extraordinary—foundational—circumstance that as regional directress I signed the page at the bottom, even though I was graded as one of the students of these classes. We knew from the Opus Dei Catechism that these internal studies had recognition within Opus Dei and to some degree outside, because, if a male numerary went to Rome to do his doctorate in a pontifical university, he only needed a maximum of two years to finish his degree, because the internal studies were accepted by those pontifical universities, but not at a state university.

What is difficult to understand is why, despite keeping such records, Opus Dei has been unwilling, when requested by someone leaving the institution, to provide the former member with a statement specifying the courses and subjects they have completed, why in order to deny it, Opus Dei even lies. Furthermore, it neither acknowledges nor certifies that former members of Opus Dei have been professors of regional or interregional centers of internal studies. This is a terrible injustice to those persons who have devoted their time to teach in accordance with Opus Dei's program of studies. If this were the practice of an ordinary educational institution it would doubtless be deemed a breach of professional ethics.

It will be helpful to keep this in mind for in the last part of this book I will discuss what Opus Dei publicly said and wrote about my studies.

An important setback occurred just a few months after I arrived in Venezuela: Dr. Moles came to our house one day after lunch and said that he had just been assigned to Rome to get his doctorate in theology. He was leaving for Rome now that vocations were arriving and there was so much to do. Out of consideration for Dr. Moles, whom I always greatly respected and appreciated, there is no need to describe our conversation in detail. The main point was that he was leaving and that the recently ordained Roberto Salvat Romero was taking his place.

To our immense regret, Dr. Moles left Venezuela and Father Roberto Salvat Romero became counselor. At his first meeting with the regional government, he told us that "Now everything is going to be different, and everything is going to change."

We did not know exactly what he wanted to change, but we all thought that Father Salvat wished to wipe out Dr. Moles' image and establish an Opus Dei image more "by the book."

Dr. Moles was a physician from Barcelona, specialized in psychiatry. Then in his forties, he was very intelligent, exquisitely mannered, tall, and handsome. Though very serious, Dr. Moles was kind and open, with a marvelous sense of humor. He was an excellent listener, patient, well-balanced, and direct. Unlike some Opus Dei priests he was not given to outbursts of scolding persons who failed to understand the institution. On the contrary, his calm understanding always managed to bring people into dialogue. A personal recollection portrays him well: I approached him once with obvious irritation and disappointment because in readying a house for a retreat for a group of ladies due to begin that very morning, I had been left alone the day before by the new vocations: consequently,

I spent the entire night working with no sleep; he listened attentively and looking at me said seriously:

"You know, that was exactly what happened to a friend of mine in similar circumstances." "To whom?" I asked. "To Jesus Christ, when he was left alone by his chosen disciples."

That was Dr. Moles.

Father Salvat was the source of a profound change in our lives. He had a low esteem for Opus Dei women. He did not say that he disliked us, but he let it be known that we had no brains.

Father Roberto Salvat was from Madrid. He had earned a law degree but never practiced his profession. Thin, of medium height, with black wavy hair, not exactly good looking; he could be polite but not refined. He was jumpy, nervous, tense, and chewed his nails. He did not exude peace, security, or calm. I attributed his behavior to immaturity. As regional vicar of Venezuela (then called counselor), he held a lot of power, but he did not help solve regional problems, largely because he lost his temper quickly. He had gone to Venezuela as a layman, went to Rome, was ordained, and came back as a priest to Venezuela to replace Dr. Moles.

I recall the first time we requested to see Constitutions, which, according to instructions from Rome, the regional advisory had the right to consult, he asked sarcastically: "Why do you want the Constitutions, if you don't understand Latin?"

I assured him, as was indeed the case, that several among us knew Latin well. He finally brought us the book, and I had to sign a receipt saying we could keep it for three days. In fact, we were checking the Constitutions in order to query Rome as to whether numerary women could wear short sleeves.

We prepared the regional government sessions carefully ahead of time. Each assessor had a copy of the written agenda. On this occasion, we considered the draft of the note to be sent to Rome. At first, Father Salvat said it was stupid to ask Rome about short sleeves. Father José María Peña, however, told us to send it. The answer from Rome gave us permission to wear short sleeves. However, Father Salvat said: "But you won't wear them."

To my question of why not, he was unable to answer.

Father Peña was the regional priest secretary in Venezuela. That is to say, he was the priest in charge of the Women's Branch. He was from Zaragoza, Spain, and came to Venezuela as part of the group that arrived to found Opus Dei. He, too, was a lawyer who never practiced law. He always tried to understand everybody and was incapable of having a confrontation with anyone. Very much the proselytizer, he treated us all with respect. Truly a man of God, he died in Venezuela a few years ago.

The first Venezuelan female oblate vocation, or associate according to the later designation, was Trina Gordils, a first-class attorney, who lived very close to Casavieja and became a good friend. I spent a good deal of time with her. She assured me that she might have become a Communist because of the love that Communism claims to have for the poor, but that when she read the gospel seriously, she realized that Christ was the one who really loved the weak and oppressed. Endowed with a delightful sense of humor, Trina was profoundly contemplative and applied the spirit of prayer in her own way and lived the presence of God with joy and simplicity. She was an associate for several years, and her apostolic endeavors brought Berta Elena Sanglade to Opus Dei.

Trina had a beautiful face and joyful, mocking green eyes, which always seemed to laugh at you. Though she suffered from asthma, she was optimistic, good-humored, and occasionally sarcastic. She was well traveled and mastered languages easily. In conversation, she made us exercise our minds in a pleasant game trying to catch her subtleties.

Trina was a good person and a meticulous lawyer who did a great deal of legal work for Opus Dei. One task for which I am personally very grateful was her efficient, quick handling of my application for Venezuelan citizenship. I well remember that when the decree of our citizenship had appeared in the *Boletín Oficial de la Nación,* and we had received our brand-new Venezuelan passports, Trina checked them and handed them over, remarking with her usual humor: "Now, my ladies, you are legally authorized to criticize the Venezuelan government."

After several years of being the first associate she informed me that she was leaving Opus Dei to become a Carmelite nun. She had contacted the recently founded Carmelite convent, being attracted to contemplative life. I fought hard to convince her not to leave, but the moment came when I realized that her wish to leave was genuine. She had made the oblation (temporary vows) as an associate and now needed a dispensation of her vows from the Father.[1] Trina did not share our affection for the Father. She said that we frequently put the Father before God and repeated with her habitual frankness that rather than saying "The Father says this" or "The Father says that" or "The Father likes things thus," we ought to say the same, substituting the name of Christ for that of the Father.

My friendship with Trina continued after she went to Carmel. She wrote a beautiful letter to me when I left Opus Dei. I always visited her at the convent when I went to Caracas, something that will not happen again,

---

1. In order for anyone to leave the institute during the period for which the oblation has been made, a dispensation is necessary that only the Father can grant, after consultation with his own council (i.e., the central government) and the regional government. *Constitutions,* 1950, p. 60, no. 98, para. 1.

because God took her in 1991. The memory remains of her contemplative spirit, her sincere and profound friendship, her affection, and her good humor. The last time I visited her and I took some pictures, she alluded to the fact that one of her eyes had remained closed as a result of her recent illness. "Please, my dear, take a picture, where the droopy eyelid doesn't show."

When the conversation became serious, she commented on Monsignor Escrivá's process of beatification: "My dear, before they [referring to Opus Dei priests] never worried about us at all. But since the Father died, all those Opus Dei priests buzz around Carmel, Father Roberto [Salvat] and the others, asking us to pray for Monsignor Escrivá's beatification. They give us pictures and all the stuff they have about him." When I asked:

"Trina, do you really think the Father was a saint?" She answered: "No, dear! How could that man be a saint after all he did to you in Rome? The man upstairs [as Trina always called Our Lord] knows that if he makes it, it will be because of some human trick or because the Holy Spirit was on vacation."

All legal matters were put before her. She was the person who conceived and composed the statutes of the first nonprofit organization, which was called and continues to be called Asociación de Arte y Ciencia (ASAC). Modesty apart, I must confess that the name was my idea. Both Trina and Alicia Alamo were of great technical help to me in the regional government.

With approval of the superiors in Rome and following Venezuelan law, I started a nonprofit corporation on September 7, 1961, the previously mentioned Asociación de Arte y Ciencia or ASAC, a copy of whose constitutions I have managed to get for my files.

I have also obtained photocopies of pages four and five of ASAC's official minutes for November 19, 1962, which describe the opening of the Dairén Residence for women university students on El Bosque avenue, a major Caracas thoroughfare. I attended this meeting. On March 1, 1963, there is another set of ASAC minutes wherein the opening of another residence for female university students, Albariza in Maracaibo, is officially approved. I also attended that meeting.

I also obtained photocopies of pages 14 and 15 of that same book of meetings of the association, which was ordinarily kept in the archives of the Women's Branch regional government. These pages contain false information. ASAC president Eva Josefina Uzcátegui says that I had submitted my resignation from ASAC as had Ana María Gibert. (We were both active members.) The minutes record that everyone present voted and unanimously accepted the resignations. The statement is false. My memory is quite reliable for this sort of detail. At that date in the fall of 1963, I was still regional directress for Venezuela, and I have no recollection that Ana María Gibert had offered her resignation and know absolutely that I had not given mine either verbally or in writing. The minutes with the signatures of a group of numeraries may have legal force, but I am certain that the account was fabricated, probably by request of Opus Dei superiors when I was no longer a member.

After reflection on this episode, I have concluded that in order to get me out of the association without stating the reasons, Opus Dei had to fabricate a date well before my departure, when I was still a member of the Work.

Opus Dei policy is to treat anyone who leaves her vocation or is dismissed as a nonperson, just as might occur in the case of someone purged under a Communist regime. So, in response to inquiries whether from the Vatican or from government officials, the ex-member might as well never have existed, as I will show toward the end of this book.

There is a rule that when superiors leave their usual residence for a short or long trip, they must sign several blank sheets of paper. I recall that before going to Rome the second time I left at least six blank sheets signed.

In the light of various events noted in this book, one of the questions that I still ponder is why Opus Dei has such fear that if a letter is misplaced, someone may discover its content. Why does concern for discretion turn into secretiveness, as shown by the codes to send reports? There is always the undercurrent of fear of being discovered, especially incongruent that an institution which describes itself as "transparent" should have such fears or concerns. Would a mother who discovered that her child takes drugs and wished to inform another child who lives far away, use a system of notes in code? The sorrow of that mother would simply be a motive of compassion, should someone open her letter by mistake.

This preoccupation with secrecy makes me think that affection is missing in Opus Dei. Which is more important to its leaders—sorrow for the faults committed by its members or fear that other people may know them?

This same consideration applies in regard to those who cease to belong to the Work. Opus Dei erases them from both its present and its past. It gives orders to those still inside to not speak about those who left. As far as I know, there are no statistics in Opus Dei about the number of men and women, who have ceased to belong to the Work. There are only figures about the total membership claimed, with rough percentages of kinds of members. They never indicate precisely how many members are numeraries, how many priests, how many supernumeraries, and how many cooperators, though the latter are not legally members of the prelature.

On December 6, 1969, when I was no longer a member of Opus Dei, the superiors modified the ASAC statutes, which practically copy the first one written by Trina Gordils. The visible heads became two supernumeraries and an associate, and as members of the executive committee, the same persons as before.

All Opus Dei pamphlets in Venezuela continue to describe at present the prelature's activities as carried out by this Association of Art and Science.

Nonprofit Organizations

The first step that Opus Dei takes on arrival in a country is to incorporate a nonprofit cultural association. Opus Dei launches all its apostolic projects from these platforms. They allow Opus Dei to operate more or less unnoticed, give it nontaxable status, and are useful in seeking economic assistance. The board of directors of those associations are ordinarily numeraries chosen by the superiors in agreement with the counselor for the country and the central advisory. Once a corporation is established, it is left to the regional superiors to decide whether a particular numerary will resign from the board of directors or continue a member. Hence, the nonprofit organizations are legal tools that Opus Dei uses for its own convenience in all countries where it operates. In the United States, Opus Dei has a nonprofit organization on the East Coast and another on the West Coast. The latter is incorporated as the *Association for Educational Development (California)* under the number D-5381860. As of December 31, 1994 the address given by Opus Dei as the legal headquarters of this association is 765 14th Avenue, Apartment 6, San Francisco, California, 94118. Its chief financial officer, Mark Bauer, declared net assets in the amount of $3,546,056 of which $800,289 has been given by donors, a list of which is stated as "confidential information, not open to public inspection," and land, buildings, and material worth $6,554,466. Although it establishes nonprofit organizations for public consumption, Opus Dei manipulates these legal tools to its own advantage and profit. Some observations are useful here:

a) On the West Coast of the United States the auxiliary corporation *Association for Educational Development* is common to Opus Dei men and women, contrary to Opus Dei's own policy which proclaims: "Men and women are like two different works,"[1] in agreement with its Constitutions. In the year ending December 1994 the tax report of this Association, dated July 13, 1995, does not mention the list of donors as done in previous years. By contrast on the list of donors, presented to the State of California on May 12, 1992, appears Janie Pansini, 2580 Chestnut Street, San Fran-

---

1. "In utraque pariter Operis Dei Sectione, virorum scilicet ac mulierum, eadem est unitas vocationis, spiritus, finis et regiminis, etsi unaquaeque Sectio proprios habeat apostolatus." Cited from Rocca, *L'Opus Dei*, p. 224.

cisco, CA. (This is the address of the Opus Dei women's house in San Francisco.) According to this record, Ms. Pansini makes a yearly contribution of $18,815. This is odd, because the Opus Dei commitment of poverty does not allow numeraries to make any kind of presents to anyone, whether or not they are members of auxiliary societies of Opus Dei. The words of the Founder are clear: "Our apostolate is the apostolate of 'not giving.' It may be, most probably, that Ms. Pansini works for this nonprofit organization, which for income tax purposes (although it is not listed as such) treats her work as a donation. At any rate, the matter is unclear.

b) In the list of donors to this corporation for 1992 were also included *The Woodlawn Foundation* (from Opus Dei in Chicago), *The Clover Foundation* (also related to Opus Dei), and *The Association for Cultural Interchange* (likewise connected with Opus Dei). In other words, funds are simply transferred among Opus Dei nonprofit associations. In the IRS 1994 official report, this information is also considered "confidential, not open to public inspection."

c) Among the directors of *The Association for Cultural Development* continued to be listed two well-known Opus Dei numeraries: Diane Jackson and Kathryn Kelly. The women numeraries work twenty hours a month and the compensation is zero. In the last IRS report, however, Kathryn Kelly received $9,240 a year for five hours work a week, i.e., under $40.00 an hour. It is interesting to note in this 1994 IRS report that on Schedule A (Form 990) they state as "0" the number of employees paid over $50,000 but on Number 26, Part II, page 2, they report as "salaries and wages" the amount of $91,698.00 which implies a monthly amount of $7,641.00 and for payroll taxes $12,337.00 ($1,028.00 a month). Since in Opus Dei nonprofit organizations there are no outside workers and the directors receive "0" income, who are the recipients of $91,698.00?

(d) The name of John G. Layter is also listed as a director of this association with an official address for the IRS 1993 report at 655 Levering Avenue, Los Angeles, CA 90024. By way of background, Dr. John G. Layter, Adjunct Professor of the Department of Physics of the University of California, Riverside, on May 22, 1992, using the letterhead of the University of California, Riverside, wrote to the editor of the *International Herald Tribune* in Paris, assuring him that I had never been a secretary to Monsignor Escrivá in Rome. On being so informed by the *International Herald Tribune,* I personally phoned Dr. Layter and asked him whether he had met me, and, of course, he said no. But, he insisted, he had been told by Opus Dei superiors that I had never been Monsignor Escrivá's secretary because that "would have implied that Monsignor Escrivá was alone in a room with a woman and that never happened." I explained to Dr. Layter that on more than one occasion, when Monsignor Escrivá

asked either María Luisa Moreno de Vega or me to get some thing or other we needed for our work, one of us had been alone for a few minutes with Monsignor Escrivá. I also had to remind Dr. Layter that it is not usual in the United States to write on university stationery on a topic related to religion and much less to lie about an employee of the same university, as this was my case. Quite curiously as an Adjunct Professor of the University of California, Professor Layter's official address is 600 Central Avenue, Apartment 270, Riverside, CA 92507, quite a different address from the one reported to the IRS in San Francisco.

Although there is freedom of currency exchange in the United States, and it is legal to conduct financial operations through foreign banks, it is interesting how this Opus Dei auxiliary operation is set up. Legally established in California, it does all its banking, including loans and mortgages in Switzerland at the Limmat-Stiftung, Patronat Rhein in Zurich about which Mr. Klaus Steigleder has written in detail[1] and most probably another style of Opus Dei auxiliary corporation. No doubt it has a very close relationship with Opus Dei's operations in Switzerland since they lent to the Opus Dei association in California, on October 29, 1981, for "general operating purposes" a twenty year *unsecured* loan of $210,000 at one percent interest. All the dealings of Opus Dei with financial institutions are totally unknown to the majority of Opus Dei numeraries, even to professionals such as Ana Sastre, a medical doctor, who made a sad statement, "in defense of the Father," in saying that "Calvinism was born in Switzerland and it burned more people than the Inquisition. Switzerland is a beautiful country with all the money in the world, especially undeclared monies."[2]

The *Crédit Andorra,* closely tied to Opus Dei, also lent money to the California association in 1989; another uninsured loan payable in 2004. The *Association for Educational Development* received several personal loans, one of them from Dr. John G. Layter's deceased mother to whom he was the sole heir. Other loans came, also uninsured, almost yearly since 1981, from Federico Vallet in amounts ranging from $5,000 to $17,000 "for general operating purposes" at 7 percent interest, payable on demand, and in December 1994 totalling $75,000. A loan from Elisa Herrera in the amount of $35,000 is also uninsured. A curious peculiarity for all these loans is that they are not only "uninsured," but all were received in "cash," which leads you think that all these persons have close connections to Opus Dei.

1. See Klaus Steigleder, *Das Opus Dei: Eine Innenansicht,* 4th ed. (Zurich: Benziger, 1991), pp. 203–11; and Robert Hutchison, *Die Heilige Mafia des Papstes,* pp. 341–46, where the author speaks in detail about Venezuela.

2. See Ana Sastre, "En defensa del Padre," *Panorama* (Madrid) March 3, 1992, p. 13.

Game Preserves

JUNIORS, CLUBS, ACTIVITY CENTERS

Opus Dei recruits young people from schools, all kinds of clubs, centers for extra-curricular activities, and university residences. These centers serve a purpose within their communities, but for Opus Dei they are places to recruit young men and women, adults, servants, workers, and diocesan priests.

The Opus Dei system of recruiting young people is almost identical to the recruitment of members to a sect. Within the church, Opus Dei is what one might call a Catholic sect.

Some thirty years ago Monsignor Escrivá explained to the numeraries in the central advisory in Rome that just as religious congregations had so-called apostolic schools, from which they derived a good number of vocations, so too, Opus Dei ought to begin a similar apostolate, but without calling them "apostolic schools," since Opus Dei's "secularity" prohibited use of religious terminology. The apostolate would be directed to very young girls, "aspirants" was Monsignor Escrivá's exact term. He was convinced that many vocations would come to Opus Dei from this contact with very young girls, especially numerary vocations.

Accordingly, in Venezuela we adopted the American term *juniors* and began to work with young girls. The category included students between the ages of 12 and 14. The term *juniors* was approved by the Opus Dei superiors in Rome and adopted by many other houses of the Work in different countries to distinguish this particular apostolate with young people. Until very recently, however, if one of these girls wished to enter Opus Dei, she could become an aspirant officially at fourteen-and-a-half years, although she was allowed to write a letter to the regional vicar at fourteen. An actual case of how Monsignor Escrivá encouraged the idea of doing proselytism with girls of this age group is that of Alida Franceschi in Venezuela. The daughter of a supernumerary woman, Alida was asked to become an aspirant at fourteen. This child was also the niece of a female numerary physician of the same name. During Monsignor Escrivá's last visit to Venezuela months before she reached fourteen-and-a-half-years, the regional superiors invited her to participate in a get-together with the Father, officially limited to numeraries. The superiors were convinced that meeting Monsignor Escrivá would give this girl the decisive push to become a numerary. That indeed happened shortly thereafter.

An excellent example of this policy is shown in the life of the current Opus Dei prelate, Javier Echevarría. Born in 1932, he became an Opus Dei numerary in 1948, at age sixteen. Two years later he was sent to Rome.[1]

---

1. See, among other places, *El Mundo* (Madrid), April 22, 1994, p. 28.

These youngsters receive a gentle, slow, subtle indoctrination. They are invited to go to an Opus Dei house with a group of their schoolmates or alone, especially on Saturdays, when there are no classes in schools. They are included in all kinds of clubs, whose official literature frequently does not say that the club belongs to Opus Dei, though it may indicate that the spiritual direction is entrusted to Opus Dei or to priests of Opus Dei. According to the interests of different age levels, there are excursions, weekend trips, spiritual retreats, get-togethers, classes in cooking, art, languages, decoration, and computers: anything that may interest girls in these age groups.

There is a well organized system to guide girls of this age group to vocations as Opus Dei numeraries. At fourteen, a girl can be admitted to Opus Dei as an "aspirant" without her parents knowing it. A written request must be submitted in a letter directed to the regional vicar (formerly counselor). The girl gives the letter to the numerary who has been acting as her spiritual older sister or to the director of the Opus Dei house she frequents. During Monsignor Escrivá's lifetime this letter was directed to him. Although the request does not entail a legal obligation and the candidate is free to leave, leaving, however, would submit the girl to intense psychological pressure by her sponsor/numerary and/or the director of the house. When a girl turns 16 years old, if she still wishes to be an Opus Dei numerary, she must write another letter, this time directed to the prelate (Father). They may tell her that she need not write a new letter, but renew the one she wrote at fourteen-and-a-half. For legal purposes of incorporation, what frequently counts in Opus Dei is the time that has elapsed since she wrote her first letter requesting to become an aspirant.

As of this writing, the policy seems to have evolved as follows: at age 16, following the procedures just explained and without notifying her parents, a girl can write a letter to the regional vicar asking to be accepted as an Opus Dei aspirant. Six months later she can receive permission to go through the official Opus Dei admission. A year later, she can receive permission to make the oblation (temporary vows), the first commitment to Opus Dei.

In the English-speaking world, this practice of proselytism with young girls led to a serious controversy to the point that it prompted Cardinal Basil Hume of Westminster to write a strong note setting down rules to be followed in his diocese. This document is probably harsher than any from the hierarchy regarding Opus Dei. His Eminence had the kindness at the time to send me a copy of his note.

Who are candidates for Opus Dei numeraries? Who are the women who possess the requisite qualities?

The answer is: cheerful happy girls belonging to well-known families, not necessarily rich, but well-off; girls without personal problems; healthy, responsible, idealistic, generous, capable of sacrifice for a higher good; if possible, these virtues should be rounded out by a sound family financial situation. Opus Dei considers that by having members from socially prominent backgrounds, it can reach out to many new places and attract more people.

Persons in poor health or with physical defects are encouraged to become associates, not numeraries. Also ineligible to become numeraries under Opus Dei's Constitutions are those persons who have belonged to a secular institute.[1] They may be considered as candidates to become associates or supernumeraries according to their individual situations. These are the rules of the game that the numeraries in charge of the work of St. Rafael must follow.

Although it is not explicitly stated as a criterion of selection, in practice a very ugly girl will scarcely be considered to become a numerary.

As I mentioned at the beginning of the present work, there is an *Instrucción de San Rafael* written by Monsignor Escrivá regarding apostolate and proselytism. This is one of the documents considered *ad usum nostrorum* (for use of members only), which we printed at the press in Rome when I was there and which provided frequent occasion for speaking to Monsignor Escrivá.

Opus Dei Schools

"One of the greatest differences between Opus Dei and religious congregations," Monsignor Escrivá repeated for many years, "is that we will never have schools."

However, Opus Dei opened its first school, Gaztelueta, for boys, in Las Arenas, near Bilbao, Spain, in 1951. Monsignor Escrivá declared: "Gaztelueta is the only exception we will make."

One must remember that children are like clay that Opus Dei molds according to its system. These children begin in kindergarten and continue step by step till they reach the university.

Obviously, my direct observations refer to the Opus Dei Women's Branch. From the time a little girl is accepted as a pupil in an Opus Dei school, Opus Dei will always follow her steps through the different levels of her education, regardless of what country she lives in or moves to. Her name will remain in Opus Dei archives forever. Even if she never becomes part of Opus Dei, the members of the Work will always try to get her to help in some way, whether as a cooperator or with money, donations, or

---

1. *Constitutions*, 1950, p. 36, no. 36, para. 1; *Constitutions*, 1982, p. 18, no. 20, para. 5.

introductions and recommendations. There will always be something that they can request from that alumna.

Opus Dei schools are the springboard for future recruitment. Officially proselytism is forbidden in these schools; what is not forbidden is the creation of an environment that strongly encourages vocations. The tutors will never speak *directly* about vocation to the pupils in their charge, but, since they are Catholic schools, the tutors will underline the necessity of having a spiritual director. The chaplain at Opus Dei schools is always a priest of the Work. In addition, the girls are encouraged to get involved at centers for extracurricular activities, which are also directed by Opus Dei. In such centers the student who is already a member tries to recruit her peers.

Opus Dei girls' schools function within the framework of the cultural organizations. They can basically be divided into two kinds:

A) *Schools exclusively directed by Opus Dei members* as a cooperative work.

B) *Schools controlled by Opus Dei.* They are not officially Opus Dei schools and are staffed by persons who may or may not be members of the Work. They used to be called "common works." In the Spanish magazine *Tiempo,* April 11, 1988, Luis Reyes published an article about the schools that Opus Dei controls in Spain. The rule is that these are single-sex schools except at the kindergarten level.

Opus Dei also operates schools in the United States such as The Heights (for boys), located in Potomac, Maryland, Oak Crest (for girls) in Washington, D.C., the Montrose School (for girls) in Boston, The Willows (for girls) and Northridge Prep (for boys), both in Chicago. All Opus Dei schools operate under the same guidance from Opus Dei superiors.

A Venezuelan example of such an institution is the Los Campitos school for girls in a residential neighborhood in Caracas. The board of trustees of the school usually consists of five members who are obliged to implement the policies set by the Ministry of Education of Venezuela. The members of the board of directors are Opus Dei numeraries, although exceptionally there may be some associates or supernumeraries. The schools' spirituality reflects the system and doctrinal emphasis of the Opus Dei prelature. Some teachers are numeraries, but the board of trustees may hire others who do not belong to the Work.

Los Campitos is well equipped in its laboratories and athletic facilities. The class size is ordinarily 30 pupils. Pascuita Basalo, a well-known ballet teacher, taught ballet there for many years, but the teaching of the fine arts is weak. The library is inadequate, and the selection of books, particularly in the humanities, is controlled by Opus Dei directors, a common practice at the Work's other educational endeavors. Even in the Opus Dei

University of Navarre in Pamplona, books considered dangerous by Opus Dei authorities are removed from the university libraries and kept in "hell," as the students call the storeroom in the cellar of that institution.

Bookkeepers do not necessarily belong to Opus Dei, and janitors and cafeteria workers have no connection with the Work.

The cornerstone of Opus Dei schools, the faculty tutors are all numeraries whose mission is to serve as a bridge between the school and the girls' families. Each tutor has a small office where the pupils who have been assigned to her can come to talk whenever they want, consulting her on anything from the classwork to God. Each month the tutor speaks to the parents or guardians of her pupils about their behavior and progress in class.

As a numerary, the tutor has great authority over the pupil whom she guides and counsels and the pupils trust and obey the tutor blindly, assuming the tutor is her best friend within the school. This blind confidence gives the tutor vast influence over the pupil to touch on all kinds of topics, whether study, family, or spiritual life. The girls discuss apostolate with their tutors, and in agreement with them attend get-togethers, clubs, days of recollection, and other events organized by the centers of extracurricular activities that Opus Dei directs. Needless to say, before a pupil from Los Campitos arrives at one of these Opus Dei centers for the first time, its director has received a note from the tutor with detailed information on the pupil, including an indication about whether she can or cannot be a future numerary.

The tutor also urges pupils to participate in direct apostolate. The most popular variety is to visit villages in the Venezuelan hinterland in order to assist modest families by teaching catechism or reading and writing. The pupils do not give any kind of present to these families. If they bring clothing or some other thing to the villages, they sell it at very low prices. With the money, the pupils might buy Catechisms, which they later would distribute free.

This is one of the apostolates that the tutors usually recommends to the pupils to be carried out primarily during vacations. Hence, contact is maintained between tutor and pupil even when school is not in session.

UNIVERSITY RESIDENCES: ORIGIN AND GOALS

It would be virtually impossible to speak of Opus Dei residences without first explaining the motive which impelled Monsignor Escrivá to begin his intellectual apostolates.

Monsignor Escrivá wanted to lead a reorientation of intellectual Spain, which had been dominated by anti-clerical liberals. He wanted to show that intellectuals can also be believers; he wanted to develop a group of intellectuals with a life of complete dedication to Christ. He wanted these new intellectuals to place the cross of Christ above all human activities.

A. THE *INSTITUCIÓN LIBRE DE ENSEÑAZA*

Monsignor Escrivá's ideal was good and ambitious, but there was a difficulty at its very root. He wanted to be the leader of this group, the only leader. As in any sect, the leader, the group's founder comes to believe that he is the only one able to communicate the message received from on high to the whole world. So, it was crucial for Monsignor Escrivá to begin his work with a residence, converting young intellectuals into disciples of Christ; he had to mold a group under his direction to make a better world. He led the majority of the original members of Opus Dei to believe that everything that he started was divinely inspired. To only a few members he expressed a more intimate desire to wage a crusade against the Institución Libre de Enseñanza,[1] founded in 1876 by Francisco Giner de los Ríos, a bold defender of freedom in culture and the humanities, who never invoked freedom for political or sectarian reasons.[2] Curiously, Monsignor Escrivá's crusade to neutralize the Institución Libre de Enseñanza ended by imitating its projects. One of them was the Junta de Ampliación de Estudios (Board for Advanced Research), which ran the still famous Pinar Residence. This residence was directed by a foundation whose president was Ramón Menéndez-Pidal and included José Ortega y Gasset among its members. The residence was famous in Spain because it housed not only students from the different departments of the University of Madrid but also Spanish intellectuals, poets, scientists, philosophers—many of them of world renown like Miguel de Unamuno, Federico García Lorca, Federico de Onis, Juan Negrín, and Calandre. It also opened its doors to foreign scholars like Albert Einstein, H. G. Wells, Henri Bergson, Paul Válery, Marie Curie, Paul Claudel, Charles Edouard Jeanneret (Le Corbusier), Darius Milhaud, and Maurice Ravel.

Its multicultural atmosphere made the Pinar Residence a place for discussions and encounters of such intellectuals and artists. There is no doubt that Father Escrivá wanted to create this type of residence, but it is impossible to equate Monsignor Escrivá's goals and his religious crusade with the intellectual approach of Menéndez Pidal and Ortega y Gasset. The defect and in a way the failure of the Opus Dei residences is that they never sheltered people of the same intellectual stature as the Pinar, quite possibly because Monsignor Escrivá was not himself a thinker of such intellectual caliber.

1. See Vincente Cacho Viú, *La Institución Libre de Enseñanza* (Madrid: Rialp, 1962).
2. See Francisco Giner de los Ríos, *La verdadera descentralización de la Enseñanza.*

B. BOARD FOR ADVANCED RESEARCH AND
COUNCIL OF SCIENTIFIC RESEARCH
(*JUNTA DE AMPLIACIÓN DE ESTUDIOS.*
CONSEJO SUPERIOR DE INVESTIGACIONES CIENTÍFICAS)

The Board for Advanced Research created the Pegagogical Museum and the Casa del Niño (House of the Child) in Madrid and the College of Spain at the University of Paris.

General Franco's government abolished the Junta de Ampliación de Estudios at the end of the Spanish Civil War. José Ibañez-Martín, the Franco regime's new Minister of National Education, founded the Consejo Superior de Investigaciones Científicas (High Council for Scientific Research) to replace it. This was lucky for Monsignor Escrivá, who was at once able to place Opus Dei under the wing of this new institution. One of the first numeraries, José María Albareda, was a close friend of Ibáñez-Martín and was appointed general secretary of the CSIC. The maneuver was extraordinarily discreet. Albareda and Escrivá were able to place their first young intellectuals in key posts in the fledgling CSIC. They were able to begin their intellectual apostolate via the new high council. We next encounter the names of Rafael de Balbín as director of *Arbor,* the general cultural journal of the CSIC, and Raimundo Panikkar as the associate director of this journal. Interestingly, Panikkar vividly recalls the meeting that took place within Opus Dei and how he thought of the name *Arbor,* symbolizing the many branches of that organization: the seal of the tree of wisdom became and continues to be the official seal of the CSIC. Rafael Calvo Serer, Florentino Pérez Embid, Tomás Alvira, and so forth, all of them original Opus Dei numeraries, were the leading intellectual figures of the new Spain. Named as architects for the new buildings were Miguel Fisac and Ricardo Vallespín, also from the first group of numeraries.

The Consejo Superior de Investigaciones Científicas was Monsignor Escrivá's most important tool in appealing to intellectuals. Opus Dei still has a strong control of it. Fairly recently, for instance, the Church of the Holy Spirit, which belonged to the CSIC, has been transferred to Opus Dei as one of its public churches. Grants for study abroad, especially at the College of Spain, as well as support in favor of people competing for professorial chairs at Spanish universities often emanated from someone at the CSIC.

This was the background of the situation which surprised me when I began to work at the Council for Scientific Research (CSIC) and discovered the proliferation of Opus Dei members within its walls.

The obsession to demonstrate Opus Dei secularity prohibits residences or corporative activities of the Work from ever being named after a saint.

They usually bear the name of the street or neighborhood where the residence is located. Zurburán was the first Opus Dei women's residence in Madrid, because it was located at number 26 Zurburán street in Madrid. Although the location has changed to Victor de la Serna, 13, the name is the same.

Student residences are places where Opus Dei women primarily do proselytism with female university students between the ages of 18 to 24. When this activity started, residences had a capacity of about 30 students, and existing buildings were adapted for this purpose. Today, Opus Dei erects new buildings for both men and women, using its own architects if possible. About a year before the first Spanish edition of this book appeared, a Venezuelan numerary woman died in an accident during the construction of a new house which was finished recently in Caracas and which houses the regional advisory. The architects are obliged to follow instructions from the books edited in Rome called *Construcciones* (Constructions), some of which were prepared when I was director of the press.

What is life like in residences for female students? How does Opus Dei recruit women students? Opus Dei's female university residences are quite similar from one country to another. In them live girls from the various departments of the different universities that exist in a given city.

Opus Dei also operates residences and centers in the United States for young men and young women. Usually these residences are close to a university: Petawa Center for women and Leighton Studies Center for men are located in Milwaukee near Marquette University; on Follen Street in Cambridge near Harvard; the Woodlawn Residence for men in Chicago was Opus Dei's first in the U.S.; in Washington, D.C., there is also a women's residence. But I must clarify that in this country it is very difficult to detect if the students are regular students or also Opus Dei members. Usually when Opus Dei says "residence," it is a combination of both. A center is just a house for men or Opus Dei women, e.g., in San Francisco the Chestnut Center, located at 2580 Chestnut Street where all are Opus Dei members or the "Office of the University of Navarra" in Berkeley on College Avenue near the university. All follow the rules indicated from the superiors in Rome.

Directors of the residences are always numeraries who have some intellectual or professional ascendancy over other students. They already have their university degree or are in the final stages of obtaining it. The local council which directs the activities and the life of the residence according to Opus Dei regulations is made up of the directress and two other numeraries.

Another group of numeraries takes care of the residence administration; their responsibility is to maintain perfect material order in the house, from cleaning and doing the laundry to the preparation of meals and the bookkeeping. Administration bookkeeping is independent from residence bookkeeping which falls to the secretary of the local council. In general, the administration is separate from the residence, but carries out the orders given in the residence leadership. Living quarters of the administration numeraries are completely separated from the house they are in charge of, although ordinarily in the same building. In addition, there are usually a number of servants within the administration, who may or may not belong to Opus Dei.

No one from the residence may enter the administration quarters, nor may the numeraries who live in the administration participate in the life of the residence or live with the residents. The regime is the same as that which is established for houses of men. Communication is conducted via the same sort of intercom, and is strictly limited to what concerns the running of the house.

Residents must observe the schedule of meals and must keep silence at night, which helps create an atmosphere of order, silence, and study that benefits the residents.

Mealtime is important in the residences. Behavior during meals is generally well-mannered. In the early years it was easy to maintain an intimate, family-like atmosphere during the meals, but this is more difficult now due to the much larger number of residents, particularly in the newly built residences. In addition, the self-service meals now set up in many Opus Dei residences does not really help. When there is no self-service, the residences require a much larger dining room, usually set up with tables for four to eight persons. Servants in uniform attend the tables. No conversation is permitted between residents and the servants.

The local council tries to watch the residents during the meals and never leave the dining room without the surveillance of some numerary, whether a member of the local council or a numerary not officially identified as such to the residents. Such numeraries come to live at the residence for family reasons and can mix and pass unnoticed among the other residents, serving the local council as informers.

Bedrooms may be single or triple, but never double to avoid the slightest possibility of lesbian relationships.

Residents are invited to weekly study circles directed by one of the members of the local council. These circles are a sort of spiritual lecture with encouragement to reflect on one's spiritual life. Girls of St. Raphael who are students may invite friends to these circles.

It is recommended in the residences that the rosary be prayed in family, that is, in the oratory, and all residents must attend.

An Opus Dei priest says daily Mass in the residence. He usually arrives fifteen minutes ahead of time so that anyone, resident or not, can go to confession. Mass is not compulsory for the residents. The regional vicar of each country selects the priests of the Work who will attend activities of the Women's Branch. Two types of Opus Dei priest are generally chosen for a women's residence: first, a youngish man, not necessarily handsome but sufficiently charming to counsel a girl who has a vocational crisis; second, the paternal priest, perhaps 40 to 50 years old, trustworthy, with the prestige of having worked in another country, or perhaps of having had a successful professional career that he had to leave when he became an Opus Dei priest.

No woman of any age may discuss spiritual matters with Opus Die priests outside the confessional. If, for any reason, a priest has to speak to a woman in a parlor, the door must remain wide open. This is an example of the constant sexual obsession within Opus Dei.

Residences also organize conferences or lecture series usually given by a college professor or someone prominent in her or his profession, business, or finance. Lecturers need not be Opus Dei members, but most probably are friends or acquaintances of a supernumerary or cooperator. It may happen that the lecturer does not know about Opus Dei and the invitation is a way of bringing him or her closer to the Work. The supernumeraries and cooperators are very helpful in this type of activity. Sometimes a group of supernumeraries are assigned to help an Opus Dei residence by organizing some activity during the academic year, obviously in concert with the local council.

What could be called "an academic group" headed by an associate may exist in the residence in order to collaborate actively in its apostolic life and to lighten the burden of the local council.

After the oratory, the most important room in an Opus Dei residence is the study hall. The study rooms of the early years of Opus Dei had only a few tables and chairs. The present rooms are very comfortable, quiet, well-lit, and encourage serious work. In the newest Opus Dei residences, the study hall is equipped with carrells as in a college library. Even architectural students have enough space to prepare their projects comfortably. The newest Opus Dei residences are those in Buenos Aires, Argentina, the men's residence Monteávila in Caracas, Venezuela, and the women's residence Albariza in Maracaibo, Venezuela.

EXTERNAL RECRUITING

Opus Dei also has a system of recruiting girls who do not live in a residence. A numerary resident will invite a classmate or even a girl from a different university department to study at the residence. The newcomer is apt to be impressed by the comfortable, pleasant atmosphere of the residence and the seriousness with which people study there. During a break the newcomer will be invited to have tea, coffee, or a sandwich and then tactfully shown where she can leave the money to cover the cost of what she has consumed.

The next step is to invite the newcomer to attend a talk by the priest in the chapel the following Saturday. At this point the prospective candidate will be informed in detail about the accomplishments of the priest whom she will hear speak, as well as his ability to understand university students.

The priest will have been previously informed, of course, that this student will attend his meditation, so that he may orient what he says toward her possible vocation. This will be the point of departure for a campaign to win over the newcomer. The numerary resident student who brought her to the residence will be extremely attentive during the school week at the university. This numerary will never reveal her membership in Opus Dei until the moment that the newcomer is experiencing a vocational crisis. Then the numerary will announce her membership in Opus Dei and help the newcomer decide to take the step of joining.

INTERNAL RECRUITING

There is a usual pattern for recruiting those living in Opus Dei residences: the local council assigns each numerary, including those not officially known as such, a certain number of residents to be "treated." To treat (tratar) means to befriend and get to know thoroughly. Opus Dei numeraries who live in the residence pray and do all kinds of mortification each day as they try to win the confidence of the girls assigned to them. Once they accomplish this, recruitment begins by posing the vocation to Opus Dei as a problem of generosity, just as I explained in my own case.

In Opus Dei residences, there are daily get-togethers, usually after supper or lunch depending on the customs of the country. These get-togethers provide the numeraries who live in the residence an opportunity to befriend those to whom they have been assigned.

INFORMERS

Yes, there are informers in Opus Dei's female student residences. They are certainly not called that, but that, in fact, is what they are.

Opus Dei numerary students who live in the residence without being identified as such fulfill this function. They help the local council keep track of what is going on and which residents are potential new numeraries. Other residents confide in them, feeling free to bring up any subject whether related to life in the residence or not. The informers are usually recent vocations whose parents are unaware of their membership in Opus

Dei. The superiors have instructed them not to inform their parents about their membership, thus making sure that the families will pay the expenses at the residence where they go to college.

When I was in Venezuela these things happened, and I cannot deny that I knew and approved. The very sad fact is that I considered it justified by the thirst for proselytism. Nor can it be maintained that the central advisory was unaware of these practices, because many of the advisors lived in residences as numeraries or were directresses in countries where such practices were followed. What I ask myself once more is whether these are not the things that outsiders intuitively grasp, without knowing them fully, and which cause rejection or doubt about Opus Dei's *modus operandi.*

Although Opus Dei emphatically proclaims to the families of residents and everybody else that there is sincerity and openness in its residences, the truth is that nothing is spontaneous in the ordinary life of an Opus Dei residence of university women or in the relations between the local council and the individual resident. Every step has been calculated and planned with the exclusive goal of recruiting the best residents as Opus Dei numeraries. Those residents who, in the opinion of Opus Dei superiors, do not possess the requisites to be numeraries will be pushed toward the vocation of associate or supernumerary. In the worst case, they are invited to become cooperators.

Sexuality

"Marriage is for the rank and file, not for the officers of Christ's army. For, unlike food, which is necessary for each individual, procreation is necessary only for the species, and many individuals can dispense with it.

"A desire to have children? We shall leave children—many children— and a lasting trail of light if we sacrifice the selfishness of the flesh" (José María Escrivá, *The Way,* no. 28).[1] It is helpful to recall that the numeraries who do proselytism keep in mind the point about marriage.

Opus Dei's activities with young people in schools, university residences, and specialized schools, which I have outlined above, respond to a pattern which Opus Dei women follow in countries where the prelature is well established, with slight variations given the inevitable differences from country to country.

My work in Venezuela moved along lines marked by Opus Dei superiors. The Women's Branch flourished because the numeraries were from well-known families, and in the majority first-class professionals.

---

1. New York: Scepter, 1992.

Father Roberto Salvat, the counselor, insisted that we try to recruit very young girls. He believed it was better for a girl "to come to Opus Dei without the slightest experience," meaning sexual experience. I was quite opposed to such young vocations, because the lack of normal contact with boys caused fantasies that complicated matters in the long run, since the girls tended to develop either exaggerated scrupulosity or a fanaticism leading them later on to harsh judgments about their sisters. I remember cases of numeraries who awakened me in the middle of the night with a sexual scruple as to whether they had let their imagination wander into improperly watching the priest celebrate Mass or because on meeting the son or daughter of a supernumerary they regretted giving up the chance of motherhood. Opus Dei instructions were that supernumeraries should never bring their children to houses of numeraries.

The principle I drew from my own observations was that the women who had had a normal social life dealing with young men were more realistic about what they were leaving when they entered Opus Dei. More than once I was morally obliged to enlighten young girls who were about to take their vows: they knew something about poverty and obedience, but were unclear about what they were giving up when they took the vow of chastity. Quite a few numeraries, discussing chastity, told me that they regretted never having kissed a man. Some who had joined Opus Dei at a very young age reacted to Monsignor Escrivá's words often repeated in meditations: "We have to love Jesus Christ with our heart of flesh," unleashing their repressed sexuality as they kissed the wooden cross in the oratory. That, in my judgment, was more dangerous than having had normal relationship with a young man.

Centers of Internal Studies

The time came when it became clear that the formation we received in Opus Dei was quite insufficient. Everything was based on the Catechism of the Work during the periods of formation, confession, the weekly talk with the priest (neither of which took longer than five minutes), the confidence, of course, and each individual member's interior life of prayer, mortification, and so on.

The members of regional advisory put on the agenda the matter of actually beginning the internal studies set out in our Constitutions and the possibility of creating a center of studies for new vocations.

Father Roberto Salvat had reservations about both ideas but said that he would not object to our beginning the internal studies of philosophy. (One must remember that the counselor has not only a vote but a veto in the Women's Branch government.)

We figured out how long the courses would last on the basis of the hours required for each subject in the syllabi of internal studies, and we chose to start with introductions to philosophy and cosmology. By then the first three Venezuelan Opus Dei priests had returned from the Roman College of the Holy Cross: Father Francisco de Guruceaga, who was subsequently a bishop, and who left Opus Dei but not the priesthood, Father Alberto José Genty, who was a Venezuelan born in Trinidad, and Father Adolfo Bueno, also a Venezuelan although a member of a Colombian family. This made it possible for the counselor to name one of them, Father Alberto José Genty, our cosmology professor. The counselor decided to give the introduction to philosophy himself. Thus, our internal studies were launched in Venezuela. Afterwards, Father Alberto José Genty was our professor in almost all the philosophy courses except for ethics and epistemology, which were given jointly by the counselor and Father Antonio Torella, the ordinary visitor (or *missus*) of the Men's Branch.

The classes called for long hours of study which we undertook diligently. The reading material was restricted by order from Rome; even when the church abolished the *Index of Forbidden Books,* in Opus Dei we could only read those authorized by the Work's internal censorship. For instance, one author who was considered "too mystical" for our spirit was St. John of the Cross.

Since we had few books to study, we tried to take abundant class notes. Different groups were formed according to the obligations of each one of us so that we could pursue our internal studies in a coordinated fashion. Basically, my group consisted of those who lived in Casavieja. We were always given serious, written examinations by the course instructor and formal records were kept in the archives, as I mentioned earlier.

For Opus Dei men, the internal studies consisted of two years of philosophy and four of theology, organized by semesters. The Women's Branch had two years of philosophy and two years of theology. I do not know whether nowadays four years of theology are required. The philosophical subjects were introduction to philosophy, cosmology, logic, ethics, psychology, history of philosophy (two full years), epistemology, natural theology, and metaphysics.

Even though ecumenism was already a burning issue, there was no discussion of world religions. Neither Judaism nor Islam, much less Hinduism were presented. We were told that Teilhard de Chardin was unsound, but given only skimpy information. When Christian Science was discussed we were told that we could not waste time on such "unimportant movements." Years later, I lived in Cambridge, Massachusetts, when I arrived in the United States. The first day I visited Boston, on a bright Sunday morning, my guide, who was a Catholic, said: "Let's begin at the beginning." He took me to visit the Christian Science Mother Church. Seeing that building with its surrounding complex, I remembered how I had once been told that "Christian Science was unimportant." Philosophy was Thomism, which meant that Gilson and Manser had the pride of place. I used to take Manser's book on the plane on my visits to Maracaibo. Father Joaquín Madoz, who sometimes came on the same flight, used to say he had never seen a book with more flying time.

Toward the end of 1961 or perhaps in early 1962, the superiors began to emphasize the study of Latin. It began years later in the Women's Branch, possibly after 1966. Today it is an obligatory subject, "refreshed" during the periods of formation.

The arrival of the Venezuelan priests was a great help in our work, because people felt more attuned to them spiritually.

Those of us who were superiors always dealt with the priests through the ecclesiastical assistants and in the weekly sessions of the regional government. Government problems were never discussed in the confessional with any priest.

Father Rodrigo, a Spaniard who was in Caracas when I arrived, was reassigned to Spain, which provoked some commotion in the work of St. Raphael, but with the arrival of Father Joaquín Madoz, who came from Ecuador, where he had begun the foundation and served as counselor, both the work of St. Raphael and that of St. Gabriel (with married women) were strengthened. Father Joaquín Madoz was a deeply spiritual man, but relaxed and friendly; he was very understanding with married women for whom he always showed great respect. The supernumeraries and a number of women who were their friends came to confession at Casavieja.

Father Alberto José Genty was assigned to the work of St. Raphael and was quite popular. He was spiritual director to many young women, and quite a few requested admission to Opus Dei. He also worked in a very unassuming way with the servants who lived in Etame and in the new house. These girls, who were from modest families, had great esteem for him and knew that he liked them.

When Father Joaquín Madoz was posted to Spain, many of the married women were quite upset. They did not want to change their confessor and complained that "they take away all the good ones." Since supernumeraries have to obey in spiritual matters, they were instructed to go to confession with Father Francisco de Guruceaga or with Father José María Peña. Some of the cooperators were not so easy to convince. Among them was a dear friend, Mrs. Ana Teresa Rodríguez de Sosa, whom I managed to convince to go to confession with the counselor, Father Roberto Salvat, whose reassignment outside of Venezuela was not foreseeable.

Mrs. de Sosa was a beautiful woman, wealthy with considerable style. Much older than me, she came from a background that had conditioned her to look down on people of color, although she was able to acknowledge their merits in many cases. I used to criticize her strongly but affectionately, when she would remark deprecatingly about someone that she or he was "colored or "inky" (tintica). I was able to convince her that racism is unchristian. She accepted my criticism very well. We were good friends and valued each other. One of the things that I most admired was her direct, sincere approach. She knew that I behaved toward her in the same way.

She was my closest contact among the married women; I used to spend my weekly outing with her, and sometimes also the monthly excursion. Her chauffeur would come to take me to her house, or we would go for a drive along the coast to Caraballeda, from where you had a magnificent view of the Caribbean.

I learned a great deal about Venezuela and its families from Ana Teresa. All I could offer in return was an account of the house in Rome, the Father, new vocations, apostolic plans in Venezuela. I encouraged her to express her reactions to these topics. She had been in Rome. She knew the house and had met Monsignor Escrivá. She realized it was important to know him, but was not a fanatic admirer of Monsignor Escrivá.

To sustain its programs, Opus Dei asked many people in Venezuela for money. When the subject came up at regional meetings, the counselor insisted that I try to get a gift from Mrs. de Sosa, which made me quite angry. Without my asking her, Mrs. de Sosa gave me no less than 30,000 bolívares each year for whatever was needed in our houses. Our friendship was genuine and I never took advantage of her for the Women's Branch. In contrast, the counselor, though he used to play tennis at her house and swim in her pool, behind her back referred to her as that "rich old woman." I was boiling inside, because Father Roberto Salvat and Father Antonio Torella used their relationship with Mrs. de Sosa to become the friends of her son, Julio Sosa Rodríguez. When Mrs. de Sosa died, she left the Opus Dei Men's Branch a piece of property, El Trapiche in Caracas. Through her son Julio the Men's Branch also obtained several other pieces of land.

I tried to inculcate the spirit of unity in the Women's Branch. When Hoppy Phelps, then very young, was going to marry Fernando Nestares, a former numerary, I brought her to our house. Hoppy was a Protestant and intended to get married in the Catholic church. Ana María Gibert prepared her for her conversion and baptism and she made her first communion in the oratory of our house. The Phelps family is prominent in Venezuela socially as well as in financial and scientific circles. The family presented us with a splendid silver service, which we sent to the central government in Rome.

After her marriage Hoppy used to come to our house occasionally and we considered her our friend. On one of the many occasions we had to solicit money, I was told to ask Hoppy for 10,000 bolívares. I was reluctant to do so, realizing that few newlyweds have any savings. Nevertheless, I was instructed that if she replied she had no money, I should suggest that she request it of her father. I did so, and on account of that Hoppy came less frequently to our house. Her husband went to see the counselor and told him never again to ask his wife for money.

When I left Opus Dei, I maintained my friendship with Hoppy and Fernando. Fernando unfortunately died a few years ago and Hoppy remarried. Our friendship continued. A few months before the Spanish edition of this book appeared, I had lunch with her in Madrid. That old request for money in Caracas came up. She told me that when her daughter was going to get married in Caracas, she asked Roberto Salvat if he would officiate as an old friend of Fernando. His answer was vague and he did not marry the couple.[1]

In times of financial crisis I have also sent women numeraries to seek funds. Several even asked for help from old fiancés or young men they had known, who by that time had attained positions of importance. That obviously required a great effort.

There were two basic causes for the need of funds. On one hand, our contribution to support the Roman College of the Holy Cross and the Roman College of Santa Maria was no less than $600 a month. On top of that, we sent substantial sums of money each month "for the construction in Rome." On the other hand, the group of numeraries who held well-paid professional jobs was still small. Nowadays the finances of Opus Dei houses are well established. The scheme is based on the idea that each numerary should support herself. This does not mean that she handles the money she receives for her professional work; rather, when the house where she lives makes its annual budget, it counts on her income to pay for her maintenance and, if there is a surplus, to contribute to the house. For her part, the numerary must make a detailed monthly expense account and does not dispose of money freely on account of her commitment of poverty.

Another major project related to our fundraising efforts was the bazar for which supernumeraries, cooperators, and their friends worked all year

---

1. Months after the publication of the first Spanish edition of this book, I learned to my deep sorrow that Hoppy Phelps was shot in Caracas. She did not die but remained in a coma for over two years. She died recently.

long. The big pre-Christmas sale was held on premises provided by Beatriz Roche's husband, José Antonio Imery.

Officially, the bazar was held to benefit the servants' school in Etame, but the truth was that all the money was sent to Rome. The same thing occurred with other events such as raffles of automobiles.

In some other countries, including Venezuela, Opus Dei has schools for domestic servants. In the Los Campitos School in Caracas, as an extra-curricular activity for the regular students, there is a school called Los Samanes. This school has a plan of studies approved by the Venezuelan Ministry of Education to allow adults to get a basic secondary education and obtain something roughly like the American high school equivalency diploma. A few of the servants in Opus Dei administrations come to these classes.

Los Samanes School has several centers. One of them is in Caracas and another in Maracaibo. The Caracas center is located in Resolana, which is the administration of Opus Dei's male student residence Monteávila, which is located on the main street of the El Cafetal area.

Resolana offers the servants a few academic classes, but most classes are practical, including taking care of centers of studies or students residences, in this case that of the Opus Dei men, who benefit by free work. Although these schools receive government subsidies and private contributions, their essential purpose is not to give the students job training, but to recruit girls between the ages of 12 and 15, and sometimes even younger, as Opus Dei auxiliaries (servants). They are generally the daughters of impoverished families, and the parents are happy that their daughters are going to school and allow them to go with Opus Dei numeraries, when the latter visit their village, usually under the auspices of the parish priest. Obviously Opus Dei gets what it wants served up on a silver platter: raw material that is rather easy to mold.

The girls are well treated, they live more comfortably than at home, and get to attend classes. The girls are not obligated to stay in Opus Dei houses. Since they are under age, if they want to go back to their parents, some numerary or associate must accompany them on their return trip.

Another group of auxiliaries lives in Caracas in a house called Mayal, which is the administration connected to the Men's Branch center of studies, which is also the seat of Araya, the regional commission, that is the Men's Branch government.

One of the Opus Dei servants in Caracas had felt ill for a long time. The numeraries took Francisca, which was her name, to an Opus Dei physician, who gave her tranquilizers, claiming her malaise was psychoso-matic. She still felt very sick, but instead of taking her to another doctor, they brought her back to the same physician who kept her so sedated that, on a visit, her mother found her in a pharmaceutically induced sleep.

One fine day Francisca said she wanted to leave Opus Dei. They took great pains to retain her, and practically forced her to stay. Finally, sick and fed-up, she got angry one day and went to the house where her mother had worked for more than thirty years. The lady of the house and Francisca's mother took her to a well-known doctor whose diagnosis was that Francisca had a large fibroma, plus appendicitis, and gall stones. The doctor said that Francisca needed an operation urgently.

When the doctor routinely asked about Francisca's medical insurance, she answered that she had none. The doctor asked where she had been working and she said that she had worked for many years in Opus Dei houses. The doctor could not believe that she had neither medical insurance nor social security. However, this is true not only of the auxiliaries but of all those numeraries who work in administrations.

When Francisca left Opus Dei, the superiors gave her 3000 bolívares. At the existing rate of exchange at that time (much devalued since my time) that was worth some $60. The cost of the operation was at least $3000. Finally, the family for whom Francisca's mother worked and Norka Salas, a former Opus Dei numerary, who had also left the Work recently, managed to negotiate with a number of medical institutions to obtain a lower rate. The family and Norka also got help for her during the period of convalescence.

After all this became public, Marisol Hidalgo, an Opus Dei numerary from Seville, has pursued Francisca to get her to join Opus Dei again in one capacity or other. Fortunately, Francisca is very level-headed and has told Opus Dei numeraries who have crossed her path and particularly Marisol Hidalgo the hard truth: Opus Dei does not have the spirit of charity and that despite their sanctity they are not at all worried about little people.

Francisca's case is not unique. Opus Dei has discharged servant numeraries after more than fifteen years of service without social security or medical insurance, leaving them virtually penniless, and with almost no possibility of finding employment.

The most they have done in certain cases has been to direct former auxiliaries to houses of supernumerary women, who did not treat them well either, so that they had to leave. I have been told, though I lack confirmation of the claim, that after the Spanish edition of my book, in Andalusia at least, Opus Dei is trying to enroll the servants in the Spanish social security system.

You must remember that I speak of an institution that proclaims its fidelity to the church and declares itself a pioneer in secularity, and used to harshly criticize nuns and friars because they were not concerned for persons as human beings. What I recount is one of the many things that you discover crossing the threshold of Opus Dei, sometimes from outside in, and in this case, from inside out.

To return to my experience in Venezuela, I continued my effort to adjust to the spirit of the Work in every way, according to the counselor's instructions. We spared no effort to upholster furniture and clean houses, and even gave the counselor's own house complete sets of valuable china, which had been given to us for the women's houses.

The counselor's demeanor in the sessions of the women's regional government was of more or less veiled contempt; he obviously believed that women were unintelligent or frivolous. This was apparent also in the way in which he spoke about people who belonged to the Work. He also showed class snobbery, saying for instance that a numerary like Teotiste Ortiz, who did not belong to the upper crust, but who was a very good person "should not belong to the Work." I remember that when Teotiste found out that I was going to Rome, she cried and said that she was afraid Eva Josefina Uzcátegui and Father Roberto Salvat would send her back home. I denied it, and she repeated as she wept: "María del Carmen, they don't like me."

I tried to reassure her, but I later found out that they did send her home. She died a few years ago.

Eva Josefina Uzcátegui strongly echoed the counselor's class and race prejudices. How often in meetings of the Women's Branch regional government, I heard Eva Josefina Uzcátegui say *tintico* (inky, darky) to refer to someone pejoratively! The expression might be accompanied by a gesture: "You know, Father Robert. Here in Caracas they aren't anybody," referring to someone who was not socially prominent.

I can honestly say that at the end of the government sessions I felt churned up inside and tried to go to my room in silence. I also remember Elsa Anselmi telling me days later that she had to make an effort to not hit Eva Josefina during the meeting. Others said the same thing.

My lack of racial prejudice was not a merit, but I just never felt animosity against people of color. On the contrary, I found the color of their skin and grace of their movements lovely.

We opened the Albariza students residence in Maracaibo, after several years of regular visits to that city by María Margarita del Corral and myself. María Margarita became directress. Another member of the local council was a numerary who came from Spain, Amanda Lobo. A very important person in the house was Cecilia Mendoza. The people in Maracaibo were especially fond of Cecilia, who continued her profession as a laboratory analyst, while taking charge of the work with married women. People in Maracaibo adored her affectionate and lovely manner.

The residence in Maracaibo was a great success. Marilú Colmenares was the first person to request admission as a numerary. She died in Caracas after a number of years in Opus Dei.

The soul of Opus Dei's work in Maracaibo was Mana Betancourt. She became a supernumerary and was always as good as she was dedicated. I became a close friend of Mana and her husband Charles. I helped decorate their house, which they were remodeling. Both of them went to Rome, while I was there, to see the Father. She already knew she had only a few months to live. She had a virulent cancer.

Opus Dei priests in Maracaibo were Father Francisco de Guruceaga and after him, Father Adolfo Bueno.

From Caracas we also began periodic visits to Valencia and Barquisi-meto, where the Opus Dei priests went frequently, because the men already had opened their first house in that city.

The growing number of vocations made the advisors realize that a center of studies for female numeraries was long overdue, but this provoked great arguments with the counselor. I never knew why he did not want us to begin this project, but, finally, after months of disagreement, he allowed us to send the proposal to Rome, where it was approved. The members of the regional advisory received the news of its approval with great joy.

For the center of studies we found a charming old house with a large garden at low rent in Los Chorros, a beautiful old suburb of Caracas. As required in Opus Dei, we submitted to Rome the proposed name for the house, "Urupagua." Urupagua is the name of a fruit from Falcón State, which is very sweet inside, although prickly on the outside. The name was approved.

Begoña Elejalde and I devoted our best efforts to the center of studies. We considered it to be crucial for the formation of numeraries in the country, especially with a view to eventually being sent to the Roman College of Santa María. Mercedes Mujica was appointed directress of Urupagua.

The courses of scholastic philosophy already described could be pursued in orderly fashion in the center of studies. Father Genty knew the first students of the center of studies well, because he had been spiritual director of many of them.

Julia Martínez used to go to Valencia with me a couple of days every two weeks. At first we used to stay at the home of a lady who was a friend of the Guruceaga family. Subsequently, to have greater freedom of movement we opted to go to a hotel.

We used to speak with some of the women in the garden of the church while the others went to confession. Julia and I would pass through the confessional before the women arrived to get information about the people Father Genty had contacted and unite our efforts on behalf of proselytism. In truth, the Opus Dei priest is the one who guides the women numeraries when Opus Dei work begins in any city.

In Valencia, a very young girl named María Elena Rodríguez from Barquisimeto requested admission as an Opus Dei numerary. So, we attended to the married women and this numerary on our trips.

The ladies in Valencia began to donate sheets and table cloths. When that happened we would notify the priest by phone to collect the bag that Julia and I left in the garden of the men's house as we passed by.

1965 brought growth to Opus Dei in Venezuela and changes in the Women's Branch. Eva Josefina Uzcátegui was appointed delegate of Venezuela in the central advisory. Reassignments of priests also took place. Father Alberto José Genty was posted to the Opus Dei men's house in Valencia. Father José María Peña, the regional priest secretary, was shifted to the job of regional spiritual director, and his old position was assigned to Father José María Félix, a recently ordained priest who had just arrived from Spain.

Father Félix was in his early thirties, of average height, blond with blue eyes. He was not friendly at all. He always had his head inclined and seemed ready to listen but not to understand. His attitude was servile toward the counselor and he was prejudiced against women, especially against me as regional directress. His last name occasioned the innocent joke, "Felix the Cat."

Father Félix scrutinized us as he spoke. It was as though he descended from Mt. Sinai holding the tablets of the law, as it were, especially, in what had to do with confessions. He contradicted everything we said.

The ecclesiastical assistants ordered a modification in the form of address to be used toward them. Instead of the Spanish "Don" with their first name, we would now say "Father" and their last name. The change pleased me because "Don" sounded completely out of place in Venezuela.

The new house of the men's regional government was located in La Castellana neighborhood. The house was called La Trocha. As a special deference, we assigned the only numerary servants we had to the counselor's house.

Venezuela began to export numeraries to other countries. We really gave the best we had in light of the needs of the country for which they were leaving. Marta Sepúlveda, a Mexican numerary, who spent several years in Caracas, was the first to leave. She was sent to Uruguay. The next numerary went to the United States, when the house in Boston was opened.

We sent Berta Elena Sanglade, who knew English fairly well, to the United States where she worked for many years and afterwards left Opus Dei forever. María Amparo, a Spanish girl, went to Brazil.

Monsignor Escrivá also decided that the Opus Dei foundation in Santo Domingo should be launched from Venezuela. After Father Francisco de Guruceaga visited the Dominican Republic for several months, the counselor asked me to go to Santo Domingo with Elsa Anselmi and Eva Josefina Uzcátegui—a few months before she was named the Venezuelan delegate—to explore the possibility of a new foundation of Opus Dei women in that nation.

I stressed repeatedly to the counselor that the political situation in the Caribbean looked very inauspicious and that the absence of diplomatic relations between Venezuela and Santo Domingo could easily involve us in a dangerous political situation. He totally disregarded my fears and considered them ridiculous.

So we went to Santo Domingo and the following day were immersed in the 1965 revolution. The airport was closed, and we had no way to leave the island. Venezuela had no diplomatic representative, so, although I no longer held a Spanish passport, I tried to contact the Spanish Embassy. To our surprise, the Spanish Ambassador had taken shelter at the Ambassador Hotel, where we were lodged. Then I called the United States Embassy to explain our plight. I was told that most probably we would be able to leave with the American civililian population, due to be evacuated in the next few days. I was instructed to submit an application for an American visa that very night at our hotel, where the American consul was to spend the entire night helping people in situations like ours. We were granted the visa. The following morning, leaving all our luggage behind and taking only documents and money, we arrived at the hotel lobby, which was packed with American families trying to leave the country. Following instructions shouted to the group, we went to the front of the hotel to wait for buses to take us to the harbor. Suddenly, we were caught in the middle of an intense crossfire between two armed groups. Our leader told us to lie flat on the ground and remain quiet. I remember Elsa Anselmi, who was quite courageous, asking me, "Do you think we are going to be killed?" I replied, "Most probably, but let us hope God helps us." For about seven minutes the shooting continued, and at the first lull, we took a chance and reentered the hotel. After a couple of hours the buses arrived, but under instructions from the government of the Dominican Republic, they could not move faster than 20 miles per hour. On the way to the harbor, people in the streets shouted insults at the United States. When we finally arrived at the harbor, no ship was visible. It was so hot that everybody was thirsty, the children were crying, and young women were distraught about leaving their husbands. We were told that a warship would arrive in an hour but that women with children and elderly people would be taken by helicopter. The announcement had no sooner ended than a kind of hurricane burst over our heads, announcing the landing of several helicopters that carried off mothers with children, the handicapped, and the elderly people to a warship anchored on the high seas.

Finally the warship arrived and we climbed on board, showing our passports and visas, leaving Santo Domingo as refugees in a warship which took us to Puerto Rico. When we embarked we had not the slightest idea where we were heading. We only wanted to get away from that nightmare. The warship was prepared to shelter civilians. We discovered how thirsty and hungry we were when we were served apple juice and a piece of pie.

The next morning we were informed that we would arrive in Puerto Rico within a couple of hours. When we got to a hotel, we were so dirty that the receptionist asked us to pay in advance. Since we had lost our luggage, Elsa went out that afternoon to buy essentials for the three of us.

From Puerto Rico we sent cables to Venezuela, Rome, and our families as well. We returned to Venezuela two or three days later on the first available flight. On arrival at Maiquetía Airport in Caracas, Dr. Héctor Font, a supernumerary was waiting and took us directly from the plane to an ambulance in order to escape the press and television, since we had become news as the only three Venezuelans caught in the revolution in Santo Domingo. This took place so quickly that we had no time to realize what was going on. The episode vividly illustrates the much vaunted Opus Dei "discretion." Despite the elaborate precautions, our names appeared often in the news during the following days.

In Caracas, not long afterwards, I went with Mrs. Laura Drew-Bear, a supernumerary, to thank the United States ambassador, Mr. Maurice Bernbaum, for his kindness in allowing us to join the American families escaping from Santo Domingo. While the ambassador's deputy, Mr. Sterling Cottrel, was talking to us, we learned that there was a demonstration against the United States at the Embassy gates. A shot was fired at the ambassador's window. The deputy, instinctively realizing the danger, shouted "Hit the deck, ladies!" The bullets struck the wall just at head level where we were seated. We ended up under the coffee table unharmed. The ambassador, who was in the next room, came in to see us at once, and the formal visit changed into a friendly, informal one.

It is my understanding that the ambassador still keeps the bullets.

When we returned to Caracas, we were told that the counselor had proclaimed he was ready to take a plane to look for us in Santo Domingo. These events brought the Opus Dei women's foundation in Santo Domingo to a halt.

The major news of the year after the trip to Santo Domingo was the appointment of Eva Josefina as delegate to Venezuela.

Father Félix had assumed full responsibility for Opus Dei women in the country. His inquisitorial attitude was difficult for us. Unhappily, friction developed when the members of the regional advisory, the local directresses, and an older numerary or two were making our annual spiritual retreat in Casavieja. This provoked his anger with me.

Father Genty was giving the retreat. According to the rescripts from Rome, we knew that members making their retreat ought to go to confession with the Opus Dei priest in charge of the retreat, but they have always had the freedom to go to confession with any of the ecclesiastical assistants or the ordinary confessor of the house. Following an Opus Dei custom, we left pieces of paper on top of a table in the hall for people to sign up for confession, with Father Genty as the director of the exercises, or with either of the other two ecclesiastical assistants. When I went to put down my name, I saw that only two had signed up for Father Félix; the rest had written their names on Father Genty's list.

Next day when Father Félix gave a meditation, we gave him the two lists for confession. Obviously, he saw that most of us had signed up for confession with Father Genty, including all the superiors of the regional advisory, except one. The following day, he came to the house and said he wanted to talk to me. I went into the parlor with Eva Josefina Uzcátegui, and without further ado he said to me: "You're an idiot. How can you give such bad example by encouraging everybody to go to confession to Father Alberto Genty, when he is not the ordinary confessor of this house?

I appealed to the rescript from Rome on this subject, but it did not stop his reprimand: "Going to confession to Father Alberto Genty is like going to confession to the priest from the parish down the block."

I responded that as an Opus Dei priest and one who was giving us the retreat, he could not be considered a bad shepherd. Father Félix responded: "Anyone who is not the ordinary or extraordinary confessor of a house is a bad shepherd, according to the Father's doctrine."

Naturally, we all had to go to confession to Father Félix. Nevertheless, I entered the confessional at another time, and explained to Father Genty what had happened.

Faithful to the Father's instructions, Opus Dei women superiors had no dealings with the church hierarchy except for the cardinal and the apostolic nuncio. We visited them, as étiquette demanded, at Christmas, Easter, and their saints' days. By way of anecdote, I recall that as regional directress, I had a dress, which we called the bishop's dress. It was a bit different from the rest of my wardrobe, discreet, but impressive. These visits were not occasions for serious exchanges; Monsignor Escrivá's advice was to "tell pleasant stories about our servants." Monsignor Luigi Dadaglio, with whom I always maintained a good personal relationship, was apostolic nuncio of His Holiness in Venezuela. On one of the official visits I made in the company of another numerary, he asked how many vocations we had had that year. With complete spontaneity I gave him the number. As was obligatory, we sent a report about the visit to Rome. Shortly thereafter, Father Roberto Salvat transmitted to me Monsignor Escrivá's indication that I had been "very indiscreet with the nuncio, because one should never give any kind of explanations about the Work to the church hierarchy." When I asked why, his answer was, "Because the Father has said so and that's enough."

We received other rescripts from Rome, specifically from the Father, in which we were told quite plainly: "Our women are not to answer any note or letter that may come from bishops or episcopal commissions. The notes or letters will be handed over to the counselor, so that he may hand them over to me."

Years later after leaving Opus Dei I went to visit Monsignor Dadaglio in Madrid, when he was serving as nuncio to Spain. He always received me most cordially. I remember that on my first visit he made a remark to the effect: "Five years ago I wouldn't have believed anything, and now I believe it all," referring, of course, to Opus Dei. I also kept him informed about what had happened in Rome and about Father Tomás Guitérrez who came for a visit to Madrid while I was visiting my family for the purpose of intimidating me.

In Venezuela, in late 1964 and early 1965, we received an avalanche of notes, rescripts, indications, letters, and so forth. I could not quite see the relevance of many of them in our country, and there was no way of putting them immediately into practice, as we were ordered to do. Other documents were issued from the press as letters from the Father, which seemed to me quite harsh toward people who had worked in new Opus Dei foundations. He insisted that they leave their positions in the country where they had worked. I shared my impressions with the other advisors.

What preoccupied me during that period was that the ecclesiastical assistants seemed more distant, especially after the return from Rome of Eva Josefina Uzcátegui. I even mentioned this one day in the confessional to Father José María Peña, spiritual director of the region. He reassured me, reminding me that the obligation of fraternal correction applied to everyone, and that if I had done anything wrong, they would tell me. Since I still had faith in the Work, I wrote a long letter to Monsignor Escrivá which I sent in a sealed envelope. In it I opened my heart completely and with utter sincerity told him how much I had suffered to get the center of studies started and that the counselor's attitude was always critical of us, particularly of me.

I also described the rather strange and mysterious air with which Eva Josefina Uzcátegui had come back from Rome, insinuating that from now on the advisors should not have contact with outsiders but follow the example of the Women's Branch central government; we should devote ourselves exclusively to work inside the offices of the regional advisory. Father Roberto Salvat had told me, I reported, that it was "stupid for me to do apostolate with married women by going to Valencia."

I had thought that Monsignor Escrivá would have responded to my letter, as he had done several other times, but nothing came.

I began to worry, but then thought I had an overheated imagination. Since I have never been able to put up with ambiguous situations, I wanted to confront the problem. In agreement with Ana María Gibert, my director, I called the counselor, Father Roberto Salvat, and asked him to come to the confessional at Casavieja because I needed to speak to him. When he came, I begged him to tell me whether I had done anything wrong and if so, to make me the appropriate fraternal correction. Father Roberto said that there was nothing wrong, that if there was anything he would tell me, that it was all my imagination. Given his manner on this occasion, I must say he was very pleasant.

However, two days later, one of the priests who came to Casavieja to hear the confessions of married women, requested that I enter the confessional and he told me something that astonished me. Eva Josefina Uzcátegui had approached his confessional to tell him that she was slipping a letter under the door to be given to the counselor. The priest said he wanted to tell me because that had seemed very strange and he was afraid that something was looming over my head.

In all my years in Opus Dei, this was the first time I had heard of anything of this sort. I thought that something was being plotted against me, but I could not understand what it was all about. I spoke to Father José María Peña again, as regional spiritual director, and he assured me that nothing was happening. I got along very well with my director, Ana María Gibert, who was and is one of the best and most intelligent people I have met in my life. She, too, attempted to dissipate my "groundless" fears.

On October 11, 1965, I was running errands with Ana María Gibert, when the counselor, Roberto Salvat Romero, telephoned Casavieja, to say that they should locate me urgently wherever I was. Whenever I went out, I had the practice of calling home to check for any important messages. This time Ana María called and received the message.

Given the urgency, we immediately went to the administration of La Trocha, the counselor's house, which was closer than ours. We notified him by intercom that Ana María and I were there. (Ana María Gibert was my internal directress, she was in the women's regional government and, furthermore, was an inscribed member.) The counselor came down and seeing me with Ana María asked me: "Can you go home now?" "Yes, of course," I answered. "Is Eva Josefina there?" "Yes, she is there," I answered. "Well, Father José María Félix and I are on our way now." Father Félix was the priest secretary in charge of the Women's Branch.

We went home and they arrived within fifteen minutes. Standing in the visitors' parlor, Father Roberto said to me: "Look, a note has just come from Rome saying you are to go there as soon as possible. The Father wants you to rest for a few days. You are to make the trip non-stop."

I was in shock.

"Doesn't it seem odd to you?" "Odd? Why? You know that the Father wants to see the older people again because, as the song says: 'Si fa sera nella sua vita' (night is falling in his life). What greater sign of kindness! You get a round-trip ticket. Logically, the plan will be to spend a couple of weeks in Rome; and I am sure, the Father, who is very paternal, will tell you to spend at least a week or two in Spain to see your parents, and afterwards you will come back."

"But do you really think I'll come back?" "Listen to how silly you are! Instead of thinking about happy days in Rome, you are going to spoil your trip. What is important is to leave as soon as possible and get to Rome this very week, because when the Father calls, he likes people to come immediately."

I told the counselor that my passport was not in order, and I did not have a visa, nor a current vaccination certificate, but the counselor insisted that I should make the trip as soon as possible.

The delegate, Eva Josefina, seconded everything the counselor had said.

What puzzled me was that he did not bring the note from Rome with him, since whenever the counselor received a note or anything dealing with the Women's Branch, he was supposed to give it to us to read.

I spoke to Father José María Peña, who told me to call the counselor and insist that he should read me the note from Rome. Also, I asked Father Peña if it would be bad spirit to tell the Father that I would like to go back to work in Venezuela, if he should instruct me to stay in Rome. Father Peña told me plainly that it was not bad spirit at all, since it was established that the members of the Work ought to live in those countries where their personality best allowed them to serve God within Opus Dei. This directive gave me great peace.

I phoned Father Salvat and in his absence spoke with Father Félix. My insistence perplexed him a bit, and he repeated almost word for word what the counselor had told me that morning. There was no way of getting them to give me the note to read, nor have them read it to me. They only repeated time and again that the Father wanted me to go to Rome to rest for a few days.

Withholding the note from me made me think that there was something in that note that they did not want me to know, and this made me very uncomfortable. I suspected that the counselor and the delegate did not like my approach to certain instructions coming from Rome, and that, instead of making me a fraternal correction according to the rules if my attitude seemed incorrect to them, they had informed Rome on the matter to get me removed from the country. This seemed likely in view of the demeanor that I had recently noted both in the counselor and the delegate when she returned from her last visit to Rome.

I had the sense of receiving a beating over the head organized with the connivance of the delegate. Although Ana María Gibert begged me to reject that idea, I was unable to do so. My old credulity had ended. Too many coincidences confirmed my fears that something loomed over me.

They gave me the news of the note on the morning of October 11, and four days later at 11:30 P.M., I was on a flight to Rome.

I made no farewells. The counselor and delegate advised me that it was not worth saying goodbye to anyone for so a short time, especially not to the ecclesiastical hierarchy. A two-week absence was anticipated. Nevertheless, I left everything in order and signed several blank sheets of paper according to standard procedure for absences of directors.

It took me three days to renew my personal documents and obtaining an Italian visa, besides buying basic winter clothing that one does not use or have in a tropical climate: a coat, a raincoat, a suit, and a few sweaters.

I had no desire to go shopping. I felt very sad, but wanted to believe what the counselor had said. Something like a sixth sense inside me said it was not true. Curiously, one by one, all of the advisors told me that my trip seemed strange, and they were somewhat frightened. We knew I would not be able to write them, but I promised without knowing how, that I would tell them what was happening. I asked them to pray for me.

One day without saying anything to anybody I went to the center of Caracas, to Plaza Bolívar. Looking at the statue of the Liberator on horseback, I smiled thinking that when I arrived in Caracas I deemed it offensive to compare him to Monsignor Escrivá. Without even realizing it in those ten years, I had learned to admire the founding fathers and realized that no country has the right to consider itself master of another. Instinctively that idea led me to reflect that in Opus Dei most national directors are Spaniards. The same thing is true in both the men's and women's central governments in Rome. Among the people in that plaza I felt as though I belonged. I felt a kind of physical need to belong and, so to speak, listen to the heartbeat of simple people. The afternoon I left Caracas I went to La Pastora, a church in a poor neighborhood in the center of the city. I looked at the image of the Virgin, a shepherdess, and asked pardon for the errors I might have committed, I begged her to take care of the young flock I was leaving behind.

It hurt to leave the country. I had given it the best part of my life. I had identified completely with it, and it had always been my intention to transmit the spirit of Opus Dei.

When news of my departure for Rome became known, Lilia Negrón, a physician, now married, whom I had known since she was fifteen, said to me gravely: "You are not coming back. They will leave you there." Lilia was a faithful friend. I followed her life closely: as a pupil, university student, engaged, then married, and most recently mother. Her first child Alberto José had just been born. Specifically, regarding Lilia, Opus Dei's judgment was that I should not devote so much time to her because she was not going to be a numerary. In reality, I ignored the indication. I always followed the practice of giving my time to anyone who asked for it or needed it, simply because I never believed that my time was my own but rather something that God had given me to administer. And I still think so.

Only with great effort was I able to refrain from calling Eva Josefina a hypocrite. In my soul I was convinced she had organized the whole thing. I was not attached to my position of authority. They renewed me in it three times. I only wanted to work in Venezuela. I never desired positions of authority and their only meaning for me was service. The counselors of Venezuela and Colombia gave me the blessing for the trip. The latter, indeed, said that I should not mention to anyone in Rome that he was in Venezuela, because only the Father and Don Alvaro would understand his trip. The counselor of Venezuela said to me: "We will both give you the blessing, one for each way."

As I look back over my years in Venezuela, my impressions and reactions are varied and complex. In regard to the country's history, I had the good fortune to witness the change from dictatorship to democracy. Personally, and because of my complete identification with the spirit of Opus Dei I had helped Opus Dei grow, not only in the Women's Branch, but throughout the whole country. I won many vocations of numeraries. I greatly encouraged the supernumeraries and cooperators and began the work with associates and auxiliaries, getting the first vocations among them. My initiative helped begin clinics in poor neighborhoods, as well as new houses and new activities, even outside Caracas. I was responsible for the center of studies, the string of students sent to the Roman College of Santa María, the achievement of financial stability, and for sending numeraries to strengthen other nations. I had carried on a genuine apostolate of friendship with many people in the country.

I learned that the Venezuelan woman is very special, combining many admirable traits. I can guarantee by my own experience. Venezuelans are people of integrity.

Sometimes the responsibility before God of having stimulated so many vocations to Opus Dei, especially in that country, terrifies me. Now I realize that Opus Dei is capable of lying and doing so publicly, especially about persons who once belonged. I also realize that the superiors are capable of fictionalizing the life of Monsignor Escrivá in such an extraordinary manner, simply in order to have their own saint. This responsibility before God terrifies me, because there are persons, who, when the mask of Opus Dei falls off, are not capable of bearing what they see, and in their fear, desperation, or impotence, take their lives or try to, as has happened in England, Spain, and the United States.

Two supernumeraries who held me in great esteem, Cecilia and Héctor Font, drove me to the airport with my director, Ana María Gibert. The wait in Maiquetía became depressing. The plane that was to carry me to Rome arrived late from Brazil. They were difficult moments for everyone, but especially for me, who embarked on an unknown course.

7

ROME II:
RETURN TO
THE UNKNOWN

At the outset, I would like to explain to the reader that I am
able to write everything that follows in such detail, because when I
left Opus Dei, I wrote down all the events that had occurred, including
conversations and names of the witnesses almost as an exercise in mental
health. I thought that years later I might forget events and names, and
something in my heart told me that I ought to record the happenings,
not out of rancor but for the sake of historic justice.

The Other Side of the Coin

Another hop over the Atlantic and the next day the plane flew over Lisbon,
affording a splendid view. We arrived in Rome after dark. It must have
been about 6:30 P.M., on October 16, 1965. According to Opus Dei custom,
no one is met at the airport. Two numeraries were waiting for me in the
bus terminal: Marga Barturen and Maribé Urrutia. Both of them were
senior in the Work and both knew me. There was jubilation at my arrival
and surprise on my part when they asked me: "Why did you come?" My
answer was sincere, "I don't know."

We collected my baggage, which was rather light. At 8:15 P.M. we arrived
at Villa Saccetti, 36. The arrival was normal for a person who had left the
central house in September 1956, and returns in October 1965, just as she
was when she left: directress of the region of Venezuela and an inscribed member.

While we were still in the vestibule, the central directress, Mercedes
Morado (whom I mentioned in the description of my stay in Bilboa),
came down to meet me accompanied by Marlies Kücking, prefect of

studies. There were hearty greetings and Mercedes asked me: "Where are your suitcases?" "My suitcases? I only brought one small suitcase for two weeks."

I saw that Mercedes looked at Marlies and smiled. Immediately she said: "Let somebody show you to your room."

Lourdes Toranzo accompanied me to the room. (Lourdes was the subdirector of the formation course at Los Rosales.)

The room was in good order: flowers, sink and shower, and so forth. I was surprised to see a thick mattress on my bed on top of the plank, something that is only assigned to people who are ill, since female numeraries normally sleep on wooden planks. Opening the door to the lavatory I saw a urinal on the floor. I was puzzled and asked: "What is that urinal doing here?"

They told me that the Father had said that the numeraries who had reached their fortieth birthday should have a urinal placed in their room. I had reached that milestone a few months earlier.

I had not finished unpacking when they informed me by the intercom in the hall, that I should run to the dining room of Villa Vecchia, where the Father was waiting for me.

I went in all haste, because the dining room was about eight minutes away at a brisk pace.

Encounter with the Father

Rosalia, the servant, told me they were waiting for me and to enter without knocking. I went into the dining room of the Villa, where Monsignor Escrivá had just had supper with Don Alvaro del Portillo. Monsignor Escrivá was seated at the head of the table, Don Alvaro del Portillo at his left, the central directress at the Father's right and the prefect of servants, María Jesus de Mer, a physician, was also present. I approached Monsignor Escrivá's chair and with the left knee on the floor, as is obligatory in Opus Dei, I kissed his hand.

The conversation went as follows:

"How was your trip?"

"Very good, Father, thank you."

"How were they when you left them?"—referring to the Venezuelan numeraries.

"Well, Father. Except that Begoña concerns me very much because of her illness." (Begoña Elejalde had just found out as a result of an operation that she had Hodgkin's disease.)

"'Misfortune,' you call it, knowing that soon she's going with God. But that is a blessing! What luck is hers! Happy is she thinking that she will soon die! And who is Begoña? How long has she been ill?" The central directress whispered something to Monsignor Escrivá. I realized that the Father did not know this inscribed member, founder of the Venezuelan region, a person who held two positions in the regional advisory. I also realized that the Father was even unaware that she was sick and had undergone an operation. I was very surprised that the Father was uninformed because we had faithfully reported to the central government about Begoña's illness and operation. But I reflected and attributed it to the fact that the Father appeared old and that they wanted to avoid upsetting him.

Monsignor Escrivá went on:

"And you, how is your health?" "Very well, Father." "I'll bet the doctor hasn't seen you." "Yes, Father, each year we have a thorough medical examination."

"Well, no matter! You, Chus," speaking to the physician, "have a look at her. Let her eat, let her sleep, and let her rest, because we are going to give her a lot of work here. Now rest, eat, and sleep." With these words he went out of his dining room with Alvaro del Portillo.

Since I knew Monsignor Escrivá well, I realized that, though he was trying to be courteous, something in his voice betrayed a certain annoyance.

As we went down the stairs from the Villa dining room to the kitchen, I asked Mercedes with the confidence of one who had known her for so many years: "Tell me something, Mercedes. Why have I come to Rome? I'll go back to Venezuela, right?" "What did they tell you?" "That the Father wanted me to spend a few days here resting." "Well, that's it. I don't know anything about anything, but you heard the Father: eat, sleep, rest."

The next day I went to St. Peter's. Paul VI was then Pope. They asked me if I wanted to stay for the Pope's blessing, but I answered that I had better get back in case the Father called after lunch. This pleased the advisor who accompanied me, who reported it later. Once again, we see that in Opus Dei good spirit means putting the Father above anyone, including the Pope.

October 18, 19, and 20 I was stuck in my room with absolutely nothing to do. I was only able to leave it at the times set for common activities, all of which I was instructed to do with the central government. Whenever I tried to leave my room to go to the garden, for instance, I encountered Lourdes Toranzo, whose room was near mine and who always asked me where I was going. If I told her that I was simply going to pray the rosary in the garden, for instance, she would find some unlikely pretext, to send me back to my room. I got up in time to attend the last Mass scheduled late for those who were ill.

In the eyes of most people in the house, I received privileged treatment, since I performed all common acts with the central government. For myself, after so long in Opus Dei, it meant that they had me under close surveillance. In fact, I had felt watched ever since I arrived in Rome.

A few days later, Mercedes Morado told me I was to make my confidence with Marlies Kücking, who was the prefect of studies in the central advisory. She was German, blond, slightly stout, but attractive; she was the only member of the central government I did not know. I realized that she was the right hand of the central directress of Opus Dei women—today she holds that post herself—and that the Father held her in high esteem.

I noticed that they slighted Mary Carmen Sánchez-Merino, the secretary of the central government, to give more importance to Marlies Kücking.

After four days of doing *absolutely nothing,* for there were not even any books in my room, and leaving the room only to fulfill the schedule of common acts with the central government, I asked Mercedes Morado to assign me some task. They gave me the whole catalogue of the book storeroom (it was not called a library) of the men's and women's sections of Opus Dei; to be done by alphabetical order and by subjects.

I realized that this was drudgery that would take months. Nonetheless, I worked at it with determination. I did the work in my room so that I was completely isolated from the rest of the house.

Missing Pieces

Two weeks went by and nobody explained the purpose of my stay in Rome. I spoke to Marlies Kücking and told her that my departure from Venezuela was so hasty that the counselor advised me that I should write my parents on arrival in Rome to save time. Marlies told me to write them, but that they would send the letter to Venezuela so that it could be sent from there to my parents in Spain. I never found out why such deception was necessary.

The Betancourts, a couple from Venezuela who had made Opus Dei's Maracaibo foundation possible, arrived in Rome. Mrs. Betancourt was near death from cancer. When someone arrived in Rome from another country, the custom was for the numerary from that country who was in the central house to accompany the visitors during their interview with the Father. In this case, I was not called, which seemed surprising, but I did not give the matter much importance.

The visits that Monsignor Escrivá received from different countries were totally regulated and organized, because the central government had established with the Father's approval, that 1) Opus Dei authorities in the countries had to explain why certain visitors should be received by Monsignor Escrivá; 2) that once back in their own countries they should make the prospective visitors understand what Monsignor Escrivá's "needs" are. This meant telling them that they should bring a gift of cash besides some other token of their esteem. Many people sent a check beforehand or handed it over on arrival when their visit was announced. Needless to say, nobody arrived emptyhanded.

When the Betancourts visited the Father, they made a most generous donation and invited me to lunch. I was advised that they would come for me at one o'clock and that I had to be back at three, an impossible time limitation in Rome, where lunch is a prolonged affair. I went out with the Betancourts, but in view of the time pressure, we decided to have just aperitifs. I was so upset at the restaurant that I became quite sick and vomited. The Betancourts brought me to their hotel to rest for a while, even at the risk of my getting back late. While Mrs. Betancourt went up to her room, her husband stayed with me in the vestibule and said bluntly that I seemed very different, very nervous. I explained that I had been in Rome for three weeks without any assigned job and still did not know why I had come. He offered to give me money. They fussed over me; and finally told the hotel manager in my presence that if I should ever turn up at the hotel, he should give me whatever I needed at their expense. They went away quite worried and called several times, once from Florence. We chose our words carefully, because we suspected that someone was listening in.

In family life within the central government I was under surveillance. I received absurd fraternal corrections, such as that my Venezuelan accent was noticeable when I spoke. Whatever the fraternal correction, they always added that "I exhibited enormous individualism and tried to squelch others." When I asked them to give me an example to understand my fault better, they never provided one. Accordingly, in family life, I spoke as little as possible.

I had yet to be told if I was to go to Spain to visit my family or return to Venezuela. Eventually, I sensed that there were plans for me that Monsignor Escrivá would tell me. They attempted to distract me like a child; the confidences dealt with silly topics. I never found out what the real problem was. One day I went out with one of the advisors to buy several things for Venezuela, a common practice when the directress of a country arrives in Rome. But I realized that it was all a charade. When we came back, the giggles among the advisors were too obvious.

I went to confession to Father Carlos Cardona, who was the ordinary confessor of the house, and who, as I recall, was the spiritual director of the central advisory. In my first confession, I told him with some anxiety about the strange treatment I was receiving from my superiors, which had no connection to the explanation for my trip to Rome given me by the counselor of Venezuela. I had not seen the Father again since the night of my arrival. During my first two confessions Father Cardona seemed kind and understanding, but suddenly he changed. He repeated unceasingly that my leaving Venezuela was providential, because my salvation was in danger due to a very sophisticated pride. As confessor he understood and saw all this in the name of God. It was clear through his change of attitude that either the Father, or the superiors on the Father's instructions, had given him directions to follow in my case. My anguish became terrible.

During my confidence and even in my confession there were insinuations that I had done terrible things in Venezuela, letting me understand that they went against the Father and the spirit of the Work. But again I pressed and requested specifics so that I might amend and repent of them; the only answer I got was: how was it possible that I didn't realize? Nobody went beyond that or specified anything to me.

My anguish grew so dreadful that one night after supper I decided to speak to Mercedes Morado, the central directress. I plainly stated that I noted great tension around me and to please tell me what they planned to do with me. A month had gone by since my arrival from Venezuela, and I didn't know what I was doing in Rome. I broke down and began to cry, but Mercedes remained cold and hard. To end the conversation, she said: "I don't know anything, do you believe me?"

I answered that it was difficult to believe that she, the central directress, didn't know why I was in Rome. But finally I blurted out: "Yes, I believe you. Just as I still believe in the Father's note that said that I was coming here to rest for a few days."

In the confidence, I mentioned several things I found disturbing at the central house in Rome. Rather than a sense of inclusiveness of all countries, everything revolved around Spain; Italian was hardly spoken. In addition, the directors lacked warmth, and there was servility rather than affection for the Father along with a cultic worship of his personality. Family life was not spontaneous, and people were not free to come and go. Above all, there was such a sense of discretion and secrecy that everything had become sheer misery. For example, you were never told when a numerary was coming from another country; you simply met her in a hall or saw her in the oratory.

Naturally, both Marlies Kücking in the confidence and Father Cardona in confession told me that what I had to say showed my lamentable critical spirit. Because I had mentioned some of these matters to a senior numerary or some servant who had reminisced with me about the years 1952–1956,

I became the recipient of extraordinarily sharp fraternal corrections, being told that this was murmuring, scandal, and bad example. The moment came when I did not know what to talk about.

The superiors never spoke to me about Venezuela. I felt like someone from another planet in those surroundings.

One night, Rosalía López, the servant who always waited on the Father at meals, said to me: "The Father has asked me how you are." (I had not seen the Father again since the night of my arrival.) "What did you tell him?" "Well, that you're very Venezuelan, and you talk the way they do there."

I was very careful not to let my tongue slip in front of her, because I knew well that she carried tales to the Father.

The atmosphere in Villa Sacchetti and the central house reminded me of the movie *The Nun's Story,* based on Catherine Hulme's novel, where she depicts the central house of a Belgian religious order and calls its superiors "the living rules." I had the same feeling: I was speaking to "living rules," not human beings.

As I described it in my confidence, the atmosphere in the house was like a police state: between the coldness of the superiors, my reclusion, the commandments from on high, and the letter of the spirit instead of the spirit of the letter, together with what I call that "mysterious discretion," and everything wrapped up in "the Father says," "the Father likes," "the Father has said," "the Father passed through here," and so forth.

Two thoughts occurred to me. On the one hand, I wondered if the Rome I had known from 1952 to 1956 was not more open than this other Rome that I met now. We worked like madwomen then, but I remembered it as more human. On the other hand, I thought that the open, warm temperament of Venezuela had changed me, and that coming back to this house of the central advisory, I felt asphyxiated. We did not speak about the church or about apostolate, but about proselytism. We did not speak as much about God as about the Father. The Second Vatican Council was taking place but it was not mentioned in a single get-together.

The eve of a First Friday, before entering the oratory, Rosalía López, Monsignor Escrivá's maid, said to me: "Miss, say goodbye to your country, because you are not going back to Venezuela."

I reminded her that what one hears in the administered house should never be repeated. When I mentioned the incident to the central directress, she responded: "To what are you going to pay attention, to what I say or to what a servant says?" "Naturally to what you tell me," was my answer. "Well then, don't pay attention to the servant."

To some degree, I went to the exposition of the Blessed Sacrament with greater peace.

Since I had not expressly been told to hand over my letters to the directress, I took advantage of the arrival of people from Venezuela and wrote two or three short letters as a major superior to my directress in Caracas, telling her the uncertainty in which I lived, the anguish I felt, and the closed atmosphere of the house.

Disillusion

One day in November just before noon, I was notified that I had been summoned by the Father. I immediately went to the central advisory sessions chamber. The room is not large. To reach it one must cross the government oratory. The walls and high-backed chairs are upholstered in red velvet. A refectory table is in the middle. In one wall there is a niche with the Virgin of the Work. The small image is carved according to the vision that Monsignor Escrivá had of Our Lady, they told us in whispers.

I entered the room. Monsignor Escrivá was seated at the head of the table. Don Alvaro del Portillo was absent. However, at Monsignor Escrivá's left was seated Father Javier Echevarría, who at that time had no role whatsoever in the Women's Branch. At Monsignor's right was the central directress, Mercedes Morado, and at her right, the prefect of studies, Marlies Kücking. Monsignor Escrivá ordered me to sit next to Marlies. The conversation went as follows:

"Look, Carmen, because I am not going to call you María del Carmen, as you like." He paused to look around as if seeking approval. "I have called you," he continued, "to tell you that I want you to work here in Rome. You are not going back to Venezuela! We brought you here under false pretenses," he said smiling, almost amused, "because otherwise, with that temper of yours, I don't know what you might have been capable of. So, now you know. You are not going back to Venezuela. You're not needed there, and you will never return. At a given point I sent you there because you had to save the day and you did it very well. Now, you're no longer needed at all! It is better that you never go back again."

My voice sounded unexpectedly strong and clear and made everyone turn their eyes toward me when I said with utter respect: "Father, I would like to live and die in Venezuela."

Visibly annoyed, Monsignor Escrivá rose from his chair and began to shout at me: "No and no! Didn't you hear! You're not going back, because I don't want you to, and I have authority"—and he pointed his finger at each of those present—"to order him and her and you, with your gigantic pride! You are not going back!"

It was as if scales had fallen from my eyes. I responded sadly: "Father, that is very difficult for me."

"Well, if it's difficult for you, it's also difficult for me," Monsignor Escrivá shouted striking his chest, "not to go back to Spain and here I am: stuck in Rome! And if you love Venezuela, I love Spain more! So, put up with it!"

Monsignor Escrivá started to leave, and we all rose. Heading toward the Relics Chapel, he turned back and exploded again: "Besides, that is pride! I'm going to say Mass now and I will pray for you. Stay in the oratory for a while." And he left through the Relics Chapel.

I waited in the oratory for about fifteen minutes, and asked the central directress if I might speak with her. In her work room I broke down and could not stop weeping. Between my sobs, I repeated that what hurt most was to find that I had been deceived and that the Father had lied and made the others lie. I told her that it seemed dishonest to circulate a printed letter which says that "people will be asked whether they want to go to a country or not," since they had not only not asked me about my preference, but had lied to me the whole time. In my tears, I kept repeating that what crushed me was to realize that the Father had lied.

I went to my room and did not want to eat. I spent the whole afternoon there. The physician, María Jesús de Mer, came to my room and forced me to swallow some pills against my will; without telling me what they were, they put me to sleep.

The next morning at ten, the central directress, Mercedes Morado, called me to the *soggiorno* of La Montagnola, the central advisory house. With her were the government secretary, Mary Carmen Sánchez Merino, and the procurator, Carmen Puente, a Mexican. The central directress asked me if I felt calmer. I said "yes," shrugging my shoulders like one who has no other choice. She also asked me if I still thought that they had lied to me in the note and that the Father had deceived me and had lied. "Yes, I still think so."

Realizing that she made these questions in front of advisors who had not been at the meeting the day before, I asked her: "What is this? An admonition?"[1]

Mercedes answered: "No, no. It is caring and wanting to see how you are. Very well, now go to your room."

I went to my room.

First Canonical Admonition

My room was at the other end of the house. I had not been back there for more than twenty minutes when they notified me by the intercom

---

1. Admonitions are official reprimands made to Opus Dei members concerning serious matters. At least three are required to dismiss a member. See *Constitutions*, 1950, pp. 62–68.

in the hall that I should go immediately to the sessions room of the central government.

I entered. Monsignor Escrivá was standing and visibly irate. Father Javier Echevarría and Father Francisco Vives were on his left, both looking very stern. At the Father's right was the central directress, Mercedes Morado, the physician, María Jesús de Mer, and the prefect of studies, Marlies Kücking. All of them looked furious. I felt terrified at the scene.

The interview went as follows:

"These people have told me," Monsignor Escrivá said, pointing his finger at the central directress and the other two advisors present, "that you have received the news that you are not going back to Venezuela with hysteria and tears." Beside himself, he shouted at me, "Very bad spirit! You are not going back to Venezuela, because your work has been individualistic and bad! And you have murmured against my documents! Against my documents, you have murmured!"

His anger affected his breathing, and he held his clenched fist close to my face. "This is serious! Serious! Serious! I admonish you canonically. Let it be so recorded," he said directing his words to Javier Echevarría, who, I insist, had no position whatsoever in the women's central government. "Next time," continued Monsignor Escrivá, "you are out! Always complications since 1948! You and that other one! Now you come to me with this. And don't cry, because your trouble is that you are proud, proud, proud . . ." Repeating these words he went through the chalice room, toward the major sacristy.

I stood frozen. I did not budge. The central directress said angrily: "What unpleasantness you are causing the Father!"

I should like to explain here the past event to which Monsignor Escrivá obviously was referring. In 1948, when I was struggling with my vocational problem, I made a trip to Valladolid to attend an alumnae reunion of the French Dominican nuns' school. Incidentally, I discussed my situation with Mère Marie de la Soledad, who, as I said, did not see my vocation to Opus Dei clearly. However, I concluded that if God sought it of me, I should surrender my doubt and stop thinking of my fiancé. I discussed the matter again with the nun who suggested that I send the news about my final decision to my confessor, Father Panikkar. So, I simply resolved to send a telegram to Molinoviejo, where he was at the moment. As I recall, the text of the telegram was something like: "I have offered everything for the missions, although more in love than ever." (Obviously, I was talking about loving my fiancé.) Naturally my confessor understood the text, but apparently not the director of the house, who opened the telegram and discussed it with an Opus Dei superior, as they told me later. Several months later, on a trip to Madrid, Encarnita Ortega, who by then lived in Rome, called me to Zurbarán and told me in the crudest fashion "that I had declared my love to an Opus Dei priest by telegram." I was dumbfounded, because nothing was further from the truth. I so informed her. When she told me what she and the Father believed, I could not believe my ears. I explained matters, but she refused to understand. I then said that I lamented that something had been so greatly misinterpreted, that I was truly sorry, and that I would present my apologies to Monsignor Escrivá, telling him that I did not wish to offend any of his priests in any way and much less my confessor. After that I did not go to Zurbarán for a while. Now, with this admonition, Monsignor Escrivá made me recall such an unpleasant incidence.

All of the advisors departed and left me alone with my anguish. They made just one indication: "Come to lunch on time."

I could not believe what I heard and saw. That good, affectionate Father, whom I had dearly loved, for whom I had done everything in my life since coming to Opus Dei, had just formulated an admonition with the threat of expelling me from Opus Dei. I could not accept that Monsignor Escrivá could be so harsh and not allow me the opportunity to speak to him alone, listening and questioning me before judging me in public. It was a trial with no defense but only prosecution. Above all, I was hurt by the Father's manners, his lack of understanding, or more precisely, his lack of charity.

I kept repeating his phrase: "Next time, you're out," but still could not believe it. The "murmuring" about the documents to which Monsignor Escrivá referred must have meant my overt comments to the counselor and regional priest secretary of Venezuela, suggesting that the members of Opus Dei be allowed to go to confession to whomever they wanted as long as the confessor was an Opus Dei priest or, should special circumstances arise, with anyone authorized to hear confessions. Although such freedom is written into Opus Dei documents, it is "bad spirit" if anyone actually uses it. I considered all this a serious lack of freedom opposed to the freedom of which Opus Dei members were supposed to be pioneers.

My comments were equally open, and in the course of my official responsibilities, with the superiors of the Venezuelan regional government, when notes arrived laying down obligations, as for example: "Our members will make a monthly outing to the countryside." Since Venezuela does not have a countryside but a jungle, we interpreted the notes by going to private beaches at times when they were not crowded, taking advantage of an apartment loaned by a friend or cooperator. Or, again, my comments referred to requests from Rome to get subscriptions for the then newborn *Actualidad Española,* a magazine edited by Opus Dei, which had no interest for anybody in Venezuela.

Incommunicada

In the afternoon of the day I received the first admonition, Marlies Kücking came to my room and told me that the Father had decided the following: *a)* that I would not write to Venezuela again; *b)* that they would not give me any letter that might come for me from there; *c)* that if visitors from Venezuela should ask for me, they would be informed that "I was sick or temporarily away from Rome"; *d)* that I must make reparation for the harm I had done in Venezuela; *e)* that they would attempt to make everyone in Venezuela forget me and that they would make clear to all what "bad spirit" I had shown; *f)* that I had deformed the spirit of the Work; *g)* that only *by prayer and blind obedience* would I save my soul; *h)* that no one in the house in Rome was to be aware of "my lamentable situation." They wanted to help me to get out of the pothole in which I was stuck because of my pride ("Pothole" means any spiritual problem you might have.) I did not respond. I accepted what Marlies said and only asked that they should tell me about Begoña Elejalde's ongoing health problems, because her illness was serious and she had recently undergone an operation. Days later Mercedes Morado responded negatively to this request, telling me that "I could not even ask how Begoña's health was; my will should force my intellect to not ask," which meant to put the will on a higher level than the intellect.

We had learned about Begoña's illness shortly before I left Caracas. When her family learned of the operation, they called from Bilbao, but I received orders from the counselor, Father Roberto Salvat, not to inform them that she had Hodgkin's disease and to downplay the gravity of her illness. I felt uncomfortable talking to Begoña's mother, since I could not tell her the truth.

I know that she was sent to Spain, and once, by chance, we met in the Barcelona airport. I was delighted to find that she was the same as always and that she was pleased to see me. However, in our brief conversation, we only exchanged generalities about her sister whom she had just seen off.

After Marlies's visit, they changed my room and put me in charge of all the oratories of the house. There were some fourteen or fifteen oratories with several large sacristies where all the vestments and sacred vessels were kept. My job was to prepare the vestments for each Mass that was celebrated in the house and to iron the oratory linens, prepare candles for each set of candlesticks, which were different in every oratory, and make all the hosts. The work was endless; the oratories were far apart; several Masses were celebrated in each of them, and the time to perform these tasks in the afternoon was minimal. Each morning I had to put away all the vestments used in the Masses and bring the dirty linen back home.

Nobody helped me in the work except on feast days when we used the best chalices, normally kept in the Chalice Chapel. There are many chalices in the Opus Dei central house, since each country has sent one to the Father or has made a contribution to have one made. Monsignor Escrivá often said that he wanted a chalice in which the screw linking the foot and the cup was a large diamond; he did not want it to be seen from the outside, but be reserved for Our Lord alone.

When a female numerary comes to Opus Dei, she turns over all the jewelry she owns, which is hand delivered to Rome. I cannot estimate the value of the jewelry that we sent to Rome in my time. Later I was humbled by being reminded by a woman who had been a numerary for many years in Venezuela that I once had told her to remove the precious stone in her ring so as to send it to Rome, and to replace the diamond with a false jewel. When she told me her mother might notice, I even suggested that she tell her mother that the ring was dirty. In my eagerness to help Rome and serve the Father I, too, lied.

The next order that I received was to take charge of cleaning the administered house. I thought that perhaps I would drown my anguish in work.

I wanted to inform my director in Venezuela and the other advisors about my situation in Rome and that I would not return again. Since it was impossible to do so through Opus Dei's "legal channels," I managed one afternoon to go out with an advisor who did not speak Italian, and on the pretense that I had to find out whether the Betancourts had left something in my name for the Father, I went to the hotel where they had stayed. I had prepared a note which I handed to the manager with the request that he take care of it, while I asked him if the Betancourts had sent anything for me. He asked me to wait for a minute. He disappeared. Two minutes later, without the paper in his hand, he said that he would remember to notify me if anything arrived, adding: "Tutto a posto, signorina" ("Everything is in order, Miss"). I know now that the telegram reached Venezuela. It said simply that I was staying in Rome under the Father's strict orders.

From that day in November 1965 until March 1966, *I was held completely deprived of any outside contact, with the absolute prohibition to go out for any reason or receive or make telephone calls, or to write or receive letters. Nor could I go out for the so-called weekly walk or the monthly excursion. I was a prisoner.*

I developed the mentality of an inmate and learned to recognize people by their steps. I learned how long each person took to complete any task. I did not ask for anything. Julia, the older servant, who had known me for so many years, said to me one day in the ironing room: "Don't forget that God sees everything and will not abandon you," and she shook her head, expressing her discomfort: "My, my!" Although no complaint escaped my lips, the people in the house knew that I was not allowed to move freely and the disrespectful treatment that I had received from Monsignor Escrivá.

Almost two weeks after the admonition, they called me to the session chamber of the central advisory. I trembled as I entered the room.

Gathered there were Father Francisco Vives, central secretary for the Women's Branch worldwide, Father Javier Echevarría, with no authority in the Women's Branch, the central directress, Mercedes Morado, and Marlies Kücking, prefect of studies, who received my confidence.

Father Francisco Vives told me to sit down because he wanted to clarify something related to the admonition the Father had given me. What followed was as close to a set of specific charges as I ever received.

a) "I had murmured against the Father's writings, and I should recall that any writings sent by the Father to the regions had been submitted to internal censorship, although that was not required. It was therefore arrogance on my part to question the Father's writings.

b) "I was very attached to Venezuela and this was deadly.

c) "I had diabolical pride because some people in Venezuela had come to be so attached to me that they didn't dedicate themselves to the Work.

d) "I had personally hurt the Work by trying to rise above it.

e) "I had to cut off all contact with Venezuela and have no further contact with anyone there.

f) "He (Father Francisco Vives) was aware that I had requested in my confidence to leave Rome for Spain, but I should realize that my personal problem would have to be resolved in Rome, since the Father, because of his special love for me, wanted me to remain in Rome.

g) "I would have to fill my day with intense work.

h) "I would have to begin at the bottom and lower than the bottom; I would have to forget everything I knew and had done and ask my director about absolutely everything as if in a spiritual childhood: from how I had to put on my panties to how to fasten my bra.

i) "I should forget my experience and past life and should ask God to give me a child's humility.

j) "This was going to be very difficult because of my diabolical pride, but everyone was going to pray for me so that I might get out of this pothole in which I had fallen.

k) "I should not think of leaving Rome or think that my stay would only be transitory. I had to remain there in the form and fashion that the Father determined.

l) "Nobody in the house could become aware of my *lamentable situation.*

m) "What I had said to the Father was unheard of, that 'I wanted to live and die in Venezuela,' because nobody in the Work had ever contradicted anything the Father had said."

To all this Father Francisco Vives added that I was "nothing and nobody in the Work." I recall his contempt and the gestures of disgust that accompanied his words during this "conversation."

It was his idea that I should go to confession immediately.

All seemed like a nightmare, although this conversation was almost a repetition of what Marlies Kücking had said to me in the previous days.

I understood that my confidences and confessions were manipulated and that, with the excuse of "helping me get out of the pothole," my soul was on public display.

It goes without saying that for a priest like Father Francisco Vives to describe such an array of past "misdeeds," he must first have spoken to Monsignor Escrivá. Of this I had not the slightest doubt.

For months the tension was brutal and the confidences with Marlies Kücking were sheer torture.

In order to make my confidence with her I had to follow a routine: I had to telephone her to remind her that it was my day for the confidence and ask her what time was convenient for her. When I arrived punctually for our appointment, almost always at the visitors' parlor in La Montagnola, the women's central government house, there were times when she made me wait more than an hour. One day I told her that perhaps it would be "lack of spirit," but that I wanted to learn about the health of Begoña, the numerary who had Hodgkin's disease. She told me that it was bad spirit, because I had to avoid thinking about anything or anybody that had to do with my stay in Venezuela.

Several Venezuelan numeraries studied in Villa delle Rose, seat of the Roman College of Santa Maria in Castelgandolfo. They had left the country a month before me. They were Mirentxu Landaluce, Mercedes Mujica, and Adeltina Mayorca. They had all belonged to local councils in different houses in Caracas before coming to Rome. Of course I had not seen them yet. I remember that the central directress told me shortly after my arrival in Rome to go with Montse Amat, a Catalonian who was prefect of studies, to visit Villa delle Rose. We arrived, and—surprise!—the students had all gone on an excursion. Only Adeltina Mayorca and a member of the local council, Blanca Nieto, who was the subdirector of the press, when I left Rome the first time were there. I might have swallowed the story better if Montse Amat, who was in the central advisory, had not told me that she "didn't know that they had an excursion." I realized that they did not want me to meet the students nor that they should meet me. I remembered the Venezuelan saying, "What is one more stripe for a tiger," and I let the matter go.

These pupils came to Rome almost weekly to lunch or an afternoon snack in the central house. Marlies Kücking ordered me not to speak to any Venezuelans. One day when she saw me speak to one of them on the staircase, she subjected me to a gruelling interrogation, as well as the other person, I later discovered.

Marlies asked me what topics we had mentioned in the conversation, if we had spoken of Venezuela, about what and about whom. She repeated the interrogation altering the order of the questions. It was a secret-police interrogation. The most normal things were interpreted as "war crimes." What I did not realize then was that these methods of asking about the same thing a thousand times is exactly what is done by the security forces in all repressive regimes. What is intolerable is that in the name of God and the church, Opus Dei would use such an approach to "obtain information." After all, the Inquisition was abolished centuries ago. Here, again, the Opus Dei system is identical to that of any sect.

A few days after Monsignor Escrivá gave me the first admonition, Marlies Kücking, called me to the central government *soggiorno* and informed me that I was no longer directress of the Venezuelan region, and by indication of the Father she was giving me a copy of the rescript, number 215, as a subject for meditation. This rather long note, written by Monsignor Escrivá, says that *cargos son cargas,* offices are burdens and should be left with the same joy with which they had been undertaken. I told Marlies that I had already done my mental prayer that afternoon, but that I would use the rescript for meditation the following day. Just in passing, I asked her: "Who is regional directress now?" The question greatly irritated her. She said:

"You must understand, Carmen, it is lack of tact and discretion to ask that question. It should no longer matter to you. How could such a question occur to you? Don't you understand?" "No, I don't understand. But it's all the same. I accept if fully."

Given the isolation to which I was subjected, I asked Marlies in one of my confidences if the canonical admonition carried any penalties. She told me it did not.

I put the same question to the central directress, Mercedes Morado, and she told me the same. Both Marlies and Mercedes told me that nobody "oppressed" me, that it was "my imagination." They also added that everything they did was by the Father's indication to facilitate my spiritual recovery. I asked permission several times to go out and the answer was always, "No."

Mrs. de Sosa's Visit

My friend from Venezuela, Ana Teresa Rodríguez de Sosa arrived in Rome in December, 1965.

She telephoned the house, and by some coincidence, I answered the phone, since I was the only one present who spoke Italian. She asked for me, but naturally, following the "rules," I did not identify myself, notified the central directress by intercom that Mrs. de Sosa was on the phone, and switched the call to her office.

That day I prayed to God with all my soul that I would be allowed to see Ana Teresa. That night Marlies told me to call Mrs. de Sosa at her hotel, saying that I was out when she called (another lie) and that she could come to see me the following afternoon.

When I called the hotel, Mrs. de Sosa—who was not bashful—told me that it seemed very odd that I had not returned her call until the evening, since she had called me several times, which I did not know.

"Child, everything seems strange. I have called you several times and you haven't answered. Are you being held prisoner so you can't answer my calls?," she added half jokingly.

Since I feared someone might be listening on the government office phone, which was connected to mine, I answered in French that indeed, I was, and that she should do everything possible and impossible to speak to me alone when she came to see me the next day.

Lourdes Toranzo was the numerary who had attended Mrs. de Sosa on her previous visits to Rome. It annoyed me extraordinarily when she referred to this woman "to whom it was necessary to attend because she made large contributions to the Work," without a touch of genuine affection. Lourdes mentioned that Mrs. de Sosa had told her she would bring flowers for the oratory in the morning. It so happened that following morning, a Peruvian numerary who had been in charge of the oratories was showing me how the electrical master switches worked. They were located near the delivery door, which the concierge had opened while she cleaned the entrance. Suddenly I recognized Mrs. de Sosa's voice. Seeing the delivery door open and the servant there, she left her orchids for the oratory and turned away. Instinctively, I rushed out that door to catch her, since I was afraid they would not let me speak with her alone that afternoon; but Mrs. de Sosa did not see me for she had gotten into her taxi and was heading toward Bruno Buozzi. Although I was outside for less than a minute and a half, the concierge had immediately reported by intercom to the advisory that I had set foot in the street. (The idiom was never more literal.)

When I rejoined the Peruvian numerary at the switch box, I said: "I'm afraid that they are going to scold me for having tried to greet Mrs. de Sosa." "The way they are treating you is ridiculous," the girl replied, "but I don't think they will." At just that moment Marlies appeared, looking incensed. (In the midst of it all God conserved my sense of humor and, when she and Mercedes were furious, they reminded me of Walt Disney's weasels showing their teeth.) Marlies asked: "What happened with Mrs. de Sosa?"

I explained I had heard her voice and gone out in order to greet her. Furious, she continued: "If you go on this way, we will have to take stronger and harsher measures with you, more vigorous measures. What you have done is intolerable! You have broken a firm order not to leave the house."

I begged her pardon, but I was sure there would be reprisals. That same afternoon I was waiting for them to announce Mrs. de Sosa's arrival. At the precise moment when the concierge announced that the lady had arrived, Marlies told me that Lourdes Toranzo would be present during the visit and would bring Mrs. de Sosa to the Villa Sacchetti *soggiorno*. I had no choice but to agree. I arrived at the visitors' parlor and Mrs. de Sosa was alone. I handed her a letter I had written and went out to call Marlies by intercom to say Lourdes had not arrived. Marlies said it didn't matter, that it was all right, but that "I should try to make the visit short."

When I returned to the parlor, Mrs. de Sosa said that Lourdes Toranzo had shown up to accompany us, but that she had told Lourdes that she had already seen her the day before and that she wanted to see me and to speak with me. We went up to the Villa Sacchetti *soggiorno* and I chose a place to sit down that was out of reach of the microphone installed in this room. (Monsignor Escrivá had ordered several microphones installed in different places in the house, all connected with his room.) One of them was in the *soggiorno* or living room, another in the oratory, another in the ironing room, another in the kitchen, another in the hall in the servants quarters; and also in several places in the central advisory house, La Montagnola.

Rapidly, I explained my situation to Mrs. de Sosa and I gave her a sheet of paper to read later, saying that the only way that they would let me go to have lunch with her was to extend the invitation in the same note that enclosed an extra donation to the Work. She sent a thousand dollars for the Work in a check made out to me. They had no choice but to let me go to have lunch with her alone, although I was instructed that, if I went out at twelve-thirty, I ought to be back at three.

I was completely open with Ana Teresa and described everything that was happening and what they had said to me: Her reaction was, "The Father must be getting senile, because what they have done to you is an injustice." She bought me stamps so that I could write as much as I wanted and told me that she would write to me care of General Delivery, Rome. She acted in every way as a true friend. Her first reaction was that I should not return to Villa Sacchetti but stay with her. I said no, that there was a general congress scheduled in Opus Dei's Women's Branch and that I was convinced that things were going to change.

But this optimism was temporary, and when I was back in my room at Opus Dei, my spirits sank as I realized I could not even phone Ana Teresa without breaking the rules that had been imposed on me. However, the prison mentality stimulated by my involuntary reclusion had made me aware that there was a brief time—not more than two minutes—when I could use the telephone without being heard. The day before Ana Teresa's return to Venezuela, while I was cleaning the entrance area of the men's house, I realized there was an outside phone, and at considerable risk, I used it. I called her very early. I told her that I was thinking of leaving the Work, because neither my mind nor my physical strength were going to last much longer. I was trying to eat as much as I could to survive, but in spite of that, from mid-October to mid-December I had lost almost twenty pounds and my hair had turned completely white. They had broken me. Although Mrs. de Sosa tried to console me as best she could, I felt profoundly alone when I hung up and she left that day.

Correspondence Retained

I wrote my directress in Venezuela, believing she was entitled to an honest account of what was happening in Rome. However, I was afraid that if she wrote to General Delivery, some Opus Dei member would discover a way to collect my mail. Mrs. de Sosa wrote me a couple of letters to General Delivery that I was able to receive through a Venezuelan numerary who picked them up for me on a trip to the main post office in Rome. Through this same numerary, I also managed to arrange to open a post office box in one of the district post offices in Rome and received a few brief notes there from some of the advisors in the Venezuelan regional advisory. Once they included a meditation letter written by a Venezuelan Opus Dei priest which gave me some hope. He encouraged me by saying that we have to live God's will and that everything would pass, because superiors are human and can err, while God is above everything and everyone. It filled me with encouragement. Needless to say, I burned this letter after I read it.

Apparently, they sent a second meditation by this priest that must have been lost. I had torn up a third meditation to shreds, intending to burn it in the wash basin at night. While I was getting undressed, two of the advisors entered my room, searched high and low, and took away the shreds of the note that I had hid at the back of the closet days before. I had made the dreadful mistake of showing one of these letters to two students who were at the Roman College of Santa Maria. Judging by the consequence, today, I am almost certain that they had reported the matter to their superiors.

Here I would recall a remark I made in the introduction that I would always use real names but to avoid reprisals by Opus Dei superiors I would refrain in exceptional cases from identifying certain persons, since they still belong to the prelature. A condensed version reached me then of the events in Caracas which paralleled my reclusion in Rome. Subsequently, I was to learn of them in detail from trustworthy sources.

The numeraries had been informed of my retention in Rome one by one in the following manner: "María del Carmen will not come back again. There is to be no comment by anyone." Obviously, that put my stay in Rome in a cloud of suspense. Here, Ana María Gibert merits a brief parenthesis. She was my directress in Caracas, as I have said. Doubtless her sending me two or three letters to Rome motivated her removal from Casavieja to a bedroom on the top floor of Etame School of Art and Home Economics, where she was held completely incommunicado for about two weeks. She could not receive telephone calls, mail, visits, or any contact with the other numeraries who lived in the house. Ana María must have been about 46 years old then. The directress of the Etame School of Art and Home Economics, Lucía Cabral, an intelligent woman who had worked in one of the most progressive schools in Venezuela under doctor Luisa Elena Vegas, acceded to Opus Dei's tactics and acted as Ana María Gibert's jailer. She had to bring her food at mealtimes.

This treatment of Ana María Gibert, a person of prestige in the academic world, who had sacrificed her professional and personal future in the interest of the Work, was one of the most unjust things I have known in Opus Dei. Beloved of numeraries and outsiders for her affability, spiritual life, and maternal character, she was one of the numeraries who began our work in Venezuela. She established a fine atmosphere at the Etame school and maintained its good reputation, along with Begoña Elejalde. After her forced reclusion, they sent Ana María to Opus Dei's Dairén students residence in Caracas and from there to Spain. Years later I met her on a Salamanca street, as I will describe later.

Eva Josefina Uzcátegui took charge of removing my photographs from the houses of the Work. Not surprisingly, given her temperament, she performed the task without the slightest embarrassment in front of other numeraries.

I was beginning to feel utterly exhausted. I thought I was being treated unjustly, but in order to repent I needed to know the specifics of my sins. I asked for examples again and again, and they never gave any. Everything was left hanging in the air; the accusations were serious but always couched in vague terms. St. Francis de Sales's phrase that you can catch more flies with a spoon of honey than a bottle of vinegar came to mind frequently.

For example, they spoke of "murmuring"—but the criticism they referred to was open and meant to be constructive. After all, I had not gone about the streets of Caracas proclaiming my opinion about the rescripts sent by Monsignor Escrivá, but discussed them frankly with Opus Dei superiors in Venezuela. I had even made my differences of opinion known in a sealed letter I had sent to Monsignor Escrivá. Perhaps the most obviously sectarian characteristic of Opus Dei is precisely the absence of self-criticism. Even more than that, the divinization of its leader and the sanctification of its Founder in life made it practically impossible to disagree with anything he might say or write.

My physical strength was diminishing, and the idea of leaving Opus Dei came to me frequently. I wept a lot at night and had dreadful headaches during the day. I thought I must ask God to take my life, because in Opus Dei it is recommended that "you must ask God for death before failure to persevere." The truth is that I asked God a thousand times to take my life. The fancy of taking my own life even passed through my head, but obviously my mental health was still intact. I requested permission to do extraordinary bodily mortification, which was granted. I believe I treated my body with brutality.

Suicides

Years later I learned of suicide attempts by Opus Dei female numeraries who did not die but who were maimed for life. One of them was Rosario Morán (Piquiqui) in England. Piquiqui threw herself out of a window of an Opus Dei women's house in London. She did not kill herself but was seriously injured, breaking her pelvis. Once out of danger, she was taken to Madrid. She died insane, although of natural causes according to Opus Dei. One of the numeraries who cared for her (and whose name I will make available upon written request) informed me in detail about Piquiqui's insanity. I do not believe the claim that she was already insane. What I do believe is that Opus Dei drove her insane, which is different. As a child, I went to school with Piquiqui in Madrid. Her brother was in my class. We met again years later at Zurbarán and requested admission to

Opus Dei at about the same time. She was able to reside in houses of the Work before me. We were together in the Molinoviejo course, when she was preparing her trip to Mexico. People in Mexico were very fond of her and she was happy there. During my last stay in Rome we met again. Piquiqui had arrived from Mexico on her way to England. I remember a conversation we had in Villa Sacchetti in 1966, while the general congress of the Women's Branch was being held. We discussed possible appointments to the central advisory. As a consequence of that conversation, I was the object of a very energetic fraternal correction by Mercedes Morado, because Piquiqui had told her that we had talked about possible changes in the central advisory. I never understood why this was so wrong and thought that when I met Piquiqui, I would call her stupid at least. Certainly, Piquiqui was not insane in 1966. You must understand that one of the requirements of those whom Opus Dei chooses as numeraries is the absence of mental illness in their families.

A case in the United States involved an American numerary who had been at the Roman College of Santa Maria. On her return to the United States, the superiors led her to believe that she was attached to her male cousin who belonged to Opus Dei. She had never considered that affection reprehensible, but it turned into a nightmare for her. She lived in Washington, D.C. Going from one Opus Dei house to another, she began to wander aimlessly for hours. She arrived at a military installation where the soldiers found her with sores on her feet, dirty, disoriented, insane. They took her to hospital from which they notified her Opus Dei house, probably because of some piece of identification she was carrying.

The numeraries from her house came and without further ado had her committed to a mental institution. One day she asked for a little mirror with which she tried to commit suicide by cutting her veins. They took her from the insane asylum to the Opus Dei house, where a Peruvian numerary, Maricucha Valdearellano, who was in the United States regional advisory, did not pay the slightest attention to her. A numerary from another South American country who lived in the house took care of her and calmed her, especially at night. Apparently, the American numerary has recovered and still resides in an Opus Dei house, but not in Washington, D.C.

Another case with which I am familiar is that of Aurora Sánchez Bella, whom the Opus Dei superiors sent to England because one of her brothers held an important post there. Aurorita was a good person but had no gift for languages; while I was in the central advisory in Rome, I remember opposing her assignment to England. However, they sent her primarily because of her brother's position there. When I returned to Rome in 1965, she seemed quite unbalanced. Her room was next to mine, and at night I could hear her pacing up and down the room.

I pointed this out to Mary Tere Echeverría, who told me that "she already knew her situation." Opus Dei creates situations that can break people psychologically. When my brother Javier, who is a medical doctor, learned about my stay in Rome, he told me: "You can certainly say that you have no insanity genes, because others have lost their mind for less."

The family life that I shared in Rome with the central advisory consisted in participating with them in all common acts, meals and get-togethers. The common acts belonging to the life of piety were limited to the visit to the Blessed Sacrament, the Preces, and the rosary. Other than that, because of my work in the administration and the cleaning schedule, I fulfilled the remaining norms in one of the two Villa Sacchetti oratories.

The women's central advisory had its own dining room by now. It was not at all attractive. The only impressive thing was a round table where thirty could easily be seated. When some advisor from another country arrived, they ate there. One of the major superiors who came most often was the delegate in Italy, Maribel Laporte, a Spaniard. Maribel was the daughter of a colleague of my father's, and I knew her fairly well. Accordingly, when I arrived, she was one of those who was pleasant to me, doubtless because our parents would talk about their daughters in Rome. Her older sister, who became a nun and whom I knew well, always inspired respect and affection because of her sheer goodness, whereas Maribel, by contrast, always seemed somewhat of an opportunist.

Tiburtino

November 21, 1965, Monsignor Escrivá ordered everyone in the house to go to the Mass that His Holiness Paul VI was to celebrate in the Tiburtino to mark the assignment of the Parish of St. John the Baptist al Collatino to the Opus Dei. The pastor was Mario Lantini, the first Italian numerary and first Italian numerary priest, currently Opus Dei regional vicar in Italy. The Father also announced the blessing ceremony of the newly constructed Elis Center buildings, devoted to vocational-technical education, some of which were apparently completed. Monsignor Escrivá informed us that Opus Dei numeraries would line the Pope's path with lighted torches. He explained to us that unless we had specifically been designated to do so, we could not go to communion at the Pope's Mass. Among the numeraries so designated was Fernanda, the first Dominican numerary, who was rumored to be next directress in Venezuela. We were also informed that the majority of the women numeraries of the Italian region, at that time Milan, Naples, and Rome as well as representatives of the international press would be in Tiburtino.

After the Father had finished his announcements, some of us remained in the Gallery of the Madonna. Mercedes Morado reported that the Father had just said: "Daughters, take care to tell your little sisters [i.e., the servants]. I know that they love me very much, but for once, let them applaud the Pope more than me. They will have other opportunities to see me and applaud me." They repeated this to us many times.

They also told us that the Pope would visit an administration of the Women's Branch for the first time in the history of Opus Dei. Consequently, *it was totally forbidden under any circumstances that anyone should go to that administration.* Maribel Laporte, the delegate of the Italian region would be with the numeraries from the local council of that administration.

Also at this time the image of the Virgin, which is now placed in a chapel at the University of Navarra, was transported to Rome to receive the Pope's blessing.

I was instructed to go to the Tiburtino parish with two servants, Concha and Asunción, both long-time Opus Dei members. When we arrived at the parish church, the huge marble statue of the Virgin occupied the middle of the nave. The Father arrived giving orders to the men about the placement of the Virgin or some such thing. The servants had learned that "for once" they had to applaud the Pope more than the Father. The majority of the women who were going to communion wore white veils and were in the central nave. The two servants and I had a good view from a lateral nave.

The Mass moved me deeply. Paul VI lauded the Opus Dei and mentioned in the homily that he had worked in the neighborhood as a priest. When he said that one of the things that he praised most highly in Opus Dei was the "spirit of freedom," I rebelled and wanted to shout out loud: "Lies, Holy Father, lies!" I realized that the world press was there and that my shout in Italian would embarrass Opus Dei but felt that in the final analysis it would embarrass the church. Although I tried not to cry, I wept uncontrollably, my Catholic loyalty being stronger than the oppression of my soul. I could not help but reflect bitterly, however, on the distorted information that the Work's superiors must have given the Holy Father.

My thoughts were interrupted by one of the servants telling me that she had an urgent need to go to the bathroom. There were no restrooms around. The poor soul was in such discomfort that I took a chance and accompanied her to the administration. I rang the door bell and Maribel Laporte opened the door. Seeing me, she said in the most disagreeable tone of voice imaginable: "As always, disobeying with your bad spirit." Maribel's words and tone of voice squelched the poor servant's problem. She kept apologizing because I had been the object of abuse on her account. I calmed her down and told her not to worry.

The following morning they broadcast the ceremonies at the Tiburtino on television, and the order was given in the ironing room for everyone in the administration to go up to the fourth floor where the central advisory offices were situated *to see* the Father (not the Pope).

The only television set in the women's area was in a large room at the end of the corridor on the central advisory office floor. I asked the directress of the administration if she was sure that I was allowed to go up and she said I was. So I went up. It was the first time I entered the office floor since 1956. I went down the hall with the Peruvian I mentioned earlier, and passing by the open door of Mercedes Morado's office, I saw her reading a letter. I felt she saw me, however. The television room was dark. I saw Marlies. Thirty seconds later someone said: "Marlies, Mercedes is calling you." The next moment everyone heard Marlies summon me into the hall. Naturally, they also saw that I did not come back. Marlies said: "You had better go down to the ironing room and continue with the oratory work." I went down, swallowing my rage.

As was to be expected, the next day after lunch, Marlies called me to the central advisory visiting parlor in La Montagnola and told me she was surprised that I had gone up to the office floor when it was clearly established that no one could go up to that floor without permission. I said simply that the directress of the administration told me to go up with the others. Then Marlies responded: "Yes, but the directress of the administration does not know that you are not like the others nor does she know about your 'lamentable situation.'"

I kept quiet.

Mercedes Morado called me two days later and asked about the Tiburtino ceremony in general. I concentrated on the Mass and the Pope, although I knew that she wanted to get to the scene in the administration, as she eventually did. I did not go into any detail but simply said we had disregarded an express order. I made no commentary on Maribel's behavior. When Mercedes insisted, I only said: "We have to realize Maribel is still very young." I knew that my understanding bothered her more than any reproach would have.

Vatican II

This occurred at the end of November 1965 and the Second Vatican Council was to be concluded on the feast of the Immaculate Conception,

December 8. I asked for permission to go to the Vatican, saying that this was a very important event for me as a Christian, and that it was the only time in my life that an occurrence of such significance would take place in the church. Marlies and Mercedes Morado said no because there was a great deal of work in the house and "more important things to do than go to the conclusion of a Council." They added that Don Alvaro and "some of our brothers would be there and that was enough."

The television carried the ceremonies live that morning and ran the tapes that night. I was the only numerary in the house who was not permitted to watch TV. Of some three hundred women numeraries in the house, nobody went to the Vatican that day. I never understood this. Monsignor Escrivá's professed love of the church and the Pope rings hollow.

My parents tried to phone just before Christmas. Apparently, the connection was broken. What probably happened was that in the rush to look for Lourdes Toranzo who was my "guardian" in matters relating to the outside, they hung up. My parents then sent me a telegram informing me that they would call on Christmas Day. I was able to speak to them but realized that somebody was listening in, possibly Lourdes Toranzo. I insisted that I wanted to see them and that they should come to Rome, but to my great surprise my mother got on the phone and said that she was still very much afraid of flying and that they would come to see me in the spring, by train. In spite of my insistence, they could not understand. They were happy to have me nearer.

I had become passive, and I barely spoke. I was meek. I helped the servants with all my strength. I just listened. The only time when I spoke up was when the superiors in the women's central advisory would say in front of Latin American numeraries that in their countries people were "soft," "tacky," uncultured. I realized that the whole house was silently on my side.

The superiors did not give me a single card or letter at Christmas. Marlies simply said there was no mail for me. I was convinced she lied but had no proof. One day I took a desperate chance. Since I knew where the duplicates of keys were kept, including the key to the mailbox, I went up to the secretary's room and grabbed the duplicate of that key. Given the arrangement of the doors in the delivery area, it was an adventure full of suspense to open the mailbox without being heard. My heart was thumping, but I did it. I saw that there were at least eight letters for me. I found out who had sent them. I opened one of them, from Lilia Negrón, who could not understand my silence for months. She and her husband asked why I didn't answer their letters. I destroyed that letter. I left the other seven in the mail box, and, of course, with more suspense I returned the duplicate key to its place. A week later I asked Marlies whether any letters or Christmas cards had arrived for me, and she said no. Then I had clear proof she was lying.

I believe they were afraid I might escape through a window. In any case they changed my room again. This one had a window onto an interior terrace.

March 19 was St. Joseph's Day, an important Opus Dei feast for several reasons. First, it is Monsignor Escrivá's saint's day. Second, on that date vows are renewed, or whatever they are now called in the prelature: contracts, sworn promises, in the last analysis still a juridical bond before God carrying responsibilities. Furthermore, the evening before there is the custom in all Opus Dei houses and centers of making the so-called list of St. Joseph. The director writes on a sheet of paper the names of three persons that each numerary gives her, for whom she will pray and mortify herself during the year to win their vocation as numeraries. Once the list is completed, it is placed in an envelope which is closed and kept by the director until the following year. Finally, the litany of the saints and the Preces of the Work are recited. Next year on St. Joseph's Day the envelope is opened and there is jubilation when some of those whose names were written on the list are now numeraries.

I decided I was not going to commit suicide but that I had to find a way of loosening the noose around my neck. Therefore, I wrote a few lines to Monsignor Escrivá, congratulating him on his feast day and telling him that I would attempt to correct my errors. (I never knew what they were.)

A few days afterward, when Monsignor Escrivá came to La Montagnola, they called all of us who were in the administration to hear the Father speak. He was on the staircase, and the whole house was gathered between the vestibule and the white marble steps. In front of everyone, he addressed me and said that my letter had given him great joy. It was all the same to me. In years gone by, I would have been overjoyed by his words. Now I was so disillusioned, so broken, that the only thing I wanted was to be left alone until the General Congress so that there could be changes in the central advisory of the Work and that thereafter my situation might be definitively reviewed.

Towards the end of March, Marlies called me to go to the visitors' parlor in La Montagnola, asking me first: "Are you dressed?" "Yes," I answered. "Well, get up there at four."

I arrived at the room and I waited for an hour. I did not know what it was all about. Suddenly Father Francisco Vives and Father Severino Monzó appeared. Surprisingly, they met with me alone.

They were conciliatory. They told me that they wanted to help me "get out of the pothole." They saw months go by, and I was the same. I didn't improve. They understood that the Father had directed special words of affection and that I did not receive them as was hoped. I was to tell them what was happening to me.

Then I spoke. I told them clearly and bluntly that *a)* I felt like a prisoner; *b)* they were wearing me down in that forced isolation; *c)* the atmosphere around me was cold; *d)* they should tell me why I cannot have contact with Venezuela and why they told me lies so that people would not see, hear, or write to me; *e)* they didn't let me talk with the students of the Roman College of Santa Maria; *f)* I cannot go out alone; *g)* they should tell what horrendous things I had done in Venezuela, because without knowing what the sins were I could never duly repent; *h)* Marlies was a torture for me; *i)* they should have sent me to any other country in the world, except Rome; *j)* I didn't want to be near the Father, because he surrounded himself with a climate of suspicion, surveillance, and lack of affection. I told them what I thought of Rome and the house. I especially insisted that they change the recipient of my confidence from Marlies to somebody else, because I was afraid I might not be sincere with her; she inspired terror in me, because I knew the rage with which she spoke to me. Finally I said to them: "You have managed to break me!" And I began to cry.

To Father Severino, I said: "Besides, you, Father Severino, have known me for years. You know perfectly well that I have faced difficult and hard times and that I am not an idiot cry baby."

Then Father Francisco Vives gave a quick twist to my words: "Idiot no, cry baby very much."

Their conclusion was that things would change. I could go out alone to Mass, and even write a letter to Venezuela. I should be very sincere and humble. They would consider a different person for my confidence. I would not leave Rome, because the Father did not want that. But if I wanted to go out, I should say so, and I would go out.

Things did not change. From a "no," when I asked to walk around the block, the answer became "let me think it over and I'll tell you later." In other words, "no," just the same. I came to think that everybody was right except me. By dint of telling me that I had to forget how I had lived and what I had known in the last ten years and of Marlies objecting to anything I asked for, I noticed that my memory for names was fading. Sometimes I remembered faces but did not recall the names. I confused places and situations. By constant insistence that it was "bad spirit" to think about the past and the present, I started to think that my problem was a matter of my imagination, just as they claimed.

The moment arrived when I doubted my sanity. My memory slipped. I must confess that it has cost me years of concentration once again to remember names that were once so familiar and events that I had lived so intensely.

Years later, I understood that Opus Dei had brainwashed me; the agents were Marlies Kücking, Mercedes Morado, and, whether directly or indirectly, Monsignor Escrivá.

Restricted Freedom

The "freedom" granted after the conversation with Father Severino Monzó and Father Francisco Vives consisted in accompanying a servant to the dentist or going out for half an hour on Saturday to buy flowers for the oratories at one of the stands on Viale Bruno Buozzi. One anecdote is from an afternoon I accompanied a servant to the dentist. Her name was Soledad and she was one of the oldest servants. On the bus she wondered if, perhaps, I had found things different in the house from what they were in 1952. She told me that things had changed very much. Now, they hardly went out, and when they did, it was in groups to Villa Borghese. They no longer went downtown. I asked her why and she said she didn't know, but that things had been that way for four or five years. I made not the slightest comment. I looked at my watch and saw that we had exactly fifteen minutes before the appointment with the dentist, whose office was near the Piazza del Popolo. The thought was father to the deed. I got her off the bus and guided her through the square. I showed her the church where Luther preached, and I brought her through one or two of the little streets nearby where she saw some store windows. One cannot do much in ten minutes. We went to her dentist and returned home.

That night at supper time, I noticed strange vibrations toward me from the members of the government. I truly could not guess why.

Next day, I will remember as long as I live. They were showing *Mary Poppins* in the aula magna (the theatre). As I was about to enter the aula magna, they told me Mercedes Morado had called me to her office. As always, she made me wait, this time some fifteen minutes. The conversation went as follows: "What do you have to tell me, Carmen?" "Nothing special. What do you want me to tell you?" "Don't you have anything to tell me, nothing that is bothering you?" "Look, Mercedes, you know everything and nothing new has come up. What can I tell you?" "You haven't spoken with someone about something that bothers you, that you think was not right?" "Well, really no." "Is your soul so coarse? Think! Let's see, Carmen, to whom have you said something incorrect?" "I haven't spoken with anybody. I only went out yesterday with Soledad, and I didn't tell her anything." "There, there. Dig deeper! Do the comments that you made to a servant seem all right to you? Let's see, tell me what happened!" "Well, nothing. She told me that they no longer go out. I told her that it seemed strange, because the Father always says that we must go out at least once a week." I went on to tell her briefly what the servant had said the day before. "But let's see. What did you say?" "Well, I already told you. That I didn't understand that, because in the Work we must go out to be in touch with people, etcetera." "No etcetera, etcetera! No! What did you tell her!" "Look Mercedes, I don't remember because I didn't have a tape recorder, but it was all about the rule that the Work gives us and that the Father would not like it if he heard."

As may be supposed, she went on to tell me I had "murmured." I had "passed judgment on the conduct of superiors and specifically the Father, speaking to a servant." I had "made comparisons between 1955 and the present." I was "giving a huge bad example." It was not the first time that similar comments that I had made in the house had gotten back to her. The correct attitude would have been to run to Marlies or her as soon as I arrived home, to report that I had made this comment to a servant. It all reflected "my great lack of spiritual finesse." I should try to imagine how hurt the Father would be when he is told.

I said I was sorry, but I had not murmured as God was my witness, but that hereafter, she need not worry, because I would speak even less than I did. I was very sorry. So, I went in to see *Mary Poppins* with a monstrous rebuke ringing in my ears.

A letter from Caracas reached my secret post office box, informing me that Father José Ramón Madurga, who was stationed in Japan, had gone to Venezuela as ordinary visitor. He had spoken to each of the members of the regional government. Different superiors wrote to tell me their particular versions. They all agreed that Father José Ramón came with his mind made up and was shooting to kill. They all told him about the trick with which I had been yanked out of the country.

In January 1966, there was a reunion for counselors in Rome. I asked to speak with Father Roberto Salvat, Father José Ramón Madurga, or Father Manuel Botas. The central advisory denied my request. As it happened, during a Mass concelebrated by Monsignor Escrivá and Father Roberto Salvat and Father José Ramón Madurga, they asked us to bring more cushions to the sacristy of Santa Maria. The sacristy was a small triangle with mirrors so you could see yourself from all angles. We brought the cushions, and when I faced Father Roberto Salvat I looked fixedly at his eyes. He could not stand my gaze and lowered his eyes. Afterwards, when they asked him in Caracas if he had seen me, he said no. To lie about the most insignificant matter is characteristic Opus Dei policy.

Another day I also saw Father Manuel Botas in the sacristy. He could not speak to me but when he reached Spain he called my younger brother Manolo and told him to tell my parents that he had seen me in Rome and that I had failed a great deal, enough to impress the most hardened person. I had aged and was much changed.

During this period I was in charge of the oratory of Santa Maria and had to prepare the first two concelebrated Masses at which Monsignor Escrivá officiated. The Father was in high dudgeon. As we were preparing the first concelebration, he said: "We will do it once, and this will not set a precedent. This is not our style." At another point, referring to the concelebrated Masses, or rather to Paul VI: "Let's see if that man rests in peace." Monsignor Escrivá let show in words or gestures an attitude of disapproval regarding the application of Council doctrine. More than once I heard him make remarks about His Holiness Paul VI similar to those I had previously heard about Pius XII. "Let's see if he leaves us in peace once and for all, and the Lord God in his infinite mercy takes him to heaven." If he considered John XXIII "a hick," as many Opus Dei members could bear witness, he considered Paul VI an "old Jesuit." So, as I have mentioned earlier, it seems presumptuous when his Opus Dei biographers insist that he had ecumenical spirit or when the present Monsignor Javier Echevarría has the gall to assure the Holy See in official documents that Monsignor Escrivá "felt emotion when he recalled his meetings with His Holiness Paul VI."

The General Congress of the Women's Branch of Opus Dei was to take place in Rome in May. At the eleventh hour they decided it would be held in the Villa delle Rose, seat of the Roman College of Santa Maria. One of the reasons for this change was that I was at Via di Villa Sacchetti, and the central advisory did not want the electors to meet me. The congress filled me with hope, because I thought that the leadership would change and things would go back to normal. The congress took place, and except for Pilar Salcedo, who dropped by Villa Sacchetti one afternoon, the other electors did not come to the central house. Unfortunately, there were no substantial changes. Mercedes Morado was reelected central directress and they named Marlies Kücking second in command, that is secretary of the central advisory. The Mexican, Carmen Puente, continued as procurator. This was a blow to me. I saw no solution to my problem without changes.

May 9, 1966, I made the customary May pilgrimage to the Basilica of St. Mary Major, to which I have always had great devotion.

Second Canonical Admonition

Toward the middle of May of that year, the earth seemed to shake beneath my feet. I was summoned on the run, as always, to the sessions chamber of the central advisory. Monsignor Escrivá was seated at the head of the table, with Father Francisco Vives and Father Javier Echevarría on his left; Don Alvaro del Portillo was absent. At the Father's right were the central directress, Mercedes Morado, and Marlies Kücking, in her new capacity as secretary of the central advisory. I was told to sit between Mercedes Morado and Marlies Kücking. Something horrible was in the air. Shouting, puffing, and beside himself, Monsignor Escrivá said: "Look, Carmen, this has to end. You are not going to laugh up your sleeve at us."

He picked up a half sheet of paper that he had in front of him and adjusting his eyeglasses said to me: "They tell me that you write Ana María Gibert, that woman, that wicked woman! And that you have a post office box here in Rome."

He left the eyeglasses on the table and began shouting at me: "What is this, you great hypocrite, you deceiver, wicked woman?"

I answered him: "Yes, Father, I have written Ana María Gibert, but she is not a wicked woman."

Monsignor Escrivá went on reading from the sheet: "And that procuress Gladys, that sow, let her come in!"

Gladys was the Venezuelan numerary who helped me with the mail. She entered the sessions chamber completely pale. Without any preamble, Monsignor Escrivá began to shout at her: "Do you take letters to the post office for her, for this wicked woman? Do you comprehend the gravity of what you have done?"

Gladys remained silent. But Monsignor Escrivá insisted: "Answer! ANSWER!"

Gladys unimpressed, remained silent, so I intervened. "Yes, Gladys, say you have taken some letters for me."

After that Gladys said: "Yes, Father," and she fell silent. Monsignor Escrivá breathed deeply before going on. "You will no longer work for the central advisory. You will not set foot upstairs, on the advisory office floor. Let them find you some other job in the house. And now, go to your room and don't leave it for any reason! Do you hear? For any reason!

When Gladys left the sessions chamber, Monsignor Escrivá told the central directress and Marlies Kücking in the presence of the priests already mentioned: "After this, take that one," he said, referring to Gladys, "lift up her skirt, take down her panties, and whack her on the behind until she talks. MAKE HER TALK!"

Addressing me, Monsignor Escrivá shouted: "I give you the second admonition, hypocrite. You write me a letter on my saint's day telling me you want to begin again, and this is what you do to me! Tell these people everything, everything. You're a bad piece of work! I warn you that I'm waiting for some affidavits from Venezuela, and you'll find out what's trouble! You're a wicked woman, sleazy, scum! That's what you are! Now go! I don't want to see you!"

It is impossible to explain my state of mind. I was terrified. Leaving the sessions chamber, I had no idea of what they might do to me, and they gave me no time to think coherently. In the best tradition of secret-police procedure, I was interrogated relentlessly either by Marlies or by Mercedes. They called me to the visitors' parlor of La Montagnola, generally after lunch. Quite often I had to wait for an hour before one of them appeared.

I do not know what they wanted me to confess about my time in Venezuela. From the drift of their questions I had the impression that they were referring to something sexual, but they were never explicit. I did my best to cooperate, but since my conscience did not trouble me regarding this unknown thing, their questions were incomprehensible.

A standard question was: "Let's see. Have you thought of anything you haven't yet said?" If I answered: "But, about what?" "But how can you have such a coarse conscience? Try to think of something you didn't tell us about." And so on.

I felt physically and spiritually drained. I got rid of everything I had. Specifically, I threw away the key to the post office box through the grill of the window of my room; it fell into a neighbor's garden. When Marlies and Mercedes requested the key to the box, I told them that I had thrown it away. They understood down the toilet, and I let them think that, because if I had said it had fallen into a neighbor's garden, they would have been capable of going over the ground inch by inch to find it. I got rid of all my notes, letters from my family, and other written materials. I kept only some photographs of my parents and the records that dealt with my studies, and addresses. Naturally, my passport had been taken from me on arrival in Rome, as was customary.

When I failed to see Gladys in the oratory or at meals, I guessed they had secluded her. Risking everything, I found out where her room was. When she saw me arrive, she told me terrified that several members of the central advisory had interrogated her for an entire day without interruption and had told her that speaking to me would be a mortal sin. With all the strength of my being I told her that no one could tell her that she was in mortal sin for speaking to me. She should stop worrying about me and be faithful to God. I closed her door and have never seen her again. She is still an Opus Dei numerary, living in Venezuela.

Mercedes and Marlies continued to interrogate me several times a day and the questions went on for hours. They repeated the questions time and again.

"Tell me the number of the post-office box at Piazza Mazzini," Mercedes Morado asked.

I emphatically said that I would not tell them. Then they threatened me, saying that if I didn't tell them I was in mortal sin. They also kept repeating that I was killing the Father with my conduct.

After each interrogation they brought me back to my room. An advisor, usually Elena Olivera, accompanied me, and stayed in the room with me. I remember that I remained seated in front of the desk with my head in my hands awaiting the next interrogation. They kept at me from May 14 to May 31, 1966. In addition to an advisor in my room, there was another one in the hall. Even when I went to the bathroom, both stood right outside. They even took charge of throwing away my tampons when I had my period, after first having checked them to see if there was anything inside.

When I returned to my room after each interrogation, I observed that things kept disappearing. My overnight bag, my academic records, family pictures, addresses, and family dates. They went through everything. I found the closet in disorder, the bed, my pajamas, even my toiletries such as face cream or toothpaste. I do not know what they hoped to find. They asked me from whom was I getting money. Mrs. de Sosa had only given me a good supply of stamps.

They relieved the servant who acted as concierge, and Mary Tere Echeverría took charge of the keys to the door. She was the local directress of the central advisory house.

Furthermore, the telephone in the room off the Galleria della Madonna was permanently watched by a member of the administration's local council. They did not allow me to do anything in the house, not even cleaning, or going to the dining room. I was confined to my bedroom. They brought me up a tray with my meals. I was completely sealed in. They did let me go down to the oratory to make my prayer.

I began to shake almost constantly as a result of my terror. I was afraid they would take me to a mental institution, as I knew they had done to other members of the Work. In my fright I remembered that Ismael Medina, the husband of an old friend from Spain, was a journalist in Rome. I had his telephone number, which by an odd and happy coincidence I had jotted down in my missal. I commended myself fervently to God and took a desperate risk, coming from the oratory. I managed to reach the telephone just as the member of the local council was called away. I called and I could barely say: "Ismael, this is María del Carmen. Come to see me. Insist even though they will not let you see me. It is serious." I hung up.

Since I shook almost constantly, Chus de Mer, the physician, who belonged to the central advisory, took my blood pressure frequently. Despite that, the interrogations continued.

One day Mercedes Morado came to my room and said: "Let's see! Give me your little reminder book, crucifix, rosary, and pen!" She took everything away.

I was just able to utter the words: "Mercedes, Tía Carmen gave me that rosary." Her answer was: "You don't deserve it."

Gathering all my courage, I told her that I had come to Rome believing in the Work and in the Father, that I was without personal problems of any kind, but they had organized a gigantic problem for me with their behavior. If I had done anything wrong, let them tell me so that I might repent. But they continued without being specific, despite the scoldings they gave me.

Visits from a Spanish Friend

Ismael Medina, the husband of my friend Conchita Bañón, came to the house several times and phoned several times. They always told him that I was not in or that I was away from Rome, and they did not know when I would arrive. Finally, he told the numerary who opened the door that he would make inquiries at the Vatican. I found this out later from him. The fact is that Marlies came to my room and asked me if I knew Ismael Medina. I said I did. Next she asked me if I had called him, and I said no, so that they would not keep me from seeing him. Marlies went on to say that he was in the visitors' parlor and that I could see him but she would stay with me during the entire visit. I warned Marlies that that would seem very odd to Ismael, since I was a friend of his wife and that once when he visited Caracas, we had met at his hotel. Marlies insisted that if, during the visit he tried to see me alone, I should say that Marlies was a very good friend of mine. With this warning we arrived at the visitors' parlor.

I cannot express the joy it gave me to see Ismael. I introduced him to Marlies. After a few minutes Ismael suggested that he would like to speak to me in confidence. I docilely said that he could go ahead since Marlies was a "close friend of mine." Ismael made the obvious reply: "She may be a close friend of yours, but as for me, this is the first time I meet this lady." So addressing her, he requested politely that she have the kindness to leave us alone for a few minutes. Marlies smiled and without saying a word, she remained seated. The strange thing is that I could have spoken to Ismael and complained in front of Marlies about what they were doing to me, but I felt too terrified.

We began to speak about the "possible divorce of my parents," a completely preposterous subject, knowing as he did how united they were. Ismael told me that I would have to go to Spain to salvage the marriage and besides begged Marlies to tell my superiors that I was the eldest and had to speak with my parents.

Obviously, Ismael realized that I did not have any freedom whatsoever in view of the absurd conversation. I will always remember him saying goodbye with his eyes and giving me his telephone number. Marlies tore the number away from me as soon as the outside door closed behind him.

That very afternoon, via Julián Herranz, a numerary journalist and priest, Opus Dei located Ismael, as he explained to me days later. They told him I was leaving for Spain to be with my family (before I knew it). He was told that I had returned from Venezuela on account of a psychological crisis, not a spiritual or religious one. To this, Ismael Medina retorted dryly that he had known me for many years as a close friend and that I had never shown any such problem.

Third Canonical Admonition

On May 27 I was again summoned to the central advisory sessions chamber. I was certain that sooner or later there would be an explosion on the subject of the written meditation sent by the Venezuelan priest, which they had found in the closet, torn into tiny pieces before I had time to burn it.

This time, gathered in the central advisory sessions chamber with Monsignor Escrivá were Alvaro del Portillo, Javier Echevarría, Mercedes Morado, and Marlies Kücking. Monsignor Escrivá went directly to the point: "Carmen, there is no solution for you other than to get out of the Work. Choose to leave by requesting your release, and say in the letter that you have been happy, because you have! Say that for some time you have realized that you don't have the strength to fulfill the obligations to the Work and you want to be released from them. If you don't ask for it that way, I will take everything to the Holy See, with documents, letters, affidavits, the names of all parties, and everyone will be dishonored—including you yourself. Your name, and the names of others, will remain marked in the Holy See. I give you from now till tomorrow noon to choose." With great irritation he added: "Don't put 'Dear Father' in the letter, only 'Father.'"

"You're still young," he continued, "and you can find a good husband out there and satisfy all your instincts." Saying this, he made gestures with his hands, like someone stroking another's body. "Besides, you're capable of taking charge of an office and managing it well."

Here he changed his tone, his demeanor, and his manners and added, shouting at me: "But let it be stated for the record. Third admonition: Out! OUT! Leave us in peace." Pointing at Javier Echevarría, he added with the same irritation and ill manners: "Write it down for the records! This should be kept on record!"

Monsignor Escrivá continued at a bellow: "So, think it over! Either you request your release or bring dishonor to everyone, including yourself. There is no other solution for you but the street! OUT!"

I went to my room shattered. Truly, I could not even pray. Chaos reigned in my mind. Of course, the surveillance inside and outside the room continued.

Not even two hours had elapsed since the scene with Monsignor Escrivá, when Elena Olivera, one of the superiors in the central advisory, arrived to ask if I had written the letter yet. I told her no. I had until the next day, and furthermore, Mercedes Morado had taken my only pen. Elena Olivera urged me to write the letter to the Father as soon as possible because he was very concerned. She loaned me her pen to write the letter requesting the release.

I managed to write the letter along the lines Monsignor Escrivá had requested. The text went more or less as he had indicated to me: "Father, although I have been very happy in the Work for many years, for some time I have realized that I don't find the strength to fulfill my obligations to the Work, and I want to be dispensed from them. I thank you for all you have done for me." I signed the letter and made a copy for myself, but Mercedes Morado took it away.

Mercedes told me that it was necessary to wait since it was the weekend and the Holy See would not give Don Alvaro the confirmation of my case until Monday. This puzzled me, because the president general's dispensation was sufficient in case of "voluntary separation from the institute," according to the Constitutions in effect at the time. But, at bottom, it was all the same to me. I was like a dishrag. I was exhausted.

They told me to write my parents to say that I was coming home. The letter did not reach my parents by ordinary mail, but someone left the letter with the concierge. I learned later that my father had sent me a telegram with the answer prepaid, asking me to send him my flight number. The answer to my father went out on May 31 at 8:30 A.M., the same day I left Rome. The superiors told me they had sent the answer. I did not even see it.

The idea of returning to my parents' home was a relief. I wanted to leave the house in Rome and the Father as soon as possible. It bothered me, however, that Mercedes Morado had kept my little reminder book, whose pockets contained my Venezuelan identity documents which were valid for several more years, my Venezuelan driver's license, my international vaccination certificate, and my international driver's license. I asked Mercedes to return those documents, which were indispensable personal identification. She paid no attention. She told me that I had enough identification in my passport. I likewise reminded Marlies.

After this admonition, Mercedes Morado and Marlies Kücking told me that I had to go to confession whether I wanted to or not. So, I entered the confessional and found Father Joaquín Alonso there, not as a priest and shepherd of souls, but as an Opus Dei major superior. I said that although I didn't know how I had been at fault, because they had never told me, I particularly repented of bad example I might have given and of harm I might have done to Opus Dei members. I likewise repented of anything caused by my bad example or behavior. I really felt that way. Father Joaquín Alonso said I had caused incalculable damage, whose extent he could not even foresee; I would experience considerable psychological trauma on leaving Opus Dei, and he hoped I would seek a good psychiatrist. God would pardon me because he was the God of mercy and pardon, but he, as an Opus Dei priest, had to tell me that I needed to live a life of penance, reparation, and prayer to the end of my days, if I desired that God might eventually grant my salvation, something that he, as a priest, saw as very doubtful.

The next to the last day, they told me not to go to Mass. The last day, I went to Mass, but Elena Olivera took me out of the oratory before I could go to communion.

"Goodbyes"

On the morning of May 31 I did not know that I was to leave for Spain in the early afternoon. That morning they told me to go to the government sessions chamber. Monsignor Escrivá stood in the Chalice Room. Also standing in a group were Father Javier Echevarría, Mercedes Morado, Marlies Kücking, María Jesús de Mer. Monsignor Escrivá said tersely:

"Here is your passport, your pen, your crucifix, the plane ticket, and the Italian residence permit, because without them you can't leave the country."

When I was going to mention my other documents to him, Marlies stopped me.

Then Monsignor Escrivá began to pace from one side of the room to the other, very agitated, irritated, red, furious, while he declared: "And don't talk with anybody about the Work nor about Rome. Don't set your parents against us, because, if I find out that you are saying anything negative about the Work to anybody, I, José María Escrivá de Balaguer, have the world press in my hands," and as he said this he made a gesture with his hands confirming the notion. "I will publicly dishonor you. Your name will appear on the front page of every newspaper, because I will personally see to it. It would bring dishonor on you before men and on your own family! Woe to you if you try to alienate your family from the good name of the Work or tell them anything about this!"

He went on: "And don't return to Venezuela! Don't even think of writing to anybody there! Because if you even think of going to Venezuela, I will assume the responsibility of telling the Cardinal what you are. And it would dishonor you!" Pacing the room he continued shouting at me: "I was thinking all night about whether to tell you this or not, but I believe it is better that I should tell you." Looking directly at me, with a dreadful rage, moving his arms toward me as if he was going to hit me, he added at the top of his voice: "You are a wicked woman! A lost woman! Mary Magdalen was a sinner, but you? You are a seductress with all your immorality and indecency! You are a seductress! I know everything. EVERYTHING! EVEN ABOUT THE VENEZUELAN NEGRO![1] You are abominable. YOU HAVE A WEAKNESS FOR BLACKS! First with one and then with the other.[2] LEAVE MY PRIESTS ALONE! DO YOU HEAR? LEAVE THEM ALONE! In peace. Don't meddle with them! You're wicked! Wicked! Indecent! Come on, look at the business of the Negro! And don't ask me for my blessing because I don't intend to give it to you!"

Monsignor Escrivá went away toward the Relics Chapel. From there he turned around to shout a final insult: "Hear me well! WHORE! SOW!"

I stood stock still, frozen to the spot. I saw and heard everything as if in a nightmare. I did not cry. I did not blink. Within me, while Monsignor Escrivá shouted his insults, I had only two thoughts: one that Christ remained silent in the face of accusations; the other that God had liberated me.

I might have stood petrified for the rest of my life, if the physician, Chus de Mer, had not taken me by the shoulders and brought me to my room, where Elena Olivera and Carmen Puente were packing my suitcase. They went over every dress, every skirt, looking in the pockets and even in the seams, as if they still hoped to find something. They even took my box of talcum powder and face cream. I let them do it. They brought my suitcase down.

At that moment Mercedes Morado entered my room and said to me:

---

1. He referred to an Opus Dei numerary priest who always defended the Women's Branch and me as its director.

2. He referred to the telegram to Dr. Panikkar, mentioned above, that so shocked Encarnita Ortega.

"Well, in spite of what you've heard the Father say, you have to remake your life because truly you have done all sorts of things, all sorts"—she said dragging out that word.

Then, she added: "Well, before you go, tell me the post office box number."

To that I responded: "Look Mercedes, I'm sick of all your questions and interrogations! I won't tell you the number of anything or about anybody. So don't bother asking me again, because I won't tell you." Mercedes persisted: "Don't forget that you're leaving in mortal sin."

She told me to go down to the car. I was not even allowed to enter the oratory to say goodbye to the Lord.

A female numerary named Fontán, who had many family members in Opus Dei, drove us to the airport. Marlies Kücking sat beside her. In the back were Monserrat Amat, a member of the central advisory who was returning to Spain, and myself.

I observed profound silence. I only spoke to tell Marlies Kücking that I needed my identity documents, and she echoed Mercedes Morado in a tone of profound disgust: "You have enough in the passport."

At the passport checkpoint Marlies half flirtingly tried to convince the police officers to let her enter the international section so that she could stay with us until we boarded the plane. To my relief they refused. So, we stayed a little longer outside the passport checkpoint. Marlies pointed out that Monsignor de Ussía, brother of a Spanish Opus Dei numerary, was a passenger on our flight. Monsignor de Ussía had an important position in the Vatican. Because of his Vatican post, Opus Dei transferred his sister to Rome. While I was still in Rome, we were told that he was kidnapped, and his picture appeared in the press as "il Monsignore rapito." He was eventually released.

The superiors would not leave me alone even on the plane, and thus Monserrat Amat flew to Madrid with me. During the trip I was pleasant to her, for I always considered her a great coward rather than an evil person. Every time she saw me go to the bathroom she trembled, because naturally, she could not accompany me.

In the middle of my own personal tragedy, I was amused by the presence of Monsignor de Ussía. I thought: "Here we are on the same plane to freedom, 'il Monsignore rapito e la signorina rapita.'"

I am grateful to God for the sense of humor he gave me, which helped me even at the most difficult turns in my life.

8

RETURN TO SPAIN

My Family. My Friends

My younger brother Manolo was waiting for me at the Madrid airport with Conchita Bañón, Ismael Medina's wife. When my brother saw me arrive with Montserrat Amat, he asked me:

"Do you have to go with her?"

I answered:

"Not on a bet!"

I grabbed my suitcase and said to Montse: "I'm going with my family." For the first time in twelve years and after the terrible events of that morning in Rome, I was able to hug my brother and my friend, who, without pretense of sainthood, loved me deeply.

When I got into the car I began to sob uncontrollably. There had been too many emotions for one day. My friend said to me: "Cry, it will do you good. Ismael has told us a great deal already."

We took the new highway from Barajas, new for me, that is, to my parents' house on López de Hoyos street, from which I had departed in 1950.

I had abandoned my parents' house in 1950, to live in houses of Opus Dei, to which I had belonged since 1948. If departure was traumatic, the return home also involved its own tensions. It meant tacitly to admit that my parents were right, that I was mistaken, that Opus Dei was not what I thought.

My mother opened the door of the house, and we embraced. I had not seen her again since that fleeting moment in 1953 in Rome. She behaved as if I had come back from an ordinary trip. I deeply appreciated it. She asked my friend to stay for lunch and had the tact to not prepare a special meal. The presence of my brother Manolo and my friend Conchita Bañón helped to make these first hours in my home more relaxed. Suddenly the doorbell rang. "It's father," I said, and ran out to greet him.

He gave me a kiss as if nothing special had happened. He asked if I had had a good trip. Then he joked with my friend Conchita, saying that she had had pretty bad luck with the luncheon menu that day and began to inquire about her husband and children. My father used to lie down for thirty minutes after lunch, but as he was about to enter his room, he took several keys off his keyring and gave them to me: "This is the house key. This is the mailbox key. Keep them. Ah! This is the car key." "I don't have my driver's license now," I interrupted. "It doesn't matter," he replied, "You already have one." He continued with a smile: "If you need money, your mother can give it to you because I don't have any small bills." Then he remembered what he wanted to tell me: "Don't be in a hurry about anything. If you want to work, work. I don't have any special concern that you should."

Luncheon was especially delicious because everything was normal and calm. Afterwards, my mother showed me which room would be mine, since, there, had, of course, been changes in the house since I left. My brother Javier had finished his medical studies, was married, had several children, and lived in Barcelona.

Conchita and my brother said they would take me for a ride around Madrid. They both realized that I had experienced too many strong emotions in one day and wanted me to relax.

That night Conchita invited me to her house for supper, where I met her children and saw her husband, Ismael, who had arrived that day from Rome.

It seemed to me that I was walking around on another planet. My head was swimming. Seeing Ismael here was certainly different from our meeting a few days earlier in Rome. He explained the steps he had taken and the difficulty he had had in getting to see me, as well as his concern that something very serious had happened to me. He told me that he urged Conchita to speak to my parents. Both Conchita and Ismael have a very special place in my heart. They were not only friends but gave me back my freedom.

I subsequently visited them in Rome several times. They told me that when Opus Dei women found out that they lived in Rome, they invited them to visit Monsignor Escrivá a couple of times. During the first visit, Ismael identified himself as a journalist and said that he would like an interview, but Monsignor's answer was somewhat brusque. On a second visit Escrivá was more courteous.

In any case, Ismael Medina never wrote about Opus Dei. As is standard practice, the Opus Dei women were assigned to keep the couple "contented" and provided the "highest honor" of a meeting with Escrivá, perhaps to prevent Ismael from writing anything adverse in view of the events related to me. Evidently, Ismael could not forget that he had evidence of how I had been robbed of my freedom, nor could Conchita Bañón ever forget how abjectly I had come back to Madrid.

During the early days at home, despite my parents' efforts to smooth things over, I wept at the slightest provocation. When I tried to sleep the first night, everything spun around in my head, particularly recalling their claims that I was in mortal sin. I resolved to speak to Father José Todolí, the Dominican priest who worked in the Council for Scientific Research. When I called his convent the next day, I was told that he was a professor at the University of Valencia. I located him, and we agreed I would go to Valencia the following day.

Before leaving for Valencia, I called Caracas to speak to Mrs. de Sosa, but the connection was so bad we could barely understand each other. I wrote a letter explaining the events of Rome. I keep as treasures her telegrams, the first of them in answer to my phone call.

Father Todolí

I will never forget that Father Todolí had the courtesy of coming to meet me at the station in Valencia. As soon as I saw him, I said that I had to go to confession, because I was in mortal sin. He looked at me sceptically, and I assured him: "Yes, Father Todolí, I am in mortal sin." Then, he said jovially: "Well, if you are in mortal sin, I am mortally hungry, because it is very late. So we are going to have supper. Then you go to your hotel and tomorrow, if you want, you can come to church and go to confession. And don't worry," he added, "I will be responsible before God for your mortal sins."

Months later he told me how dreadful an impression I made on him when he met me at the station. He had known me before I entered Opus Dei and had been in Caracas; seeing me again he had the impression of meeting a badly treated, battered prisoner.

Next day I went to the Dominican church and explained matters in the confessional. Suddenly he said, "Enough!, caramba!" He went out of the confessional. I was terrified and thought that even Father Todolí was shocked by me.

After a while he came to look for me and said: "I was waiting to give you communion. Where did you go?"

When I said that I had thought he was frightened by my confession, he made a characteristic gesture as he said: "About you no, about them. Come on, come on, come so that I can introduce you to a lady who would like to get to know you."

He introduced me to a charming woman who showed me Valencia for three days and entertained me as much as she could. Of course, I spoke to Father Todolí, who suggested that I should find some kind of a job to get back into Spanish life again so that I could begin to feel independent.

I went back to Madrid reassured and with a much more positive view of my "new" life. I established my new ground rules. I decided that my life of piety should not suffer for my experience in Opus Dei, that God was not to blame. Also, that my interior life did not need to follow a regime based on the practices of that institution.

During one of the first conversations with my younger brother, he gave me two thousand pesetas, and I asked: "Is it a little or a lot?" My brother smiled and told me I would have enough for some time, at least for transportation. Lest there should be any doubt, Opus Dei provides no social security, health insurance, or any financial assistance to anyone who leaves the institution, for whatever reason. It is also totally untrue that Monsignor Escrivá "tried to help me look for a job," as affirmed by a public statement released by the central directress of Opus Dei on the appearance of the Spanish and Portugese editions of this book.[1]

When I returned from Valencia, my mother informed me that Guadalupe Ortiz de Landázuri, my old director at Zurburán, had come to my parents' house. My mother told me that she had begun to cry, saying how sad everyone was that I had left the Work. She had asked where I was. My mother in good faith said that I had gone to Valencia. To Guadalupe's question whether anyone had called from Venezuela, my mother naively said: yes, Mrs. de Sosa. What my mother could not know was that Guadalupe had been sent by her superiors to trace my steps since returning home.

Without going into details, I told my mother that she should not receive visits by anyone from Opus Dei, no matter what the excuse. Later on that day, still influenced by Monsignor Escrivá's order that I not say anything about Opus Dei to my parents, I simply told them that I had left Opus Dei because I was no longer at ease there. My father said nothing but seemed unwilling to listen to the slightest explanation of the matter.

Soon afterwards, I went to Barcelona to spend two days with my other brother, Javier and my sister-in-law, Teresa Soler, whom I met for the first time. Their children were charming and beautiful, and still quite small. I had the great satisfaction of seeing my brother work as a physician. Monsignor

1. In *O Expresso* (Lisbon), June 5, 1993, p. 42-R.

Escrivá's threat still fresh in my mind, I explained bits and pieces of what had occurred in Rome. I found out that there were Opus Dei members within my extended family. As I was leaving, my brother and sister-in-law very generously gave me six thousand pesetas, a large amount at that time. "It's all we can do now," my brother said lovingly, "we're just beginning our life."

After a long trip to Cartagena, where I was born, to see my paternal grandmother and other family members, I decided to look for work. At my age, I could not be a burden to my parents or my brothers.

Madrid, because it had changed so much, seemed enormous to me, and I went around on foot to get familiar with it again. I resolved to set two objectives for each week: to go to a concert and visit a museum or exposition. As I rejoined normal life again, I began to discover that Opus Dei's so-called secularity was a myth. As I became part of everyday life, I was surprised, for example, to see the changes in the liturgy due to Vatican II, such as use of the vernacular instead of Latin in the Mass and that women went to church without the mantilla.

I was annoyed when my friend Mary Mely Zoppetti de Terrer de la Riva would tell me I was "immature." She observed that Opus Dei makes people immature. For example, when you leave Opus Dei, you lack a sense of the value of things and tend to feel that people are obliged to give you what you need.

I gradually realized that by isolating its members Opus Dei makes them overly dependent, even childish. Similarly, its lack of ecumenical spirit makes its members inflexible in human relations.

My first step in the search for a job was to go to the Council of Scientific Research. However, I realized that with Opus Dei members in key positions, I had no chance of getting a position there. To find work in Madrid was no easy matter for a forty-year-old woman. I did not use the recommendations I had, although my cousin Antonio Carreras helped me get a splendid one from the Marquis of Luca de Tena. I wanted to know how far I could get on my own. Finally, in July, I started to work for the prestigious law firm, J. & A. Garrigues, on Antonio Maura street. Most of the staff did not know what to make of a woman my age, who was neither married nor attached to anyone. I never spoke about my "past" and did not tell anyone that I had belonged to Opus Dei.

When I started to work for the law firm, I faced the problem of my lack of identification papers for the first time. Under treaties between Spain and Venezuela, as a Venezuelan citizen I was legally entitled to work, but the employer needed to see and keep copies of my documents. I showed my passport and was forced to lie, pretending to have lost my Venezuelan identity card and my driver's license and that, since the Consulate could not issue duplicates, I was planning to travel to Venezuela to get new copies. I was believed because of my family background, but felt manipulated by Opus Dei and cowed by Escrivá's threat.

Relations with my old friends had changed, primarily because their lives as married women with children were completely different from mine. I went to lunch with my friend María Asunción Mellado one day and she told me she was an Opus Dei associate. Her parents were dead, and her brother had been married for several years. Although we were good friends, I understood that her devotion to Opus Dei came before everything else, so that I was unable to reestablish our friendship for many years. In December 1991, the news that her only brother Antonio Mellado Carbonell had died quite suddenly moved me so deeply that I called María in Córdoba, where she had lived for years, to offer my condolences. My call surprised her very much. I found her changed, but I imagine that her regard for Opus Dei might well be the same.

In regard to my spiritual life, it was an effort to go to confession, because I did not want to speak about Opus Dei, yet it was unavoidable. Finally, one day, I went to confession to a Dominican at a church near my parents' home. First, in the confessional and then in his office, while I explained matters to him, I remember his silence. Finally, he said: "May I ask a question?" "Of course, Father," I answered. "Why do you go on believing in God?" "Because God has nothing to do with Opus Dei," was my reply.

That response, which came out of the depths of my soul, is evidently what made me preserve my faith in God and the church.

Encounter with Father Panikkar

I spent that summer in Madrid. One night at the end of September, 1966, my cousin Juan Gillman came to my parents' house with his wife. He brought a set of slides of family events from weddings to baptisms, which had occurred during my years away. The maid entered and gave me a note which the concierge had brought up. Turning on the light, I saw with astonishment Raimundo Panikkar's name and telephone number in his own handwriting. I thought it was an Opus Dei trick and with serious reservations dialed the number. To my surprise, Raimundo Panikkar was staying at a residence for priests. At the outset I told him bluntly that I had left Opus Dei a few months earlier. To my astonishment, I discovered that he had left the Work just a month later than I. He explained that he was still a priest and incardinated in the diocese of Varanasi in India.

Next day before work, I went to Mass that he celebrated at the residence for priests. We agreed to talk when I finished work that afternoon, since he was going to Argentina representing UNESCO the following day. He noted that when he arrived in Madrid he had not the slightest idea that I had left Opus Dei, but passing by my parents' house with Father Carlos Castro, whom I knew years earlier before he was a priest, it occurred to them to inquire what had become of me. They asked the concierge whether my parents still lived there and with the habitual indiscretion of concierges he said that not only did my parents still live there but that I had returned from America and was with them.

I spoke to him with my old confidence and recounted clearly the experiences of the last year in Rome, Monsignor Escrivá's outbursts, how the superiors kept my personal documents, my lack of freedom, and the accusations of which I was never informed. Under different circumstances, I might have resented Father Panikkar's own role in staging my vocational crisis, but I realized that he, too, had been disillusioned by his personal experience in Opus Dei, to which he had committed himself with the highest ideals.

Father Panikkar made it clear that he understood and sympathized with my situation. When he learned that I had not told my parents the truth about what had happened, he told me that I had an obligation to do so.

Father Panikkar left for Argentina the following day. That evening I said to my parents and my brother Manolo, who was still single and living at home, that I had to speak to them. That kind of announcement was not usual in my family, and everyone expected something grave. I tensely said that I wanted to tell them about what really happened to me in Opus Dei. Although I explained matters very summarily, I was clear and to the point. I felt too upset to enter into much detail.

When I finished, my mother and brother remained silent, but my father said: "I didn't believe a word you said when you had just arrived. That's because I knew that Miguel Fisac, who is an intelligent man, said something similar, and later I found out about some of the harm Opus Dei members have done him and still do to him."

I do not know how my father knew Miguel Fisac. Perhaps someone had mentioned him in a professional connection, since my father was an industrial engineer, and Fisac an architect.

9

REPRISALS

⚜

Correspondence Between
My Father and Monsignor Escrivá[1]

The day after the conversation with my family, when my father arrived home at lunch time, he asked me to read the draft of a letter to Opus Dei requesting my personal documents. He was outraged that they had been retained. "No matter what you may have done, they have no legal right to retain your personal documents. They don't even do that in prison."

Although the letter was addressed to Monsignor Escrivá, it was answered by Francisco Vives. A translation of both letters follows:

Madrid, October 4, 1966

Very Reverend Monseñor Josemaría
    Escrivá de Balaguer y Albas,
President General of Opus Dei
Viale Bruno Buozzi, 73
Rome, Italy

Dear Monsignor Escrivá:

I take the liberty of writing to ask you to have the kindness of ordering the following documents, that my daughter María del Carmen left in Rome and that are now most necessary, be sent to me at the address below:

    1) Her Venezuelan identity card, valid until 1970, similar to our Spanish identity document. Specifically, this document was inside

---

1. Copies of my father's two letters to Monsignor Escrivá in Spanish as well as the reply from Francisco Vives may be found in Appendix B.

a little weekly planning book, which Miss M. Morado took from María del Carmen.

2) The international vaccination certificate, a booklet with yellow covers issued in Caracas.

3) Papers recording her grades at the Madrid Central College of Commerce and other public educational institutions, Secretarial School, and so forth.

4) Birth and baptismal certificates.

5) Official Gazette of Venezuela in which her Venezuelan nationality was published.

6) Spanish Social Service Certificate.[1]

7) International driver's license, valid until April 1967, issued in Caracas.

8) Any other personal documents which I might not expressly list now, but which evidently have strictly personal utility, among which are, for example, a smallish, black notebook with addresses, etc. That is to say, I repeat, papers, documents, etc., which could only concern my daughter, as, to give another example, passport-size photos.

I would like to express particular appreciation for any inconvenience my request might cause and hope you will indicate any expense you may incur so that I can reimburse you immediately.

Signed,
Francisco Javier Tapia Cervantes-Pinelo

FRANCISCO VIVES
Doctor in Civil and Canon Law

Rome, October 11, 1966

Mr. Francisco Javier Tapia Cervantes-Pinelo
Industrial Engineer
López de Hoyos, 15, 5º, izda.
Madrid

Dear Mr. Tapia:

Your letter of October 4 arrived when Monsignor Escrivá de Balaguer was out of Rome. However, I have had the opportunity to speak with Monsignor by telephone and in his absence, would like to answer you personally.

---

1. Under Franco the Social Service Certificate was required for women as a rough equivalent of military service for men. Consequently, this certificate was necessary in order to get a passport or to obtain work.

I will send you with pleasure those things belonging to María del Carmen that are here. I will wait for the opportunity of a friend's trip in the near future, which seems more secure than ordinary mail.

However, I truly regret having to say that my conscience does not permit me to send the things related to your daughter's stay in Venezuela. What I have just said doubtless requires an explanation particularly if, furthermore, one considers that quite probably you have received a notably partial and deformed version of events.

Please believe that with these lines I do not intend to increase your concerns, but rather to contribute to your daughter's well-being. Accordingly, I feel obliged to say that if you were aware of some of the details of your daughter María del Carmen's behavior in Venezuela, you would be deeply hurt, for she not only harmed herself but also seriously wronged other souls.

You will now understand better why I cannot send you anything related to your daughter's stay in Venezuela. This is likewise the reason why your daughter was absolutely advised—and I want you to know—not to consider returning to Venezuela. I must say with all honesty that María del Carmen's going to Venezuela might lead to great unpleasantness, because matters would come to light there which until now—out of consideration for you and your wife and out of charity toward your daughter—we have diligently silenced, maintaining total discretion.

I have tried, my dear Mr. Tapia, to be clear and tactful, but not crude. In order that you may realize more fully the importance of what has occurred, I only wish to add that all of the means that might assist your daughter were employed during a long period. Finally, in view of her having lost her way, there was no choice but to open a process, fulfilling the norms of Canon Law with maximum justice and charity and using the utmost delicacy at each step.

I hope you will also understand why we have not informed you about these matters. We have wished to cover her faults with the mantle of charity, and the proof is that we have not informed even you about these lamentable events. By contrast, it is evident to me that María del Carmen does not maintain this silence—nor does she honor the truth—which astounds me, because if we permit the truth to be known, it would be most painful for her.

I must not end without expressing my deep sorrow at what has occurred and the hope that María del Carmen will finally reorient her life and forget the past, as those of us whose duty required that they be involved in this matter, have done.

Yours sincerely,

Francisco Vives

With Father Francisco Vives' letter to my father were enclosed my final examination grades from the Central College of Commerce, the weekly grade booklet from the French Dominican Sisters School in Valladolid, and a few other final examination grades of miscellaneous courses, but nothing else.

I did not find out that my father had received this letter until a couple of weeks later. My father was a very calm man, opposed to violence, unable to hurt a human being. He was a good colleague and a good superior. He was a man of integrity. Everybody under his orders deeply revered him because he was always fair. I do not recall that my father ever spoke badly of anyone. He always tried to give in to "the other side" to calm tempers. Even when he was denounced in the civil war, he never took reprisals against those responsible. Given my father's character, he could not conceive that Monsignor Escrivá had ordered that anything of this sort could be written; my father was certain that it would hurt me deeply. He resolved to go to England, where, as he had discovered, Dr. Panikkar was delivering the Tape Lectures at Cambridge. He wanted to ask him if he ought to show me that letter. He sought this advice because he knew Dr. Panikkar was a priest, had been my spiritual director, and had left Opus Dei. That my parents should travel to England did not surprise me, because they went frequently on account of my father's professional activities.

Raimundo Panikkar told my parents two things: first that they should show me the letter, and second, that Father Vives' letter was blackmail. It was important that I be made aware of its content.

When my parents returned, they gave me the letter. After my experiences in Rome, nothing surprised me anymore. After reading the letter, I finally told my parents in detail about my time in Rome and Monsignor Escrivá's insults.

At the time my father received Francisco Vives' letter the only specific charge I had heard was that I had "murmured," that is, dared to criticize notes sent by Monsignor Escrivá to Venezuela as irrelevant for that country. The uninitiated may find it difficult to believe that for Opus Dei this is of capital importance. Two years ago, in a public statement issued by the Opus Dei central directress, I heard for the first time that "I was planning a coup d'état in Venezuela." For anyone familiar with the rigid centralism within Opus Dei, it is hard to imagine a more preposterous accusation.

My familiarity with the internal workings of Opus Dei made me dangerous outside the institution. Toward me, as toward others who have left and might talk about the association, the tactic has been to intimidate and then to launch vague accusations that generally involve insinuations of mental instability or sexual deviation. Opus Dei never accuses up-front and clearly, but always uses unspecific terms that, nevertheless, can be easily interpreted.

In subsequent chapters, I will present the charges that Opus Dei made against me to the Holy See in 1981, as they are recorded in the Acts of Monsignor Escrivá's process of beatification in the Vatican archives. By describing me as a "perverse" person, Opus Dei managed to dissuade Vatican authorities from calling me as a close observer of Monsignor Escrivá's life.

The description was presented to the Vatican by Monsignor Javier Echevarría. Monsignor Echevarría never heard my confession nor talked to me alone. Curiously, his recent election to the post of Opus Dei prelate was based, according to its Constitutions, on his "prudence, piety, charity toward the prelature and zeal for his fellow men."[1]

My father was very concerned. When I explained that there were people who witnessed Escrivá's words and insults to me, my father said to me: "Those people, as in sects, are ready to give their lives for the sake of the cause, not for the sake of the truth." He was afraid that they might do something to me. We seriously considered legal action, because of my father's fear of recriminations. He preferred to wait several months, but in March 1967, since my documents never arrived, he felt it was appropriate to send another letter to Monsignor Escrivá, which follows.

No reply was ever made to this letter, although I have the return receipt confirming that it was received in Rome. My father died in September 1969 and he never received a reply from Rome.

Madrid, March 9, 1967

Very Reverend Josemaría Escrivá de Balaguer y Albás
President General of Opus Dei
Viale Bruno Buozzi, 73
Rome, Italy

Dear Monsignor Escrivá:
I have received Dr. Francisco Vives' letter of the past October 11, in which he responds in your name to my letter of October 4.

1. *Codex Iuris Particularis Operis Dei*, no. 131, para. 3.

The letter was hand delivered at my office, accompanied by some of the documents mentioned in my letter.

Since that date I have been waiting to receive the remaining personal documents belonging to my daughter, María del Carmen, also requested in my letter. I was confident that, in spite of what Dr. Vives declared in his letter, you would understand that, *as these are personal documents which belong purely and simply to my daughter,* they ought to be returned to me.

However, these documents have not been sent to me, and therefore, I beg you once again, to arrange to have them sent as soon as possible. These are personal documents that she must have at her disposal; the unavailability of these documents may cause legal consequences. For these reasons, there is no justification for their retention by you.

In regard to your reference to my daughter's possible trips to Venezuela, there is nothing I can tell you. Only God knows the future of each particular person. Neither you nor I can limit her freedom of movement. As you well know, we *all* must respect personal freedom.

While I await the requested documents I am,

Yours sincerely,

FJT/lal   Francisco-Javier Tapia Cervantes-Pinelo

Toward the end of 1966, while I was at work in the Garrigues law firm, my mother called me at work one day to say that Dr. Lilia Negrón and her husband, Dr. José Nuñez, had phoned me at home. My poor mother, burned by her experience with Guadalupe Ortiz de Landázuri, merely told them to call that evening, without giving them my work number, but they had left the number of the hotel where they were staying. I called at once with great delight and we made an appointment to meet that very afternoon.

The reunion moved me deeply. I narrated my Roman odyssey and said that while, on the one hand, I was afraid of going mad, on the other, I was terrified by the possibility that they might shut me up in an insane asylum. They glanced at each other and said: "There you go. Do you realize?"

They had been greatly puzzled by my failure to answer any of the series of letters they wrote. That was compounded by the mysterious attitude of the superiors in Venezuela—however much Lilia asked for me, they never revealed where I was—and by the fact that they had also sent Ana María Gibert and Begoña Elejalde to Spain without explanations.

Putting the pieces together, it became clear that the fact that Ana María Gibert was my directress and that I had written to her while I was in Rome led Opus Dei superiors to behave toward her in the deplorable way described earlier and then, as a punishment, sent her to Spain.

Knowing Opus Dei's modus operandi, Lilia and her husband took very seriously the possibility that they might have committed me to an asylum to get me out of the way. The idea shocked them, but they did not reject it, resolving to go to Spain. Since Lilia was a psychiatrist, they reasoned that they were the only people who could get me out of wherever I was.

The first step they took on reaching Madrid was to telephone Beatriz Briceño, a Venezuelan Opus Dei numerary, now a journalist and in Madrid for some time, to ask for my address. Beatriz said she did not know it, because "I lived in a village without a telephone." Naturally, they did not believe her. (In fact, Beatriz Briceño knew perfectly well where I lived; she herself resided in the next block from my parents' house and through my younger brother I discovered that Beatriz used to visit my parents occasionally.) So, Lilia and her husband began to go through the Madrid telephone directory calling all the Tapias listed, until my mother answered one of the calls.

Of course, when they left Madrid, Lilia and her husband went to bid Beatriz goodbye and let her know that, I didn't "live in any village."

On Dr. Panikkar's return from Argentina he asked me to work part-time for him and to take care of his publications, to which I agreed. He returned to India, where he was living, and I continued to work for the Madrid law firm until February 1967, when I became convinced that I could not do two jobs. I resolved to leave the law firm to work full time for Dr. Panikkar.

The United States

In May 1967, I came to the United States for the first time. Professor Panikkar had accepted an invitation from Harvard University and had begun to teach in February 1967.

I spent the summer of 1967 at Manhattanville College in White Plains, New York, where a routine medical checkup discovered uterine tumors that needed to be removed as soon as possible. Since I had no health insurance and was alone, I left for Caracas at the invitation of my friends, the Nuñez's, who sent me a plane ticket. Dr. Rómulo Lander, who had been my personal physician for years, was also in Caracas.

I stayed at the Nuñez's home in Caracas. The emotions at my return to that beloved country were almost indescribable.

I renewed my acquaintance with many cherished friends. Among them was Cecilia Mendoza, a former numerary, who left Opus Dei because she refused to testify against me to the Opus Dei priest who arrived as an official visitor to inquire about my behavior. Cecilia, who was in Maracaibo, was questioned about anything that she might have noticed in my behavior against the spirit of the Work. She replied that I had a strong and straightforward character and that she had not seen anything in my attitude against the spirit of Opus Dei. Persistently interrogated and asked to dig down into her consciousness about my behavior, she told the priest that she could make no other statement. She left Opus Dei, upset and furious about the grilling.

Shortly after leaving, she met Tomás Gunz, whom she married a year later. Her husband, Tomás, likes to say that thanks to me he met his wife.

The primary objective, however, for my trip to Caracas was to visit the Nuncio and His Excellency Cardinal Quintero, to tell them that Monsignor Escrivá had said that if I went back to Venezuela he would tell the Cardinal "who I was." The Nuncio listened in silence and said that I should not worry, because "God sees the truth of human beings in their hearts." At my insistence that he interrogate me about whatever and however he pleased, Cardinal Quintero repeated: "Don't forget, daughter, superiors, too, make mistakes."

Dr. Lander's evaluation concurred that I needed to undergo surgery. He offered to do it himself, but given that my parents were in Madrid, I returned to Spain, where Dr. León López de la Osa performed the surgery. Fortunately, I had no cancer.

The topic of Opus Dei faded into history, or so I thought. There followed a period of readjustment to normal life, until I came across Opus Dei again.

Responsibility for Dr. Panikkar's publications required extensive travel, since he resided in India and taught at Harvard. Eventually, I decided to stay in Cambridge, Massachusetts, for six months of the year and divide the rest of my time between Europe and South America.

The dominant recollection of the years from 1966 to 1971 is of difficulty and isolation. However, my work, the travel, new acquaintances, new countries, and my religious faith helped dissipate my inner isolation.

God helped by giving me the insight to reconstruct my new personal life: new friends in different countries and new languages; involvement again in things I always enjoyed like art, music, and reading. My time at Harvard was very interesting and helpful. I spent long hours at the Harvard libraries and attended English classes and French literature lectures.

The University of Santa Barbara offered Dr. Panikkar a position as full professor in 1971, a move that made me come to the West Coast for the first time and establish residence in California.

Correspondence to Obtain
My Certificate of Studies

The University of California started the paper work for my application as a permanent resident of the United States.

I then stumbled onto an unexpected problem while trying to fill one of the immigration questionnaires. I had to list my occupation and addresses during several years when I had belonged to Opus Dei.

It was easy to list addresses of the houses where I had lived in Opus Dei. The difficulty was to explain my professional occupation to the Immigration Service. As a secular institute, Opus Dei did not confer any juridical status on its members. So, to tell the State Department that I had been an Opus Dei numerary and had occupied leadership positions was more or less like saying that I had been a YMCA member, or rather less, since the YMCA is infinitely better known that Opus Dei in the United States. Hence, it was as if I had been in limbo for a number of years.

The dean of foreign students and scholars counseled me in this tedious process and advised that the best thing would be to explain what courses of studies I had completed during my affiliation with Opus Dei. In other words, I should request of Opus Dei a certificate—not a transcript—where those studies would be listed.

Needless to say, the Immigration Service and, in the last analysis, the State Department require such information as a condition for consideration for permanent residence status in the United States. The questionnaires are taken seriously, and vague answers are not tolerated.

Copies of the entire official correspondence dealing with the request for a certificate of Opus Dei studies appear in Appendix A in chronological order. It includes a series of replies systematically denying that I had ever studied as a member of the Work. The replies were given to government agencies. There is also a somewhat confused explanation of the matter sent by Opus Dei to the Holy See.

The affair was serious because a file developed in the international office of the university, in which Opus Dei superiors denied in writing what I had affirmed as true in the questionnaires. If my supporting material had been reviewed within a certain time period, the result would have been that I would seem to have committed perjury.

I struggled to obtain the certificate of studies for six years. Finally, an Opus Dei priest who had been a professor in the majority of the courses realized the grave harm that the groundless refusal of the Opus Dei superiors might occasion, possibly including deportation. One does not play games with the State Department. He decided in conscience to give me the certificate himself. Unfortunately, that action led to serious reprimands from Opus Dei superiors, a break in communications with me and others, and the threat that if he contacted me again, he would be expelled from the association. Since he became the object of Opus Dei's customary interrogations and isolation, I have inked out his signature in the Appendix.

You must understand that all these letters, which Opus Dei sent to persons who, in their official capacity, sought information regarding my studies, were written with the consent of Monsignor Escrivá. In Opus Dei any member, superior or not, signs anything whatever requested by "our Father" (as Monsignor Escrivá has been called within Opus Dei since his death) or the Father (as the reigning prelate is familiarly called). This is true even though the author of a letter knows that he is distorting the truth. If it "suits the good of the Work" nobody would dare not to sign or write what they are given, even though they clearly know that the facts are misrepresented. A patent example is the case of Father Roberto Salvat Romero, Monsignor Escrivá's representative in Venezuela. Besides being a Spanish lawyer, he was also my professor in the ethics course and he claimed on different occasions that I had not done any studies in the institution in Caracas.

I have often wondered why they did not want to give me a certificate for the courses I had completed, which would not have involved any degree, but a confirmation that I had taken a number of subjects based on syllabi established by Opus Dei and had obtained certain grades in them. Doubtless this is simply a reprisal, with the hope of discrediting me by making me appear as a liar before government agencies. This is the standard practice of Opus Dei. Besides, the question of Opus Dei's internal studies has not been totally resolved in regard to outside educational authorities. Opus Dei prefers not to clarify the nature of its internal studies to avoid any possible evaluation by outside academics.

A blatant example of a more violent and hurtful reprisal was the campaign organized against María Angustias Moreno, when she published her book *El Opus Dei: Anexo a una historia* (Barcelona: Planeta, 1976), which portrayed Opus Dei in detail. By order of the superiors, the volume was swept up from bookstores, exhausting an edition, thus impeding its diffusion. I managed to buy the book during a trip to Madrid. I had never met the author although she was an Opus Dei numerary for many years. Criticisms of the book or better against the book from persons who were unquestionably close to Opus Dei culminated in a campaign of character assassination, which led María Angustias Moreno to publish a second book, *La otra cara del Opus Dei* (Barcelona: Planeta, 1979), which documents these attacks.

Exclusions of Witnesses Considered Not Suitable

Opus Dei does not play fair. Though Monsignor Escrivá used to repeat that "we must drown evil in an abundance of goodness," his association engages in reprisals in order to reach its goals. It uses slander to defend itself, and given its own obsession, the slander always hints at sexual misconduct. At the risk of jeopardizing my own reputation, I believe it is important to stress the extent to which Opus Dei employs this strategy. It is very sad that an institution of the church that uses the word "pax" as the customary greeting among its members, whose Founder claimed that "we are sowers of peace and joy," can stoop so low as to denigrate persons in writing, even hiding behind official ecclesiastical secrecy.

In late 1991 and early 1992 Opus Dei stated to the press, sometimes without mentioning names, that a number of persons had not been called to testify in Monsignor Escrivá's beatification process, because the tribunal for the Process for the Cause of Beatification had decided that the persons were not suitable. What Opus Dei never said was why those persons were not suitable, nor who supplied the Tribunal with such information.

Popular wisdom is generally right. The Spanish saying that "there is nothing hidden between heaven and earth" is very true. Sooner or later things always unravel. The summary of the Acts of the Madrid Tribunal for Monsignor Escrivá's beatification (p. 2133) declares in regard to the "exclusion of some possible witnesses":

> b) *Existence of a campaign of defamation against the servant of God and Opus Dei.* In the search for other possible contrary witnesses to be cited by us, the Tribunal examined individual attitudes of several possible candidates, and after having gathered the necessary evidence, reached the conclusion that these also were to be rejected, just as Miss Moreno had been.
>
> The Tribunal further came to demonstrate the existence of a campaign of defamation seeking to put obstacles to the Cause of the Servant of God. . . . The larger part of those persons was made up of individuals who, after having been part of Opus Dei for some years, had abandoned their vocations and presently cultivate intense resentment. . . . In this regard, the Madrid Tribunal gathered a rather eloquent documentation. Particularly significant was Miss Carmen Tapia (who turned out to have been involved in the preparation of the program *La Clave* and to have suggested furthermore that Opus Dei priests lacked respect for the sacramental seal). . . . The Tribunal made the statement based on the information gathered, that the behavior of these persons made them unsuitable to testify in a Canonical Process and in fact unreliable to clarify the truth.[1]

---

1. "b) *l'esistenza di una campagna diffamatoria contro il Servo di Dio e l'Opus Dei.* Nella ricerca di altri eventuali testi contrari da citare d'ufficio, il Tribunale esaminò le singole posizioni

The actual facts are that there exists no campaign of defamation against the beatification of Monsignor Escrivá, nor against Opus Dei, nor is there a group organized to these ends.[1] Opus Dei has invented this to claim martyrdom. The simple truth is that I did not participate in any session of *La Clave,* as can easily be confirmed by the television chain that broadcasts the program. I was invited to participate in the program in May 1984, but I was not part in any way of its preparation. What is more, the refusal by its organizers to tell me who the Opus Dei participants were in the program, while, by contrast, Opus Dei did know the names of the other guests, led me to decline the invitation. Indeed, the Madrid newspaper, *El Pais,* published a note with this information.[2]

Let us consider now other paragraphs from pages 2136 and 2137 of the Documentary Appendix of the Summary of Monsignor Escrivá's process of beatification, which refer to me:

6. In effect, during the process, the Tribunal attempted to obtain information about persons who had had relations with the Servant of God and could or should be called as witnesses. We thus were able to discover that there is a group of persons that appears to be associated with Miss María Angustias Moreno in that same fundamental attitude of aversion toward Opus Dei. When they can, these individuals do not hesitate to direct such aversion against the Servant of God as the founder of this institution. . . .

The majority of these persons signed a collective letter against Opus Dei, which appeared in the *Diario de Barcelona,* January 30,

---

di diversi possibili candidati e, dopo aver raccolto le prove necessarie, giunse alla conclusione che anche costoro andavano scartati, per gli stessi motivi per cui lo era stata la sig.na Moreno.

"Il Tribunale pervenne anzi all'evidente constatazione dell'esistenza di una campagna diffamatoria mirante ad ostacolare la Causa del Servo di Dio, la cui esponente più in vista era proprio la sig.na Moreno, ma alla quale collaboravano attivamente anche altri. La maggior parte di costoro era costituita da persone che, dopo aver fatto parte per alcuni anni dell'Opus Dei, avevano abbandonato la vocazione e coltivano attualmente un acceso risentimento. Pochi avevano avuto rapporti diretti con il Servo di Dio su questi il Tribunale di Madrid raccolse una documentazione assai eloquente. Si trattava, in particolare, della sig.na Carmen Tapia (che risultava essere intervenuta nella preparazione della trasmissione "La Clave", suggerendo addirittura di accusare i sacerdoti dell'Opus Dei di mancato rispetto del sigillo sacramentale). . . . il Tribunale dichiarava doversi concludere, in base ai dati raccolti, che la loro stessa condotta li rendeva inidonei a testimoniare in un Processo canonico a comunque inattendibili in ordine all'acclaramento della verità;" "Sull'esclusione di alcuni possibili testi: I. Atti del Tribunale Matritense," in *Romana et Matriten. Beatificationis et Canonizationis Servi Dei Iosephmariae Escrivá de Balaguer, Sacerdotis Fundatoris Societatis Sacerdotalis S. Crucis et Operis Dei, Positio Super Vita et Virtutibus: Summarium* (Rome, 1988), p. 2133.

1. In the United States ODAN (Opus Dei Awareness Network), of Pittsfield, Massachusetts, has the goal of supporting persons who have suffered because of Opus Dei. They are not so much concerned with Escrivá's beatification as with alerting families about Opus Dei tactics.

2. *El Pais,* May 26, 1984.

1977, subsequently reprinted in other sensationalist or pro-Marxist periodicals and magazines. We attach a photocopy of that letter in Appendix III.

10. Although she does not appear among the signatories of the mentioned letter, Miss María del Carmen Tapia, who used to belong to Opus Dei, is also part of this group. We have found out that she had a major share in the preparation for the program *La Clave,* which Spanish Television devoted to Opus Dei (Cf. Appendices I and II). In Appendix IX there are photocopies of notes by Miss Tapia sent to Spanish Television for the development of that program. During the program she was mentioned on several occasions both by the director of *La Clave* and by Miss María Angustias Moreno. She generally resides in California (USA) but makes frequent trips to Spain and has been in contact with Miss Moreno. Her open hostility to Opus Dei and incidentally to the Cause was obvious also in two long letters, one published in the daily paper *El Pais* (February 17, 1988), and the other earlier, directed to Miss Moreno to express her solidarity with Miss Moreno's first book against Opus Dei. The letter was reproduced in Miss Moreno's second book (Appendix X).[1]

Opus Dei obstinately asserts that I belong to some group. The truth is that I ended up so burned by having belonged to their group, the Opus Dei, that today I shun the *G* in *group!*

---

1. "6. Efectivamente, durante el Proceso, el Tribunal trató de obtener información sobre personas que hubieran tenido relación con el Siervo de Dios y que pudieran o debieran ser llamadas como testigos. Pudimos así averiguar que hay un grupo de personas, en el que todas se muestran unidas a doña María Angustias Moreno en esa misma fundamental actitud de aversión al Opus Dei, que no dudan en descargar, cuando pueden, sobre el Siervo de Dios, como Fundador de esta Institución. . . .

"La mayoría de estas personas son las que firmaron una carta colectiva contra el Opus Dei que apareció en el *Diario de Barcelona* del 30.I.1977 y que fue reproducida después en otros órganos de opinión y en revistas de carácter sensacionalista o de inspiración marxista. Adjuntamos en Anexo III una fotocopia de aquella carta. . . .

"10. Aunque no figura entre los firmantes de la carta citada, forma también parte de este grupo doña María del Carmen Tapia, que perteneció al Opus Dei. Hemos sabido que tuvo una decisiva participación en los preparativos del programa "La Clave", que Televisión española ha dedicado al Opus Dei (cfr. Anexos I y II). En el Anexo IX se recogen fotocopias de unas notas de la Srta. Tapia enviadas a la Televisión española para la elaboración de ese programa. Durante el programa fue citada en varias ocasiones, tanto por el Director de "La Clave", como por doña María Angustias Moreno. Reside habitualmente en California (USA), pero hace viajes frecuentes a España y ha mantenido relación con la Srta. Moreno. Su manifiesta hostilidad al Opus Dei—y, de rechazo, a la Causa—queda también patente en las dos extensas cartas, una publicada en el diario *El País* (Madrid, 17.XI.1981), y la otra, anterior, dirigida a la Srta. Moreno para solidarizarse con el primer libro publicado por ésta contra el Opus Dei, y transcrita en su segundo libro (Anexo X)." Ibid., p. 2136–37.

I did not participate in the planning of the program. I do not recall the letter they say I wrote to *El País*. What is frightening, *really frightening*, is the spy network Opus Dei seems to have organized to check my correspondence and follow my movements.

Moreover, obvious questions remain. How does anything set forth in those Acts and Summary constitute an impediment to my testimony about a person I knew so well and for so long. My sanctity is not at issue but that of Monsignor Escrivá. Are persons not in agreement with Monsignor Escrivá *ipso facto* anathema, even though we continue to be faithful children of the church? Are slander and aggression the doctrine that Monsignor Escrivá left as an inheritance to Opus Dei? All this reflects badly on the charity which, as they maintain, Monsignor Escrivá lived heroically but which, during the six years that I spent in Rome as a major superior in Opus Dei, I never witnessed.

Doubtless, Opus Dei feared that we who knew Monsignor Escrivá so very well might tell the truth and that the likelihood of his beatification and eventual canonization would thereby be less likely. To prevent us from testifying in the cause, Opus Dei's approach was to allege deeds which would make us unacceptable witnesses beyond a shadow of a doubt. Since these declarations were *secret,* and they were convinced that the interested parties would never discover them, they did not hesitate to attack with low, disgraceful slander about sexual conduct. This is demonstrated by the declarations made regarding me by Monsignor Javier Echevarría, then general secretary of Opus Dei and now prelate. They appear on pages 610 and 611 of the "Summary of the Roman Process for the Cause of Beatification of Monsignor José María Escrivá."

> 2347. Unfortunately, it was not to be, because years later, she attempted to pervert several women with the worst aberrations. As soon as the Servant of God knew certain facts, he called Carmen Tapia—who was in Venezuela—to Rome. Here he announced to her that she would not return to that country, and from her reaction deduced that there were more important matters than those already known, in which several persons were involved. In the face of such horrendous depravity, which cost Servant of God many tears on account of the most serious offenses to the Lord, and for which he tried to make reparation with constant prayer and penance, he told this woman that she had two solutions: to seek a dispensation which would be immediately granted, or to not seek it, and then it would be necessary that she be subjected to a process, which would be sent to the Holy See, leaving her—as she deserved—completely dishonored on account of her wayward life. That

woman sought the dispensation. As the Servant of God understood that she was a person without conscience, he warned her that if she slandered the work with her corruption, there would be no choice but to inform about who was the slanderer. We have found out, unfortunately, that this woman has continued on this disastrous path.[1]

The complete lack of charity toward a fellow human being is striking. If this alleged "horrendous depravity" had been real, Monsignor Escrivá's task in charity would have been to be silent about it. But it is not Christian to employ slander and defamation to keep a person from testifying in Monsignor Escrivá's process.

The reader ought in fairness to receive two clarifications: a) Monsignor Escrivá never wept for the sins of anyone and did not wish us to weep for anything or anyone. "You must be strong, my daughters." Speaking of his death, he even used to say: "The day I die, a few tears because we are human, but then, to work, hey!" b) Bishop Javier Echevarría, or "Javi" as he was familiarly known in Opus Dei, was never my confessor nor was he a superior of the Women's Branch during the eighteen years that I spent in Opus Dei. I never spoke confidentially with him during all those years nor at any other time. He was, however, present at the scoldings and insults that Monsignor Escrivá hurled at me on the occasion of my expulsion. It was he who recorded in an official document (Monsignor Escrivá's) admonitions to me.

---

1. "2347 (p. 769). Desgraciadamente no debió ser así, porque al cabo de los años intentó la perversión de unas cuantas mujeres con las peores aberraciones. El Siervo de Dios, apenas tuvo conocimiento de algunos hechos, llamó a Carmen Tapia—que estaba en Venezuela—a Roma; aquí le anunció que no volvería a ese país, y por su reacción, dedujo que había cuestiones más importantes que las ya conocidas en las cuales había involucrado a varias personas. Ante tan horrenda depravación, que costó mucho llanto al Siervo de Dios por las gravísimas ofensas al Señor, y que trató de reparar con una constante oración y penitencia, dijo a esa mujer que tenía dos soluciones: pedir la dispensa, que se le concedería inmediatamente, o no pedirla, y entonces habría de someterse a un proceso, que sería enviado a la Santa Sede, quedando—como se merecía—completamente deshonrada por su extraviada vida. Aquella mujer pidió la dispensa; y como el Siervo de Dios comprendió que era una persona sin conciencia, le advirtió que si calumniaba a la Obra con su corrupción, no habría más remedio que informar sobre quien era la calumniadora.

"Hemos sabido que, desgraciadamente, esta mujer ha seguido por esos desastrosos derroteros." "Sull'esclusione di alcuni testi: II. Atti del Tribunal Romana," in ibid., pp. 610–11.

10

PORTRAITS

On January 13, 1902, in Barbastro, the pastor of the cathedral, Father Angel Malo, solemnly baptized a baby boy born at 10 P.M. on the ninth, legitimate son of Mr. José Escriba, born in Fonz, and Mrs. Dolores Albás, born in Barbastro, spouses, residents, and merchants of the city. The paternal grandparents were Mr. José, of Peralta de la Sal, deceased, and Mrs. Constancia Corzán, of Fonz. The maternal grandparents were Mr. Pascual, deceased, and Mrs. Florencia Blanc, of Barbastro. The baby was christened José María Julián Mariano. His godparents were Mr. Mariano Albás and Mrs. Florencia Albás, uncle and aunt, both residents of Huesca, whose authorized representative was Mrs. Florencia Blanc, to whom I directed the ritual warnings.[1]

A marginal annotation reads:

By order of the very illustrious episcopal delegate of this diocese of Barbastro, given May 27, 1943, the surname Escriba on this certificate is changed "to Escrivá de Balaguer," so that hereafter it shall be written: José María Julián Mariano Escrivá de Balaguer Albás, legitimate son of Mr. José Escrivá de Balaguer and Mrs. Dolores Albás.

Barbastro, June 20, 1943[2]
José Palacio

---

1. Luis Carandell, *Vida y milagros de Monseñor Escrivá de Balaguer, fundador del Opus Dei* (Barcelona: Laia, 1975), pp. 79–80.
2. Ibid., p. 80.

Note that the names with which he was christened were José, María, Julián, and Mariano. His biographers claim that devotion to the Virgin led him to combine the first two names. I heard Monsignor Escrivá explain that he signed internal documents of the work "Mariano" out of devotion to the Blessed Virgin.

The font in which Monsignor Escrivá was baptized was destroyed during the Spanish Civil War. Opus Dei had it reassembled and transported to the central house in Rome.

International Who's Who for 1967–68 contains the following entry on p. 387:

> Escrivá de Balaguer, Mgr. Josemaría, D.IUR., S.T.D., Spanish ecclesiastic; b. 9 Jan. 1902; ed. Saragossa, Madrid, and Lateran Pontifical Univs.
>
> Ordained 25; founded Opus Dei 28; former Superior,[1] Saragossa Seminary, Rector, Real Patronato de Santa Isabel, Prof. of Philosophy, Madrid School of Journalism, Prof. of Roman Law, Univ. of Madrid and Saragossa,[2] Doctor, h.c. of Univ. of Saragossa, mem. Colegio de Aragón, Grand Chancellor Univ. of Navarra; mem. A[c]cademia Theologica Romana, Consultor (Adviser) of the S.C. of Seminaries and Univs. of the Pontifical Comm. for the Authentic Interpretation of the Code of Canon Law, Holy See; Pres. Gen. Opus Dei.
>
> Publs. *The Way, Holy Rosary, The Abbess of Las Huelgas, Spiritual Considerations, The Apostolic Constitution Provida Mater Ecclesia and Opus Dei,*[3] and works of ascetic literature, law and history.
>
> Viale Bruno Buozzi 73, Rome, Italy.

According to Escrivá's biographer, Andrés Vázquez de Prada,[4] Monsignor Alvaro del Portillo petitioned the Holy See for the nomination of Monsi-

---

1. Monsignor Escrivá liked to say that he had been superior of the Seminary before being ordained, and so Vázquez de Prada calls him in *El Fundador del Opus Dei,* pp. 82 and 548. However, "superior" is quite misleading, and Vázquez de Prada hedges (as Monsignor Escrivá did not) by adding that the position was called "inspector" and that there were two senior seminarians each year who were inspectors.

2. Here the English-speaking numerary who composed the biographical blurb for Escrivá erroneously transcribes what we were all given to understand, namely, that Escrivá was never a professor at two universities. Vázquez de Prada (*El fundador del Opus Dei,* pp. 19, 101, and 107) says that Escrivá taught at the Instituto Amado in Zaragoza and the Academia Cicuéndez in Madrid. Such schools were tutoring services to help students cram for examinations, particularly entrance examinations for universities or technical schools.

3. No one knows of this publication. Since neither a publisher nor a periodical is mentioned, it is not clear whether it was just a manuscript, if indeed it existed. Since Opus Dei is no longer a secular institute, it is not mentioned by Vázquez de Prada.

4. Vázquez de Prada, *El fundador del Opus Dei,* p. 249.

gnor Escrivá as "Domestic Prelate of His Holiness the Pope" which was granted to him on May 25, 1947, by official letter from His Eminence Cardinal G. B. Montini.[1]

Circumstances surrounding his doctorate in law have never been clarified. One of his official biographers, Peter Berglar, mentions on page 388 of his work, cited above: "In December 1939, Monsignor Escrivá obtains the doctorate in Law at the University of Madrid." This academic degree was never discussed in Opus Dei, and it does not seem that anyone has ever seen the diploma. The topic of the thesis for the degree was also never mentioned. *La Abadesa de las Huelgas* by Monsignor Escrivá, published in 1944 by Rialp, can hardly be the doctoral thesis for his law degree. However, Escrivá did use this book as a thesis for the doctorate in theology granted by the Lateran University. In its official documents Opus Dei does not indicate when this latter degree was granted. As nearly as I can calculate, it must have been between 1957 and 1961.

The Spanish Ministry of Justice Official Guide to *Grandezas y Títulos del Reino* announced that Monsignor Escrivá had been granted the title of Marquis of Peralta on November 5, 1968.[2]

PERALTA, Marquis of
Granted: March 4, 1718, confirmed by Royal Provision of Fernando VI, December 4, 1758.
Granted to: Don Tomás de Peralta, Secretary of State, War, and Justice of the Kingdom of Naples.

DON JOSÉ MARÍA ESCRIVÁ DE BALAGUER Y ALBÁS
Letter issued: November 5, 1968.
Residence, Rome, Bruno Buozzi, 73. Tel. 87 90 42.

Several years before this public notice appeared, a brief document informed Opus Dei members that this title had been granted to Escrivá. The same document instructed us *not to speak about it.* On November 17, 1972, that is four years later, this same Ministry of Justice publication announced that the title was being officially transferred to Monsignor Escrivá's brother, Santiago Escrivá de Balaguer y Albas, previously named Barón of San Felipe.

---

1. See *Acta Apostolicae Sedis,* 1947, 39, and de Fuenmayor et al., *El itinerario jurídico del Opus Dei,* p. 538, Appendix 25.
2. Ministerio de Justicia, *Grandezas y Títulos del Reino* (Madrid: Centro de Publicaciones, 1967–1969), p. 341.

Opus Dei distributes the following profile of Monsignor Escrivá to the general public.[1]

Blessed Josemaria Escriva was born in Barbastro, Spain, on January 9, 1902. He was ordained to the priesthood in Saragossa on March 28, 1925.

On October 2, 1928, in Madrid, by divine inspiration he founded Opus Dei, which has opened up a new way for the faithful to sanctify themselves in the midst of the world, through the practice of their ordinary work and in the fulfillment of their personal, family and social duties. They thus become a leaven of intense Christian life in all environments. On February 14, 1930, Blessed Josemaria Escriva by God's grace understood that Opus Dei was meant to develop its apostolate among women as well. And on February 14, 1943, he founded the Priestly Society of the Holy Cross, inseparably united to Opus Dei. Opus Dei received the definitive approval of the Holy See on June 16, 1950. On November 28, 1982, it was erected as a personal Prelature, a juridical form desired and foreseen by Blessed Josemaria Escriva.

He guided and inspired the growth of Opus Dei throughout the whole world with constant prayer and penance and by the heroic practice of all the virtues. In doing so, he showed loving dedication and untiring concern for all souls, and a continual and unconditional surrender to God's will. When he yielded up his soul to God, Opus Dei had spread to five continents with over 60,000 members of 80 nationalities, serving the Church with the same veneration for and complete union with the Pope and bishops that Blessed Josemaria Escriva always lived.

The Holy Sacrifice of the Mass was the center and root of his interior life. His profound awareness of being a son of God, expressed in a constant presence of the Holy Trinity, moved him to seek complete identification with Christ in everything, to live a deep and tender devotion to the Blessed Virgin Mary and St. Joseph, and to enjoy a continual and confident friendship with the holy guardian angels. This made him a sower of peace and joy along all the ways of the earth.

Msgr. Escriva had repeatedly offered his life for the Church and the Pope. Our Lord accepted this offering, and on June 26, 1975,

---

1. *The Venerable Servant of God, Josemaria Escriva: Founder of Opus Dei: Bulletin on the Life of Monsignor Escriva*, no. 8 (New York: Office of Vice Postulation of Opus Dei in the United States, n.d.), p. 2. With slight variations, this same text is printed on back of the widely distributed holy picture with Monsignor's picture.

in Rome in the room where he worked, he surrendered his soul to God with the same holy simplicity that characterized his entire life. His body rests in the Prelatic Church of Our Lady of Peace at Viale Bruno Buozzi 75, Rome. There it is accompanied by the constant prayer and gratitude of his sons and daughters and countless others who have come closer to God through his example and teaching. His cause of canonization was introduced in Rome on February 19, 1981. Pope John Paul II, on April 9, 1990, declared that he lived the Christian virtues to a heroic degree, and on July 6, 1991, decreed that a cure attributed to his intercession was miraculous. The Founder of Opus Dei was beatified by Pope John Paul II on May 17, 1992, in Rome.

This is the way the world outside Opus Dei is shown Monsignor Escrivá from baptism to death. I am not going to debate this profile. I am simply going to sketch a picture of Monsignor Escrivá with a few strokes, using the colors available on my palette.

Monsignor Escrivá was called "Father" because he determined that Opus Dei was a family. This idea is foundational to the Work and everything else rests on it. Other members of the Work are "sisters" or "brothers"; Monsignor Escrivá's sister Carmen is "aunt" and his brother Santiago is "uncle." Likewise, their parents were "grandparents." The Work was a family, to be sure, the link was the Founder's family, not that of its members. To distinguish our families from the "family" of the Work, the former were called "blood families."

The way Monsignor Escrivá worshipped his deceased parents bore no resemblance to the way in which Opus Dei members were allowed to treat their own families. The "grandparents" were even removed from the cemeteries where they were interred, to be buried in the house at Diego de León, 14, in Madrid. Monsignor Escrivá told us that his mother and his siblings, Carmen and Santiago, had given everything to the Work in its foundational period, including what should have gone to Carmen and Santiago as their inheritance. I also heard Monsignor Escrivá say very often that his mother and sister made the foundation of the Women's Branch possible by taking charge of the administration of the first houses of men. I have never challenged this because I do not have data to do so, although there are members of the Work who do not share the opinion; in any case, the Escrivás were generously compensated.

Before Lola Fisac, the first acknowledged Opus Dei woman numerary, there existed a small group of women, whose spiritual director was Monsignor Escrivá. Except for Laura Fernández del Amo, a strong person who comes from an old Spanish family, cultivated by Monsignor Escrivá in his early days in Madrid, no one ever knew exactly what happened to them, nor who they were. This was one of a number of taboos inside Opus Dei. I once asked Carmen whether she had known them, and she said yes, and added: "They were crazy. They were all unbalanced." Carmen apparently knew about the earliest period of Opus Dei of which many numeraries were virtually ignorant.

I recall that the last time we sent a present for Santiago from Venezuela was after Carmen's death. Then word came from the central government in Rome that the Father had said that presents should no longer be given to Santiago. The order puzzled us, because no reason was given. Later we found out that the reason was that Santiago was going to get married, and the Father was very displeased by his choice. Monsignor Escrivá had assigned Opus Dei priests in Spain the task of finding a fiancée for his brother among eligible female Spanish aristocrats, but Santiago was indifferent to his brother's opinion in such a personal matter. Priests of the Work in Spain counseled Monsignor Escrivá, who was extremely irritated by his brother's independence; as head of the family, he ought to go to Zaragoza on Santiago's behalf to request the hand in marriage of Yoya, Santiago's fiancée. Escrivá grumbled that he would only go if he were lodged at the Palace of Cogullada in the same room where Francisco Franco had stayed. Members of the Work had to spend a great deal of time negotiating this deal, but were finally successful, and Monsignor Escrivá went to Zaragoza and was lodged at the Palace of Cogullada.

Relations between Monsignor Escrivá and Yoya were rocky at the beginning. A supernumerary, Mercedes Jiménez de Andrade y Fernández de Córdoba, wife of an economics professor, Javier Irastorza, was charged with advising the young woman about how to dress, what perfumes to use, "so as not to displease the Father."

Monsignor Escrivá did not want his brother and sister to stay in Spain and brought them to Rome. Later, Carmen wished to return to die in Spain, but Monsignor Escrivá refused. Carmen is buried in a niche in the central house in Rome. On the wall, bronze letters set in pink marble spell "CARMEN" with the date of her death. Santiago returned to Spain after his sister's death.

Santiago died at Christmas 1994. One of his sons also named after his uncle, José María Escrivá de Balaguer, attended one of the Opus Dei schools in Madrid and became an Opus Dei numerary. Although it sounds comic, José María Escrivá de Balaguer left Opus Dei as a numerary. This was kept secret by Opus Dei superiors who retained the young man as an Opus Dei supernumerary. At this writing I am not sure whether or not he is still an Opus Dei supernumerary, although for some time he dated a young woman who was one. One of his sisters, who also became a numerary and was posted to Peru, left Opus Dei as well.

Numeraries could not have family photographs in their rooms, much less in the common rooms of the house where they lived. By contrast, in every house of the Work, there are photographs of the "Grandparents" and of "Aunt Carmen." The grandmother's photograph is taken from a portrait, itself based on an old photograph, in which she appeared in a simple black dress. The painter modified the photograph by adding an ermine neckpiece over the dress to make it more distinguished. I remember clearly that while I was in Rome, we were requested via the intercom from the director's office to provide "a collar of white ermine," because the painter needed it. Once the painting was complete, it was photographed, and this is the representation present in every house of the Work.

One fine day while I was in Rome in the 1950s, Monsignor Escrivá said that we had to learn to make "crespillos," a dessert his mother used to make when he was a child. From then on, this dessert has been served at the main meal in the houses of the Work on the grandmother's saint's day (Our Lady of Sorrows).

From the time I met him at the end of the 1940s, Monsignor Escrivá planned his road to sainthood. Convinced that he would be canonized, he had his tomb built in the central house in Rome as if it were the most natural thing in the world. He instructed the superiors: "But don't leave me here for too long. Let them take me after a while to a public church so that they will leave you alone so that you can work."

He also liked to tell us: "My daughters, if when you open my tomb, you find that I have not decayed, I will have cheated the Work. They should only find skin and bones." The move of Monsignor Escrivá's remains to the church of St. Eugene—which now has the status of an Opus Dei public church—strikes me as a curious irony. He repeatedly remarked about that church that "it looks like a bathroom," to stress Pius XII's bad taste.

In the photographs, *corpore insepulto*, before his burial, Monsignor Escrivá wears Eucharistic vestments, violating his own rule that we should all be prepared for burial wrapped in "a simple white sheet." The reader may recall that it was necessary to include this instruction in one's will.

All personal items that Monsignor Escrivá ceased to use were kept as future relics in the central house in Rome and in the houses he visited, especially on his last trips to South America. Such items ranged from handkerchiefs or a bathrobe belt, to the little bottle of holy water, the soap he used, and even the ribbon from a box of chocolates he brought the women numeraries in one of the houses of the Work.

Now and then Monsignor Escrivá would give the numeraries things he no longer used, like nail scissors, pencils, as well as his photographs with an ejaculation written on the back.

Also, during his lifetime, in houses he visited and especially in countries where his visits were infrequent, plates or cups he used were set aside. Even the flowers on the altar where Monsignor Escrivá celebrated Mass would be framed, and a mark would be made on the chairs on which he had sat.

After his death and before the burial, part of his hair was cut off and distributed to different houses around the world, as were pieces of the cassocks he had worn.

Shadows and lights show up what are important for me or for persons whom I knew well. At the same time and as a backdrop, a picture of Monsignor Escrivá's successor, Bishop Alvaro del Portillo takes shape.

Don Alvaro del Portillo was a witness to and cooperated in the fabrication of this devotion to the Father.

The late Alvaro del Portillo was born in Madrid March 11, 1914; incorporated into Opus Dei as a numerary in 1935, he was ordained a priest on June 25, 1944. Upon the death of Monsignor Escrivá on June 26, 1975, Monsignor Alvaro del Portillo was elected the second president general of Opus Dei on September 15, 1975. When Opus Dei changed its status from secular institute to personal prelature, Alvaro del Portillo was named prelate of the prelature of the Society of the Holy Cross and Opus Dei by Pope John Paul II on November 28, 1982. The Pope consecrated him a bishop on January 6, 1991.

Alvaro del Portillo was close to Monsignor Escrivá ever since he entered Opus Dei and they were never separated after his ordination. One of Escrivá's biographers recalls that from 1940 on he prayed for his son Alvaro, with the idea that he might be his successor.[1]

With Don Alvaro del Portillo, Monsignor Escrivá compensated for certain personal deficiencies so he kept Alvaro nearby in part because the latter belonged to a high social class and his family connections were important to the Work; also, he was a civil engineer, a prestigious profession, particularly in Spain at that time; but principally because he was a man of diplomatic tact and good manners, who moved with ease internationally and had command of Italian and French and a knowledge of some German and English as well. Escrivá frequently described to members of the Work, as one of his biographers does,[2] the engineer's dress uniform that Alvaro del Portillo wore on June 4, 1943, when he was received by

---

1. Vázquez de Prada, *El fundador del Opus Dei,* p. 263.
2. Ibid., p. 234.

His Holiness Pius XII in a private audience along with José Orlandis. To be sure, his dedication to Opus Dei kept Don Alvaro from acquiring much experience in engineering. Don Alvaro del Portillo was a sensitive, courteous person, although one never knew what he really thought. Nobody in Opus Dei was sure who directed whom. Did Monsignor Escrivá tell Alvaro del Portillo what he had to do? Was it Alvaro del Portillo who told Monsignor Escrivá what he should *not* do? Only Monsignor Alvaro del Portillo knew, and he went to the grave with his customary tact. However, the relation between them was very peculiar. Monsignor Escrivá did not know how to be alone. When Don Alvaro had some duty outside of the house, for instance in the Vatican, Monsignor Escrivá went to the Roman College of the Holy Cross to talk to the men or sometimes even to the Villa Sacchetti, especially while the Women's Branch government offices were there.

On his journeys, Monsignor Escrivá was always accompanied by Don Alvaro del Portillo, a numerary doctor who looked after his health, and his chauffeur, Armando Castro, the first Portuguese numerary. Within the Women's Branch, Don Alvaro del Portillo enjoyed respect and affection. He was invariably polite to us and knew how to say "please," "thank you," and "excuse me." Monsignor Escrivá very seldom said "please," and instead of "thank you" he would say, "May God pay you."

Monsignor Escrivá did not have natural good manners. He was rough, brusque, and rude. When he was angry and had someone to reproach, he had no measure of charity in his language. His offensive, violent words profoundly wounded persons. I remember vividly that when I went to the Vatican in 1973 and visited His Eminence Cardinal Arturo Tavera, then prefect of the Sacred Congregation of Religious and Secular Institutes, he asked how many years I had spent in Opus Dei, and when I told him eighteen, he commented: "And you needed eighteen years to realize how rude José María Escrivá is?"

His language was frequently crude. One Easter Sunday, the numeraries of the women's central government had been told to go up to the Villa Vecchia dining room to greet the Father for Easter after his lunch. As we entered the dining room, Don Alvaro was smoking, with his usual ivory cigarette holder. Monsignor Escrivá was talking through a wide-open window that overlooked the Villa garden. He was speaking to a group of numeraries from the Roman College of the Holy Cross, although we could not see them from where we were. He said with a great guffaw: "Have a brandy as I told you, but be careful, don't do what that Monsignor Galindo, my fellow countryman, did, who used to warm up the snifter in his fly" (Monsignor Pascual Galindo was the rector of the Church of the Holy Spirit in Madrid).

We could all hear that Don Alvaro tried to tell Escrivá that we had arrived, calling: "Padre! Padre!," but he did not hear. When he realized we were there, he slammed the window shut and beamed at us piously: "My daughters, may God bless you." We were forbidden to discuss this event even among ourselves.

A former Opus Dei male numerary recalls a similar incident that took place in Pamplona, Spain, in the presence of at least fifty male numeraries. Seated in front of the group, Monsignor Escrivá unbuttoned his cassock to take off a sweater (the day was warm) and remarked: "Well, I already have the behind of an abbess." Then he dressed himself again in public.

What wounded me most deeply during the last months in Rome leading up to my dismissal were not Monsignor Escrivá's scoldings and violent insults but his lack of charity. He put his rank of president general and his prestige as Founder ahead of his priestly role. There was never a shadow of a doubt that I might be innocent; he passed judgment and sentence without hearing me, based on assessments of other people.

Monsignor Escrivá taught that one should be "intransigent with sin, but tolerant with the sinner," but this was not what he practiced. If he heard a numerary say she felt "sorry" for someone, he would say, "Be sorry for the Work!"

He was especially harsh in his attitude toward those who left the Work. He forbad all contact with them, and he did not provide them with the slightest financial assistance, whether they left the institute or were dismissed. Monsignor Escrivá was never concerned, did not even contemplate in either of the two versions of Opus Dei's Constitutions written in his lifetime, that numerary members including servants or priests should have social security for old age or sickness. Moreover, it is explicitly stated in the Constitutions that numeraries who, under any circumstances, abandon Opus Dei may not seek any compensation for the work they have done inside the institution. This injustice has led to financial problems, not only for women numeraries, but also for numerary priests who left Opus Dei. The Work not only did not help them, but in more than one case slandered them, insinuating sexual misconduct.

The Father's scoldings were famous throughout the Work. He was saintly before the multitudes, frequently calling himself a sinner, but he was capable of the most terrible insults for the slightest reason. For instance, if a fried egg was not done to his taste, he would abuse the director of the house. If an altar cloth did not hang exactly at the stipulated number of centimeters above the floor, he was capable of scolding the director; similarly, he would go into a rage if there was noise in the kitchen when the pots and pans were scrubbed. However, you could not write in the house diary, "The Father was angry or caused a row," but had to say: "The Father taught us this or that today."

One of the best descriptions of Monsignor Escrivá's character was given by Alberto Moncada, who wrote that the Father "is charming, pleasant, and persuasive when one is on his side. He is intolerant, intractable, and crude when his standards are not accepted."[1]

Monsignor Alvaro del Portillo was present at all times and by never showing disagreement seemed to condone such conduct. This frightens me even more than the Founder's own fits, because it seems to reflect a cold, calculating attitude. Could Bishop Alvaro del Portillo believe that Monsignor Escrivá's frequent behavior was justified because it reflected "holy anger"?

Power and high office attracted Monsignor Escrivá. He claimed, "I am a descendant of a princess from Aragón,"[2] and claimed that the famous sixteenth-century Aragonese physician and heretic, Miguel Servet, was an ancestor. By his express order, shields of his seven noble surnames were engraved near the main altar of the Basilica of Torreciudad in the vicinity of Barbastro, his birthplace. His residence in Spain was always listed as Diego de León, 14, purchased for the princely sum of six million pesetas. He conveniently forgot the more modest houses in Madrid, where he actually lived with his family, notably the house on Martínez Campos, 4, which survives with a modest bar, "Vinos El Majuelo," on the ground floor. Landing at Barajas Airport in Madrid, Monsignor Escrivá would enter by the hall for "Authorities." In addition, while Jesús Romeo Gorría, connected with Opus Dei, was president of Iberia Airlines, his car awaited Monsignor Escrivá at the steps of the plane.

He took care that we were frequently reminded that he was "the Founder." "In my life I have known several popes," he would say, "many cardinals, a pile of bishops, but only one Founder—me." Then he often added: "God will demand much of you for having known me."

At one of the Men's Branch general congresses, Monsignor Escrivá told Antonio Pérez-Tenessa to propose that members of Opus Dei should greet the President General by genuflecting with the left knee touching the floor. The rule was quickly adopted. When Monsignor Escrivá notified those of us who were superiors of the Opus Dei Women's Branch, he said: "My daughters, it is not for my sake; I know you love me very much and respect me. I am doing it for the poor soul who will follow me."

When the Estudio General de Navarra became a university, Monsignor Escrivá arranged to be named grand chancellor. From then on, he began

---

1. Alberto Moncada, *El Opus Dei*, p. 126.
2. In *Crónica*, internal publication of Opus Dei Men's Branch, according to a former numerary.

to appear before crowds in theaters and large lecture halls, which were recorded in movies and photographs.

Opus Dei directs an entity named UNIV, headquartered in Rome. Under the leadership of local Opus Dei members in any given country, UNIV organizes trips to Rome to attend a Mass celebrated by the Holy Father and also to visit the Opus Dei prelate: Monsignor Escrivá when he was alive, subsequently Bishop del Portillo and presently Bishop Echevarría, the current prelate. The visit to the Opus Dei prelate is a well-staged question-and-answer period in which the questions have been carefully selected by Opus Dei group leaders, who check them out first with the prelate in order to prepare his appropriate responses, which seem spontaneous to the young people who are unaware of the well-prepared operation.

The format of previously prepared questions and answers is standard when the Opus Dei prelate appears in public. For instance, when the current Opus Dei prelate, Monsignor Echevarría, visited Brussels in October 1994, a gathering was staged in a hall at a Sheraton hotel. Since Monsignor Echevarría speaks neither French nor Flemish, an Opus Dei priest translated. To questions such as "What is the difference between Opus Dei and Christian people?" or "Why do people say that Opus Dei takes children away from their parents?" standard answers were given: "We are exactly like other people and we are interested in the same problems"; "Parents wish to live a Christian life, but do not have enough time for their children, but Opus Dei has the time to give those children a strong formation, new perspectives in life." Everything is planned beforehand.

The trips Monsignor Escrivá made to different countries during the final years of his life seemed extravagant to many numerary women on account of the expense they entailed. To be sure, there was a cultic reverence for the Founder on his visits, and he considered as proof of "good spirit" that the supernumeraries chartered international flights, sent flowers for his Mass, brought organically raised chickens from villages for his meals, and had crates of oranges available in case he wanted juice, even though oranges were not in season.

An amusing anecdote may be recounted here. Monsignor Escrivá was once invited to lunch at Dr. Faelli's house. They served some cheese with "little flowers on the labels." He recommended that we buy some. After tramping all over Rome to find them, I entered Allemagna in Piazza Colonna and discovered a pile of boxes of cheese, in which one portion in each box had a label with the "little flower." Delighted, I pulled out a box and the decorative pyramid came tumbling down. Since there was only one piece of cheese with the "little flower" in each box, we had to buy several boxes to serve Monsignor Escrivá the cheese with the "little flower," which turned out to be an edelweiss.

During the last years of his life, I am convinced that Monsignor Escrivá suffered from some psychological disorder since, otherwise, it would be totally inconceivable that a priest, with the aura of a Founder, would say things such as "If I knew that my parents had not desired me when I was conceived, I would have spit on their tomb."[1]

Again, I have heard of an occurrence (in 1962) at the home of María Paz Alvarez de Toledo, who was a friend and classmate in the French Dominican Sisters School in Valladolid. My absence from Madrid has kept me from obtaining confirmation, but my source is trustworthy. Apparently, Monsignor Escrivá was smitten with a tapestry that the family had in its dining room. (In Opus Dei jargon this translated to "The Father likes the tapestry.") He did not hesitate to tell the Opus Dei Women's Branch superiors in Madrid to request it for the Work. María Paz politely and generously said that she could not give it away because it belonged to the family patrimony, but she offered a million pesetas to buy another tapestry for Monsignor Escrivá.

Alvaro del Portillo was present at many of the events I have described in this book and probably at many others I don't know of, above all, in relations with the Vatican. He, like Bishop Echevarría, myself, and others who worked closely with Monsignor Escrivá, all heard him express pejorative opinions about supreme pontiffs and even about Vatican II: "Pray for the next Pope, who will have to mend many things." Or again, he referred to the Jesuits either as "the little ones" (los pequeñitos) or the "usual ones" (los de siempre). Monsignor Escrivá was terrified—as Alvaro del Portillo knew better than anyone else—that Pius XII might appoint the Jesuits as official visitors to Opus Dei women's houses. Similarly, those around Escrivá could see his lack of affection, to put it mildly, for the Theresians, despite having been their chaplain in Salamanca during the Spanish Civil War. Escrivá never judged them to be a legitimate secular institute; one suspects that he may have been uncomfortable that their founder, Father Pedro Poveda (assassinated early in the Civil War by leftist militiamen), conceived of an apostolate suspiciously like that of Escrivá's but twenty years before Escrivá.

My concern for all these facts is that Bishop Alvaro del Portillo, whom I had always considered a thoughtful, fair person, should close his eyes to reality and push a cause, ignoring the harm that it might do to many Catholics as well as to many Christians from other denominations.

Bishop del Portillo, like his successor Bishop Echevarría, knew well how to manipulate the process of beatification, how slander and defamation

---

1. Maite Sánchez Ocaña told me this story in Madrid. She heard it from a numerary priest who arrived from Rome in 1967 and had been present himself when Monsignor Escrivá made the remark.

were used in order that church tribunals reject as untrustworthy witnesses certain persons able to supply clarifying testimony.

It is painful to read the Summary of the Process for the Cause of Beatification, where each paragraph repeats references to Monsignor Escrivá such as that he offered "his own life to the Lord and a most intense prayer and mortification to obtain the conversion of those persons" (who left the Work) or "he carried on with such heroic exercise of virtues that it stirred up those of us who were at his side." I always heard Monsignor Escrivá repeat when someone left the Work: "...only the dry branches fall. And it is best that they fall," using the image written in *The Way* in reference to tribulations.[1]

Due to my concern about Monsignor Escrivá's process of beatification I sent His Holiness John Paul II two letters included in Appendix C as a secret of conscience, to which I have received no reply, although they reached the hands of the Holy Father through his secretary, His Eminence Cardinal Angel Sodano. However, His Eminence Cardinal Ratzinger had the courtesy of acknowledging receipt of copies of those letters.

The following are directives which Opus Dei women numeraries received to expand the devotion to Monsignor Escrivá. All such directives were known by Bishop Alvaro del Portillo.

> *Devotion to our Father.* In filial piety and justice with the church, we all have the serious duty to continually expand private devotion to our Father. We must take advantage of the opportunities that arise to distribute numerous holy pictures and information bulletins. We must try to give them to persons in certain professions where their impact will be multiplied. Parishes and churches are an effective distribution center. In the case that a member has special relations with a pastor, there should be no difficulty in leaving a small pile of holy pictures and bulletins. (Not too many. It is preferable that they be exhausted and that more be requested.) If there is no objection, these can be left visible with other pious objects, books, and so forth, which are sometimes in churches or in parish centers. We should not distribute them ourselves at the church entrance. Remember that it is important to obtain donations for the expenses involved in printing the bulletins and holy pictures. The thanks for a favor received, the resolution to support a petition with the sacrifice of alms, penance, or in general, the desire to help the spread of this private devotion, which does so much good to

---

1. Josemaría Escrivá, *The Way*, no. 685.

many, many souls, can be motives to stimulate generosity, whether in the form of large or small contributions.

During his lifetime, Monsignor Escrivá started to plan for the third Opus Dei generation, or to be more precise, to train "the third Father." For this reason he seems to have chosen two young numeraries, Javier Echevarría and Antonio Ugalde. Both accompanied him on many of his trips, completed their theological studies, and were ordained priests at the same time. However, long before Antonio Ugalde, currently a distinguished sociology professor in the United States, left Opus Dei and then obtained secularization from the Holy See, Javier Echevarría had clearly been designated heir apparent.

The Most Reverend Alvaro del Portillo died on March 23, 1994, and Monsignor Javier Echevarría was duly elected Opus Dei prelate on April 21, 1994, less than a month later. Javier Echevarría was born in Madrid on June 14, 1932. He entered Opus Dei in September 1948 at age sixteen. Two years later he was sent to the central house in Rome. Unfortunately, Javier Echevarría never had the opportunity to act on his own; he always formed part of a trio accompanying Monsignor Escrivá and Monsignor del Portillo on their trips around the world. His main mission on such trips was to supervise and demand perfection in all material preparations for Monsignor Escrivá and Don Alvaro del Portillo.

Javier Echevarría, or "Javi" as Monsignor Escrivá called him, was close to the Founder, first as his secretary, later on as one of his *custodes.* He completed his priestly and secular studies in Rome in a somewhat peculiar fashion: according to a colleague of his, from 1951 to 1953, he finished two years of philosophy and four of theology, plus a doctorate in canon law at the Angelicum (now Pontifical University of St. Thomas), but no studies of law took place in Rome until 1953. He was ordained a priest on August 7, 1955. In the official biography by Opus Dei, Monsignor Escrivá appointed Javier Echevarría in 1953 as his secretary. Opus Dei also says that Echevarría holds a doctorate in civil law from the Lateran University in Rome, but it is not clear when Bishop Echevarría studied civil law nor when he obtained this doctorate. Opus Dei requires that to be ordained a person must not only have finished such studies but also to have had professional experience; Echevarría had none and may have been ordained before completing his doctorate. In regard to the Opus Dei administration, he managed to get any rescript or norm that originated in Rome transmitted to regional vicars in the shortest time.

Outside Opus Dei Echevarría is unknown. His philosophical and theological writings are nonexistent, as are his publications on civil law. It is impossible to imagine Bishop Echevarría giving a public lecture on theol-

316 · BEYOND THE THRESHOLD

ogy or law at Harvard University or any of the campuses of the University of California, where one is challenged in a question period. For somewhat different reasons, it is also difficult to imagine him giving a talk on freedom or on human rights to some world organization.

So far my brush strokes sketch the portrait of these very different men united in the exercise of power. Lamentably, that power is covered by the mantle of the church and is exercised over Opus Dei members, who, with the noblest intentions, desire to grow close to God. To this end these people leave the good things God provided for them in this life on the altar of Opus Dei. Their north star and guide has been Monsignor Escrivá. Alvaro del Portillo continued that path and did not hesitate to show those he guided a mirage of sanctity.

With his lack of charisma, Bishop Echevarría assumes now the gigantic task of living the letter of Opus Dei to the hilt in order to conserve its spirit. So I would like to add a plea to Bishop Echevarría that I made in the Spanish edition of this book in anticipation of his prelature: Please God, may he reflect on his *basic* errors and help him take a new path toward love rather than power; to be more charitable, *more Christian,* and *more Catholic.*

11

SILENCES

Sincerity, "savage sincerity," is the constant watchword repeated to Opus Dei members, the "faithful of the prelature," as they are now called. One must speak, open up, in the fraternal chat, formerly called the confidence, in confession, and in the weekly talk with an Opus Dei priest. "In order for the mute devil not to take control of our soul, it is necessary to live sincerity." "When something happens that you would not wish to be known, say it immediately—in a hurry—to the Good Shepherd," Monsignor Escrivá used to say.

Opus Dei's indoctrination of its members gives pride of place to sincerity. Sincerity is mentioned in season and out of season in Opus Dei. Its members hear unceasingly that sincerity is the cure for all evils. When I came to Opus Dei, I believed in the authenticity of that healthy, useful attitude.

Unhappily, Opus Dei fails to say many things and misrepresents others. This is a major source of the great disillusionment that sweeps over a person when the blindfold of fanaticism slips off. In Opus Dei the truth is constantly silenced. On the one hand, the member of the Work is urged to bare herself spiritually to her director or the priest. On the other, that same director is capable with holy astuteness of silencing the real motive of any of the directives that she imparts to the member.

Without any intentional bad will on the part of superiors, this Opus Dei emphasis on discretion creates a false air of mystery: people coming from other countries to the central house are not announced; nobody is informed when a member is leaving for a different country. Sooner or later, one finds out through chance meetings on the stairs or in the oratory. The ordinary members' lack of information increases the power of the directors, who feel powerful because they know what all the rest do not. Sadly, this sort of practice is familiar to citizens of totalitarian countries.

The most significant area of silence in Opus Dei was that surrounding Monsignor Escrivá. From the most trivial to the most important, many details were hushed up. Numeraries and servants who cleaned his rooms could not mention, even among themselves, that Monsignor Escrivá often took a bath instead of a shower as the rest of the members did; they had been carefully instructed not to discuss what they learned while working at the administered house.

One day he almost died. I knew that only because in the afternoon of the crisis, he came with Don Alvaro to the office of the central advisory and told us: "This son of mine, Alvaro, saved my life with his great presence of mind." The rest of the house, more than a hundred members, knew nothing until many months later; except, of course, Rosalía López, who as the maid, was present at the scene.

It was not openly acknowledged that Monsignor Escrivá had diabetes. When he fell into a coma, Don Alvaro immediately realized what was wrong. He forced open his mouth and practically poured down the sugar bowl placed on the table, sprinkling it with water to make it easier to swallow. Meanwhile, he urgently sent Rosalía to the kitchen for more sugar and to call the Father's numerary physician, who also lived in Villa Vecchia.

I learned that those who were in the kitchen—and did not know what was happening—were going to give Rosalía another sugar bowl in response to her abrupt demand for "sugar for the Father." She snatched the big can out of the hands of the person in charge of the kitchen and returned to the dining room on the run. This happened on April 27, 1954.

The Founder's childhood friends were never mentioned in Opus Dei. Did he have any? Isidoro Zorzano is the only boyhood friend, specifically from secondary school, known as such through the early biography by Daniel Sargent.[1] Zorzano's process of beatification was opened in Madrid, October 11, 1948, with a proclamation posted on the cathedral door announcing: "Cause of beatification and canonization of the servant of God, Isidoro Zorzano Ledesma, of the secular institute Opus Dei." Those of us who were members of the Work during the following decades were encouraged to pray to him as a model of sanctification of everyday life. Why has Opus Dei silenced this process?

---

1. Daniel Sargent, *God's Engineer* (Chicago: Scepter, 1954), pp. 32 ff. Sargent describes Opus Dei as a secular institute. Opus Dei eventually "silenced" this book in its houses.

Is it because Opus Dei is now a prelature, while Zorzano became a saint when it was a secular institute? Opus Dei has similarly silenced the process of Monsita Grases, while pushing forward with Monsignor Escrivá's process.

Many things and many individuals are silenced in Opus Dei. They disappear in silence. Those who left Opus Dei, those who committed suicide or tried to, those who became insane are never mentioned.

Even greater care is taken not to mention priests who leave Opus Dei. Opus Dei silences them all. Many of them continue in the priesthood. Others seek secularization, and receive dispensations from the Holy See, and marry in the Catholic church. I found out about some cases when I was still in Opus Dei. I remember that when I learned of one case by chance, I called the counselor to the confessional and asked him if what I had been told was true. He confirmed the rumor I had heard outside, but recommended that "I say nothing," although the situation was whispered about all over Caracas.

Opus Dei silences the truth. To squelch discussion inside the Work about the many people who quit the institution, the superiors—perhaps without reflecting on the consequences that their statements might have—have said that those individuals were "sick" in some cases, or "insane" in others; they never try to offer a straightforward explanation as to why they have left.

For me, the worst silences are those that hinder personal freedom. Opus Dei shows admirable zeal in trying to preserve vocations that have been a decade or more in its ranks. Its practice belies the slogan that is repeated when one joins: "The door to Opus Dei is only open a crack to come in but wide open to leave." Perhaps without realizing the danger of its strategy, Opus Dei silences persons, intimidates, even blackmails, deliberately creating a sense of guilt which leads some former members in turn to keep silence about their membership in Opus Dei. There have been those who have suffered some misfortune after they left Opus Dei and considered it God's punishment for having left. I remember only too well the case of the daughter of a friend who tormented herself for a long time with this notion.

Opus Dei's cold silence toward those who leave provokes contradictory reactions. In their resentment toward the association, some also leave the church. Others remain within the church, but their acquaintance with Opus Dei makes them regard it as a sect which has managed to lodge itself within Catholicism. But almost all former members of Opus Dei, even if they never met while they belonged to the Work, agree publicly that Opus Dei silences the truth.

None of this is meant to deny that there are not only good people but excellent human beings inside Opus Dei. Some are still blinded by their own good faith and credulity. Others, who have privileged information, do not dare to say what they think out loud for fear of being silenced by Opus Dei. A range of circumstances could be described which retain such individuals within Opus Dei. For example, one is the age of many women over fifty, including professional women, who have not exercised their profession for many years. Even if they are not in agreement with major aspects of the Opus Dei and have suffered its penalties and harassment personally, they would not know where to go if they left Opus Dei at their stage in life. It is not easy to begin a life outside especially when one carries the burden of the years spent in Opus Dei. Thus, they let their life slip by in silence, on behalf of a cause of which they are no longer convinced in conscience.

Then there are numerary priests whom Opus Dei silences when they have tried to exercise genuine charity as the church demands rather than as Opus Dei commands. Such priests have defended just causes with great integrity and energy, even at the risk of being silenced.

Opus Dei takes pains to warn them and to convince them that failure to persevere in the association is equivalent to leaving the church. They are blackmailed with the argument that if they leave Opus Dei they might end up in concubinage. It requires heroic courage for a numerary priest over fifty to leave Opus Dei. The change from the comfortable, sheltered life of Opus Dei houses to the poverty and hardship of a poor parish is very great. Accordingly, some priests accept the rules of the game, become silent, and spend their lives in inner conflict, a situation which has led to more than one case of alcoholism among male numeraries.

Some years back after I had ceased to belong to Opus Dei, I encountered a paradigmatic case of a "silenced" Opus Dei priest. He acknowledged that Opus Dei was a harmful organization but felt he could not abandon it, because he had "given his word and had to keep it." I suggested to him that he speak to the bishop of the diocese where he lived and place himself under the latter's authority, continuing as a priest but outside Opus Dei. I was shaken by some of his responses: "I would not have been a priest because it never occurred to me to be a priest before entering the Work. I was ordained as a priest *of the Work*. . . . As an Opus Dei priest, I have nothing to do with the activities of the church that have not been assigned me by Opus Dei superiors. If the children in Vallecas [a proverbially poor Madrid neighborhood] have runny noses, let their parish priest wipe their noses. I have nothing to do with that, and it doesn't interest me. If a woman has a problem, let her go to whomever she needs. It doesn't affect me as an Opus Dei priest. I'm not going to worry about it. . . . I have been ordained to serve my brothers in the Work, nothing else, nobody else. At least until the Opus Dei superiors tell me otherwise."

This doctrine that Opus Dei priests serve the prelature rather than the church is not news to me. I have heard Monsignor Escrivá express himself on the matter on several occasions, saying that "Opus Dei numeraries are ordained to serve their brothers." Of course, this is never said overtly to church authorities; rather the contrary is proclaimed.

Opus Dei claims the right to silence those members who waver in their vocation, taking their freedom away, isolating them, forcing them to submit as slaves for whatever period the supervisors deem "medicinal." They are deprived of their freedom, isolated, held incommunicado.

Why do men and women who left Opus Dei fear to tell the truth of what they saw, heard, and often suffered? As can be learned from my own case, many, understandably, fear reprisals and prefer to put painful memories behind them as they try to rebuild their lives. Some married people fear that their children might suffer abuse from Opus Dei and remain silent about their years in the institution. They may even beg that their name not be mentioned publicly because "members of their family who belong to Opus Dei would completely avoid them."

Opus Dei silences critical minds. Monsignor Escrivá used to say, "I don't want great brains in the Work, because they turn into swelled heads. Average intelligences, if they are docile and faithful, are very effective."

An engineer, banker, or scientist tends to have fewer problems with superiors in the Work than humanists, philosophers, or theologians, who are almost always frustrated within the Work. As soon as someone—who may even be a priest—is outstanding in the field of philosophy or theology, Opus Dei will almost certainly end by silencing him. He disappears. Opus Dei hides him. He frequently ends up by leaving the institution or becomes the patient of a psychiatrist. Opus Dei does not let you think nor engage in speculation. There is an "internal censorship" that reviews articles, books, lectures, or anything that a member wants to publish. Youngsters with "good spirit," mostly incompetent in academic disciplines, dare to suggest corrections and bring them to the attention of superiors. The proof is that outside Opus Dei institutions there are no Opus Dei philosophers or theologians particularly well known and respected for their work at other institutions besides the University of Navarra. Jurists can acquire some importance within the prelature but philosophers and theologians have no place. This is publicly recognized. I say nothing new but observe a fact.

I speak about what I know, because to my shame I must confess that I, too, used the weapon of silence within Opus Dei, accepting and participating in the game of discretion. It was difficult for me to swallow the rules of discretion, but I did so conscientiously, learning how to dish out the truth in small doses, or more precisely, how to keep it hidden or even make it disappear. This lasted a long time, proof of my having acquired "good spirit" in Opus Dei.

Years later, life in Venezuela freed me, it brought back my real self, and helped overcome my fanaticism. My experience there aroused my conscience, reminding me first to look to God and to consider everything else secondary.

As I said in the Introduction, I judge it my responsibility before God and humanity to unmask Opus Dei, even if I have had to undertake the sometimes tedious task of describing in detail life inside women's houses. For that, I have no other method than to follow the thread of my personal experiences.

Therefore, even at the risk of being destroyed by Opus Dei, I refused to be "silenced" by them at this stage of my life, because I believe in spiritual freedom and in the defense of human rights.

> Ese cielo tan rosado
> es que el día está rompiendo.
> Esta fiesta se ha acabado:
> Cantaclaro se está yendo.[1]

> That sky turning pink
> shows day is breaking through.
> The fair came to its end:
> Cantaclaro fades away.

---

1. Rómulo Gallegos, "Cantaclaro," *Obras Completas*, Tome I (Madrid: Aguilar, 1976), p. 996.

CORRESPONDENCE TO OBTAIN MY CERTIFICATE OF STUDIES

UNIVERSITY OF CALIFORNIA, SANTA BARBARA

BERKELEY · DAVIS · IRVINE · LOS ANGELES · RIVERSIDE · SAN DIEGO · SAN FRANCISCO   SANTA BARBARA · SANTA CRUZ

INTERNATIONAL CENTER · FOREIGN STUDENT OFFICE   SANTA BARBARA, CALIFORNIA 93106

March 1, 1973

A I R   M A I L

The Rt. Rev. Monsignor José-María Escrivá
President General
Societas Sacerdotalis Sanctae Crucis et Opus Dei
Viale Bruno Buozzi,   73
Roma,   ITALY

                        Re: Scholastic transcripts of
                             María del Carmen Tapia
Most Reverend Sir:

        This is to request an official transcript of the studies
María del Carmen Tapia completed at the Collegium Romanum Sanctae Mariae,
Regionis Venezuela, at Caracas, Venezuela, during the period from 1960
through 1965.

        It would be most helpful, if this is possible, to have the
courses listed by Title and the unit value, as well as the grade. It is
my understanding that the studies in Philosophy were completed and the
first year of Theology started.

        This would enable us to evaluate the credit in comparison
to our own curriculum.

        It would be very much appreciated if we could receive this
record at your earliest convenience and if the transcript is directed to
this office with a statement of any cost involved, an international money
order will be dispatched by return mail.

                                Very sincerely,

                                K. M. Mathew (signature)

                                K. M. Mathew
                                Dean of Foreign Students

KMM:mje

SECOND COPY

CC: United States Embassy
    Roma, Italy

UNIVERSITY OF CALIFORNIA, SANTA BARBARA

BERKELEY · DAVIS · IRVINE · LOS ANGELES · RIVERSIDE · SAN DIEGO · SAN FRANCISCO   **SANTA BARBARA · SANTA CRUZ**

INTERNATIONAL CENTER - FOREIGN STUDENT OFFICE   SANTA BARBARA, CALIFORNIA 93106

The Rt. Rev. Monsignor José-María Escrivá   May 10, 1973
President General
Societas Sacerdotalis Sanctae Crucis et Opus Dei   AIR MAIL REGISTERED
Viale Bruno Buozzi, 73
Roma, ITALY   CERTIFIED RECEIPT REQUESTED

Most Reverend Sir:

      On March 1, 1973, the Dean of Foreign Students on this University campus airmailed a letter of inquiry to you on behalf of María del Carmen Tapia. Since more than two months have elapsed without reply and the letter was not registered, we are assuming that there was some difficulty in delivery and perhaps the letter did not reach you. I am therefore taking the liberty of forwarding the same letter to you again.

      If I have directed this request to Your Grace in error, may I ask that you kindly refer to the proper authority? It is not possible to evaluate prior credits without some authorized records from previous institutions attended.

      If, on the other hand, the cost of transcripts or postage may delay this transmittal, please be assured that immediate notification of any charges will receive our attention by return post.

      Your kindness will be most appreciated.

Very sincerely,

Mrs. Muriel J. Engle
Administrative Assistant

MJE:
enclosure

cc: U.S. Embassy
    Roma, Italy

Societas Sacerdotalis Sanctae Crucis

Procurator Generalis

May 29, 1973

Mrs. Muriel J. Engle
University of California,
International Center —Foreign Student Office,
Santa Barbara, California 93106,

U. S. A.

Dear Mrs. Engle,

I wish to acknowledge receipt of your letter
of May 10, 1973 addressed to our President, and to
inform you on his behalf, and in my capacity as
Procurator General, that Miss Carmen Tapia did not
follow, in this Institution, any courses in Philoso
phy or Theology.

Yours sincerely,

Rev. Daniel Cummings

UNIVERSITY OF CALIFORNIA, SANTA BARBARA

BERKELEY · DAVIS · IRVINE · LOS ANGELES · RIVERSIDE · SAN DIEGO · SAN FRANCISCO   SANTA BARBARA · SANTA CRUZ

INTERNATIONAL CENTER · FOREIGN STUDENT OFFICE   SANTA BARBARA, CALIFORNIA 93106

                                                                June 25, 1973

The Rev. Consiliario del Opus Dei   A I R   M A I L
in Venezuela
c/o Excmo. Y. Revmo. Monsignor Nuncio
Apostolico de S.S. en Venezuela   REGISTERED
Nunciatura Apostolica   Return Receipt Requested
Caracas, Venezuela

Dear Sir:

        It is our understanding that María del Carmen Tapia was a member
of your institution, living in Caracas, during the period from October 1956,
until October 1965.

        We would appreciate receipt of a transcript of any studies that she
performed during this period. It would be helpful to have the courses listed
by Title, and the unit value, as well as the grade. This would enable us to
evaluate the credit in comparison to our own curriculum.

        It would also be appreciated if we could receive this record at
your earliest convenience and if the transcript is directed to this office
with a statement of any cost involved, an international money order will be
dispatched to you by return mail.

        Thank you kindly for your assistance.

                                        Very sincerely yours,

                                        K. M. Mathew

KMM:mje   K. M. Mathew
                                        Dean of Foreign Students
cc: Embassy of the United States
    Caracas, Venezuela

Sociedad Sacerdotal de la Santa Cruz

El Consiliario

Caracas, 7 de Agosto de 1973

Mr. K.M. Mathew
Dean of Foreing Students
University of California
International Center-Foreing Student Office
Santa Barbara. California 93106. U.S.A.

Distinguido Señor:

Acuso recibo de su atenta carta
de fecha 25 de Junio de 1973, en relación al conte
nido de la cual le informo que la Srta. Carmen Ta
pia no ha cursado estudios en esta Institución.

Atentamente, queda de Ud. afmo.

Fdo.: Roberto Salvat Romero

Translation of letter on previous page.

Priestly Society of the Holy Cross
  The Counselor

  Caracas, August 7, 1973

Mr. K.M. Mathew
Dean of Foreing [sic] Students
University of California
International Center-Foreing [sic] Student Offices
Santa Barbara, California 93106 USA

Dear Sir:
  I have received your letter of June 25, 1973. In regard to
your inquiry, I can inform you that Miss Carmen Tapia has
not done any studies in this Institution.

Yours truly,

Signed: Roberto Salvat Romero

[Original has UCSB Dean of Foreign Students date stamp of
August 14, 1973]

UNIVERSITY OF CALIFORNIA, SANTA BARBARA

BERKELEY • DAVIS • IRVINE • LOS ANGELES • RIVERSIDE • SAN DIEGO • SAN FRANCISCO SANTA BARBARA • SANTA CRUZ

DEPARTMENT OF RELIGIOUS STUDIES   SANTA BARBARA, CALIFORNIA 93106

November 29, 1973

William K. Braun Esq.
Attaché Cultural
Embassy of the United States
Via Vittorio Veneto, 119
00187 Roma (Italy)

Dear Sir,

I would like to inform you that Miss María del Carmen Tapia,
personal research assistant to Professor Raimundo Panikkar
(formerly Professor at Harvard University and now a professor
in our Department of Religious Studies) will be in Roma, January
the 1st until January the 6th. attending the Philosophical
Colloquium organised by Professor E. Castelli. Miss Tapia
will leave Roma for this country on January the 7th.

Miss Tapia is a Venezuelan citizen and as a permanent resident
of our country holds the green card.

For personal reasons which we have discussed, Miss Tapia would
like to speak with you and, on her behalf, I am requesting an
appointment to be held at your convenience.

Since Miss Tapia will leave for vacation the 6th of December,
there will not be sufficient time for an answer to arrive before
her departure. Therefore, I ask that you please send a note to
her c/o Dra. Enrichetta Valenzioni, Via Lagrange, 1. Parioli.
00197 Roma.

Miss Tapia will call you upon her arrival to Roma, January 1st.

I would be most grateful for any kind of assistance that you
can give to her.

Sincerely yours,

Gerald J. Larson
Chairman

GJL/mct

EMBASSY OF THE
UNITED STATES OF AMERICA

Rome, Italy

January 29, 1974

Professor Gerald J. Larson
Chairman
Department of Religious Studies
University of California
Santa Barbara, California 93106

Dear Professor Larson:

I am attaching a copy of my letter of January 16
to the Reverend Daniel Cummings and a photocopy
of his reply dated January 24. The subject of this
correspondence is the record of studies done by
Maria del Carmen Tapia, but you will see from Father
Cummings' reply that my inquiry has been unsuccessful.

I am sorry that I have been unable to obtain anything
more helpful.

Sincerely,

William K. Braun
Cultural Attache'

Encl.: As stated

Rome, January 16, 1974

Rev. Daniel Cummings
Procurator General
Societas Sacerdotalis Sanctae Crucis
Viale Bruno Buozzi 73
00197 Rome

Dear Father Cummings:

I am writing in response to a request from Professor
Gerald J. Larson, Chairman of the Department of Religious
Studies at the University of California in Santa Barbara.

Professor Larson and the University of California would
like very much to receive a transcript or a record of the
studies completed by a Maria del Carmen Tapia at the
Collegium Romanum Sanctae Mariae, Regionis Venezuela, at
Caracas, Venezuela, during the period from 1960 through
1965.

I am not, of course, familiar with the problem of obtaining these transcripts, but as I understand it difficulties
might have arisen because (as the University of California
has been told) Miss Tapia's records are no longer in Caracas
but in Rome. I am told that previous inquiries both in
Caracas and in Rome have resulted in the information that
Miss Tapia was not enrolled at either institutions but that,
now that her records are apparently here, your office might
have the necessary information.

Professor Larson would greatly appreciate any help you can
provide. I shall of course be happy to be of any assistance
I can.

Sincerely,

William K. Braun
Cultural Attache'

WKBraun:gb

RÉV. DANIEL CUMMINGS

January 24, 1974.

William X. Braun, Esq.,
Cultural Attache',
Embassy of the United States
of America,
Rome.

Dear Sir,

        I write to acknowledge receipt of your
letter of January 16 last, and to inform you
that neither here nor in Venezuela have we any
records of the person in question having completed courses of studies.

                    Yours sincerely,

                    Daniel Cummings

                    Rev. Daniel Cummings

On January 3, 1974, I sent a letter to the Vatican addressed to His Eminence the Reverend Cardinal Arturo Tavera, at that time prefect of the Sacred Congregation for Religious and Secular Institutes. In the first place, I expressed my thanks for his kind and warm hospitality, and then I related to him in detail my life while in Opus Dei, particularly the steps I had taken to obtain my certificate of studies.

—*Marìa del Carmen Tapia*

Prot. n. I.S. 901/74

Distinguida Señorita:

En relación a su escrito del 3 de enero pp. han sido interrogados los Responsables del Instituto que nos han enviado la siguiente respuesta.

"Los estudios de filosofía y de teología en el Opus Dei sólo adquieren efectivo valor académico, tanto internamente como externamente (efectos públicos), y por tanto sólo pueden ser garantizados por la Institución, cuando son, caso por caso, revalidados.

La frase de la carta del Procurador General, de fecha 29.V. 1973, con la que confirma que "Miss Carmen Tapia did not follow, in this Institution, any course in Philosophy or Theology", tiene precisamente ese sentido: mientras no se cursa y se supera la reválida, no llevamos constancia oficial de los estudios o de los cursos previos y, por lo tanto, resulta imposible extender ningún certificado: es como si no los hubiera hecho.

La señorita María del Carmen Tapia no ha cumplido ese requisito. Como ya se ha hecho constar a los diversos organismos ante los que ha acudido la mencionada señorita, ni en Venezuela ni en Roma hay documento alguno que acredite que esa persona haya obtenido la reválida de ningún tipo de estudios: en consecuencia, no es posible expedir ningún certificado al respecto.

Lo dicho en el primer párrafo de esta nota lo conocen todos los socios y las asociadas del Opus Dei. Por eso, ninguno ha pedido jamás en tantos años, una certificación de estudios si no ha hecho previamente la reválida. El caso de la señorita Tapia es el primero que se nos presenta."

Con el testimonio de mi consideración queda de Vd. atentamente en Xto.

J. B. Verdelli
Subsecretario

Srta. María del Carmen Tapia
900-B, Hot Springs Road
SANTA BARBARA, Calif. 93108

U.S.A.

Translation of letter on the previous page.

Rome, February 26, 1974

Sacred Congregation for
Religious and Secular Institutes

Dear Miss Tapia:
In regard to your letter of the past January 3, upon being questioned, the authorities of the Institute have sent us the following answer. "The studies of philosophy and theology in Opus Dei only obtain effective academic recognition, both internally and externally (public effects), and accordingly can only be certified by the Institution when they are revalidated[1] on a case-by-case basis.

"The Procurator General's expression in the letter of May 29, 1973, in which he affirms that 'Miss Carmen Tapia did not follow in the Institution, any course in Philosophy or Theology,' has exactly this sense. So long as the revalidation is not taken and passed, we do not maintain official notice of the previous studies and courses and accordingly, it is impossible to grant any certificate. It is as if she had not done them.

Miss María del Carmen Tapia has not fulfilled that requirement. As has already been made known to different organizations to which the cited person has appealed, there is no document in Venezuela, or Rome which accredits that such a person has obtained the revalidation of any type of studies. Consequently, it is not possible to issue any certificate.

"What is stated in the first paragraph of this note is known to every male and female member of Opus Dei. Therefore, in all these years no one has ever requested a certificate of studies, if he has not previously done the revalidation. Miss Tapia's case is the first that has occurred."

Please receive the expression of my esteem. Yours in Christ,

G.B. Verdelli, Subsecretary

---

1. *Translator's note:* The Spanish *revalida* and *revalidado* have no exact English equivalent. In centralized national educational systems, programs given in private institutions sometimes have to be validated by an examination given or supervised by public officials.

UNIVERSITY OF CALIFORNIA, SANTA BARBARA

DEPARTMENT OF RELIGIOUS STUDIES   SANTA BARBARA, CALIFORNIA 93106

March 25, 1974

The Rt. Reverend Monsignor José-María Escrivá
President General
Societas Sacerdotalis Sanctae Crucis et Opus Dei
Viale Bruno Buozzi, 73
Roma (Italy)

Reverend Sir,

I asked Dr. K.M. Mathew, Dean of the Foreign Students Office of
this University to write to you in your capacity of President
General for the evaluation of the studies that Miss María del
Carmen Tapia performed in your Association during her stay in
Caracas, Venezuela from 1956 till 1965. Dean Mathew wrote to
you on March 1st. 1973, but he never received any answer.

       1.- On May 10, 1973, Mrs. Muriel J. Engle, Admi-
nistrative Assistant to the Dean of Foreign Students Office,
wrote to you: She included a copy of the above mentioned letter
thinking that the original had been lost in the mail.

       2.- Mrs. Engle received from Rev. Daniel Cummings a
letter dated May 29, 1973, on your behalf, and in his capacity
as Procurator General of the Societas Sacerdotalis Sanctae Crucis
et Opus Dei, that "Miss Carmen Tapia did not follow any courses
in Philosophy or Theology in your Institution."

       3.- On June 25, 1973, Dr. Mathew, the Dean of the
Foreign Students Office, wrote to the Consiliario of the Opus Dei
in Venezuela, Roberto Salvat Romero (who, as I understand had
been Miss Tapia's Professor in two disciplines of Philosophy:
Introducción a la Filosofía and Etica. Dr. Mathew wrote on my
behalf asking for information regarding any kind of studies that
Miss María del Carmen pursued during her stay in Venezuela.

       4.- Dr. Roberto Salvat Romero answered in a letter
dated from Caracas, August 7, 1973, that "la Srta. Carmen Tapia
no ha cursado estudios en esta Institución."

       5.- On January 16, 1974, and on my behalf, William
K. Braun, Cultural Attaché to the Embassy of the United States in
Roma wrote to Rev. Daniel Cummings (in his capacity as Procurator
General of Societas Sacerdotalis Sanctae Crucis and Opus Dei) also
requesting information regarding the studies that Miss Tapia had

UNIVERSITY OF CALIFORNIA, SANTA BARBARA

BERKELEY · DAVIS · IRVINE · LOS ANGELES · RIVERSIDE · SAN DIEGO · SAN FRANCISCO   SANTA BARBARA · SANTA CRUZ

DEPARTMENT OF RELIGIOUS STUDIES   SANTA BARBARA, CALIFORNIA 93106

performed in your Institution during her stay in Venezuela.

6.- Mr. W.K. Braun replied to me on January 24, 1974 including as well a copy of the letter from Rev. Cummings to him. In this letter, Rev. Cummings stated that "neither here (Rome) nor in Venezuela, have we any records of the person in question having completed courses of studies."

7.- I must say that I am baffled with the information received from the Opus Dei since it does not tally with what Dr. Salvat told the Apostolic Nuntius in Caracas (that the records of Miss Tapia were in Rome) and in no way seemed to deny that Miss Tapia had, in fact, studied in Caracas. Further, we also have information here that present members of the Opus Dei in Venezuela have confirmed that Miss Tapia studied in your Institution.

8.- Allow me to explain: Indeed I am aware that those "Estudios Internos" have no academic validity as Miss Sofía Pilo mentioned in Caracas. However, this is not my present concern. What I need, Monsignor Escrivá, is to know all the philosophy and theology courses, one by one, that Miss Tapia studied in your Institution, as well as the grades she received in each of these philosophy and theology courses, even if they do not have academic validity, or have not been revalidated.

9.- I need this information in order to confirm what is already on file in this University as well as what is at the Office of Immigration and Naturalization which keeps the official records of Miss Tapia.

10.- I would also appreciate receiving your confirmation on the following confidential points: Whether Miss Tapia

a) from 1949 until May 1966 was a member of the Feminine Branch of the Opus Dei;

b) stayed in Spain until April 1952;

c) was in Rome from April 1952 until September 1956;

d) was during the first time of her stay in Rome helping you on Secretarial matters concerning the Feminine Branch of the Opus Dei;

e) afterwards she was a 'Major Superior' in your Institution;

UNIVERSITY OF CALIFORNIA, SANTA BARBARA

BERKELEY · DAVIS · IRVINE · LOS ANGELES · RIVERSIDE · SAN DIEGO · SAN FRANCISCO

SANTA BARBARA · SANTA CRUZ

DEPARTMENT OF RELIGIOUS STUDIES   SANTA BARBARA, CALIFORNIA 93106

       f) was named "Directora Regional de Venezuela" in September, 1956 leaving for Caracas, where she arrived in October 1956;

       g) was "Directora Regional de Venezuela" from October 1956 until October 1965 when she was required to go to Rome;

       h) living in Roma, Via di Villa Sacchetti, 36 from October 1965 until May 1966 when she returned to Spain.

       11.- I would like to make very clear Monsignor Escrivá, that I am interested to receive all information concerning the time Miss María del Carmen Tapia belonged to the Opus Dei as well as that specifically related with her studies.

       What I am not requesting -and much less interested-is in receiving personal or confidential information regarding the spiritual life of Miss Tapia during her stay in the Opus Dei.

       I would appreciate, Monsignor, your attention on these matters as well as for your earliest answer.

       Looking forward to receiving a detailed information of my request, I remain,

                Truly yours,

                Gerald J. Larson
                Chairman

P.S.: Since I am requesting clarification of all information we have received, a copy of this letter will be sent to the persons we consider pertinent in order to prevent any kind of misunderstanding.

REV. DANIEL CUMMINGS

April 15, 1974.

Gerald J. Larson, Esq.,
Chairman,
Dept. of Religious Studies,
University of California,
Santa Barbara, California 93106,
U.S.A.

Dear Sir,

　　　　Your letter of March 25 last has just come
to hand, and I am writing immediately to confirm what
I communicated <u>clearly and punctually</u> to Mr. Braun,
who wrote to me on your behalf. As requested, I gave
you in that letter the answer pertinent to your question; the only possible answer, because there is no
other one. There is, therefore, nothing further that
I can now add.

　　　　I fail to understand the motive, and purpose,
of the other questions which you ask in regard to points
which have no bearing on academic matters, and which are
not relevant either to the carrying out of a person's
professional work. Perhaps you think otherwise, and I
respect your opinion, while I trust that you also will
respect my point of view. I wish to make it very clear
that I am not referring to confidential information of
any kind: I refer to the non-academic matters you bring
up.

Yours truly,

Rev. Daniel Cummings

P.S. I see no objection to your sending copies of your
letter to whoever you wish.

April 17, 1974

Miss María del Carmen Tapia
Assistant to Professor Panikkar
Department of Religious Studies
University of California
Santa Barbara, California 93106
U.S.A.

Dear Miss Tapia:

Thank you for your letter of February 15, which arrived here only today, such are the vagaries and vicissitudes of the international mail.

I did write to Dr. Roberto Salvat and I received a letter from him in which he states that there was no record of your having made the studies you described. I thought I had sent a copy of this letter on to you and Professor Larson, but I am mistaken as a search of the file indicates. Enclosed is a copy of Dr. Salvat's reply.

Please be sure of my good wishes.

Sincerely yours,

Edward J. Joyce
Cultural Affairs Officer

Enc.: As stated

ROBERTO SALVAT ROMERO

Apartado 60707
Caracas

Caracas, 24 de enero, 1974

Dr. Edward J. Joyce
Agregado Cultural de la
Embajada de Estados Unidos de América
Caracas.

Estimado Dr. Joyce:

Acuso recibo de su atenta carta del 14 del pasado mes de diciembre, que he encontrado a mi regreso a Caracas.

En relación a su contenido, debo manifestarle que no hay ninguna constancia de que la Srta. Tapia haya seguido cursos de Estudios Religiosos en esta Institución.

Con los mejores deseos para este nuevo año, le saluda muy atentamente

Roberto Salvat Romero

P/D: Me consta que, con fecha 29 mayo 1973, ya fue enviada a esa Universidad, desde Roma, esta misma comunicación.

Translation of letter on the previous page.

Roberto Salvat Romero
Apartado 50707   Caracas, January 24, 1974
Caracas

Dr. Edward J. Joyce
Cultural Attaché of the United States Embassy
Caracas

Dear Dr. Joyce:
    I am in receipt of your letter of the past December 14, which I found upon my return to Caracas.
    In regard to your request, I must explain that there is no record that Miss Tapia has taken courses of religious studies in this Institution.
    With my best wishes for the new year, I am

                    Yours truly,
                    Signed: Roberto Salvat Romero

P.S. I am informed that on May 29, 1992, that University received this same reply from Rome.

Translation

Certification of Faustino Castro Gete at the request of Miss Maria del
Carmen Tapia _____

Faustino Castro Gete, of Spanish nationality, 48 years of age, by profession
lawyer, entered Opus Dei as a numerary member in 1950 and was ordained
a priest in Madrid in 1955. He remained a numerary priest of Opus Dei
until 1968, when he ceased to belong to that Institution and was
incardinated in the dioceses of Talanpantla, Mexico. _____

At the request of Miss Maria del Carmen Tapia, I Faustino Castro Gete,
manifest and declare that _____
    1. The numerary women of Opus Dei (excepting the auxiliary
numeraries) complete studies of philosophy and theology in courses
generally taught by numerary priests or by specialists in the corresponding
subjects. _____
    2. The numeraries who attend these courses undergo a final exam in
each one and receive their grade. An act is prepared which is signed by a
tribunal or professors.
    3. There is no validation examination subsequent to the courses of
philosophy or theology.
    4. The philosophical subjects or courses taught to the numerary women
(excluding the auxiliary numeraries) are the same as are taught to the
numerary men. They are the following: Cosmology, Logic, Ethics,
Psychology, History of Philosophy (two years), Epistemology or Theory
of Knowledge, Theodicy, and Metaphysics.
    5. Only those who have passed each and every course in philosophy can
take the subject or courses in theology. _____
    6. During the years in which I was a numerary priest in Opus Dei, I
was the professor of numerary women or various philosophical subjects
(noted in number four of the present declaration). On occasion, I read
written examinations of numerary women who had taken some subject or
course in theology. In all cases, I gave the grade that I thought appropriate,
and on several occasions, I signed the examination acts. _____
    Everything written here I affirm and declare, and after having re-read it,
I am in conformity with what is written, according to the normal sense of
words and phrases, and I sign it today, April 14, 1974, in Mexico City, to
all effects, knowing that everything manifested and declared is true in each
and every point, and that the truth does not harm nor offend. _____

Signed: Faustino Castro Gete

March 3rd, 1979.

TO WHOM IT MAY CONCERN

This is to certify that MARIA DEL CARMEN TAPIA attended classes
of Scholastic Philosophy at Caracas, Venezuela during the years
1963 to 1965.   The Subjects of the said Course were:

Introduction to Philosophy
Logic
Cosmology
Psychology
History of Ancient Philosophy
History of Medieval Philosophy
History of Modern and Contemporary Philosophy
General Ethics & Special Ethics
Metaphysics
Epistemology
Theodicy

HHaving passed the written examinations satisfactorily she was
allowed to enter a Theological Course.

Being, myself, one of the teachers of this Philosophical Course
and having taught most of the subjects of this said Course while
stationed at Caracas, Venezuela during the years 1962 to 1966,
I give testimony that this is a true statement with my usual
signature.

                                        Minister of Religion

ORIGINALS OF CORRESPONDENCE

BETWEEN MY FATHER

AND MONSIGNOR ESCRIVÁ

Madrid, 4 de octubre de 1966

Excmo. y Revdmo. Monseñor Josemaría Escrivá de
Balaguer y Albás,
Presidente General del Opus Dei
Viale Bruno Buozzi, 73
Roma (Italia)

Estimado Monseñor Escrivá:

Me permito enviarle estas líneas para rogarle tenga a bien indicar
el envío a mi nombre y a la dirección del membrete, los siguientes
documentos que mi hija María del Carmen dejó en Roma y que en
la actualidad le son muy necesarios:

1) Tarjeta de identidad venezolana, válida
hasta el año 1970, semejante a nuestro documento de identidad es-
pañol -concretamente este documento lo tenía dentro de una agenda
que le retiró la Srta. M. Morado-;

2) Certificado internacional de vacuna -es un
librito de cubiertas amarillas- expedido en Caracas.

3) Papeletas de exámen de la Escuela Central
Superior de Comercio de Madrid y de otros Centros Oficiales de
Enseñanza -Escuela Mecanográfica y Taquigráfica, Profesional de
la Mujer-, etc. ;

4) Partida de Registro Civil y de Bautismo;

5) Boletín oficial del Estado Venezolano en
el que constaba su nacionalidad oficial venezolana;

6) Certificado de Servicio Social;

7) Título internacional de conducir -válido
hasta abril de 1967- expedido en Caracas;

8) Aquellos otros documentos personales que
en este momento pudiera no nombrar yo expresamente, pero que ló-
gicamente sólo tienen validez extrictamente personal, entre los que
se encuentra, a título de ejemplo, un cuaderno de tapas negras, más
bien pequeño con diversas direcciones, etc. etc. ; es decir, repito
papeles, documentos, etc. que sólo a mi hija pueden interesar, por
ejemplo también fotografías de tipo carnet, etc.

Le agradezco muy especialmente las molestias que mi petición
lleva consigo y por supuesto cualquier reembolso que haya que
enviar, le ruego tenga a bien indicármelo para que pueda dar yo
las correspondientes órdenes, a fin de que le sea hecho efectivo
de inmediato.

En espera de sus prontas noticias, le saluda muy atentamente,

Firmado:

Francisco-Javier Tapia Cervantes-Pinelo

FJT/lal

FRANCISCO VIVES
Doctor en Derecho Civil y Canónico

Roma, 11 de octubre, 1966

Sr. D. Francisco Javier Tapia Cervantes-Pinelo
Ingeniero Industrial
López de Hoyos, 15, 5º, izda.
M a d r i d

Estimado Señor Tapia:
    Se ha recibido su carta, de fecha 4 de
octubre, cuando Monseñor Escrivá de Balaguer estaba fuera de
Roma; sin embargo, he tenido ocasión de hablar por teléfono
con Monseñor y, en su ausencia, deseo contestar a Vd. perso-
nalmente.

    Le envío, con mucho gusto, las cosas que había aquí de
Mª del Carmen. Espero la ocasión del viaje próximo de un ami
go, porque me parece que este sistema es más seguro que el
del correo ordinario.

    Siento de veras, en cambio, tener que decirle que las
cosas relacionadas con la estancia de su hija en Venezuela,
no puedo enviárselas, porque no me lo permite mi conciencia.
Lo que acabo de manifestarle, indudablemente, requiere una
explicación, sobre todo si -además- se tiene en cuenta que
con bastante probabilidad Vd. habrá recibido una versión de
los hechos notoriamente parcial y deformada.

    Crea sinceramente que no quiero, con estas líneas, au-
mentar sus preocupaciones, sino contribuir al bien de su hija. Por eso, ahora me veo obligado a decirle que, si Vd. co-
nociera algunos aspectos del comportamiento de Mª del Carmen
en Venezuela, se quedaría profundamente apenado, porque no
sólo se hizo daño a sí misma, sino que también perjudicó gra
vemente a otras almas.

    Ahora comprenderá Vd. mejor el porqué no puedo enviarle
nada que tenga algo que ver con la estancia de su hija en Ve
nezuela. Y ésta es igualmente la razón por la cual se desa-
consejó por completo a su hija -y quiero que Vd. lo sepa- el
pensar en un posible regreso a Venezuela. Tengo que decirle,
con toda lealtad, que la marcha de Mª del Carmen a Venezuela
podría dar lugar a cosas muy desagradables, porque allí sal-
drían a la luz hechos que hasta ahora -por consideración con
Vds., y por caridad con su hija- hemos silenciado celosamen-
te, guardando la más absoluta discreción.

He querido, estimado Señor Tapia, ser claro y delicado, pero no crudo. Para que Vd. se haga más cargo de la realidad de lo sucedido, sólo deseo añadir que, durante mucho tiempo, se pusieron todos los medios para ayudar a su hija; y que, finalmente, ante su descamino, no hubo más remedio que instruir un expediente, cumpliendo las normas del Derecho Canónico, con la máxima justicia y caridad, y extremando en todo momento la delicadeza.

Espero que también sepa comprender el porqué no le habíamos informado de estos asuntos: hemos querido cubrir las miserias con el manto de la caridad, y buena prueba de esto es que ni siquiera a Vd. habíamos dado a conocer estos sucesos lamentables. Me consta, en cambio, que Mª del Carmen no guarda este silencio —y falta a la verdad—, cosa que me deja perplejo, porque la verdad, si dejamos que se sepa, es muy penosa para ella.

No quiero terminar sin hacerle patente mi profundo dolor por todo lo sucedido y la esperanza de que, por fin, Mª del Carmen encauce su vida y olvide el pasado, como lo hemos hecho los que por deber hemos tenido que intervenir en este asunto.

Le saluda atentamente

Madrid, 9 de marzo de 1967

Excmo. y Revdmo. Monseñor Josemaría Escrivá de
Balaguer y Albás
Presidente General del Opus Dei
Viale Bruno Buozzi, 73
Roma (Italia)

Muy Sr. mío:

Acuso recibo de la carta del Dr. Francisco Vives de fecha 11 del
pasado octubre, en la que contesta, en su nombre, a la mía del
4 del mismo mes; carta quenme fué entregada a mano en mi oficina
y acompañada de algunos de los documentos interesados en mi citada carta.

Desde aquella fecha he estado esperando a recibir los demás documentos personales de mi hija María del Carmen solicitados también
en mi carta; pues confiaba en que, a pesar de cuanto indicaba el
Dr. Vives en la suya, comprenderían Vds. que por tratarse de documentos personales y de la estricta propiedad de mi hija, me de-
bían ser devueltos.

Sin embargo, estos documentos no me han sido enviados y por ello
le ruego, una vez más, disponga me sean remitidos a la mayor bre-
vedad; por tratarse de documentos personales que ella necesita te-
ner en su poder, hasta el punto de poder incurrir en responsabili-
dad legal al no hacerlo así y que por estos motivos y bajo ningún
concepto se puede justificar que sean retenidos por Vds.

Respecto a las indicaciones que me hacen sobre posibles viajes de
mi hija a Venezuela nada puedo decirles que a Vds. deba comunicar.
puesto que sólo Dios sabe el porvenir concreto de cada persona,
y ni Vds. ni yo podemos limitar, llegado el caso, su libertad de
movimientos, ya que, -como Vds. bien saben- todos tenemos que re:
petar la libertad personal.

En espera de los documentos solicitados, le saluda atentamente,

                    Francisco-Javier Tapia Cervantes-Pi

FJT/lal

APPENDIX C

LETTERS TO HIS HOLINESS

POPE JOHN PAUL II

María del Carmen Tapia

Santa Barbara, August 2, 1991

His Most Illustrious Eminence
Cardinal Angel Sodano
Secretariate of State
Vatican City

Matter of Conscience

Your Eminence:

I enclose material labeled *"Secret and matter of conscience"* with the urgent request to put it directly and personally in the hands of our Blessed Father, His Holiness John Paul II.

Given the importance of its contents, Eminence, I request in the name of God that you not entrust this material to any intermediary but rather that your Eminence be the one to present it to the Holy Father directly and personally.

Abusing your charity, I would request for the peace of my conscience that you also send me a short note at the address below, notifying me of the date on which the document was directly presented to his Holiness.

With gratitude and respect, I request your blessing,

(signed) María del Carmen Tapia

María del Carmen Tapia

Santa Barbara, August 2, 1991

His Holiness John Paul II
Vatican City

Blessed Father:

After serious deliberation, I have decided to write in order to open my soul to you and manifest before God and the Church what is for me a serious duty of conscience: that the life of Monsignor José-María Escrivá de Balaguer, which I witnessed for many years, was not admirable and much less was it worthy of imitation. His process of beatification would seriously harm the Church and souls, since it would also imply that the manner in which he lived the teaching of Opus Dei, founded by him, was exemplary.

I know Opus Dei well because I was a Numerary for almost twenty years (1948–1966), during six of which I lived in Rome (1952–1956 and 1965–66). I was Monsignor Escriva's personal secretary and a Major Superior in the Opus Dei Women's Branch Central Government. Monsignor Escrivá in person received my final vows in Opus Dei. Furthermore, I was the first director of the press that Opus Dei has in its central house in Rome and also was specially charged, when Monsignor Escrivá went to the women's house, with taking notes for posterity, on whatever I might hear him say. In 1956 I was sent to Venezuela as Director of the Women's Branch in that country, where I obtained Venezuelan citizenship, which I retain. I left Venezuela in 1965, when Monsignor Escrivá summoned me to Rome, where I remained until my departure from Opus Dei in 1966.

Now I see Opus Dei superiors rush through the steps of this beatification, exhausting all their human, social, political, and financial resources, because they judge that if they do not succeed during your Pontificate, Blessed Father, perhaps centuries will go by before they obtain the beatification. After having won the juridical change of status from Secular Institute to Personal Prelature, Opus Dei's single goal and objective is to make its founder a saint.

I wished to testify in Monsignor Escrivá process at the appropriate time and was not allowed to do so. Moreover, it was expressly indicated to me in Madrid, in October, 1981, by way of the priest Don Joaquín Aznar Cleofas, whom I visited, because he was an "advocatus diaboli," that I would not be permitted to do so.

Given the extreme importance and repercussions of the possible outcome, and understanding that my testimony may be crucial, I am ready, Blessed Father, to be directly interrogated by your Holiness in the manner in which you may choose, going to Rome on day and time that are chosen.

Opus Dei's way of acting, its great influence, and its maneuvers within the Roman Curia have been well known by everyone for a long time. But unfortunately during Monsignor Escriva's whole process of beatification, this has been especially the case in the Congregation for the Causes of Saints, where his Eminence Cardinal Pietro Palazzini was in charge. Therefore, I would beseech you, Blessed Father, if your Holiness cannot personally hear me in such an important case for the health of the Church and of souls, that you would accede to designate a judge for the hearing, *who has your strict, personal trust and who has not the slightest relation with Opus Dei.*

If Opus Dei perceives my desire to testify before your Holiness, I would not discount the possibility, Blessed Father, that they might interfere with my testimony, whether by somehow impeding my physical presence in the Vatican or else by a subtle or not so subtle personal attack that would sow doubts about my moral integrity; it would not be the first time that they recur to this procedure, as several of the documents which I have in my power show. For this reason, I have felt obliged to store the originals of the documents that I possess in different, secure places under legal protection. All this material would in the last analysis become public even in the event that something should happen to me.

For a long time I have wished to be able to speak directly to you and, like a daughter to her father, open my heart which suffers because of the likelihood of this event, and also to be able to respond to any question of yours, but unhappily, I have not been able to reach your Holiness, despite my previous trips to Rome.

It is my fervent desire, Holy Father, that at this time, for the good of the universal Church and of all souls, this beatification process, which Opus Dei so precipitously wishes to accelerate and shorten be prolonged for as long as necessary. In this way, scandal would be avoided, ample time would be given to investigate the case thoroughly. Along with the already familiar testimony of those persons who were unilaterally presented by members or Superiors of Opus Dei, testimony could be taken from those others who knew Monsignor Escrivá intimately, spent more than fifteen, twenty, or thirty years in Opus Dei, and would have wanted to declare, but were not called nor permitted to do so, because thay had ceased to belong to Opus Dei.

Opus Dei Superiors fear this testimony because true facts would come to light, which they do not like, which cast a different light on the picture they try to project of Monsignor Escrivá's life. Therefore, they do whatever is in their hand so that those persons whose point of view does not coincide with what they want to make prevail are considered to be unsuitable or untrustworthy witnesses.

Blessed Father, I attach to this letter a series of sketches of events at which I was present, lived through, and heard, during my years inside Opus Dei. Althought these events are not all I know, they can offer your Holiness a different perspective of Monsignor Escrivá's real life. I could add other events, still more serious, and individually documented, about my personal experience with Monsignor Escrivá, which I am prepared to set forth in your Holiness' presence.

Also, I attach a draft, in its current state, of a work which I prepared commenting on the document presented by Opus Dei to the Holy See with the petition for the change from Secular Institute to Personal Prelature. I can assure you, Holy Father, that my comments on each point reflect the truth.

I know a number of persons who still fear reprisals by Opus Dei, and who with troubled conscience remain silent. These persons would only speak at the request of your Holiness. And their testimony, which would be important and which could specially weigh on your Holiness' final judgment, would not become available in any other way. For example, I can place at your Holiness' disposition the name of a female Opus Dei Numerary of thirty years standing, who requested to withdraw from Opus Dei only two years ago, and who has assured me that unless she speaks with your Holiness, she would never speak with anyone for fear of possible Opus Dei reprisals.

I believe in the Holy Spirit and trusting in his intercession, I hope that your Holiness may hear my plea.

With all humilty, your daughter in our Lord requests your blessing,

(signed) María del Carmen Tapia

Attachments: 11 pages of descriptions and a 53 page draft in blue cover.

María del Carmen Tapia

Santa Barbara, September 24, 1991

His Illustrious Eminence
Cardinal Sodano
Secretariate of State
Vatican City

MATTER OF CONSCIENCE

Eminence:

With renewed confidence I attach this new material as *"Secret and matter of conscience"* with the request just as before to put it directly and personally in the hands of our Holy Father his Holiness John Paul II.

At this point it is obvious that I must insist on the importance of the enclosed material and that, abusing your goodness, it be you who give it directly and personally to the Holy Father.

I would thank you from the bottom of my soul, if you would have a brief note sent assuring me that both the material sent for the Holy Father by way of your Eminence with the date of August 2, 1991, and the present material have been personally given to his Holiness. I know with certainty from the postal service used that the material reached your Eminence. However, I have not yet received confirmation from your Eminence that the material has been handed over to the Holy Father.

Awaiting your reply, with all gratitude and respect, I request your blessing,

(signed) María del Carmen Tapia

P.S. I would like to repeat, Eminence, that I am prepared to travel to Rome at his Holiness' first call.

María del Carmen Tapia

Santa Barbara, September 24, 1991

To his Holiness John Paul II
Vatican City

Blessed Father:

While I await your Holiness' summons to testify with regard to the cause of beatification of Monsignor José-María Escrivá de Balaguer and, as a continuation of my letter of August 2, 1991 (which according to the postal service was received in the Secretariate of State on August 9, 1991), I would like to include as addenda the following account of events which I consider to be very important:

1. Monsignor Escrivá's own actions in my own process of withdrawal from Opus Dei.

2. As a consequence of the above, photocopies of the letter sent to my father by direct and specific order of Monsignor Escrivá, as also the letters sent by my father to Monsignor Escrivá.

3. Photocopies of letters sent by order of Monsignor Escrivá to different university and diplomatic authorities denying the philosophical and theological studies that I completed in Opus Dei. One must understand that such letters can only be written in Opus Dei by direct and specific order of the President General, at that time Monsignor Escrivá. In essence, what they were trying to deny was not only the studies that I completed, but that I had belonged to the institution. Indeed, his Eminence, Cardinal Tavera, may he rest in peace, tried to help me on this point and was never able to understand the lack of charity and justice in Monsignor Escrivá's actions.

It is obvious, Blessed Father, that I am ready to expand upon these events in speaking before your Holiness or, as I said in my previous letter and repeat now, before a judge who enjoys your strict, personal confidence and *who has no connection whatever with Opus Dei*. Similarly, I am ready to repeat everything under oath.

I know that a number of persons who were in Opus Dei for many years have just written you again, since the correspondence sent previously seems never to have reached your Holiness' hands.

The matter as a whole is so serious, Blessed Father, that more than ever I trust fully in the Holy Sprit to illuminate your Holiness, and to move you precisely in the direction of justice as Pope, to listen to those of your children who have made our heartfelt requests as children of the Church and for the good of souls.

Requesting humbly that you bless her, your daughter in our Lord,

(signed) María del Carmen Tapia

Attachments:

1. Monsignor José-María Escrivá's own actions in my own process of withdrawal from Opus Dei (18 pages).

2. Correspondence between Monsignor Escrivá and my father (three letters).
3. Correspondence between the Dean of Foreign Students of the University of California, Dr. K.-M. Mathew, and Monsignor José-María Escrivá (three letters).
4. Correspondence between the Dean of Foreign Students of the University of California, Dr. K.-M. Mathew, and the Counselor of Venezuela, Roberto Salvat, via the Apostolic Nuncio in Venezuela, Monsignor Del Judice (three letters)
5. Letter of the Administrative Assistant of the Dean of Foreign Students, Mrs. Muriel E. Engle, to Sofía Pilo, Regional Secretary of Venezuela.
6. Letter of Attorney Dr. Carlos Hernández Bitter to Roberto Salvat, Counselor of Venezuela.
7. Correspondence between the Chairman of the Deparment of Relgious Studies of the University of California, Professor G.-J. Larson, and Mr. William K. Braun, Cultural Attaché of the Embassy of the United States in Rome (four letters).
8. Correspondence between María del Carmen Tapia and his Eminence Cardinal Arturo Tavera (two letters).
9. Declaration of Dr. Faustino Castro, attorney and priest.
10. Correspondence between the Chairman of the Department of Religious Studies of the University of California, Professor G.-J. Larson, and Monsignor José-María Escrivá (two letters).
11. Certificate of Studies by Rev. Father [name whitened out] Numerary priest of Opus Dei.

BIBLIOGRAPHY
ON OPUS DEI

Albas, Carlos. *Opus Dei o chapuza al diablo.* Barcelona: Planeta, 1992.

Arias, Juan, "Juan-Pablo II erige el Opus Dei en Prelatura Personal," *El País* (Madrid), August 24, 1993.

———. *Un Dios para el Papa: Juan Pablo II y la Iglesia del Milenio.* Madrid: Grijalbo Mondadori, 1996.

Artigues, Daniel. *El Opus Dei en España.* vol. 1 (1928–1957), vol. 2. Madrid: Ruedo Ibérico, 1968.

———. "Que'est-ce que l'Opus Dei?" *Esprit* (Paris) November 1967.

Baeza, Alvaro. *La verdadera Historia del Opus Dei.* Madrid: ABL Editor, 1994.

Becarud, Jean. *De la Regenta al "Opus Dei."* Madrid: Taurus, 1977.

Berglar, Peter. *Opus Dei: Vida y Obra del Fundador José María Escrivá de Balaguer.* Madrid: Rialp, 1987. Original German edition: *Opus Dei: Leben und Werk des Grunders Josemaría Escrivá de Balaguer.* Salzburg: Otto Müller Verlag, 1983.

Bernal, Salvador. *Monseñor José María Escrivá de Balaguer: Apuntes sobre la vida del fundador del Opus Dei.* Madrid: Rialp, 1976, 2d edition. English edition: *A Profile of Msg. Escrivá, Founder of Opus Dei.* London: Scepter Ltd., 1977.

Bernstein, Carl, and Marco Politi. *His Holiness: John Paul II and the Hidden History of Our Time.* New York: Doubleday, 1996.

Boixados, Jordi. *Opus Dei, retrat de família.* Barcelona: Editorial Columna, 1993.

Bowers, Fergal. *The Work: An Investigation into the History of Opus Dei and How It Operates in Ireland Today.* Dublin: Poolbeg Ltd., 1989.

Burke Cormac, *Conscience and Freedom.* New York: Scepter Press and Manila: Sunag Tala Press, 1977.

Carandell, Luis. *Vida y milagros de monseñor Escrivá de Balaguer, fundador del Opus Dei.* Barcelona: Laia, 1975, 2d edition 1992.

Casanova, José Vicente. *The Opus Dei and the Modernization of Spain.* Michigan: University Microfilms International, 1983.

Casciaro, Pedro. *Soñad y os quedaréis cortos.* Madrid: Rialp, 1994.

Cierva, Ricardo de la. *Misterios de la Historia.* Second Series. Barcelona: Planeta, 1992.

Concilium: The Church as Institution, vol. 1, number 1 (London), January 1974.

Constituciones del Opus Dei, vol. 1, 1950. Bilingual edition, translation of Latin into Spanish by Lois Pérez Castro. Madrid: Tiempo, 1986.

Constituciones del Opus Dei, vol. II, 1982. Bilingual edition, translation of Latin into Spanish by Matilde Rovira Soler. Madrid: Tiempo, 1986.

Cordero, Franco. *Opus.* Turin: Einaudi, 1972.

Creach, Jean. *Chroniques Espagnoles: Le Coeur et l'epée.* Paris: Librairie Plon, 1958.

Cremades, Javier (coordinator). *Josemaría Escrivá de Balaguer, Fundador del Opus Dei: Claves de un proceso de canonización.* Madrid: Scriptor, 1992.

Cuadernos-3: Vivir en Cristo. Rome: Collegium Romanum Sanctae Crucis, 1973.

Dalmau, Josep. *Contrapunts: Al Camí de L'Opus Dei.* Barcelona: Editorial Pòrtic, 1969.

Day, Mark R. "What Opus Dei Has Done for the Church . . . and for the Sake of Its Reputation" (interview with Maria del Carmen Tapia), *National Catholic Reporter,* May 27, 1983, pp. 12–13.

Documentos Mundo Cristiano: José María Escrivá de Balaguer: Itinerario de la causa de canonización. Prologue by Jesús Urteaga. Madrid: Ed. Palabra, 1991.

Eguibar, Mercedes. *Monserrat Grasses: Christian Heroism in Ordinary Life.* New York: Scepter Booklets, 1980.

Escrivá de Balaguer, José María. *Camino.* Valencia: Ediciones C.I.D., 1939. English edition: *The Way.* New York: Scepter Publishers, 1979.

———. *Conversaciones con.* Mexico: Rialp Mexicana, 1968.

———. *Es Cristo que pasa: Homilías.* Madrid: Rialp, 1974. English edition: *Christ Is Passing By.* Manila: Sinag-Tala Publishers, 1974.

———. *La Abadesa de las Huelgas: Estudio Teológico Jurídico.* Madrid: Rialp, 1974.

———. *The Christian Vocation.* New York: Scepter Booklets, 1974.

———. *Time Is a Treasure.* New York: Scepter Booklets, 1974.

———. *Humility.* New York: Scepter Booklets, 1974.

———. *Holy Rosary.* New York: Scepter Booklets, 1974.

———. *Detachment.* New York: Scepter Booklets, 1979.

———. *Christian Respect for the Person and His Freedom.* New York: Scepter Booklets, 1979.

———. *Woman Today: Her Role in the Family.* New York: Scepter Booklets, 1980.

———. *Surco.* Barcelona: Rialp, 1986. English edition: *Furrow.* London/New York: Scepter, 1988.

———. *Forja.* Mexico: Editoria de Revistas S.A., 1987. English edition: *Forge.* London/New York, Scepter, 1988.

Estruc, Joan. *L'Opus Dei: les seves paradoxes: iun estudi sociològic.* Barcelona: Edicions 62, 1993.

———. *Santos y Pillos: El Opus Dei y sus paradojas.* Barcelona: Herder, 1994. English translation: *Saints and Schemers.* New York: Oxford University Press, 1995.

Farrell, Michael J. "What Escrivá's Beatification Says about the Church," *National Catholic Reporter,* April 17, 1992.

Fuenmayor, Amadeo de, Valentín Gómez-Iglesias, and José Luis Illanes. *El itinerario Jurídico del Opus Dei: Historia y defensa de un carisma.* 4th edition Pamplona: Ediciones Univ. de Navarra, 1990.

García Viño, M. *Josemaría o la planificación de un santo.* Madrid: Libertarias/Pro-hufi, 1991.

Garvey. J.J.M. *Parents' Guide to Opus Dei.* New York: Sicut Dixit Press, 1989.

Giacomo, Maurizio di. *Opus Dei.* Naples: Tullio Pironti Editore, 1987.

Gómez Pérez, Rafael. *El Opus Dei: Una explicación.* Madrid: Rialp, 1992.

———. *Trabajando junto al Beato Josemaría.* Madrid: Rialp, 1994.

Gondrand, François. *Al Paso de Dios: José María Escrivá de Balaguer, fundador del Opus Dei.* Madrid: Rialp, 1985.

———. *Au pas de Dieu: Josemaría Escrivá de Balaguer fondateur de L'Opus Dei.* Paris: Editions France-Empire, 1982.

———. "La réponse de l'Oeuvre (aux déclarations de María del Carmen Tapia." *L'Actualité Religieuse* (Paris), no. 134, 15, June 1995, p. 35.

Hebblethwaite, Peter. "Opus Dei: Lifting the Veil of Mystery," *National Catholic Reporter,* May 27, 1983, pp. 9 and 13.

Helming, Dennis M. *Footprints in the Snow: A Pictorial Biography of Josemaría Escrivá the Founder of Opus Dei.* New York: Scepter Publishers, 1986.

Hertel, Peter. *Ich verspreche euch den Himmel: Geistlicher Anspruch, gesellschaftliche Ziele und kirchliche Bedeutung des Opus Dei.* 4th printing, Dusseldorf: Patmos, 1991.

———. *Geheimnisse des Opus Dei.* Freiburg i.B.: Herder, 1995.

Hutchinson, Robert. *Die heilige Mafia des Papstes: Der wachsende Einfluss des Opus Dei.* Munich: Droemer Knaur, 1996. English edition: *Their Kingdom Come.* London: Doubleday, 1997.

Keenan, William. *Der selige Josemaría Escrivá: Eine kurze Lebensgeschichte.* Cologne: Adamas-Verlag, 1990.

Lernoux, Penny. *People of God: The Struggle for World Catholicism.* New York: Viking Press, 1989.

Le Tourneau, Dominique. *What Is Opus Dei.* Dublin: Mercier Press, 1989.

Le Vaillant, Yvon. *Sainte Maffia: Le dossier de L'Opus Dei.* Paris: Mercure de France, 1971.

Lo Castro, Gaetano. Le Prelature Personali: Profili Giuridici. Milan: Dott. A Giuffré Editore, 1988.

Martin, James. "Opus Dei in the United States," *America,* February 25, 1995.

Martinell, Francisco. *Cristianos Corrientes: Texto sobre el Opus Dei.* Madrid: Rialp, 1970.

Messori, Vittorio. *Opus Dei: Un'indagine.* Milan: Mondadori, 1994.

Mettner, Matthias. *Die katholische Mafia: Kirchliche Geheimbünde greifen nach der Macht.* Hamburg: Hoffman und Campe, 1993.

Moncada, Alberto. *El Opus Dei: Una interpretación.* Madrid: Indice, 1974.

———. *Historia oral del Opus Dei.* Barcelona: Plaza y Janes, 1987.

———. "Sectas Católicas: el Opus Dei," *Revista Internacional de Sociología* (Madrid: C.S.I.C.), 1992, pp. 280–330.

Morales, José, et al. *Estudios sobre "Camino"* (Madrid: Rialp), 1988.

Moreno, María-Angustias. *El Opus Dei: Anexo a una historia.* Barcelona: Planeta, 1976.

———. *La otra cara del Opus Dei.* Barcelona: Planeta, 1978.

———. *El Opus Dei: Creencias y Controversias sobre la canonización de Monseñor Escrivá.* Madrid: Literarias Prodhufi, 1992.

Moynihan, Robert. "In Search of 'the Father,'" *The Catholic World Report,* May 1992, pp. 10–23.

Oberle, Thierry. *L'Opus Dei: Dieu ou César?* Paris: JCLattès, 1993.

Ocariz, Fernando, and Ignacio de Celaya. *Vivir como hijos de Dios: Estudios sobre el Beato Josemaría Escrivá.* Pamplona: Ediciones Universidad de Navarra, 1993.

O'Connor, William. *Opus Dei: An Open Book* (a reply to *The Secret World of Opus Dei* by Michael Walsh). Dublin: Mercier Press Ltd., 1991.

Olaizola, José Luis. *Un escrito en busca de Dios.* Planeta, 1993.

Opus Dei. *21 preguntas a Mons. José María Escrivá de Balaguer.* Semana (Caracas) number 239, November 1972.

Opus Dei. Excerpts from press interviews on *Twenty Questions to Msgr. Escrivá.* New York: Scepter Booklets, 1977.

Orlandis, José. *Historia y espíritu.* Pamplona: Eunsa, 1975.

Paulus Akademie, ed. *Opus Dei: Stosstrupp Gottes oder "Heilige Mafia"? Macht und Einfluss des Opus Dei in der Schweiz und anderswo.* Zurich: NZN Buchverlag, 1992.

Portillo, Alvaro de. *Faithful and Laity in the Church.* Ireland; Ecclesia Press, 1972.

———. *Escritos sobre el sacerdocio.* Madrid: Scriptor/Palabra, 1990.

———. *Monseñor Josemaría Escrivá de Balaguer.* Pamplona: Ediciones Universidad de Navarra, 1976.

———. *Intervista sul Fondatore dell'Opus Dei* (by Cesare Cavalleri). Milan: Ares, 1992. German edition, Cologne: Adamas Verlag, 1996.

Portillo, Alvaro del, Francisco Ponz Piedrafita, and Gonzalo Herranz. *En memoria de Mons. José María Escrivá de Balaguer.* Pamplona: Eunsa, 1976.

Rocca, Giancarlo. *L'Opus Dei: Appunti e documenti per una storia.* Rome: Edizione Paoline, 1985.

Roche, John J. "Winning Recruits in Opus Dei: A Personal Experience," *The Clergy Review,* October 1985.

Rodriguez, Pedro, Fernando Ocariz, and José Luis Illanes, *El Opus Dei en la Iglesia.* Madrid: Rialp, 1993.

Romano, Giuseppe. *Opus Dei: Chi, come, perché.* Milan: Edizioni San Paolo, 1994.

Ropero, Javier. *Hijos en el Opus Dei.* Barcelona: Ediciones B, 1993.

Ruiz, Carlos M. *Yo Argentina, esclavo del Opus Dei.* Valencia: Brolisa, 1980.

San Francisco Chronicle. "Opus Dei's Roots in Francisco Franco's Spain," June 1, 1986, p. A–10.

Sargent, Daniel. *God's Engineer.* Chicago: Scepter, 1954.

Sastre, Ana. *Tiempo de Caminar: Semblanza de Monseñor Josemaría Escrivá de Balaguer.* Madrid: Rialp, 1989.

Seco, Luis Ignacio. *La herencia de Mons. Escrivá de Balaguer.* Madrid: Ediciones Palabra, 1986.

Steigleder, Klaus. *Das Opus Dei: Eine Innenansicht.* Zurich: Benziger, 1983. Italian edition: *L'Opus Dei: Vista dall'interno.* Turin: Claudiana, 1986.

Tapia, María del Carmen. *Tras el Umbral: Una vida en el Opus Dei.* Barcelona: Ediciones B, 1992; Portuguese edition: *Do lado de dentro: Una vita na Opus Dei.* Lisbon: Publicaçoes Europa-America, 1993. German edition: *Hinter der Schwelle: Ein Leben im Opus Dei.* Zurich: Benziger Verlag, 1993; German paperback edition: Munich: Goldman Verlag, 1996.

———. "Goodhousekeepers for Opus Dei . . . and Recipients of the Father's Rages," *National Catholic Reporter,* May 27, 1983, pp. 10–11.

———. "El poder del Opus Dei: Encuesta," *Temas para el Debate* (Madrid), no. 3, February 1995, p. 44.

———. "Opus Dei: Révélations sur 20 années passées au coeur de l'Oeuvre" (press conference). Paris, Press Club de France, February 13, 1995. Translated into Italian and published in *Adista* (Rome), no. 24, April 1, 1995.

———. "Sectaire l'Opus Dei?" *L'Actualité Religieuse* (Paris), no. 134, June 15, 1995, pp. 32–34.

Urbano, Pilar. "En defensa de Padre," *Panorama* (Madrid), March 9, 1992, p. 13.

———. *El hombre de Villa Tevere.* Barcelona: Plaza y Janes, 1995.

Urteaga, Jesús. *Josemaría Escrivá de Balaguer: Itinerario de la causa de canonización.* Madrid: Scriptor, 1991.

Various authors. *Escrivá de Balaguer ¿mito o santo?* Madrid: Libertarias Prodhufi, 1992.

Vázquez de Prada, Andrés. *El fundador del Opus Dei: Mons. José María Escrivá de Balaguer* (1902–1975). Madrid: Rialp, 1983.

Walsh, Michael. *The Secret World of Opus Dei.* London: Grafton Books-Collins, 1989. Spanish edition: *El mundo secreto del Opus Dei.* Barcelona: Plaza y Janes, 1990.

West, W. J. *Opus Dei. Ficción y realidad.* Madrid: Rialp, 1987.

Woodward, Kenneth L. *Making Saints: How the Catholic Church Determines Who Becomes a Saint, Who Doesn't, and Why.* New York: Simon and Schuster, 1990.

Ynfante, Jesús. *La prodigiosa aventura del Opus Dei: Génesis y desarollo de la Santa Mafia.* Madrid: Ruedo Ibérico, 1970.

———. "Résurrection de l'Opus Dei an Espagne," *Le Monde Diplomatique* (Paris), July 1996, p. 3.

———. *Así en la Tierra como en los Cielos.* Madrid: Mondadori, 1996.